The Study of Tourism
Anthropological and Sociological Beginnings

TOURISM SOCIAL SCIENCE SERIES

Series Editor: **Jafar Jafari**
Department of Hospitality and Tourism, University of Wisconsin-Stout, Menomonie WI 54751, USA.
Tel: (715) 232-2339; Fax: (715) 232-3200; E-mail: jafari@uwstout.edu
Associate Editor (this volume): **Robert E. Wood**
Rutgers University, Camden NJ, USA.

The books in this Tourism Social Science Series (TSSSeries) are intended to systematically and cumulatively contribute to the formation, embodiment, and advancement of knowledge in the field of tourism.

The TSSSeries' multidisciplinary framework and treatment of tourism includes application of theoretical, methodological, and substantive contributions from such fields as anthropology, business administration, ecology, economics, geography, history, hospitality, leisure, planning, political science, psychology, recreation, religion, sociology, transportation, etc., but it significantly favors state-of-the-art presentations, works featuring new directions, and especially the cross-fertilization of perspectives beyond each of these singular fields. While the development and production of this book series is fashioned after the successful model of *Annals of Tourism Research*, the TSSSeries further aspires to assure each theme a comprehensiveness possible only in book-length academic treatment. Each volume in the series is intended to deal with a particular aspect of this increasingly important subject, thus to play a definitive role in the enlarging and strengthening of the foundation of knowledge in the field of tourism, and consequently to expand its frontiers into the new research and scholarship horizons ahead.

Published TSSSeries titles;

Leisure Migration: A Sociological Study on Tourism
József Böröcz (Rutgers University, USA)

Contemporary Tourism: Diversity and Change
Erik Cohen (Hebrew University of Jerusalem, Israel)

Exporting Paradise: Tourism and Development in Mexico
Michael Clancy (University of Hartford, USA)

Anthropology of Tourism
Dennison Nash (University of Connecticut, USA)

Tourism Community Relationships
Philip L. Pearce, Gianna Moscardo and Glenn F. Ross (James Cook University of North Queensland, Australia)

Empowerment of Sustainable Tourism Development
Trevor Sofield (University of Tasmania, Australia)

Tourism and Religion
Boris Vukonic´ (University of Zagreb, Croatia)

Tourism and Modernity: A Sociological Analysis
Ning Wang (Zhongshan University, China)

The Study of Tourism
Anthropological and Sociological Beginnings

Dennison Nash, Editor
University of Connecticut, USA

ELSEVIER

Amsterdam • Boston • Heidelberg • London • New York • Oxford
Paris • San Diego • San Francisco • Singapore • Sydney • Tokyo

Elsevier
The Boulevard, Langford Lane, Kidlington, Oxford OX5 1GB, UK
Radarweg 29, PO Box 211, 1000 AE Amsterdam, The Netherlands

First edition 2007

Notice
No responsibility is assumed by the publisher for any injury and/or damage to persons
or property as a matter of products liability, negligence or otherwise, or from any use
or operation of any methods, products, instructions or ideas contained in the material
herein. Because of rapid advances in the medical sciences, in particular, independent
verification of diagnoses and drug dosages should be made

Library of Congress Cataloging-in-Publication Data
A catalog record for this book is available from the Library of Congress

British Library Cataloguing in Publication Data
A catalogue record for this book is available from the British Library

ISBN-13: 978-0-08-044240-2
ISBN-10: 0-08-044240-4

For information on all Elsevier publications
visit our website at books.elsevier.com

Printed and bound in The Netherlands

07 08 09 10 11   10 9 8 7 6 5 4 3 2 1

Working together to grow
libraries in developing countries

www.elsevier.com | www.bookaid.org | www.sabre.org

ELSEVIER   BOOK AID International   Sabre Foundation

To the Memory of Malcolm Crick

Preface

Those of us who have been privileged to be among the first from anthropology and sociology, as well as other social sciences, to be involved in the study of tourism may have some idea of how it came about. We may even have some notion about how our own personal odyssey compares with that of some of our colleagues in this regard. But no one has yet attempted to study the whole process in such a way as to provide an adequate inside picture in scientific terms of the emergence and development of this new field of study. Like all scientists, those involved in this process have had to deal with forces that shaped their recognition of a new subject and how it was to be seen, and treated (Barnes, Bloor and Henry 1996). True, one hesitates to say that where the subject is tourism, the innovation involved is as significant as that for the creation of the Double Helix in biology or Relativity in physics; but some of the specific processes would seem to be not unlike other scientific developments, as for example, the discovery and progressive understanding of some new and debilitating disease. How much or how little, of course, remains to be uncovered in this book as well as others.

Those of us who have become students of tourism, as of any other subject, have much to learn from a project of this kind. It can be a sort of self-examination with all the pleasure and pain that that implies. But there could also be implications for others not directly involved in such study. Tourism is said to be one of the world's largest "industries," and the number of people involved in it, one way or another, is very great and increasing. One cannot be unaware of this potentially great audience of interested parties consisting of other tourism researchers and academics, workers in various aspects of the tourism industry, and the increasingly large number of tourists themselves. One hopes that all of these people will find something personally involving in reading this book.

Our project follows a small, but vital tradition of intellectual autobiography in the sciences and humanities—a line of production with what amounts to its own evolving subculture and associated problems (Berger, ed. 1990). It also represents a contribution to the growing field of tourism research, the excitement of which often has been contagious. This is how I described it for anthropologists in an earlier work (Nash 1996:vii):

> Those of us who have been pioneers in the study of tourism have found the air of discovery and sense of freedom associated with being on the frontier enormously exciting. Being on the margin of our professional cultures, with all the looseness of social ties that this implies, we have had an opportunity for adventure which may be even greater than that which is routine for anthropologists who are well-known for their adventurous natures.

And indeed as it has turned out, there have been many satisfactions during the production of this book—satisfactions not entirely unaccompanied by problems, some anticipated and some not (see Appendix B and Aguilar 1981:15–26). But in the end, I hope that we have here a collective accomplishment that does credit to all of us and to the emerging field of tourism research, which we represent.

Acknowledgments are, for me, always a pleasure. First, I would like to thank all of the participants for their collaboration in what has been an unusual and often demanding project. Second, thanks are due Jafar Jafari, the editor-in-chief of the TSSSeries and of *Annals of Tourism Research*, as well as a participant in this book, whose encouragement and editorial acumen during the course of publication has been invaluable. Third, I am deeply grateful to Graham Dann, a friend and former collaborator during the days of his Barbados existence, as well as a participant in this book, who has helped me in various ways. Fourth, I am particularly grateful to two of the participants who, despite battling serious maladies during the course of production of the book, made a special effort to get their personal histories to me on time and in good order. Fifth, thanks are due to my University of Connecticut where, after formal retirement, I have had studies, offices, an available library, and computer resources, which have provided the necessary ambience and support for scholarly production. Sixth, there are those who provided computer and secretarial help, library, and translation assistance: Asha Shipman, Bambi Billman Terese Andrews, and Geoffrey Meigs and his team of computer wizards. Seventh, thanks are due to colleague René Baretje, now head of the Centre International de Recherches et d'Études Touristiques, for his keen archival assistance. Eighth, I am indebted to the "formal" reader of the complete manuscript, Bob Wood, for his critical review and helpful comments, as well as a long-time colleague and collaborator, Jerold Heiss, who has been no less important in a less formal capacity. Ninth, Tom Selwyn provided a useful account of the impressively productive activities associated with the Roehampton Institute and its successor at London Metropolitan.

Tenth, thanks are due to friend, colleague, and former reader, Seth Leacock, for his sharp remarks from time to time during discussions of the evolving manuscript. Finally, there are a host of friends too numerous to mention, whose simple presence and occasional aid (not necessarily in matters pertaining to the production of this book) have helped me immensely. The creation of this book has been an unusually long and difficult endeavor, and without the help of all of these people, this book might never have seen the light of day.

Kudos to all of us! Dennison Nash

Contents

Chapter 1

Prologue

We are dealing here with a small aspect of Western intellectual history. It concerns the creation and development of a field of inquiry in the social sciences, the main facts for which have been provided in personal histories of some of its creators, written especially for this book. Its subject, in the broadest sense, is the development of a tourism social science. More narrowly, it concerns the early study of tourism by anthropological and sociological scholars who, having a good deal in common and ties to the other social sciences, have played a part in the creation and development of a multidisciplinary tourism social science. Though a number of social sciences have been drawn on in formulating the approach of this study, the main thrust comes from the knowledge produced by scholars associated with the disciplines directly involved, which means that, in its basic orientation, our effort qualifies as a kind of anthropology/sociology of knowledge.

It would seem that the study of tourism by practitioners in these fields began in a manner similar to that for other new-found subjects, that is, as a refiguring of established understandings about the world. This was a development that took place in the twentieth century, and as an empirical science, in the second half of that century; and despite an increasing involvement of scholars in the non-Western world, it continues to be dominated by Europeans and North Americans. Since no major "paradigm shift" appears to have been involved in the creation of this new field of inquiry, its emergence appears not to meet Thomas Kuhn's (1970) criteria for an intellectual "revolution," but rather (the staking out of a new field of study excepted) to have begun in a way that is closer to the workings of what he calls "normal science," which involves the more mundane working—through of "revolutionary" ideas. Such an observation, however, should not be construed as in any way diminishing the significance of our study.

Certainly, the project has implications for the emergence of any area of research pertaining to new subject matter, but it also has relevance for the development of anthropology, sociology, social thought in general, and perhaps other intellectual endeavors. Further, it will be seen to touch on the broader phenomenon of sociocultural change, which has been of interest to social scientists for their intellectual operations since the beginnings of their work a little more than two centuries ago. So much by way of introduction to our project.

Tourism as a Social Fact

These days, the fact of tourism is hard to dismiss and seems to have acquired a taken for granted quality, which some social scientists (Schuetz 1964) have emphasized in dealing with the essentials of everyday life. Putting aside arguments over its definition, which have certainly not been settled, it probably would be fair to say that even the participants in such disputes, as well as the proverbial (man) people in the street, would agree that tourism exists as an important social fact in today's world. Almost any contemporary society or sub-society we look at seems to be involved with what most people would think of as tourists, and most are receiving them as well. North Americans and the French visit each other. Germans go to exotic places like New Guinea, among a host of destinations. Northern Europeans and North Americans go south in the winter. Japanese tourists are seemingly everywhere—in and outside of Japan. Some Westerners have even visited North Korea on tours. And people from many other countries also seem to be involved.

Tourism has become one of the world's largest "industries" in a comparatively short time. Cohen (1984:377), for example, says, "The rate of expansion (of international tourism) has been spectacular: in 1950 there were only 25.3 million international tourist arrivals … and in 1981 an estimated 291 million." More recently, the World Tourism Organization (2001) estimated that there were approximately 700 million international tourist arrivals with tourism receipts of approximately $475 billion; and the same organization has the confidence to forecast (a tricky thing to do these days) a growth rate that could reach one and a half billion tourist arrivals in 2020. Statistics for domestic tourism, which according to Smith and Wanhill, editors (1986:329), in a special issue of *Annals* on the subject, comprise "the bulk of the world's tourism," are even more impressive.

Of course, there are also varieties of tourism to be considered such as ecotourism, cultural tourism, sport tourism, mountaineering tourism, ethnic tourism, and tourism for health, to name only a few in one classificatory scheme, but all have shown impressive growth rates, which suggest that tourism in all of its manifestations is indeed on the march and that it has come to play an increasingly important role in our lives.

The tourism we know in the West carries with it considerable historical weight. Looking at the subject more specifically as a kind of sightseeing, a notion made popular in the works of authors such as Boyer (1972), MacCannell (1976), Adler (1989). Löfgren (1999) traces it back in Western history through the nineteenth century excursions of Thomas Cooke to the travels of young aristocrats and their tutors on the European continent beginning as early as the latter part of the seventeenth century. His historical account, which follows a frequently used path of analysis, would seem to be only a bare beginning for Western history, however.

True, the first written mention of the word "tourist" in the West, according to Böröcz (1996:39–41), can be traced only to the beginning of the nineteenth century in the English and the French languages, with associated words like "tourism" and "touristic" appearing in those languages shortly thereafter. But one can identify people most of us would call tourists, as well as their actions, before that. Hunt (1984), for example, reports on European pilgrimages (which seem also to have had a secular-touristic side) to the Holy Land in the fourth and fifth centuries; Balsdon (1969) examines what appear to be touristic diversions among ancient Romans; Friedlander (1965), the emergence of second homes among the more affluent of those Romans; and Becker (1895), similar phenomena for ancient Greece. Some might at first think that these older tourisms have a special quality which makes them different in kind from the tourism of our time, but close examination of the historic reports reveals that it is often difficult to distinguish them from the tourism we know—all of which suggests that, without a great deal of legerdemain, we can demonstrate that something like the tourism we in the West have come to take for granted has a good deal of historic depth.

Such depth is not unique to the Western world. Graburn (1983a:18) says that the foundations of Japanese tourism can be found in historic documents over a thousand years ago on travel, military activities and religion, the last of which could take the form of what we know as pilgrimage. Indeed, in line with Cohen's (1984:377) argument that pilgrim and tourist activities have important commonalities, Pfaffenberger (1983) sees present-day tourism in Sri Lanka arising out of a long tradition of religious pilgrimage.

The existence of the essentials of tourism, or something prefiguring tourism, in human history, therefore, is a fact that anyone with a broad interest in the subject ought to be aware of. Additionally, they might want to go back still further into the realm of prehistoric societies in their examination of the subject, as does Nash (1979). Based on reports about the ways of life of peasants and foragers in the contemporary world, who often are used as models for the reconstruction of ancient social life, his study suggests that if one accepts the broad view that tourism is centered around the activity of leisured travelers, it may be possible to identify it in the earliest human societies, including those of peoples like the aboriginal hunting and gathering San of southern Africa. This might force us to the unanticipated conclusion that the rudiments of tourism have always been with us and that it may, in fact, be a cultural universal, which makes it an important social fact indeed—grist for the mill of scholars concerned with the unity and diversity of all human societies from the time they first appeared.

Though there are different views of tourists and tourism among scholars, some of which are revealed in the personal histories of our participants, all those interested in the subject probably would agree with Crick (1989) that it is a multifaceted phenomenon; and Chambers (2000) has done well to remind us that not only tourists and those who provide them with hospitality are involved in touristic activities, but others (air and boat crews, tourist agencies, developers, guides, vendors, porters, etc.) as well. So pursuing our broad-based interests and persisting in our thinking of tourists as leisured travelers, we can view tourism as a pan-human, historically conditioned *social process* that can include a variety of social actors, which, as Nash (1981:462) sees it:

> ... originates with the generation of tourists in some society or sub-society, continues as these tourists travel to other places where they encounter hosts with a different culture, and ends as the give and take (in the various social relationships along the way) affects the tourists, those who serve them, and the various societies or subsocieties involved. In addition, this touristic process may evolve into a *touristic system* which itself can be embedded in some broader social context. Those who focus on any aspect of this system will be wise to keep in mind the larger contexts of which it is a part.

Anthropological and Sociological Inquiry

To continue, some explanation should be given that accounts for our decision to consider both anthropological and sociological approaches to tourism *en bloc* in this study. It is because, first of all, as we conceive them, and as anyone who is familiar with the fields knows, they have histories which overlap considerably. Indeed, speaking in the 1940s of the (social) anthropology and sociology they have known, two American sociologists (Parsons and Barber 1948:246) say, "... at the present time, social anthropology and sociology are, as conceptualized disciplines, so close together as to be almost fused." The nature of this "fusion," which we intend to deal with in some detail, has been reflected in their approaches to the subject of tourism. Speaking of disciplinary boundaries in the social scientific study of tourism in a volume dealing with Tourism Social Science (Graburn and Jafari, eds. 1991), Nash and Smith (1991:13) say, "As is apparent from this volume, anthropologists and sociologists are especially inclined to mine each other's territory." This becomes apparent also in "state-of-the-art" reviews of the early study of tourism for sociology (Cohen 1984) and anthropology (Crick 1989), which though offering somewhat different discipline-oriented points of view, are based on what many acquainted scholars would say were both anthropological *and* sociological publications, often without any indication of their particular disciplinary provenance.

But because the disciplines of anthropology and sociology have been variously defined and labeled in the present and past, some of which is evident in the personal histories of participants in this project, and because even so, some of the participants in this study seem not to question their own disciplinary identities, it might be wise at this point to consider the natures of the disciplines involved shortly after the middle of the twentieth century when some of their practitioners had begun to look into the subject of tourism. By that time, they had become more or less scientific–humanistic in their orientations. Merton (1968:29), for example, sees sociology as "poised between the physical sciences and the humanities;" and anthropology may have become even better known for embracing these two approaches. As with other social scientific disciplines, their approaches to the social world often are traced back to the thinking of Enlightenment figures such as Locke, Hobbes, and Rousseau (Harris 1968:8–52; Rossides 1978:503–518). The development of this line of thought took place primarily in Europe and, subsequently, North America, that is, in regions where, according to Bottomore (1993a:633), industrialism developed most rapidly.

In Europe, the conception of anthropology as a social science, has been called variously sociology, ethnology, and social anthropology while in North America it has been called cultural, social, or sociocultural anthropology, which distinguishes it from other categories of (American) anthropology, namely archeology, physical anthropology, and (somewhat less definitively) linguistics (Schippers 1991:146–152), work in all of which has so far had only a little to do with tourism. However named, this kind of anthropology, like sociology, refers to the study of the social activities of human beings.

One often encounters other notions of anthropology and sociology that have different affinities. Indeed, one wonders why the version of sociocultural anthropology offered in an encyclopedia article by Zabel cannot also be applied to sociology. He (Zabel 1996:170) says, "Sociocultural anthropologists study social relationships, the structure of society, and the function of individuals and cultural variables within a society." Any informed reader would take this description as conflating, not distinguishing the two disciplines.

Fields of study have sometimes been distinguished in terms of their subject matter, but as we see in Zabel's attempt at definition, this turns out to be a difficult task where anthropology and sociology (as well as the other social sciences) are concerned (Levi-Strauss 1963:347). However, one can make some progress in distinguishing the disciplines in terms familiar to anthropologists, that is as overlapping cultures, behavior in which is normatively regulated, but variable and contested (Nash 1999:12–16). Seen in this way, one might say that each discipline is identifiable by its outlook on the world. So

Zabel (1996:169) also says, "Anthropologists employ the comparative method and maintain a relativistic view of human cultures. Under the relativistic approach, anthropologists consider all people and cultures valuable to study." Along the same line, Nash and Smith (1991:13), among many others, speak of anthropology as embracing all of the cultures of humankind.

The distinctiveness of this pancultural purview is persuasive as far as anthropology is concerned, but it might be news to members of the International Sociological Assn. and those who have published in the *International Journal of Comparative Sociology*. And it might also have been news to Pierre Bourdieu, the late, lamented "sociologist," whose cross-cultural range of subject matter was not considered inadequate for many an "anthropological" dossier. Perhaps a more persuasive distinction between anthropology and sociology might be fashioned, not by the range or extent of peoples included, but in terms of the kind of cultures or societies studied. Among sociologists and anthropologists the editor spoke with before writing this chapter, the notion that anthropologists (in contrast to their sociological colleagues) are supposedly preoccupied with simpler, non-Western societies was quite evident. Levi-Strauss (1963:347) qualifies this by insisting that anthropologists tend to be concerned with societies that are remote or different from the observer's home society—a view which suggests that, as compared with sociologists and other social scientists, anthropologists have been more cosmopolitan in their research.

One must be careful even with such a distinction, however, because it seems to have become less and less viable in the second half of the twentieth century, when according to Bain and Kolb (1964:678), anthropologists had begun work in "contemporary literate 'folk' societies and even modern societies." But despite the inevitable problems of overlap with sociology, the view of anthropology as a cross-cultural intellectual operation still carries considerable weight (Parsons and Barber 1948:246).

So much by way of a preliminary rumination about anthropology and sociology for the time with which we are primarily concerned, that is, when some of their practitioners were beginning to come to grips with the subject of tourism. It has its inadequacies, but other distinctions—all of which have their proponents (e.g., in terms of methodology where ethnography is sometimes mistakenly thought to be exclusively associated with anthropology)—would seem to be no more adequate (see, e.g., Borowsky 1994; but also Hammersley and Atkinson 1995). Rather, in the words of Talcott Parsons (1937:473), this sketch will "content itself with selecting by the ideal-type method, a few major theoretical strands which are particularly relevant to the problems of this study."

In their Enlightenment beginnings, of course, the question of similarities and differences between anthropology and sociology would tend to be a non-issue because the various social sciences, as we know them, hardly were distinguishable then; it might be better, therefore, to think of these beginnings as taking place in a proto-cultural period of social thought produced by various kinds of social philosophers such as Vico, Diderot, Montesquieu, Turgot, and Locke (Harris 1968:8–52), in which principles of what we know as science (rather than religion or metaphysics) were increasingly relied on to study the social world. Subsequently in the nineteenth century though, the disciplinary differences and similarities with which we are concerned become more readily identifiable, not only in terms of their ideas, but also the sociocultural structures associated with them.

The crucial issues concerning the nature of social life and how to study it were already established by the beginning of the nineteenth century in the thinking of Westerners such as Auguste Comte, whose work can serve as an introduction here (Harris 1968:59–66). For Comte, the substance of social life was to be found scientifically in the ideas of its participants by using a combination of theory and empirically based methodology. A society was thought of as something like an evolving organism with both static and dynamic aspects, neither of which could be treated at the expense of the other. Though claiming to be involved in dealing with a universal social history, Comte was in fact preoccupied with Western or Western-related social arrangements. Because of this, many present-day social scientists (perhaps favoring the view that sociology deals primarily with modern Western societies) probably would have little trouble agreeing with his claim to being a sociologist.

A good deal of Comte's thinking can be seen to anticipate the work of a group of nineteenth century thinkers such as Herbert Spencer, E. B. Tylor, Henry Maine, Lewis Henry Morgan, Karl Marx (and Friedrich Engels), and possibly even a 'Diffusionist' like Wilhelm Schmidt who stressed borrowing, rather than independent invention as the source of new customs. These so-called "Evolutionists" (Harris 1968:108–249) offered various grand theoretical schemes for analyzing changing human sociocultural realities (including aspects such as religion, kinship, technology, political organization, etc.) and for tracing their history and pre-history. Whether emphasizing the notion of cultural borrowing or not, all of these thinkers have been "tagged" here as Evolutionists largely for their all-encompassing views of sociocultural change.

In their analyses, these thinkers saw various forces at work producing different evolutionary trajectories, often toward some valued sociocultural arrangement in the present. For example, Morgan, a favorite of Marx and Engels, suggested a universal path from savagery, through barbarism, to civilization, with each stage exhibiting certain complexes of ways of acting. Sociocultural traits, which did not integrate as expected into a predicted complex and were, therefore, thought by some to be survivals from a previous stage in an evolutionary sequence, excited a good deal of controversy in this evolutionary undertaking (Harris 1968:164–170).

Though the Evolutionists have been subjected to considerable criticism in regard to their use of evidence, it should be pointed out that some of their evolutionary schemes were derived from a good deal of ethnographic and archeological evidence. Indeed, E. B. Tylor and Herbert Spencer are notable for their cross-cultural and archeological erudition. But their use of contemporary ethnographic evidence, as well as their inferences from archeology, in support of general diachronic schemes continues to raise serious questions, even though general notions of some kind of sequence (or sequences) in sociocultural evolution and ideas that one can find the past in the life of contemporary "primitives" have not entirely disappeared.

As far as the early part of the twentieth century is concerned, grand theoretical approaches in anthropology and sociology (i.e., cross-cultural treatment of societies or cultures) were dominated largely by the theoretical work of three Westerners with close anthropological and sociological affinities: Karl Marx (together with his associate, Engels) and two main interlocutors Emile Durkheim and Max Weber. All three of these men offered general schemes for analyzing the static and dynamic aspects of sociocultural reality, which have had considerable influence in the two disciplines, as well as others. Indeed, shortly after the middle of the twentieth century when our study begins, any committed practitioner in either of these fields would have been acquainted with the thinking of at least one of these masters, and probably more (Coser 1971). Clearly they provided the theoretical foundation for modern anthropology and sociology.

Any summary exposition of the contributions of Marx, Durkheim, and Weber (Coser 1971) would show that even though these thinkers were primarily concerned with the society around them, in which they were both intellectually and more or less politically engaged, they all brought to the table a considerable cross-cultural sophistication (none of it involving their own fieldwork, however); and all offered evolutionary or revolutionary schemes that were related in some degree to their political aims, which in the case of Durkheim, involved movement toward a liberal, solidarity-enhancing socialism, for Weber, a form of liberal nationalism, and Marx, the revolutionary overthrow of capitalism, which would come about through political and paramilitary action exploiting contradictions in the capitalist economic base. It should be pointed out, however, that though all three were engaged politically, the bottom line—even for Marx, an active revolutionary polemicist—was some kind of scientific understanding of society.

Marx saw society as composed of three major sociocultural aspects: the material (economic) base, social structure, and ideology, of which contradictions in the first were the ultimate determinants of its evolution (Coser 1971:43–88). For Durkheim (1938:lvii), the ultimate determinant of a society's character was to be found in its "collective representations, ... which although immaterial (ideas), are nevertheless real things." Weber was an eclectic concerning the paramount determinant of a society's character. He is quoted by Bendix (1962:46), for example, as saying "not ideas, but material and ideal interests directly govern men's conduct." For him, any aspect (religious, economic, or whatever) could dominate depending on historical circumstances; and his demonstrations of the factors at work (as, e.g., religion as an enabling force in the rise of the spirit of capitalism in the West (Weber 1958)) are always impressive. Of the three, Weber, in his view of social action, tended to give personal, rather than institutional agency, more of a role in his analyses of social activity. The more collectively oriented Durkheim argued that, as far as sociological analysis was concerned, social facts should never be seen as involving individuals (Lukes 1972:19–22). A society, usually conceived in idealistic terms, was an entity *sui generis* according to this sociologist par excellence (see, e.g., Durkheim 1938 [1895]. His view pervaded the journal *Année Sociologique*, in which he, along with Henri Hubert and Marcel Mauss (Durkheim's nephew), who were important scholars in their own right, played key roles.

Though considerable, the influence of the thought of Marx, Weber, and Durkheim did not spread equally in all directions. For example, until comparatively recently, revolutionary Marxist thinking did not fall on fertile ground in England and America. In the early history of American anthropology, for example, one is hard put to find any other Marxist than Leslie White (who did not always identify himself as such) at work in the first half of the twentieth century. On the sociological side, the American mid-Westerner, Thorsten Veblen, provides a similar example. Though major elements of his work reveal his debt to Marx, he often rejected any connection. Now, however, it is easy to note many neo-Marxist anthropologists and sociologists (Frank 1972; Mintz 1986; Rojek 1985:106–139; Roseberry 1996; Wallerstein 1974; Wolf 1982; Worseley 1984). The initial reception of Marx in Western Europe, not to mention Russia, was much more positive (Merquior 1993:710), however; and it is important to note the important influence of various critical and contending Marxists of the "Frankfurt School" (Horkheimer, Adorno, Marcuse, and Habermas) who were active between the great wars and after (Bottomore 1993c).

Problems of translation at first hampered the spread of Weberian thought into America, but once these problems were resolved, it was favorably received by the more person- or agency-oriented American sociologists (e.g., C. Wright Mills, Talcott Parsons) as well as some French (e.g., Raymond Aron), and, of course, Germans (e.g., L. von Wiese). Concerning Durkheim, some indication of the influence of his thinking is indicated by Parsons and Barber (1948:253) who, writing from their vantage point in the mid-1940s, say that "much of Durkheim's influence has diffused to the point where it is so taken for granted that its source is no longer identified." Whether implied or not, this observation would appear to apply to anthropology as well as sociology.

Considering the influential weight of Marx, Weber, and Durkheim, one might expect that their intellectual production was associated with the security of some kind of academic tenure. Not so with Marx, of course, whose entire productive life was spent outside of academia and whose range of interests went beyond what we think of as sociology or anthropology; and when one learns that Weber, whose interests were at least as broad, was only infrequently involved in academic life and that his good friend, the eminent sociologist, Georg Simmel, whose "pure" or "formal" sociology is justly famous, and whose concern with the fundamental patterns of social interaction continues to challenge social scientists, students of tourism included, had to struggle to find academic employment, one begins to suspect that academic tenure was not so important a distinguishing feature of scientifically based social thought—at least until further on in the twentieth century. Only with Durkheim, the sociologist par excellence, do we find a comparatively secure academic base (in universities at Bordeaux and Paris) for intellectual work as writer and teacher.

Finally, in regard to the triumvirate just discussed, one should note, as Rojek (1985) is at some pains to point out, that though none of these authors dealt directly with the subject of leisure, the relevance of their work for the study of tourism-related subjects are not insignificant; and as we are beginning to find out, especially from a variety of neo-Marxists, present-day researchers on tourism also can benefit in many ways by referring to their theoretical contributions.

The German–American anthropologist Franz Boas, a contemporary of Durkheim, also managed (though not without difficulty) to find secure academic posts for his intellectual activity (ending an academic career at Columbia University in New York City). For many present-day anthropologists, especially Americans, Boas is one of the classic figures of their discipline; and indeed, this transplanted German, who was nourished on the hard sciences in German academia and later (through geography) became committed to the humanistic social sciences, contributed important work in all of what were becoming the four fields of American anthropology. Here, we will be particularly concerned with his role in the development of sociocultural anthropology, in which the list of his students and publications is long and distinguished.

Marvin Harris (1968:250–289; but see also Bee 1974:67–93) characterizes Boas' approach in sociocultural anthropology as "Historical Particularism," a point of view, which tended to put off the search for the kind of general regularities in human behavior we have noted earlier for the Evolutionists in favor of particular historical situations. Though Boas is sometimes referred to as "anti-Evolutionist" in his thinking, the truth is a bit more complicated in that he was not so much opposed to the ideas of social evolution as against the inadequately supported demonstrations of overall sociocultural change, which were rife in his intellectual world. Above all for him, there had to be support, derived from rigorous ethnographic and archeological fieldwork, for any assertions about sociocultural reality. Boas style of research was so often lacking in theoretical underpinning, however, that Harris (1968:301–318) has referred to him as a "methodological puritan." Perhaps an overstatement, this bias in terms of methodological rigor and against the many dubious theoretical claims that pervaded anthropology in those days may be one reason for the statements of a number of his students (e.g., A. L. Kroeber and Margaret Mead) that there never was a Boasian "school" of anthropology. Such a view requires serious qualification if for no other reason than Boas' relentless arguments in favor of the autonomy (and, indeed, primacy) of the sociocultural realm (conceived idealistically as embracing all learned social activity), without the biological underpinnings that often were assumed by the Evolutionists. The Boasian position against racist arguments, which perhaps reflects his immigrant background as well as his own studies of the subject (Boas 1982), was enormously influential in the social sciences and has continued to inform much anthropological and sociological work up to the present.

Boas also was influential in his acceptance of methodological individualism (in which sociocultural realities were recognized as composed of individual agents) that characterized, for example, the field of psychological anthropology, which found particularly fertile ground in a more individualistic America. This movement, often referred to as Personality and Culture, involving the wedding of an idealistic notion of culture with an often psychoanalytic view of the individual, had as its early central problem the question of how group-patterned social arrangements (called cultures) shaped the developing individual through the course of socialization or enculturation. Later, however, it became more broadly concerned with the give and take of culture and the individual, not only in psychoanalytic terms, but learning theory, as well as forms of social psychology involving self and role theories, such as those offered by social philosophers Charles Horton Cooley and George Herbert Mead (Wallace 1970:165–206). Besides his emphasis on culture, Boas' contribution in this regard mostly took the form of an enabling presence for some of his many students, Margaret Mead, A. I. Hallowell, and Ruth Benedict among them; and it is further testimony to the variety of his contributions to the developing field of anthropology.

In America on the sociological side, early decades of the twentieth century were dominated by what amounted to something of a collective enterprise at the University of Chicago that revolved around the names of Albion Small, W. I. Thomas, Robert E. Park, and Earnest Burgess—often referred to as the "Chicago School"—who devoted themselves especially to the study of social problems in urban America that, according to Coser (1993:69) were associated with "the rapid wave of urbanization, industrialization, and capitalist expansion after the

Civil War." For them and their students, Chicago became a gigantic laboratory in which a myriad of social problems could be studied—often in an ethnographic fashion (Vidich and Lyman 1993:33). The social psychological side of their views regarding the analysis and solution of these problems seems often to have been aided and abetted by John Dewey, Charles Cooley, and George Herbert Mead whose thinking about the social aspect of the self, as in the tourism-relevant work of scholars like Ervin Goffman (1959), came to carry enormous weight in America. Some indication of the influence of this "school" is given by Coser (1993:70) when he says, "The Chicago dominance was overthrown in the 1930s when Harvard, Columbia and other eastern universities began to institutionalize sociology, but it had dominated for so long that even afterwards, it was often still seen as the epitome of American empirical sociological research." One should add, however, that such research often involved, as Hammersley and Atkinson (1995:251) point out, an attempt "to combine a humanistically inclined scientific orientation to the study of human behavior with the heritage of German idealism and historicism, as in the work of Max Weber."

The thinking of another anthropological figure of renown will be used here to stand for the "Structuralist" paradigm in the social sciences, which according to Bottomore (1993b:648), "has emphasized ... the identification and analysis of (mental) structures that underlie observable phenomena. Originating in linguistics ..., it has made its way into anthropology through the work of Claude Levi-Strauss, and sociology, mainly in the form of Louis Althusser's structuralist Marxism." Now we are talking about historic figures who some of us regard as contemporaries. Here, we will refer primarily to the work of Levi-Strauss, which is derived not only from a certain kind of linguistics, but also the tendency to approach social phenomena in idealistic terms, which reflects a French tradition that emerged significantly in Durkheim's later work.

Though Levi-Strauss had carried out some anthropological fieldwork in the classic, ethnographic mode, and though he often praised the work of masters of this genre of research, one would have to say that this was not a salient feature of his contribution. Instead, it was his "armchair" cross-cultural theoretical work, carried on in the qualitative tradition in academic departments in France and America, on which we will concentrate. In this regard, he developed his own brand of structuralism (Levi-Strauss 1963), which rejects normal biopsychological motivational analysis in favor of what Harris (1968:493) refers to as "the basic propensity of the human mind to build logical categories by means of binary contrasts underlying large portions, if not the totality of sociocultural phenomena." Such a paradigm, of course, tends to minimize the role of observable historical and functional factors in comprehending sociocultural phenomena; and indeed, according to Bottomore (1993b:648), "it was anti-empiricist ... by virtue of its insistence on the causal efficacy of a deep (perhaps undemonstrable) structure underlying the immediately given surface appearances."

Durkheim's influence on French structuralism certainly is clear, but it may be even more evident in the history of British anthropology where, throughout the time of a declining British empire in the earliest decades of the twentieth century and beyond, functionalism was preeminent. Functionalism provided a theoretical coherence to what had been a multifarious (British) discipline, especially so with the "structural-functionalism" of A. R. Radcliffe-Brown, for whom the role of social structure replaced Durkheim's idealistic notion of social solidarity as the ultimately "requiring" factor in any sociocultural system. Though this brand of functionalism was later to be disputed by Malinowski's ultimate requirement of certain psychobiological needs, the tendency to use the notion of function in an analysis of any sociocultural system, the normal condition of which was thought to be a bounded, evolving, and ultimately harmonious whole, became widespread in British anthropology and beyond.

The fact that such analysis might be tied to the historical condition of the societies being studied, most of which were African colonies of an imperial Great Britain, and was often justified in terms of the lack of adequate historical information about them, tended to be overlooked until English critics such as E.E. Evans-Pritchard, Fred Eggan, Raymond Firth, Max Gluckman, and Edmund Leach, among others (Asad 1973; Harris 1968:514–567), began to raise problems with this paradigm.

So much for the anthropological side of things. A similar American-inspired functionalist perspective had also been coursing through the sociological community at the same time. As in anthropology, it was not so much a refusal to acknowledge that societies or cultures were not entirely harmonious, did not have problems, and did not change, only that an evolutionary analysis in terms of what often was thought to be some ideal-typical organic whole tended to clash with what seemed to be going on in the world, in which, as a number of critics have pointed out, the guiding question in social research could just as well concern the forces that make society fall apart as hang together (the latter of which many functionalists seemed to assume). As anthropologists and sociologists began to take seriously this alternative point of view, the notion of society as a fissionable and changing entity began to grow.

The functional sociology which had come to dominate in America and elsewhere after World War II during the period of the Cold War between the United States and Russia is typified by the thinking of the American Talcott Parsons and his associates, as well as students such as Edward Shils and Robert Merton. Though under increasing criticism, this mode of thought remained significant throughout the period when the study of tourism began to emerge in anthropology and sociology. In Parsons' recognition of personal agency in the functioning of sociocultural systems through social psychological concepts of role, personality and self (Parsons 1949, 1951:201–248), his multidisciplinary connections, and his vision of sociocultural reality as a functioning whole (Parsons 1951:326–383), this paradigm, which flourished for two or more decades, represented something of an Americanization of sociocultural analysis; but the notion of sociocultural change as "a moving equilibrium" (Parsons 1951:481) of a rather harmonious whole shows a tendency toward the kind of analysis that was also characteristic of the British (anthropological) functionalists.

Bottomore (1993a:635), who might as well have been speaking also about anthropology, points out that the decline of the functionalist paradigm in sociology began in the 1960s when social conflict and change, instead of consensus and the regulation of social equilibrium, became a central issue. Then, conflict-based theories of change, sometimes nourished by an evolving Marxism, began coming to the fore. He also notes that as the discipline flourished, there was a proliferation of new and redefined areas of research accompanied by an increase in intradisciplinary disputes.

In anthropology, there had developed an increasing number of sociocultural areas of inquiry (e.g., religion, kinship, economy)—more than a hundred having been defined for cross-cultural investigation in its Human Relations Area Files (Murdock 1982), and significant divisions between its biologically and culturally oriented practitioners, its scientists and humanists, those favoring human agency and those giving primacy to institutional structure in sociocultural analysis, the politically oriented and the apolitical, the diachronic and synchronic analysts, the ideographic and the nomothetic, the interpretivists and the positivists, the literary and the rational-scientific, etc. Indeed, though anthropologists have always had their disagreements (Lewis 2001:401), it would seem that this discipline, too, had changed in a similar manner from the not too distant time when heroic figures such as the Americans Boas and Linton and British functionalists like Radcliffe Brown and Malinowski still seemed to cover everything (at least primitively) human everywhere with views that had come to assume an almost taken-for-granted quality. It is no wonder that with all this dissonance Marcus and Fisher (1986:16) speak about a decline in "paradigmatic authority" within the discipline of anthropology, a trend also revealed in Friedrichs' (1970:11–56) analysis of the sociology of that time.

So by the time when anthropologists and sociologists were finding their way into the subject of tourism, the regnant theoretical worlds, which provided them with the tools of social analysis, were being challenged more and more, and questions even about the basic nature of scientific inquiry, as in the already established distinction between qualitative and quantitative methodologies, began to come to the fore. It was in this period of theoretical and methodological flux that anthropo-logical and sociological study of tourism of historical significance arose. Naturally, there was more or less commitment to different schemes of social analysis and rigor in carrying them out in early tourism research by anthropologists and sociologists (Cohen 1984; Crick 1989; Dann and Cohen 1991; Dann, Nash and Pearce 1988; Nash and Smith 1991). Undoubtedly, more specific qualities of the theoretical and methodological orientations assumed by anthropologists, sociologists, and perhaps others will be revealed as we move forward in our study, especially as we delve into the personal histories of our contributors.

A glance over the very general view of the subject of tourism presented earlier should confirm that any social scientific approach to this subject would have to acknowledge that it is, indeed, as Crick (1989) says, "a multifaceted phenome-non" and that whatever aspect of the available theoretical pool was tapped for inspiration, any investigation would depend—at least in part—on the facet of tourism selected for investigation, as well as the particular conceptions of tourism and tourists involved (Cohen 1984:374–376). As an example, consider what has been the most frequent form of tourism study, i.e., the consequences of tourism development for some host culture. Consider further our notion of tourism as cen-tered on leisure travelers who, in their touring, get involved, directly or indirectly, with other peoples. Their contact and that of various tourism associates such as travel agencies, airline crews, hotel chains, site developers, etc. has relevance for sociocultural change—a view that can be easily derived from the general con-ception of tourism as a process given earlier.

Consider still further that "host" partners in exchanges with tourists and their associates from more developed countries are people in less-developed societies, perhaps as in a tourist destination such as the Seychelles or some island in the Caribbean—the kind of "host–guest" touristic encounter which has been mini-scule when compared with those between (or within) developed countries, but nevertheless important to anthropologists and sociologists with development on their minds. The social exchange in this kind of relationship is bound to be asym-metric as far as power is concerned, and the researcher, possibly involved in some applied project, may be concerned with the consequences of this touristic encounter for the less developed host people.

A variety of theories of development (Novak and Lekachman 1964; Seligson and Passé-Smith 1993), available to change-oriented anthropologists and sociolo-gists interested in tourism, were at that time gaining currency for analyzing this kind of sociocultural change. For example, the sociologist Forster (1964:218), who often is mentioned as an early practitioner in the field, begins a study by saying, "The position from which I begin is that the tourist areas of the Pacific are essentially undeveloped." A related view could have been found in the various notions of acculturation (Bee 1974:94–119; SSRC Seminar 1954), which were circulating in the social sciences of that time, with economists, perhaps, tending to emphasize the positive side of such development or acculturation for the hosts and anthropologists and sociologists the negative (UNESCO 1966). Such theories, while perhaps not entirely eschewing functiona-list assumptions, began to incorporate contestation and change and could be adapted for analysis of asymmetrical colonial or neo-colonial relationships, a subject that was of increasing interest to a new wave of anthropologists and sociologists. All that was necessary was to hook up some conception of tourism, an increasingly obvious fact in the contemporary world, with one of these theories and get on with the developmentally—or acculturatively—oriented study.

This was only one line of research that has been readily available to interested anthropologists, sociologists, and other social scientists. It also has been the line most frequently taken. A host of other possibilities, for example, the consequences of tourism for tourists and their cultures, the generation of tourists and tourisms, the nature of tourism networks, the nature of tourist groups, tourist motivations and their sources, etc. In Chapter 4, the issues are discussed in further detail.

The Discovery of Tourism by Anthropologists and Sociologists

Even though something resembling the tourism we know, had at the time already become a significant fact of life in the world around them, it must be said that it appears not have been a readily available fact of social life for social scientific researchers in the middle of the twentieth century. There also appears to have been a delay in coming to terms with the related subject of leisure (Lanfant 1972; Rojek 1985:4), which, along with travel, has been taken here to be an elemental aspect of tourism. Certainly, by the mid-twentieth century something like what even the most naive among us would take to be tourism was being practiced in many parts of the world; and in the West it had already become a well-known and named fact of life. Certainly, it was also becoming increasingly apparent in the Developing World in which anthropologists and some sociologists had developed a strong interest not only for practical, but theoretical reasons (Wallerstein 1984). And when the World Bank, the Organization for Economic Cooperation and Development (Pouris and Beerli 1963), and the United Nations (UNESCO 1966) began to show an interest in gathering basic facts associated with it, some possibilities for social scientific study of tourism, particularly on the applied side, would seem to have been readily apparent.

For the social sciences as a whole (Baretje 1981; Graburn and Jafari 1991:1–11; Towner and Wall 1991:71–84), it is possible to note some "anticipatory" studies of tourism (a good number of them without a clear disciplinary provenance) from the early part of the twentieth century, as, for example, those by Pimlott (1947) on "The Englishman's Holiday," destination areas of those English such as Nice and its surroundings (Musée Massena 1934), Pau in the French Pyranees (Duloum 1963), and the French Savoie (Miège 1933), in various inland and coastal resorts in Britain (Gilbert 1939), and British Hill stations in the Orient (Spencer and Thomas 1948). There were also early studies that took on the entire subject of tourism (Duchet 1949).

Discipline-related activity was not entirely absent in these anticipatory studies, however. What may be the earliest such indication is an economics-related article by Bodio (1899). As far as sociology is concerned, Cohen (1984) has noted only scattered earlier production from sociologically related scholars (e.g., von Wiese 1930, as well as a few other Germans) with the first empirical work on the subject (on tourism development in the Pacific) provided by Forster (1964). On the anthropological side, there was no work of consequence until that derived from the fieldwork of Nuñez (1963) concerning Mexicans at the beach and Kottak (1966) on the development of second homes in a Brazilian fishing village. Over all, Cohen's (1984:374) view on the lack of earlier systematic development of tourism research in sociology, can be accepted for anthropology as well. He says, "The study of tourism as a sociological specialty rather than merely as an exotic, marginal topic emerged only in the 1970s."

But though Lett (1989:275–279) speaks of an "explosion" of interest among anthropologists in the subject of tourism in the 1970s, though Cohen speaks of a rapidly growing field of research in the second-half of the 1970s, though a number of publications of significance appeared (DeKadt 1979; MacCannell 1976; Noronha 1979; Smith 1977; Turner and Ash 1975; Young 1977), though there were academic gatherings of consequence such as the section on tourism at the Meetings of the American Anthropological Assn. in Mexico City (1974), and though there were inauguration of journals such as *Annals of Tourism Research* (1973) and *Journal of Travel Research* (1970), exclusively devoted to tourism, it seems to have taken a rather long time (especially when one considers that this was a period of burgeoning anthropological and sociological specialties) for tourism study to get off the ground; and though research productivity has increased enormously since then (Goeldner 2003), one still hears complaints about problems in developing and carrying through a social scientific interest in the subject. For example, a colleague in a personal communication about the lack of tourism research at a well-known university in an American state that is well-known for its tourist destinations, reports an academic Dean saying recently, "If our benchmark schools don't have it, we shouldn't have it."

One way of curbing one's enthusiasm about progress in the field of tourism research would be to think in terms of some "bottom line" indication such as academic employment opportunities for candidates with degrees in anthropology or sociology who are specializing in tourism, articles on tourism in disciplinary journals, etc. For anthropology, sociology, and any other social science, any such accounting would likely confirm the notion that tourism study by anthropologists and sociologists has not been exactly taken for granted by their disciplinary establishments, however defined. In disciplines more directly related in a practical way to the subject, such as Hospitality and Tourism Management and Recreation, Park and Tourism Sciences, the outlook would appear to have been somewhat better.

Before entering too deeply into the question of delayed recognition in Anthropology and Sociology, it might be useful to make comparisons with other disciplines, especially those in the social sciences. One has to move cautiously with such a project, however, because though we do have some information, data are often inadequate and no systematic comparative study has been undertaken. What is clear, however, is that European social scientists seem to have gotten involved in the study of tourism earlier than North Americans. But the geographer Mitchell (1979:326), for example, even while tracing an interest by geographers in tourism back to the 1930s and noting that European geographers were ahead of North Americans in considering tourism, indicates that progress was slow in this field; and Richter (1983) has complained about the disinterest and total neglect of tourism research by the political science establishment, which produced only a few studies in the 1970s.

The question about the comparatively slow uptake on tourism study in Anthropology, Sociology, and the other social sciences in a period when the subject was so obviously significant is intriguing and merits consideration as a problem for intellectual history. On the conceptual–theoretical level, social scientists would seem to have been well prepared to take up the study of tourism at that time. As mentioned earlier, Cohen (1984:374–375) has suggested a variety of sociological issues associated with different aspects of tourism that were ready-made for tourism research; and Nash (1996) has suggested several anthropological perspectives, in which the discipline was already tourism-friendly. So it appears that, shortly after the middle of the twentieth century, these disciplines were prepared to digest a subject that was clearly evident to people at large, if not yet to certain academicians.

Additionally, there were applied interests of institutions such as those already mentioned above in tourism-related issues such as development, a subject which had come to the fore only a little earlier. With so many encouraging factors, how can one explain the comparatively slow development of tourism study in anthropology and sociology, as well as other social sciences? Put more generally, this question would take the form of an investigation into the sociocultural forces that spawn an interest in new subjects and work for or against their continued consideration.

Theron Nuñez, an anthropologist, who was exactly at the point of entry of the study of tourism in anthropology, offered a hypothesis accounting for the delay. Speaking from the vantage point of Valene Smith's (1977:208) first edition of *Hosts and Guests: The Anthropology of Tourism* (which is widely thought to have established some legitimacy for the field), he argued that the discovery of tourism by anthropologists had occurred largely by "accident" and that the delay in its recognition was due to "the impropriety of the subject within the traditional purview of the discipline." Further specification obviously is needed if we are to turn this into a working hypothesis to be considered not only for anthropology, sociology, and other social sciences; but the idea is persuasive enough to give some direction to the present investigation. We will begin with the notion that at the time when anthropologists and sociologists and possibly other social scientists were beginning to consider the all-too-obvious subject of tourism scientifically, there existed some kind of tabu against its scientific consideration.

Nuñez' hypothesis can be used not only to open up the question of the contextual basis for the development of tourism study in the social sciences, in which questions can be raised not only about sociocultural forces aiding or inhibiting such research, but also, perhaps, how it has shaped by those forces. And, of course, in a study that is pregnant with issues of persistence and change, we may also venture to note broader implications that pertain to other areas of sociocultural life beyond the subject of tourism research itself.

By Way of Summary

In this introduction, we hope to have established tourism as an increasingly impressive social fact, which can be studied by theories and methodologies available to social scientists. It exists not only in the Western world, but elsewhere as well; and if we adopt a fairly loose definition, which takes tourism to be centered around leisured travelers, it would seem to have prevailed in all historic and prehistoric societies.

The serious and continuing consideration of tourism as a social scientific subject began only a half century or so ago in the West. Here, we have taken two fairly representative social sciences, anthropology and sociology, which have many affinities, to commence an exploration of the discovery and early treatment of the subject. This exploration is based primarily on the personal histories of pioneers in the field who, fortunately for this enterprise, were still alive and able to convey them directly to the editor.

After briefly tracing the main lines of social thought in the two disciplines, it was possible to outline the relevant theoretical pool, with which the discoverers of tourism as an anthropological/sociological subject had to work. Different aspects of this pool could be applied to different facets of tourism. For example, it was shown how theories of development could be related to studies of host populations in destination areas.

A most striking fact, derived from our exploration of the beginnings of the study of tourism, was the obvious delay in the recognition of some aspect of tourism as a subject for investigation through some anthropological/sociological perspective; and this was thought to be a possible key to the analysis of the early history of the study of tourism provided by the personal histories to follow. We hope to be able to use it as a starting point for our analysis of the beginnings of the field of tourism research, which could have implications for the development of science, intellectual history, and perhaps sociocultural change and persistence generally.

Chapter 2

The Study

One can, of course, look at the emergence and development of new fields of study by simply noting and tracing intellectual currents revealed in published works. Thus, following Kitcher (1993:114), one could isolate areas of inquiry which "typically begin with big, vague questions followed by the introduction of explanatory schemata that suggest new, more precise inquiries to undertake." Good enough, but as was indicated in Chapter 1, that is only a beginning. Scientific ideas are not only things that exist in a disembodied world of their own. They also should be seen as created and maintained by human beings who, besides thinking and feeling more or less deeply in ways that we may call scientific, religious, artistic, etc., may respond, individually and collectively, to other aspects of their natures and to the world in which they are involved. The fact that they are scientists, mystics, artists, etc., should not in any way provide immunity from research procedures aimed at analyzing other aspects of their humanity. This point, which is developed cross-culturally by the anthropologist Frederick Barth (2002), can be extended beyond scientific disciplines to extra-scientific factors, as is suggested by Thomas Kuhn's (1977:xv) observation about complaints that his account of scientific development "is too exclusively based on factors internal to the sciences themselves." His response acknowledges the importance of "external" factors in the development of a scientific idea world, which suggests a line of inquiry that is well illustrated in, for example, Strozier's (2001) study of the often acrimonious debates associated with the development of a new form of psychoanalysis by Heinz Kohut and his followers, the study by Shapin and Schaffer (1985) of Robert Boyle's struggles with the Royal Society over the results of his experiments with the Air Pump, or Roseberry's (1996) analysis of the development of American anthropology after World War II as an intellectual endeavor situated within a framework of material, social and political relations and processes. All of these, of course, may be seen in terms of a paradigm for science, which has been developed by Robert Merton (1996:208–209).

A useful way of looking at the development of an anthropology/sociology of tourism from this broader perspective is to adopt the point of view of social action alluded to earlier, which conceives of the scholars involved in studying a particular subject such as tourism as dealing with a mix of social forces while engaged in purposeful, subjectively meaningful action. This social action point of view, which owes a good deal to Max Weber (1958; but see also Barth 2002; Dann 1981), considers socially situated actors to be thinking, and perhaps feeling about their own actions as they pursue their subjectively informed courses of action. Using this perspective, we can try to comprehend more fully what anthropological and sociological scholars were up to as they were coming to grips with the (for them) new subject of tourism, which is the nature of the specific reality they had chosen to investigate.

In our study, the informant-actors who will provide the information about this process were mainly selected to represent a somewhat broadly conceived category of social scientist who shared qualities of character derived from anthropology and sociology, which tended to set them off from colleagues in the other social sciences. How "set off" these scholars were according to discipline was not always easy to discern because of the multidisciplinary nature of the early study of tourism, not only by sociologists and anthropologists, but by members of other social scientific disciplines as well. In the end, however, it does seem that our participants, though sometimes marginally situated between disciplines, have not raised too many difficulties about their identification with single disciplines.

Participating informants were also selected because they were among the earliest to deal with the subject of tourism scientifically (being on the spot, so to speak), and (as a token of their insider knowledgeability) have been involved with the subject up to the present. This qualification, which left one or two living "pioneers" out of our projected "sample," was adopted in order to ensure some similarity in developmental perspectives, as well as survivability in the new field of tourism study. As a result, we can say that all of those selected for the sample, have been involved in the field of tourism study since its beginnings and have left a recognizable mark in it by their writing, teaching, or other scholarly actions. However, questions about the importance or seminality of their contributions, though at times an issue, have been considered largely extraneous to the selection process; and indeed, considering Merton's (1996:318–336) discussion of the complexity of the issue of scientific reputations, would be better left for history to decide.

All of the participant-informants turned out to be creatures of what may loosely referred to as Western culture and involved in scholarly, tourism-related activities in its academic institutions, which as suggested earlier, have been the main institutional locus for social scientific study, including that concerning tourism. It might be wise to point out here, however, that the editor was not entirely intransigent in the process of selecting informants. Insiders will note, for example, that the name of one well-known pioneer, the deceased Theron Nuñez, who may have been the first to study tourism anthropologically and who also has commented publicly on early developments in the field (Nuñez 1977), is missing from the participating informants listed in the book. The absence of anyone with his qualifications, for whatever reason, from our group of informants certainly is to be lamented, but we do not intend to ignore him as an informant. Neither will we ignore certain knowledgeable others who, for one reason or another, were not fully qualified as participants, but who possessed information pertaining to our investigation. Their contributions will be properly noted as we move along.

The Use of Informants

The use of informants in ethnographic field research has been well established in anthropology and sociology, and to a lesser extent, in some of the other social sciences since early days and is in accord with Coser's (1971:219) characterization of Weber as taking a stand that "man, in contrast to things, could be understood not only in external manifestations, that is, in behavior, but also in his underlying motivations." Though sometimes criticized, the use of the well-placed, or situated informant has been an important part of this methodological tradition (Harris 1968:585–589). There can be many reasons for following this procedure, but we should now know that it has to be used with care because of the inevitable problems with sampling faced by anyone studying group ways of life, often called cultures, which though normative, are also variable and contested (Nash 1999:12–14). The tendency of ethnographers to seem rather helter-skelter in the selection of informants can raise questions about the accuracy of their sociocultural depictions, especially among those scientists who are prone to use more systematic sampling procedures.

These critics, however, may be operating in more controlled situations, say, in public opinion polling or laboratory experiments, where more systematic procedures for gathering information are well established. Anthropologists, sociologists, and other social scientists doing ethnographic research under more "natural" conditions where research questions are less likely to be fixed beforehand, universes studied are small, and associated parameters less well-known may find that less systematic procedures are actually called for. In such situations, the judgment of researchers who have immersed themselves in a peoples' lifeways and acquired at least a beginning understanding of their natures may turn out to be the best way to go, especially in the early history of a developing field with amorphous boundaries like tourism study.

Considering the complexities and difficulties of typical ethnographic research in the field where one may have to deal with cultural differences between researcher and subjects, the variability and contested nature of cultures, differences between cultures, the variety of potential research questions, situational differences, and the different natures of researchers, it would seem that, however fallible, the informed judgment of the ethnographer could, indeed, turn out at times to be a more desirable method of selecting informants. It should be emphasized, however, that it is not suggested here that qualitative research, which is a term often used for the methodology in this kind of study (Denzin and Lincoln, eds. 1993; Phillimore and Goodson, eds. 2004), should be hit or miss in choosing informants, but rather that it always should employ justifiable criteria for their choice in discussing some phenomenon- a stance which, unfortunately, as Nash (2000) points out, has not always been taken in ethnographic research, including the study of tourism.

In our study, which despite some obvious differences still has many of the qualities of a typical ethnographic investigation, the overriding question for choice of informants was the nature of the research problem, which concerns the emergence and development of a new object of intellectual concern among certain social scientific researchers. Since little had been written on the beginnings of an anthropology/sociology of tourism, and since it was no longer possible to observe the process directly, the use of available informants who had been directly involved was an obvious procedure for acquiring information; and the fact that the editor was one of these, though raising some special problems, could only help to improve the general quality of the investigation.

Research Procedures

Beginning with a pool of participant who had been suggested by a variety of "experts," the editor, considering issues of coverage and manageability, began a process of selection, which also involved questioning those approached for other possible informants who might be added to our list. Some suggestions about participants by referees of the book proposal also were considered before concluding a selection process, which in the end, resulted in a projected sample of anthropological/sociological informants, including the author himself, plus a few others, who though not meeting all formal criteria for participants, nevertheless could be used to help out on certain issues. The editor himself was acquainted personally with almost all of these people, worked strenuously to forestall attrition, but in the end, one person from those originally selected as participants, as well as another who had been added later were unable to complete the writing of their personal histories which were at the heart of our project. This resulted in a final formal "sample" of 13 participant-informants. In the end, information from these participants, as well as some "outsiders," where available through personal communication or published sources, would be considered in constructing the early history of the study of tourism in anthropology and sociology.

Perhaps it is important to mention once again that all informants who were selected for the working sample of participants met all of the criteria for selection, which meant that they were scholars who had participated in the beginnings of an anthropological/sociological study of tourism and had continued their involvement in such study up to the present. It is important to remind readers here that these informants are not the earliest to have engaged in tourism study, which according to Towner (1996) can be traced back to its (rather spare) beginnings a century or more ago. Nor does it include several sociologists and anthropologists who are known to have preceded those in our sample, who for one reason or other, are no longer involved in the study of tourism.

Though there are some minor problems of lifetime mobility, it can be said that at the time of the study our participants were working in six different countries—all of them Western or Western-oriented. With the exception of one or two people, all could use English without assistance. This meant that research business could be carried on, for the most part, in English, with only occasional translation problems to be handled by the editor and a more expert associate (see Appendix B).

In glancing over the listing of participating informants, some of those acquainted with the anthropological and sociological study of tourism, as, for example, a referee for this project, might raise questions about the importance of one or another participants for this field of study; but considering the preceding discussion, this issue was not considered relevant. The guiding question for the selection of informants was only that they be among the more knowledgeable about the early development of tourism study in anthropology and sociology through their direct involvement in it; and because they had been directly involved, they could, therefore, help the editor to construct as full a picture as possible of this particular development in Western intellectual history from an insiders point of view. Further discussion of the selection process is included in Appendix B.

Techniques for Acquiring Information

As mentioned earlier, this study does not actually involve fieldwork, but it does share some aspects of research in the ethnographic mode, which is generally thought of as small-scale, first-hand, involving an active give-and-take between researcher and subjects, and usually employing at least two basic techniques: participant observation and the use of informants (Nash 2000:19–20). Of such techniques, the study leans heavily, but not exclusively, on the latter of these. Though the author has been directly involved with a number of the participants and acquainted with them and their work during the formative years of the field, his involvement with them has been nothing like the daily, face-to-face interaction normally employed in ethnographic fieldwork, which the anthropologist Frederik Barth (2002:436) discusses as follows:

> There seems to be no alternative for us but to depend heavily on our personal social capacity so as to achieve that degree of resonance and intersubjectivity that gives access to our primary, empirical data on what people are indeed doing, that is, their subjectively purposeful and meaningful acts.

Nevertheless, the editor has found that the rapid give-and-take by e-mail with familiar others that sometimes obtained in this study, as well as direct contact with some of them at meetings and elsewhere, has been a useful way for developing and maintaining the kind of intersubjectivity that seems to be valued in Barth's model for ethnographic fieldwork.

The research involved in this study also may be characterized as making use of personal documents, which is a procedure that has been widely employed in the social sciences (see Gottschalk, Kluckhohn and Angell, eds. 1945; Langness 1965; L. Smith 1993), as with, for example, diaries (Pearce 1982:41–46) or letters (Thomas and Znaniecki 1927). There are varying views about how much "reality" can be unearthed by this method. Though sympathizing with Smith's (1993:302) comment that "doing biography is an active constructionist activity," this author has not yet given up on the belief that there are social realities that can be apprehended, probably imperfectly, and that some social scientists are especially capable of doing that with certain subjects, as, for example, Max Weber's "religiously musical" researchers (investigating the subject of religion) who in our case, might be called "touristically musical."

Here, the personal document produced by participants was partially directed in that they were asked to prepare a loosely structured written narrative (personal history) about themselves and the contexts in which they acted as they came to be involved with the subject of tourism and developed their interests in it. The plan was for their personal histories to follow a very general Guide (see Appendix A) given them by the editor, as well as comments and subsequent directions sent out to them in a number of e-mail Missives from time to time. Problems that emerged over such matters as coverage, style, organization, and clarity were to be handled through the mails and are discussed in Appendix B.

The personal document required of the participants was not exactly what has been referred to in the literature as a Life History. Rather, it was to take the form of a portion or slice of that history, as discussed by Davies (1999:167–173)—in this case, that part in which participants became involved in the study of tourism and began their work in an emerging field. One of the better known of such studies, that of the Hopi Indian Don Talayesva (Sun Chief) by Leo Simmons (1942), though dated in some respects, turned out to be unexpectedly useful for purposes of orientation. Though Simmons' ultimate aim was to reconstruct the life history of an individual personality (and not the development and prosecution of a particular interest during that history), and though there are differences in the way we have gathered and organized our data, there turned out to be something rather useful in his work for a study such as ours. In particular, there is his suggestion (Simmons 1942:389–390) that "the life course ... may be viewed as a successive series of linked situations in which the individual makes (situational) adjustments, and these adjustments may be studied as single units." Such a "slice of life" approach seemed to be particularly applicable in a study which seeks to integrate relevant aspects of an individual's life course with a developing interest in a new subject of study. As he (Simmons 1942:389–390) says, "If it proves unprofitable to attempt to explain a whole personality over an extended period of time by means of a few sweeping and simplified formulas, the life course from birth to death may yet be viewed as a successive series of linked situations in which the individual makes adjustments, and these adjustments may be studied (by situational analysis)."

In some cases, a good deal of give-and-take of participants with the editor was necessary for using this more limited perspective. One problem occurred with several participants who seemed to have had early childhood experience (e.g., travel) on their minds, and it was not always easy to convince them that some more proximate dispositions, experiences, and inclinations could be more relevant, and indeed effective for tracing the course of their increasing connectedness with the subject of tourism. For these participants, the editor, somewhat jokingly, suggested the tactic of ruling out "kid stuff" from their personal narratives, a suggestion that has not been entirely successful.

Another problem was posed by several participants who argued that their development as tourism scholars had not been a matter of successive, coherent stages, one evolving from the other, in a simple "step-by-step" fashion. Rather, it was argued that the development of their tourism interest was at times apparently non-coherent and involved multiple, apparently, unrelated actions, and that it also could involve advances and regressions. In this regard, the personal experience of the editor in various "paraclinical" situations, including those with artists whose development sometimes could appear rather chaotic (Nash 1954), undoubtedly was useful; but readers should keep in mind that our intention of seeing a participant's increasing involvement in the subject of tourism in terms of stages was more a descriptive than analytic strategy. Nevertheless, the job of eliciting the story of their discovery and increasing involvement with tourism was not always easy to accomplish. Here, the book's aim of getting participants to produce simple, direct discourse in what Bennett Berger has referred to as a "natural" register (Berger, ed. 1990:xiii) that was also interesting and understandable to readers, as well as useful for constructing the early history of tourism research, sometimes conflicted with problems of personal revelation. Further discussion of this issue is included in Appendix A.

In our investigation, participating informants were asked to provide written information mainly about a part of their life (the single unit referred to by Simmons) that had to do primarily with their developing interest in tourism. Asked to think of themselves as informants, they were supposed to provide an account about their discovery of, and subsequent involvement with the subject of tourism. The Guide asked them to cover certain essentials of the process. These included their earlier academic background, the sociocultural (including disciplinary and theoretical) context associated with their discovery and developing study of tourism, and the developmental processes involved. Finally, they were asked to look back over their own intellectual development since they had became involved with the study of tourism and locate themselves in intellectual currents of the present, not only in tourism study, but in broader fields as well. Subsequent directions were given to keep explanations and interpretations to a minimum in their accounts—the overall aim being to keep the narratives as much as possible in a "natural voice," rather than a "professorial" one, as Berger calls them. At the time of this writing, it is possible to say that some participants succeeded better than others in accomplishing this, but most of the participants (with more or less help from the editor) ultimately adapted to this "requirement" reasonably well.

Generally, the editorial intention was to intervene as little as possible so that participants would be able to give a natural account of what had transpired in their tourism-inspired lives, much as in open-ended interviewing; but for some, a good deal of direction from the editor in getting the life history on track was necessary. When problems in the preparation of a personal history became particularly severe, a rough draft of the editor's own personal history was made available on request. The ideal agenda was to follow a course dictated by the Guide with a minimal amount of intervention from the editor in the first draft. Then, all first drafts would be revised in terms of the editor's suggestions, a process sometimes strewn with difficulties. Further editorial intervention was increasingly one sided, with the aim of the editor being to produce a clearly written document in keeping with the subject's intentions.

One might have thought that, given the sociocultural location of the participants and the earlier association of the editor with most of them, the Guide and various Missives sent out from time to time would have been enough to get everyone together on the same page in this autobiographical operation. But this turned out not to be always the case, and some significant interventions were required to keep the participants on track and on time. Your editor must admit that this all came as a surprise to him, and he has been speculating about why the problem existed in this particular sample. Again, further discussion of these issues will be found in Appendix B.

As far as the contribution of Leo Simmons is concerned, one is surprised to find how useful his work has turned out to be. After all, there has been a good deal of change in anthropology and the social sciences since he did his work. Certainly, it lacks much in the way of "post-positivist" reflexiveness and other approaches giving a larger role to observer observations and interpretations, which are important elements in qualitative methodology (see, e.g., Davies 1999; Giddens 1995; Hammersley and Atkinson 1995; Nash 2000; Nash and Wintrob 1972; Phillimore and Goodson, eds. 2004). And Simmons used a theoretical orientation from the field of Personality and Culture that is not very much in vogue these days. But the empirically oriented will be drawn to his knowledge of subject matter and the care he took to ensure the accuracy of his situationally derived constructions. His analysis and interpretations seem always to be well grounded in the life of his subject, Don Talayesva, a Hopi Indian Chief, and the sociocultural world in which he lived. Also, Simmons seems to have managed to strike an optimal balance between distance and involvement, an always-desirable quality in ethnographic fieldwork. In sum, there is much to admire in this author's work, and the fact that it was "old" did not keep it from being useful in this study.

Any reader perusing this chapter concerning the methodology used in this investigation of the origins and development of a certain social scientific approach to tourism, should not be surprised to find that many of the ideas informing it reflect the disciplines of the participants, particularly those of the editor. Both anthropology and sociology now have developing traditions concerning the analysis of the production and dissemination of knowledge, the study of which has a precursor in German *Wissenssociologie*, more specifically, the writings of Max Scheler (1980 [1924]) and Karl Mannheim (1936). Its point, according to Berger and Luckmann (1967:1), is that "reality is socially constructed and that the sociology of knowledge must analyze the processes in which that occurs."

What someone knows, according to Bertrand Russell (1948:9), depends on "what a person has seen and heard, what he has read, what he has been told, and also what, from these data, he has been able to infer." The sociological study of this process and its inevitable attachment of knowledge to certain social arrangements has become the stuff of the sociology of knowledge, which is discussed authoritatively by Barnes, Bloor and Henry (1996) and informs a good many contributions to the International Journal for the Study of Science (ISIS).

All of the work of the sociologists in this area can be viewed from the perspective of the Sociology of Science—or Knowledge, which obviously informs our study. The tradition of an Anthropology of Knowledge is not nearly as long and deep. Crick (1982:287), in reviewing its shadowy beginnings, is wary about the establishment of a new sub-field, which will become "increasingly remote from the main stream." Franklin (1984) speaks of the early development of the field in terms often used by the sociologists involved, that is, conflict between those looking at science as "science," in which the veracity of some view of reality is paramount, and those looking at it as a "culture," in which the aim is to connect the view, whatever its ultimate veracity, with particular social arrangements. Though there have been scattered anthropological contributions along the way (see, e.g., Hallowell 1965; Stocking 1983; Vermuelen and Alvarez Roldan 1995), a fuller, more formal, cross-culturally viable framework for the same kind of analyses such as those carried out for Western society by sociologists has only recently appeared (Barth 2002). Except for its broader, cross-cultural framework and associated details, however, there appears now to be little except the range of cultures involved that distinguishes this anthropology from a sociology of knowledge, both of which will provide the pool of ideas for our analysis of the development of early thoughts about tourism in anthropology and sociology in the concluding chapter of this book.

Advances in the sociology/anthropology of knowledge have undoubtedly been associated with the relativization of researchers' observations and interpretations and the development of a more critical realistic perspective on subject matter. In this regard, the editor has been at all times aware that in the flux and diversity of our present historical condition, any privilege we might have thought we had as observers has come into question, and we must increasingly accompany accounts of what we scientists are doing by referring to the existential situation of the researcher (see, e.g., Giddens 1995; Nash and Wintrob 1972).

Accordingly, it might be wise at this point to give some idea of the posture aimed for by the editor in this study, in which he considers himself as one of the various actors who have, directly or indirectly, contributed to it—a project which is coming to be increasingly necessary in social scientific research (Hall 2004). As one of these actors, he should know that he is not exempt from forces that move other humans, that he should be aware as possible of those that affected him throughout the study, and that he should be prepared to discuss his research experience and inclinations openly. Even so, it is incumbent on him to accept full responsibility for his views.

Second, it is hoped that some optimal combination of theoretical and methodological acumen will prevail. Third, an attempt will be made to achieve some balance of detachment and involvement, which is always desirable. Fourth, it is hoped that there will be as much transparency as possible where research procedures and the investigating self are concerned, a requirement which has already been discussed to some extent in the present chapter and is further discussed in Appendix B. And finally, there is the requirement that researchers should be as familiar with their subject matter as possible, a quality which the editor of this study, having, himself, engaged in the study of tourism, fortunately possesses. With such an outlook in mind and carried through in practice, it is to be hoped that the editor's claims as an investigator of the early development of an anthropology/sociology of tourism, however flawed, will be considered as not entirely without privilege.

Having taken care of the necessary preliminaries of this study, the editor, in the proximate chapter, will be seen as one of our participating informants, who has written his own personal history, a task not entirely consonant with his role as editor. After that, he will reappear as a presumably more informed, if possibly more distanced editor in the ultimate, analytic chapters of the book, in which he will attempt to make sense of information provided in the personal histories of our participants. In doing all this, he may even be thought to have gained the additional privilege of speculating a bit about the present and future of the comparatively new field of tourism study.

Chapter 3

Personal Histories

Jeremy Boissevain (1928–) is Emeritus Professor of Social Anthropology, University of Amsterdam, Singel 176-B, 1015 AJ, Amsterdam, The Netherlands (e-mail: jboissevain@fmg.uva.nl). Once CARE Mission Chief in the Philippines, Japan, India, and Malta, he has also held appointments at the University of Montreal, the University of Sussex, and the University of Malta. His work has dealt with local politics, ethnic relations, small entrepreneurs, ritual change, tourism, and environmentalism. Recent publications include *Revitalizing European Rituals* (Boissevain, ed. 1992), *Coping with Tourists: European Reactions to Mass Tourism* (1996), and (with Tom Selwyn) *Contesting the Foreshore: Tourism, Society, and Politics on the Coast* (Boissevain and Selwyn, eds. 2004).

SAINTS, FIREWORKS, AND TOURISTS

Beginnings

I was born in London of a Dutch father and American mother. Together with my two younger brothers we moved around a good deal between England, Holland, and America. By the time I graduated from high school in Huntingdon Valley, Pennsylvania, I had moved twelve times. In these shifting cultural settings we were always newcomers, half outsiders, always slightly different from our neighbors and classmates. We were continually observing, comparing, and discussing the customs and behavior of the others among whom we lived. At the same time, my brothers and I tried to blend in with our changing surroundings. In Holland, we were welcomed and looked up to as exciting school companions from the land of cowboys, Indians, and gangsters. In America, at least in the beginning, we had quite the opposite experience. To our class, most of whom had never been out of Pennsylvania, we were foreigners, "dumb Dutchmen," who didn't know the score and had different family customs. In retrospect, I think these experiences and the somewhat aloof, detached outsider's orientation they inculcated were in part responsible for my later interest in anthropology. They also help explain my reluctance to join organized groups like the Boy Scouts and debating clubs, fads, theoretical schools, and guided tourist excursions. I still feel you have to live in a place, or at least to have been there on a working visit in order to gain an appreciation of its culture and people, even of its monuments and landscape.

After an 18-month stint with the US Army, during which I was sent to Trieste, I attended Haverford College, a small liberal arts men's college in Pennsylvania. I majored in French under Lawrence Wylie who, during my final year, was writing up his research on a little village in the south of France. He had lived there with his family to learn just how the French, whose literature and culture he had studied for years, actually became Frenchmen and women. So he observed them in their daily life, visiting schools, spending time with them in cafés and in their homes. He had done this research very much like an anthropologist. He lectured to us in French about his experiences and the intricacies of French politics. I found it altogether fascinating. During part of my time at Haverford I lived, along with other students studying French, in the 'French House,' where on several evenings I looked after the young Wylie children.

I spent my third year at college in Paris at the Sorbonne. During my year in France, besides learning to speak French, I rediscovered my European roots in the course of a Christmas holiday trip to Amsterdam to visit my aunts and cousins. But most important of all, I met Inga, a Swedish girl studying journalism in Paris. She was adventurous, had hitchhiked widely around Europe, spoke several languages, and was interested in continuing to explore the world. In short, she was refreshingly different from the dating obsessed American girls I had met while at college. In June she left for an apprenticeship on a newspaper in Sundsvall, northern Sweden. After sitting my final examinations at the Sorbonne, I hitchhiked to Sundsvall and worked in a paper mill, the job Inga had found for me until it was time to return to Haverford for my final year. Later on she entered the United States as an immigrant, clutching the required envelope of x-ray photographs to prove to the uninterested Immigration authorities that she was not diseased. A month later we were married.

After graduation, I worked for about six months as a management trainee for Pan American World Airways at New York's Idlewild Airport. My duties involved weighing baggage, checking tickets, examining passports, and in other ways serving and enviously assisting people to depart for abroad. Many of the passengers were holidaymakers bound for Europe and the Caribbean. This was my first contact with organized tourism. But after nine months on the ticket counter, during which Inga worked as a guide in the United Nations building, our turn came to leave Senator McCarthy's America—to our joy.

CARE

Through my father's contacts, I was fortunate enough to find work with the Cooperative for American Remittances Everywhere (CARE). In the late spring of 1953, I flew to Manila. It was my first long flight. In those days trans-Pacific flights were luxurious for all passengers. We had all the legroom we could use, free slippers, and an ominous engine cowling glowing red just outside our window. During the next five years as CARE Mission Chief in the Philippines, Japan, India, and Malta, I directed food aid and development programs. My most exciting activity during those interesting years was helping establish a successful program to introduce hothouse cultivation to Maltese farmers. With CARE we led a very interesting, comfortable, and somewhat unreal life. We had semidiplomatic privileges, substantial housing, a car and driver, household help, and for me, a trained office staff. After almost two years in Malta and about to be transferred to Lebanon or Turkey, Inga and I, now with two daughters, were beginning to crave a slightly more settled future. I was also growing frustrated with always being a visitor—an outsider looking into fascinating, but closed societies. Moreover, I was becoming increasingly disillusioned with the negative developmental impact of food aid programs and the way they invariably reinforced the position of local elites.

I wrote for advice to Lawrence Wylie, by then Dillon Professor at Harvard University. After hearing me out, he strongly advised me to study anthropology, something he said he would do if he could start over again. I followed his advice and, with the help of the US consulate in Malta, began to research US anthropology departments. Information gleaned from a team of University of Durham research students studying land use in Malta convinced me that a British university best suited our needs. The anthropology graduate programs there were swifter, much less expensive, and more in line with my interests in applied anthropology. Thanks to Wylie's strong recommendation, I was offered a place at the London School of Economics and Political Science.

Interestingly enough, shortly before leaving I had a discussion with the Malta government Director of Information. He mentioned that he had just been asked to take over responsibility for promoting tourism, which it was hoped would cushion the economic effects of the decline of the British Military establishment on the Island. Somewhat discouraged, he asked me, "Jeremy, do you think Malta can ever become an interesting tourist destination?" I had recently been to Greece and Libya, and had been impressed by their hotels, the scenery, and the antiquities. I mentally compared those experiences with the shabby decor and service at the hotel we had stayed in when we first arrived in Malta, and also the Islands' neglected megalithic monuments, tatty countryside and crowded beaches. I replied, "No way. Definitely not!" The first of my many failed prophesies.

Back to School

In the summer of 1958 we sailed from Malta, our most comfortable and pleasant CARE posting, to London to gamble on a new career as an academic and/or enlightened community development worker. My first step was, as a very green, foreign graduate student at a British University on a tight budget, sourced entirely from personal savings. At the LSE I worked most closely with Raymond Firth, the Head of Department, and my supervisor, Lucy Mair, who was then Reader in Applied Anthropology. Both had been students of Malinowski. As a callow American graduate student without a background in the social sciences, I had much to learn. For the previous five years I had lived a quasi-colonial life, responsible for a complicated aid program. I had suddenly become an ignorant student. Just how ignorant was made clear to me the first time I attended the undergraduate class to which I had been assigned in order to catch up with what I was supposed to know already. It started off with a student reading his essay on a recent article by Meyer Fortes about unilineal descent groups. After he finished, Maurice Freedman, who ran the class, turned to me and asked, "Well, Mr. Boissevain, what do you make of that?" I was stunned. I had not a clue of what the essay had been about. Many of the words the student had used were totally foreign to me. I felt my face begin to turn red and mumbled something. Maurice Freedman, mercifully, asked another for comments, and the girl started a learned discourse on the essay. Duly humbled, I dashed to the library after the class to look up the meaning of "agnatic" and read Fortes's article.

The staff at the LSE provided me with the most essential anthropological tools: the importance of asking apposite questions and the careful use of language in order to communicate the answers to others. Raymond Firth's constant probing questions during his weekly graduate research seminar taught his students to look beyond discourse at people's actions to discover the motives that articulate behavior. "Why did they do that? What did they get out of it," he would continually ask. Lucy Mair had a ferocious reputation. It was rumored that she literally threw books at students, especially at Americans, when she disagreed with their language or analysis or their work. She eventually taught me how to write clearly and succinctly, but not without some painful encounters. Once I described Maltese festa celebrants as joyously "careening" down the street. She objected loudly, and demanded to know what I meant. I explained that they were weaving along wildly from side to side. She snorted and stated that careening meant to turn a boat on its side in order to scrape the barnacles off its bottom. "You mean careering! Here, you look it up," she exploded. I sputtered. She then leapt up and, with force, thrust the *Concise Oxford English Dictionary* at me. She was, of course, right, but then so was I, for I was using American English. After that I always kept a dictionary very close to hand. But through this encounter I also discovered the origin of the "Lucy-throws-books-myth." Outside her office she was a warm, charming woman, who invited us to visit her at home and smiled benignly when one of our daughters spilled strawberries and cream all over her carpet. Several years later, on her way home from Africa, she stopped over in Malta and stayed with us for a few days.

With the wisdom of hindsight, and sadly now too late to credit and thank Raymond Firth and Lucy Mair for it, I realize how much I had been influenced by their Malinowskian legacy of vigorous and persistent questioning and observation that exposes how people behind a facade of discourse manipulate rules for personal gain. This legacy, in fact, was part of the foundation for my own rejection, much later, of the structural functionalism that I had absorbed via the - literature during my crash course in social anthropology while at the LSE (Boissevain 1974).

I survived the first year and passed the written qualifying examination, which permitted me to register for a PhD. That summer, I was able to replace the CARE representative in Libya for three months during his home leave so that I could scout around for a possible fieldwork site. Libya proved to be too costly for our savings and logistically too complicated for research with a family. Fortunately, I was granted a Colonial Social Science Council fellowship for a year to carry out research in Malta into local-level politics and their relation to the troubled national political scene that was causing a severe headache to the British government. At the time the Island was still a British Colony. The award was in no small measure due to contacts I had made while I was with CARE with the former Lieutenant Governor of Malta, Trafford Smith. I had passed through Malta on my way home from Libya and called on him to discuss the possibility of doing research in Malta. I wanted to keep my research options open. He indeed thought it would be a good idea. As it happened, when I applied for a grant the next year, he had left Malta and was back at the Colonial Office in London. I listed him as one of my references on my grant application, which Lucy Mair vigorously defended on my behalf. In fact, two years later, he was one of the examiners of my thesis. So, after two years in London, we returned to Malta.

The 15 months we spent in Malta were as hectic as they were fascinating. At the outset, the new British Lieutenant Governor warned me that if I were observed contacting the General Workers Union or the Malta Labour Party I would be expelled immediately. (Later I heard from the United States' Consul that the man's churlishness was probably due to the severe case of hemorrhoids from which he was then suffering!) We lived in two different villages, Kirkop and Naxxar, had our third daughter, Maria (named after Naxxar's patron saint), attended some 25 festas, and learned much about fireworks, festas, factions, and political infighting. We also renewed contact with old acquaintances, made many new friends and learned a great deal about the Maltese Islands and their inhabitants, forming a deep and lasting attachment to them.

Back at the LSE, I naively worried that the material I had gathered on little Malta would not be adequate for a PhD. How could it ever hope to match the complex material my fellow students brought back from places like Fiji, Ethiopia, Yemen, or Indonesia? I need not have worried. My accounts of the way rival festa factions schemed to outdo each other to honor their respective patron saints and the pettiness of the corrosive encounters between Malta's Archbishop Sir Michael Gonzi and Labour leader Dom Mintoff were quite as exotic and complex as anything my colleagues presented. A year later, the University of London accepted the results of my research and I was granted a PhD in 1962 (Boissevain 1965).

Settling Down: Sicily, Canada, England, and Holland

The month after I handed in my PhD manuscript, we departed for Palma di Montechiaro in Sicily. There, I worked for 10 months researching the difficulties facing a community development project. This, I thought, was an opportunity to apply anthropological insights to help solve practical development problems, with which I had some experience whilst working with CARE in the Philippines and India. A very energetic Dutch Franciscan priest, Salvinus Duynstee, to whom I had been recommended by two friendly Maltese priests, directed the project. Unfortunately, after six months, his work and my income were cut short when local priests, angry at my employer's (wise!) refusal to share with them the funds donated to his project by the German Bishops, denounced him as a Communist to the Cardinal Archbishop of Palermo who forced him to leave. I was able to stay on for two extra months with a grant from The American Philosophical Society (obtained, thanks again to Lawrence Wylie's support) and a consultancy that old friends at CARE arranged for me with its Rome office. In July 1963, Inga and our three daughters joined me and we sailed from Palermo as emigrants to Canada with an anthropology lectureship at the University of Montreal in store—something I had located the previous November at the American Anthropological Association conference in Detroit.

I began my new career as an academic by lecturing on kinship in French, laced with Italian, to students whose Canadian French gave me considerable problems for some time. I soon discovered that life as a university lecturer, in spite of the petty squabbles and point scoring, was much more congenial than that of a peripatetic community development worker. I was able to continue to research on things Sicilian, supplement my modest salary, and arrange for secretarial help by contracting to carry out research on Italian immigrants in Montreal for the

Canadian Commission on Biculturalism and Bilingualism. The research provided insights into the difficulty of adapting into a new country, a problem with which I could certainly empathize. It also helped me to conceptualize the role of social networks in structuring the relations among a locally and globally dispersed community. Though seduced by the intriguing puzzles of academic anthropology, the work I did with this immigrant community, and later with Surinamese immigrants in Amsterdam, together with my study of the impact of tourism, is the way I have periodically been able to realize my wish to apply my anthropology to the real world *we* live in.

Two years later, and two months after the birth of our fourth daughter, we gave in to the desire to return to Europe, and I took up a lectureship in Sociology at the new University of Sussex. The following year, we moved to the Netherlands where I took over the chair of Cultural—later Social Anthropology—at the University of Amsterdam. And there we have remained, mostly, ever since.

After arriving in Amsterdam I concentrated on gaining acceptance for, and developing, two personal interests. The first was the anthropological study of Europe in general, and the second concerned the Mediterranean region in particular. In the Netherlands, at that time, Mediterannean areas were considered the private academic hunting preserve of sociologists and geographers. Anthropologists were supposed to confine themselves to the non-Western (preferably tropical) world. I worked hard to legitimize this European orientation. Helped by Anton Blok and later by Jojoba Verrips and others, as well as by academic changes following the student revolution at the University, we succeeded. By the early 1970s, our European Mediterranean faction in the large Sociological–Anthropological Center formally became a small, active Department of European and Mediterranean Studies (Euromed). But that is another story. Our little department was active and thrived. It focused on Europe, the Mediterranean area, and the Middle East. Our policy was to let many research flowers bloom. Although we worked on very different projects, we formed a closely-knit team for many years. My second objective was to work out an analytical framework (emphasizing structure and agency) to the structural–functional paradigm that was then dominant. I believe I accomplished that with the publication of *Friends of Friends* in 1974, after which I was somewhat at loose ends as far as subject matter was concerned.

Coming to Grips with Tourism

Thus, it was no coincidence that my active interest in tourism began roughly in 1974. One of my MA students, Peter van der Werff, was then writing up the field research he had carried out on the polarizing impact of tourism in a Tuscan seaside community. We had long, sometimes heated discussions about the developmental framework he employed, which dominated much of the early writing on tourism in the late 1960s and early 1970s. It postulated that poor, peripheral areas and countries were locked into a structural relation with rich metropolitan areas, which contributed to the development of underdevelopment. In this process, the rich metropolitan center drained wealth from the poor periphery, while increasing the gap between rich and poor there. This analytical model, elaborated by, among others, Andre Gunder Frank (1972), was very popular among European staff and students. In it, tourism flows were seen as controlled by outside metropolitan forces, which perpetuated the dependence and poverty of peripheral areas. In short, it was a mechanism furthering a neocolonial development or underdevelopment.

This paradigm had been elegantly elaborated and had much to recommend it. But it was too rigid. Patently, tourist zones prosper, even though metropolitan interests siphon off much, if not the lion's share, of tourist-generated income. Moreover, the scheme conceived of development purely in economic terms. Quality of life, health, and education were left out of the model. But the theory did bring back echoes of the situation I had encountered in the Philippines, India, and Sicily. My chief objection to the center–periphery concept was the almost sect-like behavior of its adherents who used it as a framework in their research. It provided a set menu for students who simply went to the field to find the ingredients. They set out not to test the model, but to assemble facts to support it. They became believers, not investigators. Anyway, it set me thinking about tourism and its effects. Van der Werff presented his MA dissertation in 1976 and eventually published an account of his research (1980). But our association had gotten me involved in the subject of tourism development and the realization that the Malta I had been visiting and researching for years could be an ideal location to investigate its impact.

For the time being, however, I had other plans. In the spring of 1974, I returned alone to Malta for a short period of fieldwork, in which I focused on social, political, and economic developments following the return to power in 1971 of the Malta Labour Party. Toward the end of this stay, I gave a talk to the Malta Institute of Directors on social trends, one of which was the growth of tourism. Since my last research in Malta in 1961, annual tourist arrivals had risen tenfold, from just under 21,000 to 211,000, and they now figured prominently in Malta's development strategy. I urged the assembled businessmen to seriously consider the long-range effects of this rapidly growing sector. The country's small size, extreme population density, and weak economy made it vulnerable to the pollution, overcrowding, foreign economic domination, and exchange leakage that had recently been reported in the literature. Malta's development policy, I argued, should be based on complete information derived from research that included the social and cultural consequences of tourism . But it was to take almost 30 more years before the penny dropped and the Maltese began to carry out that type of research themselves, which was indeed a paradox because their country's economy had increasingly come to depend on tourism.

In 1976, I became thoroughly involved with tourism research in several different ways. In February, I was confined to bed with a slipped disk. Since I was planning to run a seminar on tourism the following year, I decided to use my down time to read up on the subject. The dozen articles, books, and reports I examined made grim reading. Many were of mediocre quality and were overwhelmingly negative (quite a few reflected the pessimistic (Frank) developmental paradigm). They warned of foreign exchange leakage, unstable employment, foreign dominance of the industry, a growing gap between rich and poor, rising resentment towards tourism, and growing class antagonism. Clearly, the contribution of tourism to most development goals was problematic. My response to this was to call for more research and to take a long, critical look at the economic, social, and political consequences of tourism. Feeling very pleased with myself and thinking I had neatly distilled the essential consequences of tourism, I optimistically sent a copy of the paper to a contact at UNESCO, who had written to me that there would shortly be a call for research papers on tourism, and others to friends at the University of Malta.

Barely out of bed, and still feeling rather delicate, I went to Malta for five weeks with a BBC team to film the preparations and rituals associated with the celebration of Good Friday and Easter in the village of Naxxar. This expedition was to present me with a theoretical puzzle which, together with my new interest in tourism, was to occupy me for years to come. I discovered that these celebrations had grown enormously since I had last studied them in 1961. I learned also that the annual festa celebrating the parish's patron, The Nativity of Our Lady, had been associated with an increase in similar revitalizing celebrations in many other Maltese parishes. This surprised me, for in the 1960s there were good reasons to think that such religious pageantry would decrease, not increase.

Some Maltese intellectuals commented that this increase, as well as the use of biblical costumes in Holy Week celebrations and the growing commercial activity at festas, was due to a desire to entertain tourists for profit. They maintained that this was robbing the celebrations of their religious anchorage, divorcing them from the solemnity that had given them birth. Was this the commoditization thesis (see, e.g., Greenwood 1977) in action at the grass roots? A busload of German tourists had indeed attended the 1976 Naxxar Good Friday procession and been seated on chairs specially placed for them on the church parvis. The loudspeaker commentary that year was in German as well as English and Maltese. Looking at the tourists watching the exotic pageantry, the BBC soundman whispered to me,

"I wonder how long it will take before the locals realize that tourists are looking at them as though they were animals in a zoo." His comment annoyed me, though I fully understood what he meant. I empathized with these "animals in the zoo." They were friends and former neighbors who were very serious about their roles in the pageantry and had spent a great deal on their costumes. I also knew, unlike the intellectuals voicing the commoditization argument, that the desire to dress up in biblical costumes antedated the arrival of tourism and that the band club had only earned a few pounds renting the chairs out. Moreover, since on Good Friday the clubs and stores are closed, they earned nothing from the tourists. So my brief visit obviously had given me much to think about.

That summer I returned again to Malta, this time on holiday with the family. The "discussion paper" I had sent to UNESCO had achieved a response. The Rev. Peter Serracino Inglott, Professor of Philosophy at the University of Malta, and I were invited by IBRD and UNESCO to prepare a study on the impact of tourism on Malta. We swiftly formed a team of interested students and staff and went to work gathering relevant documents and statistics, interviewing key stakeholders, and talking to friends. During this research, I was astounded by the extent to which people were willing to go to accommodate the wishes of tourists. One of my oldest village friends vigorously defended what I considered an outrageous plan to build a large hotel overlooking the beautiful, intimate inlet of Wied iz-Zurrieq, a favorite local swimming place. " But Jer," he shouted excitedly, "We must do it. It's modern! It's good for tourism!"

Father Peter and I spent much of the summer working on the project and discussing our findings. Toward the middle of August, we met in a hideaway he had located in a hot, musty old building in Valletta, one block from my former CARE office. There we organized the results of the research and begin to draft our report. Father Peter then left to teach for a term in a US college and I returned to Amsterdam, where I wrote up the report for UNESCO. Our overall conclusion was that tourism was contributing substantially to the government's economic and employment targets, that the government had adopted measures to curb some of tourism's negative effects, and that tourism stimulated Maltese arts and theatre. Generally, this report (Boissevain and Serracino Inglott 1979) was welcomed by the Maltese whose views of the positive impact of tourism profoundly affected my thinking and our conclusions. Certainly, it provided a healthy antidote to the overwhelmingly antitourism bias of the literature I had surveyed and recommended to UNESCO just six months earlier.

That November, I gave a paper at a symposium organized by Valene Smith at the 1976 meeting of the American Anthropological Association in Washington, D.C. My presentation reflected our favorable evaluation of the impact of tourism in Malta. It also aired my developing misgivings about much of the current literature on tourism and development (Boissevain 1977). I argued that much of it was a spin-off of research focused on other topics rather than on tourism; that much of it was second-hand; that it often ignored indigenous evaluations of the effects of tourism; and that in evaluating the relation between tourism and development, the authors conceptualized development exclusively in economic terms. For the first time I met colleagues working on tourism, including some of the contributors to Valene Smith's *Hosts and Guests*, which was to be published the following year.

During a family break in the South of France that Christmas, I visited the Centre des Hautes Études Touristiques at the University of Aix in Provence. There I met Jean Maurice Thurot who was just back from a trip to Africa. He asked me if I knew why there were so many five-star hotels, rather than more affordable modest hotels, in Africa. I didn't, but he suggested that it was because consultants recommended them because the commissions on luxury furniture, fixtures, and bathrooms were so "interesting." This sharpened my critical view, and I often thought of his cynical observation as I watched the luxury hotels taking shape around Malta's St. Georges Bay, and the developers growing wealthier and more powerful.

That semester I finally gave the seminar on tourism and anthropology, about which I had been thinking for some time. In the Netherlands, it was then the custom for Professors to give a *capita selecta* course to the more senior students. This amounted to being obliged to think up a new subject each year, upon which we were then expected to shed our professorial light. With the help of two student research assistants, I had by now done a good bit of reading on the subject. Moreover, after several years of twisting and turning in theoretical debates, the study of tourism had begun to appeal because of its "down to earth" qualities and practical possibilities. It was certainly the first time that an anthropology seminar course on tourism had been given in the Netherlands. The students, travelers all, reacted quite enthusiastically to it. Many of those who took the course chose to focus on tourism when they subsequently did the fieldwork for their MA dissertations. In contrast, tourism was not a subject that interested my colleagues at the Institute. Most were indifferent to it, and a few were quite negative about it, regarding it as a form of neo-colonialism. So I pursued tourism research for quite a while on my own, stimulated by the work of students reporting on their findings, and by the contacts I had with those outside Malta. In time the students produced a number of MA theses, and one wrote a book on foreign second house owners and "settlers" in Malta (Esmeyer 1984).

For the academic year 1977–78, I again returned to Malta, this time as visiting professor at the University. It was to be a busy year. Among other things, I organized research to assess the impact of tourism on Malta's small, underdeveloped sister island, Gozo. This was part of a larger research project on Gozo conducted by the University of Malta for the Human Habitation section of UNESCO, the direc-tor of which was Salvino Busuttil, formerly Head of the Economics Department of the University. Together with an enthusiastic team of students we interviewed tour operators, bus companies transporting visitors to, from, and in Gozo, tour guides, souvenir stall holders, women knitting pullovers for sale to tourists, and tourists returning to Malta by ferry. On one tour, I heard the guide tell the English visitors some very strange things about Gozo and its inhabitants, which reflected the middle class prejudices Maltese have about their poor and more rural sister island. Among other things she maintained that they looked different from Maltese, that they were devious and they spoke an unintelligible language.

I also gave a course on tourism, together with a young economist, John Grech, who later would become chairman of the Maltese Tourist Board. I think this was pos-sibly the first course on tourism ever given at the university. That winter I arranged for a class of Gozitan secondary school students to write a short essay about what they thought of tourists (they liked the foreign tourists but loathed Maltese day trip-pers). I also gave a talk to the youth section of Malta's leading heritage organization, NGO, Din l-Art Helwa (This Fair Land), on some of the unpleasant effects of tourism on the social environment. In the spring, I helped organize a research sym-posium at the university at which I presented the first results of our Gozo research, detailing among other things, the exploitation of the lucrative tourist link to Gozo by Maltese entrepreneurs (Boissevain 1979a). It nicely illustrated certain aspects of the center–periphery thesis I had criticized earlier. As part of my personal mission to get the public thinking about some of the potential negative consequences of tourism, I also wrote a long article for the *Sunday Times of Malta* on tourism in Malta and the Mediterranean. Later that year, I gave a paper at a symposium on Core–Periphery Relations in Europe organized by the Institute of Development Studies (IDS) at the University of Sussex. Still influenced by the generally positive effect of tourism in Malta and the measures the Labour government was taking to limit its negative aspects, I took a position rather contrary to the negative image of tourism held by many of the development economists present (Boissevain 1979b).

For the next 10 years, except for supervising several MA projects, I scarcely thought about tourism. During 1980–1981, I was a visiting research fellow at the IDS, where, among other things, I wrote a long discussion paper on small entrepreneurs in Europe. Upon returning to Amsterdam, I organized a project via the Ministry of Economic Affairs to study problems facing self-employed immi-grant Surinamese entrepreneurs. It was a practical project, which provided employment for several recent graduates, the alleviation of some of the problems of immigrant shopkeepers and, in time, a number of articles. At the same time, I continued to explore the literature on public rituals in Europe, seeking an expla-nation for the resurgence of ritual pageantry in Malta that I had noted in 1976.

Then, in 1986, Marie-François Lanfant invited me to a URESTI conference in Paris on the social and cultural impact of international tourism. Two years later, Tom Selwyn asked me to give a paper for the conference on the anthropology of tourism he was organizing for the Group for the Anthropology of Practice and Policy (GAPP) at Roehampton Institute, London. These two events brought me back into discussions on tourism, as I was able to combine my interest in the consequences of tourism and the revitalization of public ritual. In Paris, making use of Turner's and Graburn's notions of *inversion* and *antistructure,* I argued that there was little evidence that overregimented North Europeans out for a vigorous fortnight of antistructure in Malta were "undermining the most firmly established systems of reference," which were tied up with family faction, party, and religion. (Boissevain 1989). This was the main thesis of the conference organizers. At Tom Selwyn's meeting, using notions of play and ritual developed by Turner, Manning, and Handelman, I examined the commoditization thesis in more detail. Religious pageantry and public celebrations were increasing, I argued, not because Maltese were selling their culture to tourists, but because such celebrations strengthened community solidarity and identity in the face of the rapid social change and political turmoil that Malta was experiencing. Tourists were part of the change, and they were welcomed because they enlarged the audience and so publicly enhanced the community's local prestige and, thus, its self-esteem (Boissevain 1996).

Retirement

When I retired from the University of Amsterdam in 1993, we again moved to Malta, where for some time we had owned a house in Naxxar. Formal retirement was to become the most active period of my engagement with tourism. For a long time I had been concerned that, except for the work by the Rev. Joseph Inguanez, a sociologist at the university, there was a notable absence of any serious, organized research by government or the university into the social and cultural impact of the booming tourist industry. By doing something about this perceived shortcoming, I hoped to make myself useful and make a positive contribution to the country that we, as a family, had grown to love, and whose people had helped me so much with my research, and thus with my academic career.

In anticipation of this work, I organized a workshop at the biennial conference of the European Association of Social Anthropology in Prague in September 1992 to explore how other tourist destinations in Europe were coping with their visitors. The workshop showed that, like Malta, the inhabitants of most tourist destinations eventually developed strategies to protect their privacy, self-esteem, and cultural heritage, if not always their environment. These strategies included covert resistance, hiding events from tourists, aggression and organized protest toward tourist-related developments. Most governments were more concerned with pleasing and protecting tourists than trying to understand and deal with the problems these visitors caused for their own citizens (Boissevain, ed. 1996).

Later that year Carmel Fsadni, a senior member of the University of Malta's Department of Management Studies, and I successfully applied to the European Union's Med-Campus program for funds to establish a project to promote sustainable cultural and ecological tourism in the Mediterranean region. Primarily designed to train personnel already involved in the tourism industry, the project also provided funds for secretarial and administrative assistance, including substantial office hardware. By the summer of 1993, our Euromed program was up and running. We thus created a partly self-financing tourist studies niche within the university. During the following decade the Med-Campus link fell away, but tourism studies at the University, with some funding from the Tourism Ministry, continued to expand. By 2003, it included a popular BA (Honours) tourism studies degree program, a full-time lectureship and growing research activity. It also enabled Nadia Sammut (now Theuma), a Maltese anthropology graduate, to carry out research for her PhD. Together we had examined the reaction of the residents of Medina, the old walled capital city, which had become a prime attraction with close to a million annual visitors and a venue of considerable reinvented pageantry. The residents complained that their town was being commercialized, that tourists were immodestly dressed, that they left rubbish behind, and uninvited, sometimes entered their houses to look around (Boissevain and Sammut 1994).

Our other research included a study of the conflict between environmental NGOs and developers over the refurbishing and extension of the Malta Hilton Hotel. The NGOs maintained that the $120 million project, which included a 21-story office tower and a marina, would destroy a historic fortification, pollute an important local swimming area, kill off marine vegetation, and deprive the area of the only remaining open space. Moreover, they argued, the Environmental Impact Study was incomplete and the Planning Authority had completely ignored the negative advice of its own advisors. The encounters between NGOs and developer were protracted, often violent. I attended the final Planning Authority hearing on project. The developer had been able to pack the room with his rough supporters. When the Friends of the Earth (Malta) spokesman began to explain the irregularities in the planning application, the developer, a hulk of a man, rose and, spewing obscene insults at the slight young lawyer, advanced on him followed by many of his followers. The atmosphere fairly crackled with menace until the Planning Authority chairman and ushers managed to restore order. Ultimately, after some rear guard actions by an NGO, the project was approved and was completed in 2000. Though defeated, the NGOs succeeded in exposing some of the dubious practices of the developers, obtained copious media coverage, and gained valuable experience, which in subsequent encounters they put to more successful use (Boissevain and Theuma 1998).

Living in Malta of the 1990s gave us a different perspective on life there. We ourselves experienced the toll that industrial and commercial development, modernization, relative affluence, and tourism were exacting from the island and its inhabitants. Vast areas of open land had been covered with new housing, roads and industrial complexes, or destroyed by ruthless quarrying. Largely unplanned and uncontrolled, tourist developments had despoiled much of the accessible foreshore, and were contributing to the already severe environmental pollution. While acknowledging its economic benefits, I became less and less convinced of the expanding tourist industry's social and cultural benefits for the island. Furthermore, I was depressed by the way most Maltese passively accepted the crowding, loss of privacy, flouting of their values, and damage to their cultural and environmental heritage. The two major political parties, intent on satisfying the powerful building and tourism lobbies, and obsessed with fighting each other, did little to alleviate these problems. The powerful Catholic Church remained silent. Only a few NGOs and the embryonic Green Party, Alternattiva Demokratika, that was not even represented in parliament, openly protested against what was happening.

Stimulated by a workshop in 1998 on landscape held by the Anthropology Department of the Jagiellonian University, Kraków, I began to focus on the environmental impact of tourism and, particularly, on the growing tension between tourist developers and environmental NGOs (Boissevain 2000). During the early 1990s, I gave a number of papers on the dark side of tourism to local workshops organized by environmental NGOs and stakeholders in the tourism industry. I also accompanied the Alternattiva Demokratika delegation to a seminar of Mediterranean ecologists organized by the European Federation of Green Parties in Barcelona. In it I argued that cultural tourism is not sustainable, that governments should pay serious attention to environmental NGOs, and that domestic tourists should be given priority by curtailing further increases of international tourism to established Mediterranean tourist destinations. In 1999 at a conference on Mediterranean anthropology at the University of Aix en Provence, I discussed the initial reluctance, but now growing interest, of anthropologists to study tourism in the region (Boissevain 2001). This brings me to 2004. At the moment I am following the campaign that Maltese NGOs are waging to prevent the construction of a second golf course. Since we moved back to Amsterdam in 2000, and now only visit Malta for eight weeks a year, I am doing this research largely via the Internet.

Retrospect and Where I Now Stand

Looking back over my career, I now see that there were many elements leading to my involvement in tourism studies. To begin with, I had just completed a major intellectual exercise and was open to a new challenge. Second, I personally experienced how Malta, to which I returned almost annually on holiday, was rapidly becoming a major mass tourism destination. Third, compared to many academics I had a favored position: a senior appointment, a relatively light formal teaching load, excellent secretarial and research assistance, generous sabbatical possibilities and available research funds. Fourth, the theoretical interest of my Dutch students in the developmental aspects of tourism, and the enthusiastic help volunteered by Maltese students (bored by their traditional regime of lectures) stimulated me enormously. Finally, invitations to lecture, to participate in focused workshops, and to discuss tourism at conferences provided stimulating incentives to continue writing about tourism even though no fellow Dutch anthropologists shared my growing interest in the subject until the 1990s.

Later, the postmodern shift in the focus of mainstream academic anthropology toward an interest in deconstruction, reflexivity, interpretation, and discourse, while opening new agendas, sidelined a concern for the social and economic developmental impact of tourism, which had engaged me. Most anthropologists (and I include myself here), during the 1970s and early 1980s, were ambivalent about tourists. They found it more comfortable to ignore them, much in the way Malinowski overlooked Trobriand white traders. The Maltese authorities, while helpful, were primarily interested in attracting and accommodating more tourists, not in hearing about the social and cultural impact of the visitors. In fact, the Minister of Tourism was quite annoyed by the unsolicited report detailing the complaints of Medina residents about tourist visitors that Nadia Sammut and I gave him. I remain ambivalent about tourism. I personally deplore what tourism and the related building development has done and is still doing to the landscape and environment. On the other hand, I welcome the economic benefits it has brought to the Islands.

My early work dealt with questions raised by propositions on the relation between tourism and development. It argued that development was more than just economic progress, that tourism made substantial contributions to well-being, to local and national identity and culture, and that there was a reciprocal dependence between areas sending and receiving tourists. After virtually a 10-year absence from the field, my work shifted to explore the complex relation between tourism and ritual. It challenged the notion that tourism necessarily destroys meaningful rituals, the commoditization thesis. Finally, during the past decade, I have increasingly focused on the dark side of tourism. This was no doubt due our move to Malta and personal experience with the growing pressure on population and infrastructure. Malta, with a land area of only 365 square kilometers (120 square miles) and a population of 380,000, is already the most densely populated country in Europe. I am still concerned about the tourist-related loss of privacy, leisure area, landscape, and heritage, as well as the passive willingness of most Maltese still to accept discomfort and offensive behavior just to accommodate tourists. The growing reaction to this of civil society, and not just in Malta, is what now continues to fascinate me.

In a certain sense, there has been regression in Malta. Since the early 1970s, especially along the coast, the conclusion must be that tourism has irrevocably denied the Maltese access to large areas of their coast. This reminds many of the way the British colonial establishment expropriated their foreshore for military purposes and for their own pleasure. Tourism is threatening the islands' limited agricultural land and recreational space, seriously mutilating and polluting the scenic landscape and, at times, even its monumental heritage. Increasingly, tourism in Malta has come under control of foreign tour operators, and the major hotels are dependent on foreign capital. With a surplus of accommodations, and in order to keep their Malta operation competitive, tour operators are obliging luxury hotels to offer lower market prices. This in turn is causing smaller hotels and rooming houses, most of which are wholly Maltese owned, to close, or to convert to sheltered accommodation for pensioners. In spite of the obvious benefits of tourism, Malta in 2004 reflects more of the negative characteristics sketched out by development economists and others in 1970 than in a later period of optimistic expansion.

Civil society's growing concern for and defense of the country's physical and cultural heritage is encouraging. What I have written and some of the activities in which I have engaged may have helped encourage and legitimize civil action to curtail tourism's dark side. But probably it has made little difference. I have written chiefly for academic audiences. Environmental and cultural activists, as well as tourism planners, developers, and hoteliers, are too busy doing their own thing to delve into scholarly texts. But my stature as a foreign academic, and long-standing friend and observer of things Maltese, perhaps helped establish tourism studies at the University of Malta. If so, that is a positive contribution.

Acknowledgments

My very warm thanks to Inga for her companionship, for sharing my interests for so long, and for continuing to subject me to Lucy Mair's stern linguistic regime.

Erik Cohen (1932–)   is Emeritus Professor of Sociology, Hebrew University of Jerusalem, Israel 91905 (e-mail mserik@mscc.huji.ac.il), currently residing at 61/149 Senaniwet, Soi Senanikhom 1, Pahon Yothin Rd 32, Bangkok 10230, Thailand. Besides administrative appointments, he has taught a range of courses in sociology and anthropology dealing with strangerhood, theory, and urban affairs. He has also taught at the University of Singapore, the University of the South Pacific, and the University of Bielefeld. Among various editorships, he is an editor (for sociology) in *Annals of Tourism Research*. His broad range of research interests throughout his career is well-illustrated by his recent *Contemporary Tourism: Diversity and Change* (2004). He is a founding member of the International Academy for the Study of Tourism.

YOUTH TOURISTS IN ACRE
A Disturbance becomes a Lifelong Preoccupation

Introduction

"May I dare to walk alone in the Old Town?" asked a young female German tourist in the vicinity of the bus station of the mixed Jewish–Arab town of Acre in Israel. She had heard that Arab youths, unused to foreign women walking unaccompanied in their ancient neighborhood, tend to harass them, though she had not heard that anyone had been raped. It was the summer of 1966. I was in the second month of my first anthropological field study (after having conducted sociological research for close to 10 years), and I resented the German visitor as an intruder into "my" community. I felt its "authenticity" had been impaired.

I was obviously aware that Acre, an ancient town with a long and turbulent history, significant archeological remains, and imposing architecture was an important tourist attraction (Rubin 1974). But I perceived tourism to be related to the material remains of the past, not to the living community. The girl's question made me aware of tourism in the latter sense—and I saw it as a fortuitous intrusion, interfering with the main topic of my study, Jewish–Arab relations in the town. Tourism appeared to me as an exogenous factor, irrelevant and disturbing.

Not that I hadn't already come across tourists. As a beginner in fieldwork, I took copious field notes on everything and anyone encountered in the town. My diary shows that already on the third day of my sojourn in the town, I saw a German girl, leaving an eating place, who was embraced by an Arab youth. I commented ironically in my diary that "I doubted that they could exchange even a single word," but at that stage I did not give the observation any further thought.

As my study progressed, notes on Arabs associating with young tourists became more frequent, especially after I befriended a group of male Arab "street-corner" youths, meeting in the evening in a lane in the Old Town. Though these youths often talked of their adventures with tourists, I showed very little interest in this during this period of my research. Even after its completion, when I developed a detailed classificatory system for indexing my field notes, I failed to assign "tourism" to one of the substantive categories. Rather, I relegated it to a residual "miscellaneous" heading.

The principal question of my present reflection on field work conducted close to 40 years ago is, therefore, how did tourism emerge from a merely marginal interest during field work and even the initial analysis of field notes to become the topic of what, in retrospect, appears have been the most important publication of the study (Cohen 1971); and further, how did it, in turn, became the point of departure for a life-long preoccupation with tourists, as well as other kinds of strangers such as expatriates, missionaries and foreign workers?

Social and Intellectual Background

I was born in Zagreb, Yugoslavia, in 1932, as the only child of a socially mobile, middle-class, secular Jewish family whose way of life was harshly disrupted by the Second World War. My secondary education was interrupted in 1949 when I emigrated with my parents to Israel (more to escape the stultifying ambience of communism than for any deep Zionist motives). Soon after my arrival I was drafted into the Israeli army; in which my initial shock and rejection of army life was gradually overcome by the acceptance of military training—especially in the officers' course. I eventually stayed on in the army for about two years beyond regular service, first as an instructor in the armored corps training camp, and later in an armored reconnaissance unit. Here I found what I desired—the appealing combination of being outdoors and studying in the desert. I also completed my secondary schooling as an external student. This pattern of being outdoors and studying has remained, to a large extent, my basic lifestyle up to the present.

The confrontation with the unfamiliar, hard life in early Israel made me aware of social problems, and for a while I embraced communist ideals, even though I had escaped from communism as practiced at the time in Yugoslavia. Those pre-occupations led me to decide at an early age, before joining the army, to study sociology and economics after army service. Completing my B.A. at the Hebrew University in 1958, I continued on to an M.A. in sociology and philosophy, grad-uating in 1961. My intellectual interests at the time were broad, but unfocused. My specialization at the master's level was in the sociology and philosophy of religion. My research in the Department of Sociology, in which I got involved before completing my studies, was in the area of collective settlements and the so-called development towns, i.e., new towns in the peripheral areas of the country. My Ph.D. was related to the latter. It was a comparative sociological study of the power structure of these new urban communities, which I completed in 1968.

Weaned from my turn to communism by overdoses of Parsonian structural functionalism, which dominated the theoretical approach in the Department at the time, I eventually embraced a nondogmatic, critical attitude about Israeli society, toward which I felt an obligation as a citizen, without necessarily identifying with its Zionist ethos. Over the years, however, this critical attitude became increasingly acute, which contributed to my turning away, professionally as well as personally, from the country until after retirement, when I *de facto* moved to Thailand.

During my student years I worked on several research projects at the department, at first as a research assistant and later as an increasingly independent researcher. In the spirit of the times, these projects were related to the larger national goals of institution building, and were of practical as well as broader scientific interest (see Yair and Apeloig-Feldman 2005). They were thus not of my own choice, but solicited and supported by governmental and other public institutions. Work on these sociological projects (despite my later "conversion" to anthropology) left an undeniable mark on my methodological approach. For example, my inclination to develop typologies was doubtless influenced by my work with my teacher, Yonina Talmon, who developed a typology of collective settlements, which I further elaborated after her premature death.

The large-scale studies in which I participated or conducted were based primarily on questionnaires administered by canvassers, mostly undergraduates, to a sample of the population of the investigated communities. My direct contact with the field was restricted. I usually visited the communities only at the preparatory stage of the study—a circumstance that prevented me from observing the "real life" out there. In 1965, however, there came an unexpected break: Max Gluckman, at the time Head of the Department of Anthropology at the University of Manchester, invited me, together with a group of other young researchers, for a six-month stint in his Department within the framework of a broadly conceived anthropological project on Israeli society.

The stay at Manchester brought me in touch with British social anthropology, which at the time was at its zenith, and I was attracted by the directness of contact with the field, and the experience of fieldwork of British anthropologists, which in the virtual absence of anthropology in Israel at the time, was new and refreshing to me; but at the same time, I was reluctant to embrace anthropology because of my worry about the "objectivity" and "representiveness" of anthropological findings. However, while still in Manchester, I decided to have a try at anthropological fieldwork upon my return to Israel—even before completing my Ph.D thesis in sociology. I chose for my study the historical town of Acre on the Mediterranean coast of northern Israel, which was then a "development town" with a mixed Jewish–Arab population. The choice was not random. I was at the time involved with urban studies; and my critical stance towards Israeli society attracted me to the problematic theme of Jewish–Arab coexistence—the Arabs of Israel being a relatively neglected topic at the time. In addition, the ancient town of Acre, with its architecture and long and turbulent history, appealed to my romantic inclinations. On the first of July 1966, I moved with my family to Acre for a six-month stretch of fieldwork.

Looking back, there was an element of risk involved in that move. By the mid-1960s, the Department of Sociology at the Hebrew University was under the sway of a few eminent scholars, who directed the large-scale sociological projects on which the younger staff worked. Though I enjoyed a good deal of autonomy in my own work on various projects, there was a general sense among the younger staff that their professional future depended upon close collaboration with their seniors, who directed them toward specific research topics in the seniors' general field of interest. This engendered a considerable degree of dependency, stifling to some extent the quest for an independent choice of topics and directions of research. Departure from the "normal" course hence involved a gamble. Only a significant original contribution could compensate for such nonconformity and offer a reasonable chance for appointment, tenure, and promotion in the Department, which at the time was the only department in Israel with an international reputation.

My own predilection for independence and experimentation induced me, even before I completed my Ph.D. in sociology, to turn to anthropology and engage in a subject, which at the time did not generate much interest in the Department: Jewish–Arab relations. However, as I will show in some detail below, this departure from the "normal" course had an unexpected, serendipitous consequence, and proved eventually to have been a turning point in my professional life: it led to an awareness of tourism as an anthropological and sociological subject. As I increasingly engaged in the elaboration of a theoretical groundwork for this new field and initiated research projects explicitly concerned with touristic topics, the study of tourism became my principal preoccupation for many years; and my work in this field was a significant factor in my academic advancement in the Department from the time I bumped into tourism—at that time, a strange and underestimated topic—during my first experimental excursion into anthropological fieldwork.

Relevance of Arab-Tourist Interaction for the Research Project

In 1966, the bulk of the Arab population of Acre, most of it Muslim, lived in the walled Old Town. This was a quarter of much historical significance and touristic "charm," but dilapidated and unhealthy for its mostly impoverished inhabitants. The focus of my study was Jewish–Arab relations in the broad sense, including the Arab perception of their position and future in the Jewish state. From that perspective, the Arabs (who appeared to me of greatest interest) were youths in their early twenties, who were about to enter adulthood in an adverse economic, political, and cultural environment, which offered them few attractive opportunities in life. In my early thirties myself, I found it easy to join an Arab "street-corner" group and conduct long conversations with these youths on a variety of topics that preoccupied them, an important one of which concerned their encounters with tourists. But I mostly failed to grasp the relevance of this for my study.

Tourism in Acre was at the time clearly divided into two kinds of sightseers: Israelis and foreigners touring the Old Town's archeological and historical sights, and young tourists, whom I later called "drifters" (Cohen 1973) and to whom local Jews referred to with the contemptuous term of "beatnik," which had been applied by Israelis to young foreigners camping in the desert in the environs of the southernmost town of Eilat (Cohen 1973:97–98).

The Arab youths in the Old Town sought to earn some money as informal tourist guides. Sometimes, they also offered to sell them drugs. Mostly focusing on young, female tourists, they would volunteer to take them around town, invite them to their parents' homes, and even offer them free accommodations. After their guests' departure, they would continue to correspond with them. I quote here from my field notes of August 14, 1966 (translation from Hebrew):

> A. is intensely engaged with [foreign] tourists in Acre. He used to invite them to his home, to sleep there. 'But I did not do anything to the [female] tourist—she was in my house like my sister [he claimed].' On some occasions there were up to twenty tourists there. He likes to converse with the tourists—that way he learned English and French.

And again, on August 15, 1966:

> The conversation [with two Arab youths] turned to female tourists in Acre. Both stressed their considerable interest in contact with them. They emphasized that they primarily learn languages from them— both youths speak English and possess the basics of some other languages—all of which derives from interaction with tourists.
> One of the youths pointed out his particular interest in Denmark— he wants to visit there, and is therefore interested in Danish tourists. Once he is there, he will see whether he can stay on...

[The youths said that] there were various kinds of tourists: those who were interested in archeological sites and those who want only to go to the beach. The youths were disdainful of the latter. There are those who sleep with the Arab youths and those who say explicitly, "Don't touch me!" The Scandinavian girls in particular come here to get laid. The Arab youths explained to me that the Scandinavian boys are not good, not hot.Therefore, the girls come to look for boys here—they like Sephardis. However, even when the youths sleep with them they do not do it in their parents' homes; if they bring the girls home, the parents receive them with much honor, explained the youth. [It should be noted, a propos, that he alluded to himself as a "Sephardi", thus apparently hinting at the similarity in skin color between Arabs and Sephardi Jews from Middle Eastern or North African origin].

Though the Arab youths' interest in the foreign girls was primarily sexual, it was not limited to just sex. Indeed, what eventually engaged my attention in the course of the analysis of the data was the recurrent attempts of the youths at what would nowadays be called 'networking'—the establishment of as many contacts as possible with visitors from different countries, and especially with those from western and northwestern Europe. Their aim was to get an invitation to visit those countries and stay there. Such imagined "escape attempts" (Cohen and Taylor 1978) from their unpromising predicament in Israel, rather than their sexual adventures, related directly to the principal aims of my study. So, it is correct to say that I came to tourism as an anthropological topic indirectly, that is, through its relevance to the predicament of the Arab youths in the town rather than as a subject of interest in itself.

Another, even more indirect link between tourism and my research interest was the role tourism played in the relationship between the Arab youths and the local police, who were predominantly Jewish. The police, for reasons of their own, did not look benignly on the Arab youths' engagements with tourists, and frequently intervened, though they hardly had legal grounds to do so. One of the youths who had invited tourists to his home complained of the police conduct, as I report in my fieldnotes of August 14, 1966:

A year ago the police started to trouble him [because of his relationship with tourists] and demanded that he cease meeting tourists. He complained bitterly over this, claiming that he neither touched the tourists nor stole from them. Why did they prohibit

him meeting tourists, he asked? In fact, he keeps on meeting
tourists, but does not take them home any more. He claimed that
the incident with the police broke his spirit. From that point on he
ceased dressing up as he had in the past; and a month had passed
since he last showered.

The police confirmed to me their policy of preventing Arab youths from meeting tourists, justifying this by claiming that the Arabs constituted a threat to the
tourists. They allegedly offered or supplied *hashish* to them; and there was also the
additional suspicion that they might rape the tourist girls. The Arab youths, however, claimed that the police had ulterior, political motives for their policy, that is,
to prevent the Arabs from discussing politics with the tourists and telling them
unfavorable things about the state of Israel. The police sought to prevent the Arabs
from having contact with the outside world and to isolate them. The conduct of the
police was thus seen as part of the policy of Israeli authorities towards the Arabs
of Acre. The apparently innocuous contacts between the Arab youths and the
tourists thus became relevant for my study of Jewish–Arab relations in the town.

Arab Boys and Tourist Girls: The Article

In the course of the analysis of my field data, I started to change my attitude
toward tourism in the town: I came to realize that rather than a disturbing, exogenous factor, tourism played a significant role in the context of Jewish–Arab relations. This was a decisive step, which led to the inclusion of tourism in my
analysis. Even though my concern with it was derived from other interests, it
became more central to my research; but at no point did tourism become an independent topic of study. In fact, it couldn't, since I did not interview the tourists
themselves.

My first article on tourism, *Arab boys and Tourist Girls in a Mixed
Jewish–Arab Community* (1971), reflected this changed perspective on tourism.
It analyzed the unexpected role the tourist girls played in the precarious life-sit-
uation of the Arab youths of Acre; but it was primarily a contribution to Israeli
sociology rather than the anthropology of tourism. The principal point of the
article was that the encounter with the foreign girls did not merely offer a sexual opportunity to the sexually frustrated Arab youths, who could not avail themselves of either the Arab or the Jewish girls in the town; but it also provided them
with what they saw as an opportunity to escape from their predicament in Israel,
which offered them few, if any, chances of sexual fulfillment, economic
advancement, or political influence. The girls were perceived as a means of
access to the world, through which they hoped to be able to establish a foothold

abroad. They hoped that one of the girls would send them an air ticket, find work for them abroad, or marry them. The few youths, who indeed succeeded in leaving Israel through the assistance of their foreign girlfriends, gave some substance to their hopes.

Toward the end of the article I drew attention briefly to the significance of tourism, illustrated by my case study as a "mechanism through which localities and nations become intertwined into a huge, super-national system of social interaction" (Cohen 1971:233), about the impact of which on local communities we know little. I ended by expressing the view that intersocietal contacts such as tourism merit more attention by anthropologists and sociologists studying communities.; and I only later managed to take up the challenge in circumstances different from those that prevailed in my first anthropological study.

The Emergence of Tourism as an Autonomous Concern

Arab Boys and Tourist Girls did not, strictly speaking, belong to the emergent field of "tourism studies." However, as I worked on the article I realized that the young tourists, who had associated with the Arabs and slept in their homes, differed from "ordinary" tourists staying in hotels and using tourist-oriented facilities. I searched in vain in the literature for a sociological categorization of tourists within which I could place the foreign youths in Acre whom I had called "drifters" (1971:225). This astonishing deficiency led me to a decisive step for my later engagement with tourism, in which I sought a theoretically informed basis for a sociological typology of tourists, which would also reflect empirically recognizable types of tourists.

It struck me that virtually all tourists face a fundamental dilemma: the attractiveness of their trip is to a large extent predicated on the experience of novelty and change from their home situation. However, while the exposure to strangeness on the trip may be stimulating, it may also be threatening, inducing tourists to seek a degree of familiarity in the host environment. Strangeness and familiarity, which, according to Schuetz (1944:507) are general categories of our interpretation of the world, thus provided a theoretical basis for a tourist typology—the tourist types themselves representing characteristic combinations of degrees of readiness for exposure to the strangeness of the host environment as against envelopment in an "environmental bubble" resembling the familiarity of home. The types ranged from the "organized mass tourist" whose exposure to strangeness was conceived as minimal (being ensconced in a familiar environmental bubble) to the "drifter," conceived as marked by the characteristics of maximal exposure to strangeness and minimal adherence to the bubble offered by the tourist establishment (Cohen 1972).

The idea of the drifter derived from my study in Acre, but the prototype was a massive German youth, whom I later met during a stretch of fieldwork in the Andean city of Ayacucho in Peru in 1969. He had single-handedly crossed the Amazon basin from the Atlantic coast of Brazil to the Peruvian Andes. However, I soon realized that I had to qualify the concept, and distinguish between the "original drifter," as exemplified by that German, and the growing phenomenon of mass drifting, presently called "backpacking," which has engendered a separate system of routes, infrastructure, and destinations, paralleling the tourist establishment and providing these young travellers with an environmental bubble of their own (Cohen 1973).

Though these articles constituted the point of departure for my continuous concern for the varieties of tourists (as against the attempts of others to propose a comprehensive concept of "tourist"), I did not follow them up immediately with anthropological fieldwork, which would empirically substantiate my theoretical constructs. In fact, I did not conceive any "research program" on tourism, nor did I see tourism as the principal topic of my professional work. Rather, fortuitous circumstances again induced me to turn to tourism as a research concern. In 1973 during a trip to Thailand, I joined a few youths on one of the first hill-tribe tracking tours in northern Thailand. Though just a tourist and ignorant about the hill tribes, I took detailed notes of the trek, including the mode of operation of our Thai guide (Cohen 1996:IX–X).

As my interest in Thailand grew, I visited a friend at the Tribal Research Center (now the Tribal Research Institute) in Chiang Mai to discuss possible research topics. Dr. John McKinnon, then foreign advisor to the Center, suggested that I conduct a study of hill-tribe tourism. Remembering my trekking tour a few years earlier, I gladly agreed, and a year later I engaged in a brief, two-month stretch of field work, trekking the hills and staying briefly in a Lisu village, which at that time constituted the hub of the increasingly popular "three-day-two nights" hill-tribe trekking tours. More than 10 years after my first encounter with tourists in the field, I started my first field project directly oriented to the study of tourism. In the years that followed, I continued to work on hill-tribe tourism in the north of Thailand, and in 1979 added the study of "bungalow tourism" on an island in the south of the country, thus for the first time being able to look at drifters and other youth tourists in Thailand at both sightseeing and vacationing locations (Cohen 1996).

These studies gradually branched out into a variety of other projects, which engaged me during the next quarter of a century, as tourism and various kinds of strangers became my dominant research interest, and Thailand my principal research field. Much of this work was brought together in two collections of articles, one devoted to different aspects of tourism in Thailand (Cohen 1996), and the other to the commercialization of hill-tribe and lowland crafts in the country (Cohen 2000). I have also recently published a monograph on the Chinese Vegetarian Festival in Phuket, which includes a chapter on tourism (Cohen 2001).

To round the story up, after many projects related in various ways to tourism, I returned in 2002 to the contemporary counterparts of the young tourists who first engaged my attention in Acre in 1966, but whom I have since put aside to study "backpackers." I started a study of the town of Pai in northwestern Thailand, which recently became an increasingly popular haven for backpackers, young and old, and hope to extend my project to some other backpacker enclaves in Thailand in the future.

Conclusion

My path to the anthropological study of tourism went through several stages, which were by no means a part of some well thought out, long-range research program or strategy. Rather, every stage involved serendipity, a fortuitous configuration of circumstances, which were unrelated to the preceding or following stages. In retrospect, however, the stages reveal an accumulative pattern. At the initial stage, tourism appeared during fieldwork as an exogenic and unwelcome disturbance of "my" community by outsiders. At the second stage, I realized that the tourists in town played a role related to the principal topic of my study, but tourism did not, in itself, excite my interest; in fact I failed to study the tourists in town. In the third stage, I discovered to my surprise the absence of a theoretical framework, which would enable me to place the young tourists in Acre into a broader context of the sociology of tourism, so I developed a typology of tourists. This stage appears to have been the decisive one in that it involved a reorientation in my treatment of tourism from an incidental factor (playing an unexpected role in the context of a mixed Israeli community) to a topic of intrinsic interest in itself (Cohen 1984).

But though this step was followed by some other theoretical articles (Cohen 2004), it did not lead to empirical research focusing expressly on tourism. Such a project was engendered by a chance touristic experience and a suggestion by a friend. It took more then 10 years between the initial and this fourth and last stage, which eventually committed me to the anthropological study of tourism. This study was followed by a series of loosely interrelated projects—some of which lasted for years, shifting interests, and newly emergent topics, precluding the formulation of some systematic, theory-oriented research program on tourism. Serendipity, and the perception of opportunities that it opens, remained to a large extent the decisive factors in the choice and execution of my empirical studies of tourism.

Malcolm Crick (1948–2006)   was Associate Professor of Anthropology, Faculty of Arts, Deakin University, Geelong, Victoria 3216, Australia, where he taught courses on religion and ritual, systems of meaning, death, colonialism and post-colonialism, and international tourism. Besides articles and chapters on witchcraft, anthropology of knowledge, post-colonialism, and the anthropology of tourism, his publications include *Resplendent Sites, Discordant Voices: Sri Lankans and International Tourism* (1994), (co-editor with B. Geddes) *Global Forces, Local Realities: Anthropological Perspectives on Change in the Third World* (1997), (co-editor with B. Geddes) *Research Methods in the Field: Eleven Anthropological Accounts* (1998), and *Maldon Memories* (2003). When he died in May 2006, he had been working on a study concerning the impact of heritage legislation and tourism development on Maldon, a small "gold rush" town near his home.

A DIFFICULT PASSAGE, LARGELY UNASSISTED

One of the more memorable annual rituals of my English childhood during the 1950s was the weeklong seaside summer holiday with the family. Invariably my father's annual leave fell during the school term, so my first touristic experiences were always disruptions to my education. That apart, my strongest recollection was an inability to enjoy such breaks from normal life. I was then, as I still am today, pretty nigh incapable of "just having fun" or "doing nothing," so instead I used holidays as periods in which to catch up on school work. I remember one year even packing my Latin vocab books in an effort to stave off boredom. By my mid-teenage years, when my dysfunctional reaction to holidays had become only too clear to my parents, I won a reprieve; henceforth they would leave me behind at home instead of taking me with them.

I mention these childhood memories simply because, on the face of it, it might be thought a little odd that someone so constitutionally averse to leisure activity should go on to spend some twenty years as an academic specializing in the anthropology of tourism. Except, of course, that many people in their professional lives often deal—whether consciously or not—with areas of life which are problematic for them. Perhaps my own gravitation to the anthropology of tourism is such an instance of someone engaging intellectually with phenomena that are difficult on the experiential level—an "anthropology of non-experience," as it were. And if anthropology involves, at some level or another, a struggle to come to terms with "otherness," then someone such as myself studying tourism becomes quite intelligible: the distance between myself and the phenomenon to be investigated being established in the very depths of my bookish, reclusive, introverted, super-serious, achievement-orientated, fun-averse personality. Such an under-standing may solve the seeming paradox of my research specialization, but I still have to remain super-vigilant lest unconscious baggage sneak into my tourism work, resulting in significant bias in how I present my research. It is an awareness of that ever-present danger that led me, I believe, to write a series of reflexive and overview pieces on tourism before publishing anything based upon my own ethnographic work.

These autobiographical remarks are the more pertinent because, when I took my doctorate in anthropology at the University of Oxford in 1974, it was for library-based research on culture, language, and meaning. I had not done field-work; I had not gone away anywhere; I had stayed behind, even though fieldwork was the "baptism by fire" for virtually everyone entering the anthropological pro-fession. Not only had I not been away to the field, it had never even occurred to me to go; I was more than happy reading and thinking a field, which at that time went under the label of "semantic anthropology." When, some three years after gaining my doctorate, I left the UK to take up a teaching appointment at the newly created Deakin University in Australia—an institution with a mission similar to that of the Open University in the UK—it was my first time on an airplane.

Given all the personal adjustments needed for a new job in a new country, and given my top priority, which was to establish a major sequence of units in anthro-pology along with two other colleagues, it was some years before a clear research focus formed. After leaving Oxford I had had a series of jobs outside academe, so I had no ongoing anthropological research project on the boil when I arrived in Australia in 1977. My first object of research attention was what was occurring within the university itself, and to that was then quickly added an interest in con-temporary Aboriginal affairs. But the semantic interests of my doctoral thesis, which had been published in 1976, strongly reasserted themselves when I real-ized that, after three years of service at Deakin, I was entitled to apply for six months research leave. I was determined this time to do fieldwork and planned to study the relationship between Buddhist notions of personhood and the ways in which Sri Lankans, in the ordinary course of their lives, think about social rela-tionships. I paid a brief visit of five weeks duration to Sri Lanka in December 1980/January 1981 in order to establish some connections, with the intention of conducting research there in 1982. During my first trip, I was given a present by a Buddhist monk resident in Melbourne to carry to his ex-teacher living just out-side Colombo. In the course of delivering that gift, I had an experience that sub-stantially changed the direction of my inquiries. I had already begun to have some doubts about the viability of my planned topic, given the fact that I was employed in a university which had no departments of Asian studies or Asian languages, and given that I would be able to get at the very maximum only eight months in the field. However, my encounter with a novice monk in 1981 was more decisive. He greeted me as I walked through the streets of a west coast Sri Lankan town with the words "Hello hippy." I thought of myself at that time very much as someone with both strong personal and scholarly interests in Buddhism; but that apart, I was quite specifically in Sri Lanka in order to set up an anthropological research project; and it had never occurred to me that I would be mistaken for some kind of a tourist.

That, in retrospect, I now concede was astonishingly naïve. In Sri Lanka in 1981, the assumed identity of almost any white person would be "tourist." Tourists and tourism were matters of immediate concern to very large numbers of locals: why did these Europeans behave as they did? How was catering to so many people from overseas changing local culture? Here, for many Sri Lankans, was an interesting form of personhood or otherness, and I was pigeon-holed as part of it. It soon became clear that here was a research project that I could quite reasonably pursue within the eight months at my disposal, not least because English would serve me quite well for most, if not all, of my interactions. Back in Australia, at the start of the university term in February 1981, I was quick to formulate my research proposal as being in the anthropology of tourism.

Like all anthropologists intending to go to the field, I would have dearly loved the opportunity to properly prepare myself, but for a range of reasons that simply did not occur. The writing of new undergraduate courses proceeded unabated throughout 1981, but that apart, my past caught up with me and I found myself for the full twelve months prior to going to the field committed to three widely divergent writing projects, none of which had anything to do with the anthropology of tourism. I had to draft a policy on Aboriginal access to higher education for the national academic staff union; then, completely out of the blue, came a request from Annual Reviews to do a piece on the anthropology of knowledge, after which I was asked to present a paper in the UK at a Conference of the Association of Social Anthropologists of the Commonwealth, the theme for which was semantic anthropology.

I felt unable to turn down any of these time-consuming offers, but that meant that I had to proceed to the field almost completely unread in the area of my chosen research. More than that, although in my ASA conference paper I was able to think about a number of fieldwork issues (Crick 1983), the economics of international airfares meant that I spent five weeks in the UK instead of three days, and that time was thus lost from what I had left for fieldwork. Instead of a full eight months I had less than seven, between April and October 1982, and I even had to spend the first week in Sri Lanka revising my conference paper for publication. Technically, my initial tourism fieldwork was conducted during a stopover in Sri Lanka on the return part of my Melbourne–London journey.

As a result of all of these "extras" to my normal workload in the period before setting off for the field, I arrived not only poorly read in what useful literature then existed in the anthropology of tourism, I had also, despite much-appreciated help from some colleagues at the University of Adelaide (where several Sri Lankan research projects were being undertaken), been unable to progress very far with learning colloquial Sinhala. I should add, too, that at Deakin University there was no one else working in the field of tourism studies, off whom I could bounce my initial ideas. It really was a case of someone, entirely isolated professionally, having to follow his own instincts. To cap it off, although Deakin University granted me six months of study leave in combination with accrued recreation leave, they would not support my research by providing any fieldwork funding.

I had applied for an extremely modest amount, but was summoned to the office of the chairman of the Leave Committee the day before my interview and was told that my application would be unsuccessful because the Committee would not be supporting any research in Asia. Although I did manage to get reimbursed to the tune of approximately $300 out of faculty funds for a number of minor expenditures on my return from the field, the absence of any significant funding up front had an effect on how I conducted my research. I would probably have emphasized the "informal" tourism sector in any event, but without a grant I simply could not afford to spend any appreciable length time in the licensed, and thus more expensive kinds of tourist accommodations. That being so, it was purely for financial reasons that a significant slice of the tourism "industry" is missing from my analysis.

It may seem here that I am attempting to excuse personal failings by invoking institutional constraints, but it seems to me that when attempting to account for how research gets done, how knowledge emerges, how publications come about, and so on, we need to go well beyond vapid generalities about the social construction of knowledge, and that one way to do this is to be absolutely concrete when describing context. In my ASA Conference paper (Crick 1983:29–31), which did not go down well at the time, I argued that we should be far more candid about the nature and workings of the specific institution that employs us, for it is an obvious fact of professional life that different academics are very differently placed with regard to research opportunities and funding.

My particular situation at Deakin University has had a direct impact upon what I have—and have not—been able to contribute to the emerging field of the anthropology of tourism. For a start, Deakin has no large department of anthropology where a "critical mass" of colleagues could stimulate active field research programs. Indeed, given the founding brief of the university to provide quality "distance education" materials to students who had missed out on a tertiary education, for many years there was very little "research culture" at all to speak of. I have already related how my Sri Lankan project was denied funding by Deakin. But nearly two decades later in 1999 when I applied for research leave to undertake my current research project in Maldon, the university had been so over-taken by a punitive, managerialist, accountancy-gone-berserk culture, that I was denied the opportunity to undertake a prolonged period of fieldwork altogether.

The fieldwork I did in Sri Lanka in 1982, during which time I based myself in the ancient "Hill Country" capital of Kandy, was of a very open-ended kind. Since I was not then steeped in the available scholarly literature, I was not in a position to test any specific hypotheses or examine the adequacy of any frame-works suggested by others. But since this was my first fieldwork experience, I wanted to undertake something far less focused than that and thus, in a sense, just jumped in, following my nose, and simply waiting to see what struck me as wor-thy of further investigation. If forced to put a conventional "descriptor" on that, "community impact" would possibly come closest to revealing which aspects of tourism interested me most anthropologically. That phrase, however, is mislead-ing in that although clearly working on a new topic, tourism, my erstwhile seman-tic interests also came center stage, and thus I was more into investigating the general problem of what tourism 'meant' to a broad range of people in a com-munity than doing a conventional impact study. Fairly early on in the piece I had clear ideas about the sorts of material that would fit into a book I could write about international tourism in Sri Lanka, and so I employed the range of research strategies that would allow me access to a "multiplicity of local voices." I did not then, and I have not since studied the tourists themselves; my focus has always been on responses to the touristic presence.

The chapter structure of the monograph that finally resulted from this piece of research (Crick 1994) corresponded very strongly with those guiding ideas I had in the field. The book allows senior officials in the Ceylon Tourism Board, the Mayor of Kandy, hotel owners, the owners of unlicensed guesthouses, shopkeep-ers, touts, school children, beggars, and others, to speak on the subject of tourism. But, apart from capturing that broad array of views and attitudes, the research also endeavored to explicitly capture the complexity of tourism on different levels. Tourism is thus explored in the rhetoric of politicians in the context of national pronouncements about cultural and economic policy, as well as in the context of the specific urban locality of Kandy. Then the operations of tourism are investi-gated within the so-called informal arena in Kandy, which operates largely out-side the controls of the tourism authorities. At a lower level still, I sought information as to how tourism had affected the lives of specific individuals.

One other thing I was determined to do in my book was to bring together the literature about tourism in Sri Lanka and the anthropological literature about that country more generally. I was very struck when, after leaving the field, I began to read as voraciously as I could before actually drafting the monograph, how in the entire corpus of anthropological work on Sri Lanka, tourism—a significant industry in the country by any measure—seemed to be almost invisible. It almost seemed as if anthropologists went out of their way to ignore tourism and tourists, although some managed a very brief derisory note. And, on the other hand, the literature on tourism in Sri Lanka—much of it, admittedly, quantitative and highly technical—seemed to make no significant connections to other bodies of literature about the country. Whatever the shortcomings of my book and the fieldwork upon which it was based, I feel that modest aim of bringing two separate bodies of literature into some sort of dialogue was achieved.

If publishing a sizeable monograph is a marker of successful research, then one would have to conclude that my tourism fieldwork in Sri Lanka was successful. However, it is more than appropriate to state in an exploration of the personal and professional contexts that have contributed to the growth of the social scientific analysis of tourism that I did not much enjoy my time in the field. Being bookish and somewhat introverted, the accepted routines of normal academic existence sit far more comfortably with me than the unpredictabilities of life in the field. If the open stretches of time involved in being on holidays had always been anxiety-provoking to me, the "nonroutine" character of much participant observation was similarly so. The contrast between reading quietly about language, culture, and meaning in a library in Oxford and standing on a street corner in an Asian city alongside touts, pickpockets, con men, prostitutes, beggars, and all the rest, could hardly have been greater. I am prepared to believe that some anthropologists put up with the daily chores of academic existence because it permits them a periodic escape to the field; in my own case, it was almost a matter of wanting to be out of the field in order to once again be in a world of familiar routines. I say this not to indulge in any amateur psychological speculation, but simply to make the point that such inner realities of the investigator must play a part in influencing which aspects of any phenomenon he/she chooses to concentrate on and also how those aspects are portrayed. In my own view such realities are properly considered fieldwork data.

I stuck unswervingly with my tourism project for the full duration of my time in Sri Lanka, but have to confess that what shaky self-confidence I had took a number of pretty severe blows, particularly early on in the project. I seemed to be constantly bumping into people from Australia, all of them far more experienced in overseas travel than I, and some of whom were fairly forthcoming in their assessment that with a rigid personality like mine I would not find out anything about tourism in Sri Lanka. And then there were also a number of postgraduate anthropology students in Kandy at the same time as myself, mostly from the UK, one of whom roundly declared that researching Buddhism would be a far safer project because asking too many questions about tourism could disturb the local elite who might not appreciate close scrutiny of some of their business activities. Having already turned from a Buddhist project to a touristic one, the thought of reversing direction did not appeal to me. I therefore soldiered on in a single-minded way, sheer stubbornness being an entrenched character trait of mine.

It was several years before I published anything based specifically on my Sri Lankan fieldwork. A second period in the field would have added immeasurably to the extent and quality of the ethnographic material I possessed, but the worsening level of ethnic violence made a second visit distinctly unattractive. In 1986, therefore, when research leave again became a possibility, I chose instead to spend six months trying to produce the first draft of a monograph while based at the University of Adelaide. Prior to that, a number of specific articles had begun to take shape, but I felt that a complete break from normal duties would be required to make any substantial progress with a major work.

My first tourism publication (Crick 1985), though certainly shaped in part by fieldwork experience, was an intensely reflexive piece, and given its deliberately playful postmodern style, it annoyed some colleagues (even to the point of their recommending nonpublication), particularly the suggestion that "anthropological" and "touristic" selves were significantly overlapping identities, and hence the anthropology of tourism could shed light, not only on the nature of tourism, but also on the nature of the anthropological quest as well. I have no doubt that my fascination with this topic, which had two further airings, far more soberly expressed than the first (Crick 1991, 1995), was in part a matter of the anxiety I had felt in the field—a context, which by placing a person into substantially altered circumstances, must cause some level of self-scrutiny, even amongst those who enjoy a change. But I was conscious at the time of an entirely different reason for pursuing such a reflexive line of inquiry, namely, a perplexity, widely felt I should imagine, amongst the pioneer writers in the emerging field of the anthropology of tourism, as to why the field was only now coming into being.

Tourism, after all, was one of the largest industries in the world and was having an impact in most of the societies where anthropologists did their research. Yet, somehow the profession almost invariably described those societies as if tourism and tourists did not exist. That neglect, or as I suggested in my 1985 article, "avoidance," needed an explanation, and my hunch was that the unacknowledged kinship between tourism and anthropology might have something to do with it. Nowadays, the many ways in which anthropological and touristic selves overlap are so obvious it almost seems trite to harp upon the issue, but in the mid-1980s it was felt to be fairly threatening by some.

The other major intellectual development in the years after my Sri Lankan research, which must be mentioned, was my strenuous effort to get on top of what anthropological (and more broadly, social scientific) literature on tourism then existed. It was an effort to get under my belt the work of colleagues, which I would love to have taken with me to the field. Several years of intensive reading as widely as I could about how the social sciences had dealt with the phenomenon of international tourism resulted in my "literature review," which appeared in the Annual Review of Anthropology (Crick 1989). I am conscious of the provocative nature of some of my reflexive pieces and am more than aware that my ethnographic writings lack a certain richness because of the circumstances in which I undertook the research, so I am more than pleased to have been able to make a contribution to an emerging field which was acceptable to such a prestigious journal. Clearly, the time was right for such an overview to appear. Today, of course, my summary is already much dated, such has been the progress over the past decade or so; but from the frequency of its citation, that article appears to have been useful to others in coming to grips with the relatively new field of study.

It is common in accounting for the growth of new fields of knowledge to point to interpersonal links with significant others as being crucial to unfolding developments. In my own case, because I was employed in a university where tourism studies were not a part of the curriculum, being a member of the Australian Anthropological Society where no critical mass of colleagues had yet found tourism interesting, and living in Australia, so expensively remote from most major centers where the subfield was developing, the context in which my own interests blossomed were of necessity very much a matter of literary encounter rather than personal acquaintance. I remember well the first two books on tourism which I read that significantly motivated me to stay in what was clearly a social scientifically fascinating field. One was *The Golden Hordes* (Turner and Ash 1975), the other *The Tourist: A New Theory of the Leisure Class* (MacCannell 1976). The tourism industry has a very high opinion of itself, so much so that analysis often seems indistinguishable from "PR." That being the case, the sheer irreverence of Turner and Ash's work appealed to me greatly, although one would have to say that nowadays, in these times of more balanced appraisals of tourism, the overriding negativism of their book would be unacceptable. With MacCannell's work, although not completely persuaded by some of his central claims about authenticity, tourism, and modernity, there was a very palpable sense of a phenomenon, which I personally did not find that interesting in itself. But being used to conduct intriguing explorations of core areas of social theory, that demonstrable linkage MacCannell so well made between tourism and time-honoured concerns in the social sciences meant that I was well and truly hooked.

Not long after these initial forays into the available literature, I became aware of a small number of anthropologists who had been writing on tourism for a number of years. Those whose work I found especially valuable, largely in part because it stemmed from a concern with basic anthropological issues, would include Pierre van den Berghe, Jeremy Boissevain, and Edward Bruner. Though somewhat dissatisfied with the "hosts and guests" framework in the anthropology of tourism (Smith 1977), nonetheless, *Hosts and Guests* was indubitably a foundational text for this new subfield within the discipline; and for me, it had an added value because, as some chapters in that book so amply demonstrated, tourism was a phenomenon that could occasion diametrically opposed representations. If Graburn could see it as a "sacred journey," while Nash felt forced to point out the fundamentally neo-imperialistic nature of tourism, then clearly this was a field not only of absolute fascination for an anthropologist, but one where the territory was only just beginning to be mapped out.

My early influences did not comprise only anthropologists. The taxonomic and theoretical work of sociologist Erik Cohen was stimulating, not least because of his having one foot squarely in the anthropological camp with his fine ethnographic work on tourism in Thailand. The ever-lively sociological writings of Graham Dann, too, were always inspiring, especially with his more recent move into sociolinguistic aspects of tourism. I also found especially thought provoking the work of Linda Richter, a political scientist. The above six names stand out, and no doubt with more reflection I could add to them without much trouble, but I must place on record the crucial role that the journal *Annals of Tourism Research* had for me personally because of the way in which it kept me in touch with an exciting and expanding area of social science scholarship. From the early 1980s right up to date, articles focused upon tourism have appeared in the mainline anthropology journals once in a blue moon. The articles in the more industry-orientated tourism and hospitality journals were almost, without exception, dull and uninspiring to someone of my intellectual interests. Thus, to have a social science tourism journal of high academic standards, which could keep me in touch with the writings of my anthropological colleagues, which, via "special" issues, could demonstrate the full array of approaches and concerns in different social scientific disciplines, and which, via its "reports," "reviews," and "calendars" could tell me what was going on around the world in this emerging field, was priceless. Those of us who have now had an interest in the social scientific study of tourism for some twenty years probably all owe Jafar Jafari (and his large team of editors of various types) an incalculable debt of gratitude for establishing and keeping that most important medium of communication going.

Before leaving the matter of important influences, I must make mention of one specific context in my own development which was inter-personal. Edward Bruner invited me to offer a paper in the tourism section at the World Congress of Sociology in Madrid in 1990, which I gladly did. As a result of that trip I was able, for a short time, to be a member of the small group of academics who made it their business to ensure that the study of tourism became a firm fixture in the International Sociological Association's firmament. That goal was achieved, but alas, the sheer distance of Australia from everywhere else and the relative paucity of conference and travel funds at Deakin University, soon meant that my personal involvement with that group was at an end. My tourism research, therefore, became a matter of soldiering on in virtual isolation while writing up my Sri Lankan material. This sense of isolation quickly took its toll, for I started to decline invitations to write articles in edited compilations, encyclopedias, and the like, because, given my location, I did not feel that I could contribute well-researched and cutting-edge material of the kind that institutionally and geographically better-placed individuals could. There was a considerable professional sadness in this, for even as I was turning down requests, nearly everyone writing in the anthropology of tourism field was citing my Annual Reviews piece.

I should add, too, that my research interests in the anthropology of tourism were quarantined from my other academic duties. In a university, teaching and research ideally sustain each other, but the reality was that at Deakin it was 1995 before I had an opportunity to incorporate a significant amount of material about tourism into the undergraduate anthropology curriculum. The fact that I had been working in an academic field for some fourteen years before getting an opportunity to teach about my particular interests goes, I think, some way toward explaining why I was so tardy in completing the Sri Lankan phase of my work with the publication of *Resplendent Sites, Discordant Voices* in 1994. Had teaching the anthropology of tourism been a central part of my weekly academic duties I am sure that my completion of the monograph would have been hastened. The reality was, though, that in 1994 I was teaching a range of anthropological subjects, which gave no indication of what my research focus had been for more than a decade. Not only was I remote from most other practitioners in the field, but also my research interests were isolated from my teaching duties.

I was, nevertheless, delighted when *Resplendent Sites, Discordant Voices* was chosen for inclusion in Harwood Academic's prestigious "Studies in Anthropology and History" series. At the same time, I was very conscious of the fact that the year the book appeared—1994—was already some twelve years after my fieldwork. I endeavored, to fill in the temporal gap by using documentary material, but this strategy could never be more than marginally successful. The reality was that 1982, the year of my fieldwork, was the peak year for international tourist arrivals to Sri Lanka, and since then a decade of serious ethnic conflict and other factors had altered things on the ground appreciably. As remarked earlier, I did not wish to do return fieldwork in such a troubled society to bring my account a little more up to date, so my monograph was noticeably not current, as well as lacking the ethnographic richness I would have achieved had I been longer in the field.

There was a strong sense of irony in all of this too, for one of the things which had first steeled my determination to study tourism was coming upon a speech by the Sri Lankan Minister of State (who also held the Tourism Portfolio), in which he offered a consciously Buddhist theory of tourism, according to which tourism was an ennobling venture, indeed the 'greatest movement for world peace and understanding' (de Alwis 1980). I thought that such a recently developed industry, so conscientiously wrapped up in such political rhetoric, had to be of profound anthropological interest. Whatever one thinks of the notion that tourism is inherently linked to peace and understanding, Sri Lanka soon became a significant example of how warfare adversely affects visitor numbers.

By the time, in the second half of the 1990s, when I was teaching a major section of a third-level anthropology unit on the subject of anthropology and tourism with, not unnaturally, frequent reference to my own research, my publications stemming from the Sri Lankan fieldwork had all but dried up. With the book published and my previously pressing need to provocatively explore the problem of the overlapping identities of 'anthropologist' and 'tourist' now exhausted, there was nothing left that I wanted to write at reflexive, theoretical, or ethnographic levels. When my Annual Reviews piece was reprinted in 1996 I realized that what I needed was a new research project to get my teeth into. Being now married and with a family I decided that whatever fieldwork I did would have to be fairly close to home so that it would not be too disruptive of domestic life. Tourism in another exotic country was certainly not on with my new domestic responsibilities. On the other hand, while resolving to do something within Australia, I did not want the expertise I had built up in regard to the social scientific study of tourism to go by the board.

So in mulling over a few ideas for a new research project, I remembered that in my filing cabinet there was a file labeled 'Maldon' that had had in it just one newspaper article. Maldon is a small country town in central Victoria, less than two hours drive from where I live. Born in the gold rushes of the 1850s, like many similarly sized settlements in Australia, Maldon spent much of the latter half of the twentieth century attempting to create a viable future for itself. When I first visited the town in the late 1970s, the one thing I knew about it was that in 1966, because of the architectural intactness of many of its buildings, it had been classified a "notable town" by the Victorian National Trust. Then in the mid-1980s, during one or two weekend visits shopping for antiques, I could sense, an enormous tension in the town. As I later found out, not only had the people of Maldon been living with a detailed planning scheme based rigorously on heritage conservation principles, but that for two decades, the town had been attracting a high number of "lifestyle" residents. For some ten years too, there were attempts to develop a local heritage tourism industry, with Maldon now sporting the label "Australia's First Notable Town," in which it endeavored to base its future on its past. The newspaper article that came to my attention—and it was in a national, not a local newspaper—suggested that the town was almost in a self-destruct mode.

That article and the general idea that Maldon was an extremely promising place for an anthropological project had obviously slumbered in the back of my mind for many years until 1997 when, as I have indicated, I was consciously looking for a new research project. Maldon, with a population of around 2000, felt about the right size for participant observation, and its distance from my home would not make for massive domestic problems. Here was a good site where I could study heritage issues and tourism development in the broader context of social change and community conflict. The more I discovered from the little literature available on the town, the more I knew I had a good project.

I found out that in 1972, the Shire Council had resolved to ask the National Trust to take back its "notable town" classification, given that the strict planning controls which came in its wake were seen by many as an infringement on personal liberty. Some fifteen years later, Maldon was clearly a town with serious divisions between urban and rural interests, between pro- and antimining groups, between pro- and antiheritage groups and between pro- and antitourism groups. Maldon, indeed, had acquired a national reputation for disputatiousness. For some residents Maldon's economy was based on tourism; for others tourism had created not a single genuine job. For some, visitors came to see local history; for others, commodifying the past was undermining all notions of heritage and authenticity. My instincts were that this would prove a first-rate field project, so I was pleased to find no evidence of any academic doing social research in Maldon.

Given my dissatisfaction with the "stop-over" status of my Sri Lankan fieldwork, I decided to properly plan and prepare for the Maldon project, and apart from spending a considerable effort to acquaint myself thoroughly with all published sources of information about the town, I also decided to apply for substantial fieldwork funding from the Australian Research Council. Up to this point in my career I had done all of my research with no such sources of additional income. Now, in order to maximize my chances, I devised a collaborative project between myself and the Professor of Australian Studies at Deakin. A historian; he could supply the much longer time frame that I wanted, namely, a historical study of Maldon from its origins in 1853, which would contribute importantly to my contemporary anthropological study about development and social change over some three decades since the attainment of "notable" status in 1966. Jointly we put in for a large research grant to cover a three-year project, which was unsuccessful.

One reason for the rejection would appear to be that the collaborative nature of the proposal made assessing the application difficult. Though the referees' reports were, of course, anonymous, it was fairly clear to me that the proposal had been vetted by an economist, a geographer, a historian, a tourism studies person and a heritage consultant (I could not detect any informed anthropological commentary). If one thing is clear from a cursory glance at any issue of *Annals of Tourism Research*, it is that different academic disciplines have widely disparate interests in tourism; the questions that preoccupy them, to say nothing of actual methodologies used in research, are quite diverse. Our project, having been evaluated from at least five completely different points of view, did not stand a chance of being financed.

While solid funding for three years would have been very welcome, given that it would have enabled concentrated spans of time "in the field" by virtue of providing adequate funds for "teaching release," I felt I could still proceed with my part of the project on a more modest scale. The larger collaborative scheme was, therefore, buried. But I was not very successful in obtaining a more modest grant from Deakin, and in the end, instead of the $120,000 we had first hoped for with the collaborative project, I ended up with a mere $500 "incentive award." Deakin University, by 1999, was consciously trying to foster a "research culture," and staff who attempted to gain major external research funding were rewarded, if unsuccessful, with minor sums to encourage them to keep going. The $500 I received was (as with the $300 gained in 1982) no more than petty cash, but it did, in fact, assist with the purchase of local newspapers, and gain me effective research entrée into the Maldon Museum and Archives.

Of course, such a small amount could provide no appreciable assistance toward traveling, let alone accommodation. I have now been engaged in the Maldon project for over five years and that "compensation prize" is the only funding I have received; the rest has been from my own pocket. When one thinks of the institutional contexts in which knowledge is produced, it is worth reflecting that my twenty-year contribution to the anthropology of tourism has been based on a grand total of only $800 in research funding.

Although I (then in 1999) realized that I would not be receiving any substantial additional fieldwork funds, I did not know that I would have to conduct my Maldon project without *any* prolonged period in the field at all. As I have already remarked, the failure to win a large ARC award was not fatal, for it is not necessary to secure a grant for 'teaching release' when your university has an "outside studies program" (OSP), under which research leave (eligibility for which is accrued at the rate of six months every three years) can be applied for. Since my six months of leave in Adelaide in 1986 to write the first draft of *Resplendent Sites, Discordant Voices,* I had applied for no further research leave and, in fact, made it clear to the faculty that I was deliberately not putting in triennial applications for six months leave because I wished to build up my accrual so that extended fieldwork of one year's duration might be possible.

In 1999, however, whilst Deakin was certainly endeavoring to build a stronger research profile, it had, as an institution, like all other institutions of higher education in Australia, been thoroughly overtaken by "managerialism," "economic fundamentalism" (the usage of the term 'rationalism' in this context seems absurd), and at a more micro level, "audit culture" (Strathern, ed. 2000). All aspects of academic life were now subject to endless quantification, and academics, who were once the core "assets" of a university, were now being conspicuously managed as "costs," requiring their conspicuous subjection to an ever-expanding and arbitrary set of constantly changing benchmarks. In 1999, in order to get study leave one had to be an "active" researcher, which was measured by a complex panoply of things ranging from bringing into the institution large amounts of extra income for its managerial class to consume (most important) to far less valued activities, such as doing quality research and publishing scholarly books and articles.

As it happened when I submitted my application for OSP, I was an active researcher in terms of the publicized criteria, but what I had not reckoned on was that in the less than three months between the submission of the application and the meeting of the Faculty of Arts' Leave Committee, my status would be transformed by the release of new mid-year audited data. As a result, when my application was actually considered, I had been a fraction of one point below the required score, and so was denied research leave. So whereas my Sri Lankan project had received some institutional support by way of an opportunity to go to the field, plus some years later, leave specifically for "writing up," my Maldon project received no institutional support other than $500. Therefore, as a result of being denied access to the field in 1999, I have, in the past four years, carried on my research project despite Deakin University rather than because of it.

Discovering, close to the commencement of a major research project in which fieldwork will be an intrinsic element, that one's employer will not grant one any research leave, is, to say the least, somewhat discouraging. But, in this day and age, and particularly given the large amount of anthropological research now done in what are normally referred to as "complex societies," fieldwork to yield results does not have to be of the "eighteen months in an exotic place with a tent" variety. I needed very quickly to work out a very different research strategy, which without institutional support would allow me a "presence" in the field so that I could observe and participate. Luckily, early on in my Maldon work, I encountered a resident, trained as a lawyer, but also with a passion for local history. He generously encouraged my research, and given that he was an active member of the Maldon Community Forum, Maldon Museum and Archives, and the Maldon Heritage Committee, I gained instant entrée to three strategically important sites from which to conduct some of my work.

My fieldwork, over some three years, thus became a matter of traveling to Maldon for two days of research twice a month, essentially so that I could attend the meetings of those bodies. Two-day trips with an overnight stay each time would not only enable me to observe the ongoing work of those organizations, but would also allow sufficient time for participant observation of a more diffuse kind, reading local newspapers and other pertinent archival material, as well as making possible some formal interviews. In regularly attending various committee meetings, I became a direct witness to some of the crucial decision-making that went on in the community.

Involvement with Maldon Museum and Archives became most critical because I quickly discovered that the local archives were in a poor state, uncataloged and with very little covering the previous 30 years (as distinct from the gold mining period in the latter half of the nineteenth century). Faced with that situation, I busied myself with building up and organizing Maldon's historical records, not only because they were important for my research work, but as a service to the local community. In fact, in the Community Forum and on the Heritage Committee, my status changed rapidly from being that of an outsider with mere "observer status" to that of an active participant in the town's affairs. Indeed, people began to forget why I was in Maldon, as I was increasingly regarded by some as a kind of member of the community. I must say, given the way in which present-day university managers seem to enjoy disparaging old-fashioned academic skills, it was wonderful to find that my skills and energies were appreciated by people I met in Maldon.

Participant observation requires two somewhat different activities—participation and observation, and the ratio between the two probably varies enormously both from anthropologist to anthropologist and from project to project. However, I found that after two years of fieldwork, during which I had read through fifty years of local newspapers and fifty years of local government records, other aspects of my project were not developing at the rate I would have liked. The reason was that I had become so actively involved in a number of projects in the town that I spent most of my time in Maldon working on those, rather than getting on with my own research. Additionally, I was increasingly wary of ending up in a "crossover" situation (Cameron 1997) where, because of the additional roles one adopts in a community as a result of carrying out research there, one risks ending up studying a field that has been appreciably affected by one's own presence. I did not want that to happen, and given that I also wanted more time to pursue specific research strategies, I decided midway through 2002 to wind down my committee involvement in Maldon.

Thus, 2003 was to be a year for a series of semistructured interviews with important people in the town and use of published records concerning the general historical background of the past 30 years. 2004 was to be the year in which I formally terminated the fieldwork stage of my research and commenced writing in earnest. Unlike in my Sri Lankan project, where a diverse number of smaller publications preceded the monograph, in the Maldon research I intended to proceed straight to the book itself. I already have far more information than I need to be able to write a rich anthropological history of how the small community of Maldon has come to terms with numerous "blow ins" (new residents), how the locals have coped with an increasingly significant tourism industry, and how heritage issues and tourism developments have, on occasion, come into serious conflict.

My rate of progress in writing the Maldon monograph was always going to be influenced considerably by workload and issues concerning morale at Deakin University. Like all universities in Australia, Deakin is now undergoing almost non-stop organizational change. An ever-growing managerial class has for some years now induced staff to take early retirement packages and not replacing them; curriculum reform to make savings is constantly on the agenda; bewildering, seemingly arbitrary, and costly structural change seems a daily occurrence. No one knows when or where the axe will next fall—on an individual or even an entire discipline. This clearly is a situation in which low morale is only to be expected and therefore where academic output of quality becomes more and more difficult to sustain.

Whether or not I shall still be at Deakin when my Maldon book is finished, I have no way of knowing. But another factor, which may prove to be more decisive, has recently entered the picture. As I write these words, I am battling cancer, which was diagnosed early in 2003. I was delighted later in that year to be able to launch in Maldon my *Maldon Memories* (Crick 2003), a book through which I have given to the community some of its early twentieth century oral history in a more accessible and permanent form. I had hoped in a few years time that I would be able to return in order to launch my account of the town's more recent history, and in so doing to make a further contribution to our anthropological understanding of tourism and its impact in small communities. However, now that my cancer has entered the inoperable, terminal phase, that will most likely not occur; indeed, the time I have left sadly may allow only half of my intended book to be completed. While that will obviously be a major personal disappointment, as I look back over my twenty years' contribution to the anthropology of tourism, I am quite satisfied. On that journey, I have probably been weighed down somewhat by a personality that few would envy me, but then all personalities yield strengths as well as weaknesses. I am also bound to say that being at Deakin University for more than a quarter of a century has probably not helped my output, for what I have added to the anthropology of tourism over that time span has been as a result of a mere $800 in research funding and an absence of any research leave for the past seventeen years. All things considered, however, I am reasonably content.

Graham Dann (1941–) is Emeritus Professor of Tourism, International Tourism Research Institute, University of Luton, Putteridge Bury, Hitchin Rd., Bedfordshire LU2 8LE, United Kingdom (e-mail: graham.dann@luton.ac.uk), where he has taught a number of graduate courses on tourism. His tourism research interests chiefly lie in the areas of motivation and the semiotics of promotion, and he has recently been awarded a higher doctorate (DLitt) for contributions in these areas. He is the author of numerous publications, among which are *The Language of Tourism: A Sociolinguistic Perspective* (1996) and (as editor) *The Tourist as a Metaphor of the Social World* (2002). He is on the editorial boards of four tourism academic journals, a member of the Research Committee on International Tourism of the International Sociological Association, and also a founding member of the International Academy for the Study of Tourism.

THE LIFE AND TIMES OF A WANDERING
TOURISM RESEARCHER

The Early Years

I was never very good at geography. All those mountains and rivers, plains and valleys, details of fruit production, coal mining and average rainfall—they were all so boring. It was thus not surprising that I nodded off one day at my minor English public school during a crucial geography test prepared by an ex-RAF officer that had been designed to identify suitable candidates for the forthcoming General Certificate of Education examination. Needless to say, I failed the exercise and, as a result, that was the only subject that I did not take at GCE "O"- level.

Some nineteen years later, and now aged 34, I had just responded to a couple of academic position announcements—one in New Zealand, the other in Barbados. Geography was still a weak point, and I confess to having to look up the location of that West Indian island in an out-of-date atlas, which is now even more *passé* and still in my possession. However, at least it was not so ancient that it colored those nations in pink that belonged to the British Empire.

Even so, that year—1975—was a good year. I successfully defended my sociology PhD, directed by an amiable slave driver called Asher Tropp, before a reputed ogre of an external examiner—Ernest Gellner, who, in that event, turned out to be a real pussycat. I took up a temporary post at the prestigious Social Science Research Council (SSRC) in London and I landed the job in Barbados. Mind you, with the telegram from Down Under coming through on the same day and also indicating acceptance, I had to consult colleagues at the University of Surrey as to which of the two appointments to take up. "New Zealand is a backwater," said one. "It's only a research position," observed another; "and the center could fold just as easily as the SSRC, starved of government funds." On the other hand, Barbados seemed more promising. As far as I could tell from the dot on the map, it was roughly half way between the United States and South America, and it would provide relative security in a newly created teaching department at the University of the West Indies.

And so it was, on one late September morning, that I boarded a British Airways jet bound for Barbados and Caracas (the latter I seemed to recall was the capital of the equally unknown Venezuela). At the other end, there was no one to meet me. Darkness had fallen in a soon-to-be-familiar Caribbean instant, and I discovered through an extremely well-spoken student at the small airport that the head of department was sick. My instructions were to proceed to a hotel called *Coconut Creek* for two days while the University sorted out my more permanent accommodation. Little did I realize at the time, but the very name of that establishment, like so many others bearing similar titles such as *Buccaneer Bay* and *Sam Lord's Castle*, would provide me with sufficient inspiration to write my very first tourism paper – "The Holiday was Simply Fantastic" (Dann 1976).

I am also happy to report that today my geographical knowledge has improved through travel, to the extent that I have now visited between 78 and 91 countries (depending on the way that they are territorially classified) and have been on 69 different airlines—a record admittedly exceeded by some other globe-trotting participants in this volume—but still not bad for a hitherto hermit and geographical ignoramus.

The Barbados Years: 1975–1996

Context   The guidebooks that still rely on imperial measures all say that Barbados is a 21-by-14-mile tropical island. Situated at approximately 13 °N and 59 °W, it is the most easterly of the Caribbean chain and, as home to some 260,000 people inhabiting 166 square miles, is one of the most densely populated territories on earth. It is also one of the few places to have experienced continuous British colonial rule for a considerable period—from 1627 until 1966, when it gained Independence. However, what this material tends to omit is that for over 200 of these years, Barbados—a jewel in the imperial crown—suffered some of the worst effects of plantation slavery. Furthermore, in excess of 90 percent of its inhabitants can trace their roots to different areas of West Africa (the present territories of Sierra Leone, Guinea, Ivory Coast, Nigeria, and the Cameroons) via the notorious Middle Passage. The result of this ignominious history—what one local novelist has described as *Growing up Stupid under the Union Jack* (Clarke 1980)—is that Barbados is more British than Britain itself. Its educational system, its legal system, its political system, its religious system, its division into parishes are all prime exemplars of the best of British culture and, in most cases, well exceeds standards in the Mother Country. Far from being ignorant, the populace can boast a literacy rate of over 99 percent, free education is provided from primary to doctoral level, the civil service is efficient, the buses run on time, and elections are held smoothly every five years. The hospitals function well and Edinburgh-trained consultants can be accessed by free phone on the same day by calling them at home. Refuse is collected regularly twice a week, the water supply is of potable excellence, and life expectancy is on par with most of the so-called "First World." In short, everything works. No small wonder, then, that Barbados ranks the highest on the UN quality of life indicators among all developing countries.

And yet the "Little England" image, so endearingly and uncritically recycled by generations of travel writers, is only half the story. Although the island still retains local place names such as "Hastings," "Worthing," and "Trafalgar Square," and even though judges continue to wear wigs, and though Anglican rituals may be more orthodox than Canterbury, a more accurate description of "Bimshire" or "Cheltenham by the Sea" might be "Little America." By finding itself in the United States' backyard, Barbados currently has far closer trade and communications links with that country. Its never-devalued currency is pegged at 2 to 1 parity with the US dollar, its television and radio stations relay US programs, and most of its visitors come from the US—complete with the demonstration effect of affluent lifestyles. No small wonder that Barbados was using e-mail and mobile phones long before Europe, or that many of its people, with relatives in New York, Miami, and Toronto, regularly take shopping trips to North America in order to make purchases of widely advertised goods in readily available US magazines.

Thus, on entering Barbados in 1975, I found myself, a minority person from Big England, having to adjust to this rapidly changing society—one that had thrown off the shackles of imperialism, only to exchange them for a state of dependency on its massive neighbor to the North.

The Academic Arena   Back in 1975, the University of the West Indies was, jokingly at least, said by its staff and students to be the "largest" tertiary level institution in the world, since its principal Mona-Jamaica campus (opened in 1948) was separated by some 1200 miles from the subsequently established campuses in Trinidad and Barbados. The latter commenced operations in 1963 in a few buildings near the Bridgetown harbor before moving to its elevated position four miles outside the capital and overlooking the West Coast. This Cave Hill Campus, as it was known, had six faculties: Arts and General Studies, Natural Sciences, Law, Education, Medicine, and Social Sciences. The last mentioned had only been a few days in existence when I first arrived, and simply comprised the departments of economics and sociology. Sociology required expansion and was combined with the discipline of government (inclusive of public administration). At that time, there were only two other sociologists and both were female (a strange anomaly in an otherwise macho society). One was English—Christine Barrow who had received her mainly anthropological training at Sussex. The other, Joyce Cole, was from the island of Tobago and had graduated from McGill in Canada. Together we put together a program for a BSc degree in sociology. I was to teach the bread-and-butter course, "Sociological Theory", and help Joyce with another entitled "Methods of Social Investigation". Back in those Neo-Positivist days, I additionally lectured in a general course known as "Scientific Method and Statistics". The most interesting was definitely the one on methodology.

Joyce and I prepared a series of lectures that included not only philosophy of science issues, but also all the stages of the research process from problem formulation to write up. However, of greater significance was our shared belief that any methods course worthy of the name had to contain a practical component, one that would involve each student in a group project which would produce hands-on experience for all the techniques learned in class. At that time, such an idea was fairly innovative. Indeed, visiting scholars from Europe and elsewhere were quite amazed with the results. One, Arnaud Marks, Director of the Department of Caribbean Studies at the Royal Institute of Linguistics and Anthropology in Leiden, the Netherlands, even offered to publish them as an edited collection. I subsequently came to appreciate that these students and those who eagerly followed them in ever increasing numbers were, unlike their counterparts elsewhere, highly motivated, willing, and able. They regarded education as a privilege, and for me, teaching them was a corresponding honor.

Our first methods *practicum*—something that was to change the course of my life—was one on tourism. As a native of the Caribbean with left-of-center political views, Joyce was intrigued by the then emerging argument, voiced by the likes of fellow West Indians, Lloyd Best, Frantz Fanon, and Neville Linton, that tourism was an exploitative force with negative sociocultural consequences for destination societies. My emphasis was altogether different. It centered on the question of why people should come to the region when all the islands seemed pretty much the same, offering a similar menu of fun-and-rum-in-the-sun attractions. Given that it did not appear to matter where they went, the answer to the problem surely had to reside in the conditions obtaining in their societies of origin.

Where there was too much political control at home, freedom could be found elsewhere. Where there was urban crime, a state of paradisical innocence could be sought. Where there was the anomic monotony of a 9-to-5 work regime, time could be suspended in the laid-back atmosphere of continual *joie de vivre*. Joyce soon caught my enthusiasm, and in no time we were thrashing out our variant of "push" and "pull" motives. As sociologists, we were familiar with the classical works of Durkheim, Veblen, and Simmel, and thus had little difficulty in formulating our views in these terms. We decided there and then that the methods project would likewise focus on the central unanswered issue underpinning all tourism: "why do people travel?"—a point that Lundberg had raised some three years earlier, but one which had been virtually ignored.

Since part of the methods course that I taught encompassed the domain of interviewing, I was left to extend the lectures into the practical training of interviewers for the project. In January 1976, the team was ready to go into the field. By that time, too, my future wife Elizabeth had joined me in Barbados after resigning a deputy headship in Camberley, Surrey, UK.

The interviews went without a hitch, and with response rates in the high nineties, (what was to become the norm for survey work in the region), the data set produced some equally elevated and reliable findings. However, Joyce was less interested in analyzing the data, and it was subsequently agreed that after we had co-authored a preliminary paper in a regional journal, I would be free to write a more detailed account on my own and seek a suitable international outlet. Besides, she had to direct her attention to preparing courses in the sociology of education and the sociology of development in order to meet rapidly expanding student demand in the department. As far as I know, she never authored another tourism paper.

The rest, as the cliché has it, is history. I submitted the article to the recently established *Annals of Tourism Research* and it appeared under the title *Anomie, Ego-enhancement and Tourism* (Dann 1977). It is probably the most widely cited of all my publications, and the subsequent empirical testing of the push–pull paradigm by others has only served to reconfirm its status. I gather that Valene Smith used to refer to me in her class of tourism undergraduates at Cal. State, Chico, as "push–pull Dann", and I was once even greeted at a conference in Bornholm, Denmark, as "Dann 77"—something of a two-edged compliment.

Spreading the Net   The editor of *Annals*, then as always, was the indefatigable Jafar Jafari. In that same year, he decided on the basis of that paper, and no doubt also wishing to internationalize his journal, to invite me to the University of Wisconsin-Stout. There he asked me to become a member of *Annals'* editorial board, and I have remained with that publication ever since. Over the years, I like to think that I have helped shape editorial policy and contribute toward making it the leading academic journal on tourism that it is today.

Joining *Annals* also had the advantage of placing me in contact with a number of scholars who were making a name for themselves in different parts of the world. I was able to correspond with them, meet them at conferences, but above all to follow them in their writings. This intellectual camaraderie, along with occasional differences of opinion engendered by the cut and thrust of debate, had the effect of not only increasing my interest in the field, but also of reducing my number one enemy—academic solitude.

Living on an island can easily lead to isolation and cabin fever. Fortunately, the University provided a generous annual study and travel allowance for both employees and their spouses, and I made sure that I used every cent of it each year without fail. Being the only person in a small department to have a consuming interest in tourism, and with no one else on the entire campus sharing such a passion, it was essential to get out and meet colleagues at conferences beyond the narrow insular confines of my immediate working environment.

In those early days, my conference attendance was limited mainly to my discipline (sociology) rather than my field (tourism). Then I belonged to the American Sociological Association (ASA), the largest professional association for sociologists, and went to a few meetings in the United States. However, there was no tourism specialization within the ASA and this lacuna led to a corresponding reduction in my own participation. Fortunately, in its place, the International Sociological Association (ISA) did provide something of a niche for which I was looking. Operating with a system of research committees, it had a group dedicated to the sociology of leisure with such household names as Joffré Dumazedier involved. In 1982, I joined and attended its session in Mexico City and soon discovered a couple of kindred spirits, notably Marie-Françoise Lanfant and Kryzstztof Przeclawski; and before long we began plotting the creation of a separate tourism unit within the ISA. In 1986, in Delhi, these plans were further developed, and by 1990, in Madrid, we had formed a working group recognized by the ISA. The 1994 meeting in Bielefeld, witnessed our promotion to a full research committee, an unprecedented rapid gain that was consolidated some four years later in Montréal.

In the meantime, Jafar Jafari had established the International Academy for the Study of Tourism (IAST), and I, along with many of the contributors to this volume, was invited to become a founding member. In 1988, our charter meeting was held in Santander, to be followed by biennial meetings in 1989—Warsaw, Zakopane, Krakow; 1991—Calgary; 1993—Seoul; 1995—Cairo; 1997—Malacca; 1999—Zagreb; 2001—Macao; and 2003—Savonlinna. To the best of my knowledge, I am the only member of IAST to have attended all these gatherings, and my wife is certainly the only spouse to have been present for every meeting. In each case I prepared a paper for the academic sessions, and on the six occasions when a book of proceedings resulted, I had a chapter published in it (see, e.g., Dann 1995).

Of course, contact with colleagues took place outside the conference circuit as well. Apart from the previously mentioned trip to visit Jafar Jafari, I also visited Valene Smith, Nelson Graburn, Bryan Farrell, and Paul Wilkinson in their natural habitats. There were, as well, colleagues who came to see us in Barbados. I think, for example, of Dennison Nash, Bill Gartner, Chuck Goeldner, Valene Smith, and Paul Wilkinson. One person who journeyed to the island every year, but who was not a fellow tourism researcher, was Rob Potter from Royal Holloway, University of London. Beginning with our first encounter in 1982, he stayed in our ramshackle home in the rural parish of St John overlooking Martin's Bay and the Atlantic Ocean on the East Coast of the island. Rob was a human geographer and, despite my earlier aversion to his discipline, was interested initially in several of my nontourism exploits, particularly investigations that I had conducted on quality of life. After a while, we began collaborating on projects of mutual interest. Indeed, it is true to say that he is the individual with whom I have co-authored the most publications—some eleven in all—including one or two eventually on tourism.

After much sweat and tears, we also jointly compiled an annotated bibliography on Barbados, a monumental task that involved each of us reading about 1500 pieces of work covering a wide range of topics. At one stage we had all the entries covering two flights of stairs in his three-story house in Egham, Surrey, England. That was definitely the first and last time that I will ever prepare a bibliography. Maybe I would be better advised to leave such a task to those more gifted—the likes of René Baretje and his archival tourism centers, for example.

Another colleague who came to stay was Klaus de Albuquerque, a Caribbeanist, tourism researcher, and fellow sociologist from the College of Charleston. He it was who offered to teach my courses (still the same old theory and methodology) in 1995, the only year that I was on sabbatical from the University of the West Indies. Regrettably, in 1999, Klaus was stricken down with a lethal cancer that robbed him of life at an early age and lost me a true friend.

Academic Development   During the first few years in Barbados, and despite an initial foray into tourism research, it became quite clear to me that if my career were to advance I would have to continue, for a while at least, with projects that belonged to mainstream sociology. Indeed, most of my colleagues appear to have thought that tourism was a trifling topic unworthy of serious research. I therefore decided to diversify and produced a number of studies on a variety of topics such as everyday life, alcoholism and quality of life, and even race and class in the Barbados Telephone Directory. One of my wackiest projects—one that was literally "off the wall"—was an investigation I undertook of religious graffiti in North East Brazil. Knowing a bit of Portuguese, I was fascinated by the imported African slave cults of Umbanda and Candomblé. Since both were illegal at the time, adherents had discovered an ingenious way of avoiding suspicion from the police. By visiting Catholic shrines that were replete with inscribed messages declaring gratitude for various miracles wrought, they found that they could also leave written communications to their own spirit deities under the guise of Christian saints. The only thing that betrayed these syncretic inscriptions was their content and the similarity of the formulae they employed to other cultic mantras that were easily available in specialist books. I decided to copy down as many of these graffiti as I could and then to compare them with the originals.

Unfortunately, one morning while I was so engaged in a well-known church in Recife, who should come along, but a man with a bucket and brush who proceeded to whitewash the walls, a duty he apparently performed four times a year. It was only by bribing him to refrain from his task until I had completed mine that I was able to finish my business. Ever since in my methods classes, I have always given this experience as an instance of an occupational hazard.

Another example had occurred several years earlier in the Basilicata region of Italy when I was part of an international team studying superstition and witchcraft. On one occasion, in a village near Potenza, I was consuming some spaghetti in which, unknown to myself, a love potion had been placed by a Lucanian *strega*. I was ill for the following three days. My coresearchers informed me that while I was asleep on my bed of sickness, a lonely Scottish lassie living in the vicinity had come to visit me. Apparently the witch had decided that, since she had heard that I was originally from Edinburgh, the two Scotties would make a good match. She was wrong in her assumption, but the others had a good laugh.

Anyway, and in spite of these distractions, I could not keep tourism out of the picture for very long. Some of the projects I conducted were in fact just a stepping stone to tourism. One of these compromise studies was on the emigration of Eastern Caribbean nationals to the United States—a field that shared much in common with tourism motivation, my area of initial interest. Another was on expatriates—persons I later found to be akin to permanent tourists, living a similar non-integrated existence on the margins of the host society (analogs of beach-boys whom I also studied). Barbados had its fair share of these characters, some quite eccentric and a few of whom I counted among my friends; and it was not long before I had my methodology students working on such a project. It was then also that I discovered that both Dennison Nash and Erik Cohen had independently written on expatriate communities. Indeed, Dennison, on one of his visits to the island, spoke to my students on the topic prior to their commencing fieldwork. But as far as my day-to-day living was concerned, I resolved never to mix with fellow Brits, Americans, or Canadians, to the exclusion of members of the host society. As things turned out, this was a correct decision, and I enjoyed my time in the unsophisticated company of local farmers and fishermen in the Barbadian countryside.

Once I had gained promotion and tenure (after just three years), I became almost exclusively tourism oriented in my research. By then, however, three changes had occurred—important milestones which were to characterize my subsequent work: (1) a search for the supply counterpart to tourist motivation demand (2) the development of an eclectic approach to theory and (3) the shift from quantitative to qualitative methodology.

A Search for the Supply Counterpart to Tourist Motivation Demand   The more I looked at tourist motivation, the more convinced I became that push factors were not only logically and temporally prior to pull factors, but that without them there would be no travel at all (Dann 1981). Destination authorities therefore, in seeking to promote their various attractions, had somehow to match their offerings with the sociopsychological needs of their potential clients. Furthermore, it did not matter so much whether their place attributes were factually accurate. What became more important was how they were selectively portrayed. In other words, the crucial element was imagery and the way that it was transmitted via verbal and pictorial representation.

In the late '80s, I therefore undertook a couple of studies of tourist brochures. One focused on how indigenous people were featured (which was not published for eight years; Dann 1996). The other was a case study of Cyprus and how that country was thematized for the British and German mass markets (Dann 1988). Interestingly, when the latter was initially presented at a 1988 editorial board meeting of *Annals* in Nicosia before an additional audience of the Cyprus tourism authorities, the immediate reaction was that they, rather than external tour operators, should be supplying their own photos and copy for outside consumption. That is to say, the issue had become one of determining self-imagery, a point that I continued to emphasize in subsequent publications, though admittedly to little effect.

From images in brochures, I next turned to imagery in other promotional media. In particular, I examined travelogs and advertising—even some postmodern variants of publicity. However, I still had to remember that such messages were targeted at individuals who had their own ways of defining in motivational terms the locations they intended to visit. I therefore conducted a large in-depth investigation of tourists in Barbados and asked them, *inter alia*, what images they had entertained of the place before they came to the island and now that they were here. I additionally confronted them with four pictures taken from a catalog produced by the local Tourist Board and asked the visitors what these representations meant to them in the above two time sequences. This projective technique yielded over 200 pages of single-spaced transcripts—an enormous amount of very rich sociolinguistic data that I was able to compare with the official language of promotion, right down to the use of specific nouns and adjectives (Dann 1995). I was also able to unearth latent motivation expressed *a posteriori* in the subjects' own words, rather than responding to an *a priori* checklist of the researcher. In such a manner,

I could additionally link this verbal framing with two other motivational features of the tourist that I had been exploring—nostalgia and "the tourist as child."

The stage was now set for my most ambitious project to date—to write my first tourism book which would somehow build on all the work that I had been carrying out over the years. *The Language of Tourism* (Dann 1996) was researched and written in 1995—some very useful material being discovered in the unique and extensive collection of René Baretje at the Centre des Hautes Études Touristiques (then of the University of Aix-Marseille) who did everything possible to facilitate my efforts. The volume appeared the following year. It was well received and represented a turning point in my career.

The Development of an Eclectic Approach to Theory   During the course of my research on motivation and its promotional counterpart that culminated in *The Language of Tourism*, I was very much aware of the theoretical roots of my discipline—sociology. Like every other student, I had been exposed to the various schools of sociological theory at both the undergraduate and graduate level. In such study, I very quickly realized that there were some useful elements and some bad bits in each paradigm. I rebelled against being tied down to any given orthodoxy. For me, there was a desire to pick and mix, to be eclectic, and carry on as an intellectual wanderer and wonderer.

I became even more convinced of this position after spending a delightful summer evening in 1977 in the sole company of Alvin Gouldner in a St Louis tavern. He and Erving Goffman were very much the *enfants terribles* of sociology, refusing to accept the Functionalist party line and causing consternation among the orthodox ranks of the American Sociological Association. Gouldner's sympathy for the European student protests of the '60s and his monumental *The Coming Crisis of Western Sociology* (1971) made a lasting impression on me.

Another significant influence, though of a more methodological nature, came in the eccentric persona of Norman Denzin. Quite by accident, I found myself in the hotel room next to his at the 1982 ISA conference in Mexico City. Later, I had a chance to discuss more fully our mutual interests on an invitation to the University of Illinois at Urbana-Champaign in 1995. Although it was snowing outside, Norman was in his chaotic office in just a pair of shorts and with nothing on his feet. On that visit I also got to know much better someone whose work I have always admired—Ed Bruner. He always sends me off-prints of his papers as and when they are published.

I also came across someone who shared eclectic views similar to my own and had been expounding such an approach since the '70s—Erik Cohen. Having so far only admired his work from afar and through correspondence, my association with *Annals* and the Academy made it possible on a couple of occasions to have face to face contact. We also had the opportunity to collaborate on a "sociology of tourism" module that we jointly delivered to the World Leisure and Recreation Association's International Centre of Excellence (WICE) candidates one cold winter week in Leeuwarden, The Netherlands, in 1989. There followed the co-authorship of a piece on sociology and tourism for a special issue of *Annals* dedicated to tourism and the social sciences. The realization that we were similarly eclectic in outlook presented no difficulty. In fact it was a decided advantage. Nevertheless, we were both perfectionists, and that did render our collaboration more problematic. To cut a long story short, the paper went through three self-inflicted revisions, and there were times when we considered giving up on the project. Eventually it appeared (Dann and Cohen 1991), and it has been frequently cited ever since.

Erik's eclecticism was evident in the different phases that he went through—his reliance on Schutz and Simmel for his typologies, his fascination with phenomenology and the sociology of religion, his flirtation with Postmodernism. My own trajectory was just as varied. A little bit of Maslow and Parsons here, some Conflict Theory there, fairly large dollops of Symbolic Interactionism and Formalism, a sprinkling of Postmodernism—altogether quite a theoretical *pot pourri*.

Of course not all my colleagues appreciated this higgledy-piggledy approach. They wanted to anchor me to a given framework, thereby making me that much easier to critique. It thus came as no surprise that on one occasion I was accused of being a Marxist. For an eclectic like myself this charge was quite absurd since I had merely cherry picked the sections of *Das Kapital* that I found useful and had abandoned the rest as decidedly unhelpful, if not highly problematic. The pieces that I liked about Marx were his early writings on "alienation," given that they neatly complemented Durkheim's notion of "anomie" (which I had employed in my motivational studies). They also supported my argument that tourism represented not just an escape from the restrictions of Western society, but that it had its own system of social control that it conveyed to its clientele through various media. I am still of that belief.

The Shift from Quantitative to Qualitative Methodology   I have already made reference to the Neo-positivist phase that characterized my early development. My first study of tourist motivation was survey-based and the data analysis was largely statistical with tests of significance galore. A similar approach was adopted in my study of alcoholism in Barbados, in which I additionally employed path analysis, a relatively new technique that I had learned during my 1975 stint at the Social Science Research Council in London. My work on quality of life was also largely quantitative, as was (though to a lesser extent) that on the sexuality of the Barbadian male and a future-oriented study that had employed conversational analysis. After all, I was in the first generation of students that had been exposed to the wonders of SPSS, and I wished to avail myself of the full potential of this Statistical Package for the Social Sciences. When I initially began the computer analysis of data via this software on a mainframe at Surrey linked to an even more massive machine at University College, London, the information had to be entered via punch cards. Later, matters were considerably simplified (though still rather tedious) since data could be tapped in directly from code-sheets.

However, none of the foregoing studies was exclusively quantitative. There were many open-ended questions in the interview schedules that lent themselves to content analysis once the transcripts had been laboriously assembled and the difficult process of classification had commenced. I soon began to realize that the creation of categories from the data was a far from mechanical exercise, and that precisely because it was theory driven (either from above or below), no amount of numerical wizardry could take the place of insight. Besides, after a table had been presented, flesh and blood had to be put on it, and this task could only be accomplished by recourse to what respondents had actually said in their own words. Alternatively stated, I had been persuaded by the likes of Alma Gottlieb and Philip Pearce that it was far more important to approach such topics as tourist motivation according to the meanings held and communicated by the participants than to impose my own armchair schemes upon them—a lesson I have always remembered.

It was thus logical that my next methodological phase should be devoted to a series of content analytical studies that could be combined with semiotic analysis at the qualitative level in order to tease out the subjective interpretations. Elsewhere, I have outlined the advantages of such a complementary approach, the most important of which was its very low cost. Naturally, this feature appealed to the Scot in me—after all, I had been born and bred in Edinburgh. More important, however, I soon appreciated that being starved of research funds could have its own rewards, because such a situation could and did lead to innovative ways of carrying out projects on a shoestring. In fact, the more I was obliged to rely on my own resources and creative imagination, the more convinced I became that there was an inverse relationship between quality of research and the financial quantity of its support– a belief that is heresy in the minds of many, but one that I nevertheless still hold today. Indeed, I have only once received any direct remuneration for contracted research. That was for a collaborative study on the sociocultural impacts of tourism in Barbados, Curaçao, St Lucia, and Tobago, conducted under the aegis of the United National Commission for Latin America and the Caribbean (UN-ECLAC). With some 2000 interviewees, this three-survey investigation among residents, hotel managers, and employees is still probably the largest of its kind.

The topics of my early content/semiotic analyses were nearly all tourism oriented. They comprised a bibliographical overview of trends in Caribbean tourism research, images of Cyprus, travelogs and the management of unfamiliarity, hyping the destination through the rich and (in)-famous, and tourists' knowledge of destination culture and the people of tourist brochures.

During this quantitative to qualitative transition in my work, I had an opportunity to appraise the situation in collaboration with Dennison Nash (an anthropologist) and Philip Pearce (a psychologist). (Of my collaborative publications, 15 have involved sociology, 11 geography, 6 political science, 6 psychology, 2 anthropology, 2 business studies, and 2 marketing.) Jafar Jafari had asked me to prepare a special issue of *Annals* on methodology, and in keeping with that journal's multidisciplinary mission, it was agreed that such a team suitably fitted this requirement. The resulting lead article (Dann et al 1988) has been quoted on numerous occasions, as has the model it supplied. Commentators from then until now have also concurred with our conclusion that most tourism research to date does not fulfil the criteria of theoretical awareness and methodological sophistication.

My increasing qualitative orientation was also associated with a more emic approach to research. Being an outsider (which did have some advantages), I had to somehow obtain an insider perspective by crossing the racial, class, and sometimes gender divide that separated the minority from the majority. I never totally achieved this virtually impossible goal, but I made several ethnographic attempts, notably in my work on everyday life, quality of life, and male sexuality in Barbados.

As a postscript, I should add that probably the most important methodological lesson that I learned during my sojourn on that West Indian island was one of time management. Due to climatic and organizational conditions, it was essential to divide the day into prime time and the remainder. The former extended from sunrise to noon, and it was during this six-hour period that I undertook most of my teaching and research at twice or thrice the rate that I could have done during the rest of the day or night. Here punctuality became essential, and when in doubt "the earlier the better" was my general maxim. I thus brought forward my originally scheduled 9am lectures—first to 8 o'clock, then to 7am—and, unlike my other campus colleagues, started class when the big hand was on twelve. I have consequently never experienced any problems with deadlines, but I must admit to being occasionally frustrated by, and intolerant of those who procrastinate and who, in their disordered and chaotic lives, thwart my own agenda.

1996—The Wanderer's Return

After 21 years of living and working in the Caribbean, I had become restless and frustrated. My pedagogy (sociology) and research (tourism) had become two distinct worlds that rarely overlapped and led to an intellectually schizophrenic existence. Such a dualism was also heightened by a growing awareness that there was temporal conflict involved, since most of my sociological investigations had terminated in the 1980s, and yet here I was in the 1990s still lecturing in sociological theory. In order to resolve this issue, I would therefore have to look for a tourism department where, with preferably no teaching (or even with no students), I could carry out my inquiries in a relatively undisturbed manner. I had already explored some job possibilities in the United States but, due to the "affirmative action" policies of these institutions, I quickly came to understand that these openings were effectively closed to Anglo-Saxon, foreign males. At the same time, I realized that social conditions were deteriorating in my island paradise (increases in drug taking, crime, etc.); and my own parents and those of my wife were not getting any younger and would soon require our filial presence.

Thus, when an opportunity arose to move to Luton, the most recent of the UK's new universities, to boost the research profile of its fledgling tourism department, I decided to apply. Some of my international colleagues thought that I was crazy, and one even said so in print. However, I soon recognized that I could only explain my position in terms of the push–pull paradigm that I had nurtured over the years. After all, return migration is not unlike tourism.

The interviews were held in February 1996 and I was appointed with immediate effect as a Visiting Professor, the position becoming permanent in September of that year. After my return to the UK after a 21-year sojourn in the Caribbean, I was often asked what change I had noticed most that had taken place during my absence. When I replied that it was increasing lack of freedom, my questioners inevitably expressed amazement. They had expected me to answer in terms of the weather or some such banality, and they could not see how their own liberty had been gradually eroded by the growing surveillance and control of successive British administrations. My only other apprehension was that the tourism department lay within a Business Faculty, an area virtually unknown to me. As things turned out, I need not have worried unduly since the then Dean was extremely generous with tourism and encouraged me to persuade some of my international colleagues to come and join me.

The first to arrive was Tony Seaton who had been the Director of the Tourism Research Centre at the University of Strathclyde. He and I had corresponded for quite a while and had met on a couple of occasions. It was clear that we saw eye to eye on most topics and shared a sense of humour. Further, we had a common interest in "dark" tourism, one that came to fruition a few years later in a special issue that we co-edited of the *International Journal of Hospitality and Tourism Administration* devoted to tourism and slavery.

Peter Burns came next and took over from Peter Grabowski as head of department. He was followed by Keith Hollinshead, Andrew Holden, and Peter Mason—the last of whom assumed the headship on a permanent basis. When their considerable talents were combined with those of Marcjanna Augustyn and Philip Alford, already on the ground, it was clear that a strong team was emerging. In fact, it was not very long before the University granted us the status of the *International Tourism Research Institute*, one that included our doctoral students who were also increasing in number. Apart from a variety of methodologies that we brought to bear, one area in which we specialized was tourism theory. Keith in particular had a great deal to contribute here, as I had come to realize through my contacts with him as a fellow executive member of the research committee on international tourism of the International Sociological Association.

Throughout this period, we were building upon an already established research profile that would provide a useful base for our collective evaluation in the all-important Research Assessment Exercise. Since this RAE was the way that the government ranked UK university departments and proportionately allocated research funds, it became essential for us to do well. It also meant that I had to argue the case for separate assessment as a research institute, rather than being entered with Leisure or submitted along with the rest of the Business School. Here, the internal politicking was successfully overcome, and we emerged victorious with a score of 4 out of a maximum of 5. Given that no other tourism department had been rated higher, this result put us on par with Strathclyde, Surrey, and Sheffield Hallam, and top of the league among those institutions submitting separately. Additionally, such an outcome indicated that we were the most improved tourism unit in the country when compared with the previous entries in 1996, and fully justified the confidence that had been placed in us.

At a personal level, the period that I had spent at Luton was certainly my most productive in terms of research, the output of which yielded on average of seven publications a year. I had carried out some follow-up studies that focused on the language of tourism. There were a couple of papers on "Greenspeak" (that register which addressed an increasing consumer interest in eco-tourism). There were some that examined the manner in which destinational difference were handled by national tourism organizations, and one that looked at a particular niche market (seniors) and how they were targeted. I also returned to travel writing in order to explore a number of literary trends—in one instance to examine the way that possibly the world's most written about city, Venice, employed the touristic themes of dreams, love, and death.

During this period, I decided to prepare three theoretical papers—this time on my own. Two were for the Academy; another was at the request of the ISA, which had asked the president of each research committee to write a state-of-the-art chapter that would eventually appear in a handbook. Although only half of the peer-reviewed submissions were accepted, I was pleased that mine was included in the collection (Dann 2000). The only revision that I was required to make was to enlarge the coverage in order to include French contributions to the sociology of tourism. This justified criticism stung me to the core. Such an oversight was quite out of character since I had for a long time been persuaded by the likes of Marie-Françoise Lanfant that there was far more to tourism theory than was to be found in its anglophone dominated offerings. Indeed, my knowledge of a few European languages (French, Italian, Spanish, and Portuguese) had allowed me to read, cite, and present material not written in English, and even to have some of my own work published in Hungarian, Japanese, Norwegian, Polish, and Russian (languages with which I was not familiar).

At this time, I was additionally able to continue my work on content/semiotic analysis. There were, for example, studies of the images of destination people in travelogs, tourists' images of a destination, Greenspeak, the green, green grass of home, dark tourism, othering, the language of differentiation, senior tourism, and others.

During this period, I was also invited to join the editorial board of six tourism journals, half of which I accepted. I additionally acted as external examiner for seven PhD theses in the UK and elsewhere; and I helped the tourism department in Finnmark College, Alta, Norway to establish a vibrant Masters program and improve its research profile. However, with further demands for referee work for journals and publishing houses, and attendance at and the organization of conferences, I soon saw that even my delicately honed time management skills were coming under mounting pressure. I therefore reluctantly had to cut back on my temporal involvement in all these activities or else face the possibility of increased stress and associated risk to health.

Consequently, I decided that if I wished to operate in a deadline-free environment where I would be able to follow my own schedule rather than someone else's, the only sensible course of action was to work part time. I thus set the date for December 31, 2002, and accordingly informed the University authorities, who acceded to my request by granting me emeritus status. I also told Jafar of my plans and that I intended winding down my commitment to *Annals*, a journal that I had served for 24 years. However, the Editor-in-Chief was not so easily convinced and indicated that while I might wish to release myself from *Annals*, indeed, *Annals* was not prepared to let go of me.

There was one other allied consideration that persuaded me that I was taking the right steps. At the 2001 July conference of the Academy in Macao, where several *Annals* editors were present, a board meeting of that publication was arranged. The session that followed turned out to be rather acrimonius, and it became crystal clear to me that my views were very much in the minority. I cannot remember exactly what prompted the heated discussion, but I seem to recall that someone had observed that no longer were the big names in tourism research (among them, a number of contributors to this volume) submitting to the journal as frequently as they once did, and that as a result there was a real danger of standards declining. My view was that if our journal wanted to retain its position of leadership in theoretical devlopment, it should continue to rely on anthropology and sociology for its insights. Social scientific pieces with an emphasis on management and marketing should be submitted elsewhere. Additionally, I maintained that where papers had a methodological component, it should be of a qualitative nature (the approach, which recently had been flourishing, and which had become an important thrust in my research, being, in my opinion, more conducive to theoretical development). I therefore proposed that *Annals* should reject quantitative papers and encourage their submission to alternative outlets, a suggestion that seemed to me to be quite consonant with *Annals'* mission statement and editorial guidelines. However, for reasons best known to themselves, and without any discernable disciplinary or methodological trends for support, most of my fellow editors disagreed with my views.

Realizing that this was the first time that we had ever had a crucial debate of this nature, and that I was a voice in the wilderness, made me aware that it was time to go. The Editor-in-Chief probably shared my views, but with such opposition from board members, there was little he could do. The lesson was important, not least because it drew attention to the fact that tourism research must still overcome some challenges from some of its own key players if it is to progress academically. We should stop regurgitating the work of pioneers (surely an indication that stasis has occurred) and encourage the next generation to critically revisit their original insights, develop them further, and provide superior alternatives.

It was precisely at this juncture that an invitation arrived to contribute to this volume—an undertaking that could not have come at a better time, since it provided a unique opportunity to give meaning to my intellectual wandering at the zenith of my career. I had always admired those who got out while they were on a high, and now seemed the perfect occasion to follow this self-administered advice. The foregoing account should thus be considered as something of a swan song, an *apologia pro vita mea*. Indeed so individualistic has this project been that many of my colleagues will recognize that this is the only occasion that I have written a paper in the first person and included so many references to my own publications. Prior to this moment, I have always considered this kind of thing to be rather pompous, egotistical, and pontifical. I am thus breaking my own rules as an instance of the end justifying the means, though in the doing, probably injecting a greater reflexivity than is normally evident in the remainder of my work. Now like Pontius Pilate, I can at last sit back and say, "What *I* have written, *I* have written."

Nelson Graburn (1936–) is Professor of Anthropology and Curator of North American Ethnology, Hearst Museum, Berkeley, CA 94720, USA (e-mail: Graburn@uclink.berkeley.edu) where, besides administrative duties, he has taught graduate and undergraduate courses on art, culture change, tourism, as well as others. Besides articles and chapters on ethnic arts, museums, tourism, modernity and identify, circumpolar peoples, Japan, and China, his published works include *Ethnic and Tourist Arts* (1976), *To Pay and Pray: The Cultural Structure of Japanese Tourism* (1983), and *Relocating the Tourist* (2001). He is a founding member of the International Academy for the Study of Tourism, active in the International Sociological Association, and on the editorial board (for Anthropology) of *Annals for Tourism Research*.

TOURISM THROUGH THE LOOKING GLASS

I have a first memory from when I was 3 (1939). I recall watching my Nanny (who was 22) standing beside the bed in which we had been sleeping. She was putting on a blue robe. My parents were in the next bedroom when we were staying in a beach house at Wittering on the coast of Sussex.

Introduction

My engagement with both anthropology and with tourism probably stemmed from my early experiences being brought up in England by a family and their friends who had spent much of their adult lives elsewhere in the "Far East"—in Amoy from 1896 and in Malaya for the first three decades of the twentieth century. Ironically, while surrounded by memorabilia, stories of life abroad, and of my parents' voyages to the Antipodes and around the world, for much of my early childhood I was hardly able to travel at all: during the Second World War. Then, no one had private cars except for official duties, long distance pleasure travel was banned, and we were not even allowed to visit towns near the coast. Thus there was a tension, a desire, and a powerful imagination built up in a time of personal privation—forces that perhaps propelled me to travel for work and pleasure later in life.

This chapter is written with the presumption that my various experiences and later intellectual projects tended to follow in turn, one leading into the next. I know many of my colleagues appear to work like that, but my own life experience has been much more "helter skelter." My projects do not neatly begin and end. This personal history will show that my professional life has always involved multiple overlapping projects, starting with two or three, mounting to five or six competing, intertwined, unbounded ones at the present time.

Desire and Distance

Though I was raised in an old farmhouse in a village in Surrey, my family called themselves "Malayans" after their collective century or more of residence there. I was surrounded by photos and objects from Malaya, conversations in the Malay language, the monthly *British Malaya* magazine, visits from other "Malayans," and nostalgic talk about "the Natives." From what I could gather, the Natives were masters of esoteric arts, with interesting clothing and splendid physical abilities, able to run fast on bare feet, climb trees, and see far distances without glasses, all of which I attempted to copy. My family defended the Natives against slurs and derogatory questions from local people who had not lived "in the Empire." Indeed my darker-skinned Uncle Percy, who had married my father's elder sister and was admired for his brilliance (he was retired Chief Justice of Malaya), his linguistic abilities, and his reading of the lessons in the local Church of England, was sometimes called a Native behind his back. Like many of his Singhalese relatives, my cousins, he settled in England, but because of travel restrictions during World War II, we were not allowed to visit my aunt and uncle on the coast, any more than we could visit Malaya or Ceylon.

During the War, our village was home to German prisoners of war who, along with refugees from Poland and other countries, became farm laborers and sometimes married local women. The only domestic "others" were the Gypsies who frequented the area buying rags, old batteries, and empty bottles. At boarding school (ages 8–13), I found others who were connected to other parts of the Empire, and knew other languages and climates. After the War was over I was able to visit my relatives on the coast, and the cousins sometimes spent their holidays with their parents overseas. At school we learned Greek and Latin five days a week, opening our imaginations to yet other civilizations we could never visit. Only compulsory French, using the blue textbook with stories of English families visiting France, opened a window of possibility for us.

At thirteen I went off to the King's School, Canterbury for five years. There I boarded with other teenage boys in dormitories organized as "houses" (totemic teams). We all had pinups next to our desks, some of film stars such as Diana Dors, but I had more dusky pinups cut from *National Geographic*. I dropped Latin and Greek as soon as I was allowed to and specialized in Chemistry, Biology, and Physics, with occasional courses in music, French, and German. Immediate attention was turned less toward travel and the outside world and more toward school sports and swotting for the required "O," "A," and "S" level exams and university entrance exams.

This led to State and University Scholarships for entering Clare College, Cambridge, where I studied the Natural Sciences for two years and took my

Tripos Part I (first degree level) exams. For my third and last year, I was free to study anything. I switched to Social Anthropology, with which I became familiar through a housemate's interest. I had helped him as he swotted for his final exams by reading ethnographic books and testing him on his knowledge. After receiving his degree, I believe he went to work for Shell, helping them explore for oil in Borneo. I went to see Professor Edmund Leach at the end of my second year, asking if I could take the "Long Vac. Term" (compulsory summer term) courses in Social Anthropology. He replied that his department didn't have any summer courses, but he gave me two books to read and comment on: Bartlett's, edited, *The Study of Society*, a series of methodological chapters covering anthropology, sociology, psychology, and mass observation, and Malinowski's *Sexual Life of Savages*. I returned in the autumn to be supervised by advanced graduate student Nur Yalman and then by his adviser Leach, himself. At Cambridge, the undergraduate curriculum required that one meet with a supervisor (tutor) in one's major, alone or with a few other students, for about an hour every week. The supervisor usually required some reading and a weekly essay, which served as the foundation for discussion. Leach also mentioned lectures one ought to attend—there were no regular courses with exams—which, most importantly, prepared one for the year-end week of exams called Tripos (Part I or II). I attended lectures by Jack Goody, Meyer Fortes, and others, and studied statistics under another graduate student.

Although the exotic ethnographies of Africa, Oceania, and even the research methods were exciting, I was never too sure what anthropology was about and why. For instance, one had to collect the kinship terms for "mother's brother." In retrospect, I determined that when I taught anthropology I would make sure the students understood the context within which such research questions arose.

During these same years in England, travel and tourism became more of a reality. Petrol was no longer rationed and exchange controls on the pound were slightly relaxed. Every summer of the mid-1950s, I traveled to the Continent with my uncle and aunt and my younger cousin Raymond (my own parents were separated and my father was in his mid-seventies). We drove through France to stay in Cassis-sur-Mer for two summers, and through France, Germany, and Austria to stay at St. Wolfgang in a third. My teenage tourism was probably typical, with attempts to speak the local languages, especially with youth of my age group, inevitable comparisons with home, and taking tons of black and white photos.

As my Cambridge career drew to a close, because I had spent a number of years studying the sciences with considerable success, I wondered if I might be able to find a career applying my anthropology as a consultant to the chemical industry. But the prospect of being called up for National Service became imminent and drove me to other plans. Leach told me to wait until the results of the

Tripos Part II (second degree) exams came through in the early summer and he'd probably be able to place me in graduate school in Australia or somewhere. But I didn't want to wait! I consulted UNESCO's manual *Studying Abroad* in the University Library. I wrote to a number of universities in Europe and North America where I might pursue graduate level anthropology. A few replied to my handwritten letters, but McGill University in Montreal was the most welcoming.

This invitation suited me because there was a long tradition of men of my family emigrating to Canada: the oldest male Graburn of each generation went off to Canada. Unfortunately, my great-great uncle, my great uncle, and my uncle, all named Marmaduke Graburn, had all gone and all had died young (shot by a Blackfoot Indian, in an opera house fire, or of some ailment). Luckily I was named Nelson after my second uncle "Bang Bang" (former officer in the Malay militia) rather than my deceased senior uncle Marmaduke. Also, my cousin and travel companion, Raymond, left Eton and decided to go to McGill as an undergraduate. We sailed on the Empress of Canada to Quebec City and Montréal, during which time my call-up papers arrived, and my father wrote on the envelope: "My son is studying abroad—Return to Sender."

The Inuit Art Experience: Export and Tourist Arts

My first direct experience with the commoditization of non-Western arts came in 1959 when I was sent to study the Eskimos (now Inuit) of the Hudson Strait in the Canadian Arctic. I went by ship specifically to carry out a "community study" of the village of Sugluk (now Salluit) for the Canadian government's Department of Northern Affairs (DNA). Although this was also ostensibly my MA thesis fieldwork, I was given little direction by my McGill professors and even less by my Government employers. In studying the changing economic bases of Inuit life, I encountered the widespread Inuit occupation of carving figurines in the local grey-black steatite for sale. These sold either directly to customers such as the crews of visiting ships and the five or six non-Inuit village residents, or indirectly in southern Canada through the Hudson's Bay Company or the DNA Northern Service Officer, who handled all Inuit welfare and employment.

The carvers liked the fact that they could get paid for their efforts, though by my calculations, they got less than 50 cents/hour. Later in *Eskimos without Igloos* (1969a:156–160), I showed that carving and handicrafts had constituted up to 50% of the total village money income in some years. The following summer, I flew to Baffin Island for a community study of Lake Harbour, NWT on the other side of the Hudson Strait, where I found very much the same patterns, though their available carving stone was a more attractive greenish serpentine. What piqued my interest in this topic were the very different stories about the "art" form found in the literature, stores, and museums that constituted the growing retail market for ethnic and tourist arts in southern Canada and the United States. The contrast with "reality" was so great that I vowed to research the topic and present the "other" or Native point of view.

While engaged in doctoral work at University of Chicago (1960–1963), my focus, as at Cambridge, was on kinship and social structure. Using data from my Salluit research, I carried out a kind of "componential analysis" comparing the fit of a purely genealogically based analysis versus a social grouping residence-based analysis, done earlier by Leach, finding in favor of the latter. I also supported myself by working for David Schneider's American Kinship Project. I became one of his fieldworkers, interviewing middle-class Chicagoans about their families and their roots. Again, alterity favored me for, unlike the other fieldworkers, I was able to ask "Well, I'm from England. Tell me how do Americans ... name their children, celebrate Christmas, remember their family history, . . . and so on?" I was pleased that some informants treated me as their "personal anthropologist" and invited me to see all their family heirlooms or to meet other relatives. I even served as a pall-bearer for the mother of one of my informants! This was my first experience in the direct practice of anthropology within the "home" society, something that became an integral part of tourism studies a decade or more later.

I probably never thought of the anthropology of art or of tourism at that time, nor did I even know they existed! However, immediately after finishing my Ph.D., I carried out a year of field research (1963–1964) in the Inuit and Naskapi-Cree communities of the Hudson Strait and Hudson Bay areas as a fieldworker for the Cooperative Cross-Cultural Study of Ethnocentrism headed by psychologist Donald Campbell of Northwestern University and anthropologist Robert Levine of the University of Chicago.

In the fall of 1964, I took a position teaching anthropology at Berkeley, still determined to carry out research on Inuit tourist arts. I planned to learn about the anthropology of art by teaching it, and I took over "The Anthropology of Art" course from my Africanist colleague Bill Bascom. It was probably not until the publication of my article *The Eskimos and 'Airport Art'* in the journal *Trans-Action* (Graburn 1967) that I was made aware of my contributions to the nascent study of tourism. Many people have informally credited me with the invention of the touristic phrase "airport art," however the credit must go to the editors of *Trans-Action*. I had originally delivered the paper *Eskimo Soapstone Carving: Innovation and Acculturation* at the American Anthropological Association meetings in November 1966, based on my research among the Canadian Inuit in 1959, 1960, and 1963–64. My motivation was to publicize the conditions and motivations for *production* of these commercial ethnic and tourist arts, as against the extraordinarily inaccurate and exoticized accounts that accompanied their *consumption* in the galleries and souvenir stores of Southern Canada. Canadian art historian George Swinton cited one of my early papers in an attempt get the Canadian government to keep me out of the Arctic (because I had "the wrong attitude").

In September 1967, my Japanese-American bride, Kathy, and I traveled from Berkeley to the Canadian North for a year's research on Inuit arts, supported by an NSF Fellowship. We lived in Povungnituk, Hudson Bay, where she was a Federal Day School teacher. Using it as my base, I took trips of up to two months each to other important commercial tourist art–producing communities. This research and shorter stays in the Canadian North in 1972, 1976, 1986, and 2000 provided the data for most of my publications on the subject.

Ethnic and Tourist Arts

After my return to Berkeley, Peter Lengyel, editor of UNESCO's *International Social Science Journal,* asked me to write a follow-up on my original much republished 1967 paper on Canadian Inuit art. To him, I suggested a broader view of these ethnic and tourist arts; a comparative context in which I wanted to place the analysis of the Inuit case. It was published as *Art and Acculturative Processes* (Graburn 1969). This in turn drew more attention, perhaps because UNESCO published it in many languages. While bent on publishing the Canadian Inuit data, I also aimed toward a broader work with comparative case studies. My paper *Art as Mediating Mechanism in Acculturation Processes*, delivered at the 1969 AAA meetings in New Orleans, emphasized the positive role of tourist arts in economically transitional contexts because (a) they provide a monetary livelihood, (b) but are not subject to wage labor discipline, and (c) they bring prestige and pride of identity to minority peoples rather than the low status attached to forms of manual labor usually left to such people.

In order to build or even to "create" the academic field of such "tourist arts," I organized a session for the 1970 AAA meetings in San Diego—inviting papers on case studies for the session "Contemporary Developments in Non-Western Arts." Two years later, I was asked to organize an "advanced seminar" on the same topic by the School for American Research, Santa Fe, and invited a group which consisted of some of the earlier collaborators—Kate Peck Kent, Renaldo Maduro, Bill Bascom, Paula Ben-Amos—and some new ones—Edmund Carpenter, Ulli Beier, William Davenport, and Richard Beardsley—suggesting a topic title "Contemporary Developments in Folk Art." When submitted for publication, the press suggested major revisions for the collection as a whole. Only Ben-Amos's "Pidgin Languages and Tourist Arts" was recommended for immediate publication.

After the AAA meetings in San Diego, I prepared a prospectus for an anthology, called *Art and Change in the Modern World: the Arts of Non-Western Peoples*. I should point out the important role taken by Berkeley graduate students, many of whom started with no particular interest in non-Western commercial arts. I taught graduate seminars in 1970 and 1971 on "Comparative Study of the Ethnic Arts." Later, I worked especially closely with graduate student anthropologist and photographer Mari Lyn Salvador, who entered graduate school after three years in the Peace Corps working with the Kuna *mola* makers of Panama. Together, we produced a fully illustrated 442-page draft version *Contemporary Developments in Non-Western Arts* (1972) for use in class. At this time, the staff of the Lowie Museum of Anthropology at Berkeley read my work on the subject and invited me to join in creating a major exhibition illustrating many of the processes of artistic change and pluralism. This resulted in not only an exhibition, but a published catalogue *Traditions in Transition* (Dawson, Frederickson and Graburn 1974) which may have been the first monograph published on tourism and ethnic arts. My advancement of the study of non-Western arts made for sale attracted attention within the University and amongst local groups such as San Francisco's Friends of Ethnic Art. I was written up in campus newspapers, asked to join conferences and to give talks on and off campus, perhaps as much through curiosity about the seriousness of studying tourist arts as shared scholarly interests.

Meanwhile the manuscript version of *Contemporary Developments in Non-Western Arts* made the rounds of many presses, including Abrams, Praeger, Columbia University Press and the University of Washington Press. Though expressing curiosity and interest, publishers found all sorts of excuses not to publish it: many citing the risk of producing a large book with so many plates, or the unknown and very limited readership (see Graburn 1999 for a detailed version of the publication process). I was not used to such rejections, but I was not discouraged; I had many enthusiastic students, and increasing numbers of colleagues were showing a serious interest in the subject. Eventually, the University of California Press, after originally rejecting them, published the revised and augmented papers from the San Diego symposium as *Ethnic and Tourist Arts* (1976).

Valene Smith and the Anthropology of Tourism

I was invited by anthropologist-geographer Valene Smith to serve as discussant in her session on the "Anthropology of Tourism" at the AAA meetings in Mexico City in 1974. Ironically, this was the last time the meetings have ever been held abroad, probably because the radical students trashed the "imperialist" Sheraton Hotel and harassed the upper class Mexicans who thought of it as an elite venue for their social functions! Valene Smith gathered a group of anthropologists who had often tangentially run across tourism as a factor in otherwise more orthodox field sites. We also met Jafar Jafari who appeared as a mild-mannered graduate student who had just founded the *Annals of Tourism Research*. After the meeting, I worked with Valene in Chico (not too far from Berkeley) on the first edition of the book eventually known as *Hosts and Guests: the Anthropology of Tourism* (1977).

My role as discussant to the papers in Smith's collection took a number directions. I had already done considerable field and comparative research on the "acculturation" of non-Western arts, including both direct and indirect forms of tourist arts. My own collection *Ethnic and Tourist Arts* (1976) was in press by then, and I attempted to apply a parallel analysis to the impacts of tourism in general. I wrote a synthetic chapter comparing the different forms of impact—on stratification, on gender relations, on economic livelihoods, on material culture, and so on—for Smith's book, but it was not chosen for publication. I also edited a paper presented at the 1974 AAA meetings by Berkeley graduate student Jane Teas. This paper *I'm Studying Monkeys—What do you do?: Youthful Travelers in Nepal.* is an analysis of the culture and behavior of "drifter" tourists, full of insights and insider experiences complementary to Erik Cohen's pioneer paper *Nomads from Affluence* (1973). Her paper was included in the "classroom draft" of *Hosts and Guests* but not the published version. I later published it in a volume of Berkeley student papers (Teas 1988).

Tourism: the Sacred Journey

My chapter (Graburn 1977) "Tourism – the Sacred Journey" in *Hosts and Guests* arose from my consideration of how the study of tourism fit into sociocultural anthropology. At this time, I was also researching other "tourist experiences" such as shopping or visiting museums. I found that different publics could treat these occasions either as a learning experience, an opportunity for socialization, or an awesome meditation on revered historical or natural objects in a "cathedral-like" setting. This analysis of museum visitors so paralleled tourist experiences that I drew upon the analysis of time and ritual as put forward by my former Cambridge supervisor, the brilliant iconoclast Edmund Leach. In his *Rethinking Anthropology* he wrote "Time and False Noses" (1961:132–136), which suggested that the regular occurrence of "sacred-profane" alternations and inversions marks important periods of social life or even provides the measure of the passage of time itself. As a general theory of ritual, it drew on the foundational works of Hubert and Mauss, as well as those of their mentor, Durkheim (1915 [1912]), who dealt with religion more broadly, and Arnold van Gennep (1960 [1908]), who had provided an analysis of the ritual structures in his work on rites of passage. My analyses, very specifically, did not then draw upon the writings of Victor Turner who, using the same sources, presented a theory of ritual, but paid little attention to the issue of time.

While I was writing my chapter for Valene Smith on tourism as a kind of ritual in 1975, I gave the plenary after-dinner address on the anthropology of tourism to the Kroeber Anthropological Society in Berkeley. Without telling the audience ahead of time, I used the draft of my *Sacred Journey* paper, replacing the word "tourist" in almost every instance with the word "anthropologist," suggesting, as others later did, that anthropologists were a kind of "super-tourist" who treated their fieldwork as a kind of adventurous ritual break from teaching. I showed the parallel motivations and the boasting stories back home, and pointed out the kind of "souvenirs" called "material culture" that they brought home with them. I even suggested that anthropologists engage in symbolic "one-upmanship" when they bring their colorfully dressed, exotic informants to professional meetings, as did some of my colleagues. Most of the audience enjoyed the comparison and roared with laughter, seeing themselves "skewered"; one senior man came and congratulated me saying that he thought every example was pointed directly at him. Only the wives of two archaeologists thought it was not humorous to make fun of the serious matter of fieldwork.

Though I hadn't yet read MacCannell's *The Tourist* (1976), my *Hosts and Guests* chapter showed the historical development of holidays out of structurally similar Holy Days in the European world, taking into account the evolution of class structures. It showed the ritual structures of leaving home, the "liminal" out-of-time experience on holiday, and the reentry into mundane home society—all a process of "recreation." I claimed that this structure of alternations was "normalized" by adult European middle classes, differentiating themselves from the poor, the unemployed, the criminal, the aged, the sick, and even babies and pets who don't "take holidays." The late Stanford anthropologist Shelley Rosaldo (personal communication) pointed out that I had not emphasized gender differences enough, because for women/wives such holidays might not be a complete break from housework and child-rearing in the same way that employed men are on a break from "real work."

At the same time, the theoretical posing of tourism and holidays as "re-creation" and as compensation for things lacking in the home environment (climatic warmth, access to nature, freedom from time-constraints, and so on) began to emerge from my use of Leach's concept of "symbolic inversion." I outlined the different kinds of contemporary tourism (historical, ethnic, environmental, etc.) as responding to "felt needs" of holiday travelers. I added the concept of tourism as a "Rite of Passage," e.g., a honeymoon or retirement cruise (or *couvade*, see below), particularly evidenced by the countercultural, self-imposed long-term "drifter" travel of college-age youth in their "prolonged moratorium on adulthood" as claimed by Cohen and Teas (see above).

Teaching the Anthropology of Tourism

In 1976, I used a manuscript draft of *Hosts and Guests* in teaching my first course on the "Anthropology of Tourism". After much academic opposition, I was allowed to teach the course as a one-time experiment. The opposition was not just from colleagues in my own Department, whose attitudes were more of amusement than support. All new courses had to be approved by the multidisciplinary Course Committees. Here the seriousness of the subject matter was severely questioned, as though studying "mere play" was in itself mere play! The course drew over 170 enthusiastic students and soon became a regularized upper division anthropology offering.

My Reader-Assistant was graduate student Niloufer Ichaporia whose doctoral research was on the history and functioning of Cost Plus, a successful low-rent chain of "warehouse stores," which started in the San Francisco Bay Area selling cheap touristy "folk arts" mainly from Asia. Her original work was ahead of its time both in the study of commercial folk arts and crafts and tourist arts and souvenirs. Though she gave a paper on the subject, her main work has never been published. It also happened that Peter Stringer, an English sociologist, audited part of the course. So did visiting British novelist David Lodge, whose *Paradise News* (1984) about an anthropologist of tourism doing research in Hawaii, was based on me and my class readings.

The class was structured then, as now, into two parts. The first half dealt with the anthropology of tourists. In it, I used my own work and that of MacCannell (1976) and others, and included the origins and history of tourism in the Western World and in East Asia and Third World countries—the theoretical basis for this topic developing out of the preexisting anthropology of ritual and time, especially from the work of Leach. The second part of the course focused on the broader and more applied consideration of the impact of tourism on anthropological studies such as acculturation, economics, and colonialism, using many of the chapters of Valene Smith's (ed. 1977) collection in both its draft and published forms.

Soon after the appearance of my *Ethnic and Tourist Arts* (1976), Peter Lengyel of UNESCO again wrote, asking me for an article on the topic. I replied that I had already published a similar article in his journal in 1969, but I was more interested in the emerging Anthropology of Tourism, about which I was teaching. I asked him whether he would like an article on this new sub-discipline? He replied by asking for an article about the class itself, which was eventually published as *Teaching the Anthropology of Tourism* (Graburn 1980). Here, I explained how I taught the subject in two halves, based on MacCannell's *The Tourist* and Smith's *Hosts and Guests*. I also explained the difficult process of getting the new course accepted at the University of California and the opposition I had faced at first. This article had wide repercussions because it described the first such course regularly taught anywhere, and with its readership in multiple languages, it stimulated the teaching of tourism in many countries, especially the Third World, and in a number of social science disciplines.

Japanese Domestic Tourism

In spring 1974, just months before Valene Smith's epic AAA meeting, I had the opportunity to travel in Asia for two months. My wife, I, and our two preschool children, accompanied my mother-in-law to her natal family and village in rural Kagoshima in Kyushu. After spending two weeks with relatives there, we left her behind and traveled to stay in Kyoto for a week, and then on to Tokyo where she rejoined us. We then went on together for another month to Singapore and Malaysia (where we visited my late father's tin-smelting company), and on to Thailand and Hong Kong. We enjoyed Japan and realized that being fluent but illiterate in Japanese, like my wife, was not enough. We started to learn to read and write Japanese and sent our children to the Saturday *Nippongogakuen* (language elementary school) at the Oakland Buddhist church for the next twelve years.

In 1979, I was invited by Prof. Shuzo Ishimori to spend a sabbatical as a visitor at the new National Museum of Ethnology in Suita Expo Park outside of Osaka. I had few duties at the Museum and wanted to work on publications on Canadian Inuit tourist arts. However, we lived in a town house in Kyoto where my children were in school next to the Imperial Palace. From Kyoto I commuted by two buses, a train, another bus and a long walk to get to the Museum, more than three hours round trip. I did not go to Suita every day. Instead, we spent many days exploring Kyoto, often with our friend Mikio Kimura who dedicated himself to showing us behind the scenes of shrines and temples and introducing us to traditional and modern artists and craftsmen. We also visited friends and family— traveling by train to nearby sights such as Nara and to more distant places such as Tokyo, Nagano, Iwakuni, Miyasaki, and Kagoshima. We enjoyed the slow-paced, crowded, but convivial atmosphere of Japanese holiday trips with friends and family members. This stay in Japan was a kind of fieldwork in the anthropology of tourism; I took many notes and numerous photographs intending to illustrate not only Japanese as tourists, but their mundane home world too.

Back in Berkeley, I lectured to the Department of Anthropology on "Japanese Domestic Tourism." Though I saw this as just a slide lecture, I was surprised to find out that there were no current analyses of Japanese tourism either in English or Japanese. The attention of the social sciences and humanities was all directed towards traditional pilgrimages, which while still extant as my presentation showed, had become a factor in burgeoning domestic travel. The temporal structure, the organization of travel, and the vocabulary of Japanese tourism still resembled that of pilgrimages. I wrote up the lecture as an article, but at eighty pages, it found no takers, and presses would not consider it seriously as a book. Fortunately, during my sabbatical leave that year, I was in contact with René Baretje of the Centre des Hautes Etudes Touristiques (CHET), which had already published my earlier piece on the museum and the museum experience. CHET published the monograph in English as *To Pray, Pay and Play: The Cultural Structure of Japanese Domestic Tourism* (Graburn 1983b). This analysis followed my previously published tourism-as-ritual framework (in Smith, ed. 1977) and showed the connections between religious and secular travel patterns in parts of East Asia.

A Comparative Anthropology of Tourism

In the early '80s, Jafar Jafari, editor-in-chief of *Annals of Tourism Research*, asked me to serve as Associate Editor for Anthropology and to put together a special issue devoted to the "Anthropology of Tourism" (Graburn, ed. 1983). In preparing the issue, I again saw an opportunity for research and publication on tourists and tourism systems, rather than on tourist impacts (which had already been the topic of two or three special issues of *Annals*). As an anthropologist, I saw my role as the editor of this issue and of the journal as the encouragement of a truly comparative analysis, including tourisms originating in countries other than the much discussed "West" visiting and exploiting "the rest." Given the wide scope of my original theoretical approach, I asked a number of Berkeley students to develop articles based on their doctoral research in the non-Western world (e.g., Passariello in Mexico, Pfaffenberger in Sri Lanka, Ichaporia in India, as well as colleague Brian Moeran in Japan). In addition, better known tourist systems were analyzed in the Caribbean (Lett) and New Mexico (Van Kemper). Established scholars Albers and James wrote a pioneer article on photographic images of Great Lakes Indians. Jean-Maurice and Gaétane Thurot, acquaintances through my sabbatical at the Centre des Hautes Études Touristiques in Aix-en-Provence in 1980, submitted a condensation of her dissertation which challenged MacCannell's (1976) analysis, which focused on the single, dated model of "sightseers." Examining French tourist advertising since World War II, the Thurots were able to establish a sequence of ideologies and styles up to and including the postmodern period.

In my Introduction (Graburn 1983a) to this collection, I again emphasized tourism as one variation of those human behaviors grouped together with ritual and play as a form of expressive culture and travel, which alternates with more mundane "serious" pursuits at home. I buttressed my argument with the inclusion of further theorists such as the Turners and Nash, whose major works had appeared since my original theoretical formulations in 1974. Though appreciative of MacCannell's view of the "[probably middle-class Western] tourist as sight-seer," I not only looked at varieties of tourism around the world, but attempted to differentiate them by looking at the roles of discretionary income, cultural self-confidence, and the endless variety of "ritual inversions" that might satisfy the range of needs of tourists from many different backgrounds. I specifically brought to bear the topics of class, generation, and culture when examining the dynamics of change in Western and non-Western tourism-generating milieux.

Since then, I've studied more about the Japanese tourist system, and since the 1990s, the burgeoning Chinese tourist system. Relatively speaking, I have touched more lightly on the "other side" of tourism, that of its impacts, except in my undergraduate and graduate teaching and in my continuing research on Canadian Inuit and other Native North American artists who are responding to internal ethno-political and external tourist demands.

Conclusion

Skepticism about the scholarly value of studying tourism still exists. Recently at a Congress of the International Sociological Association, I ran into a sociologist colleague from Berkeley who asked me: "What are you doing here? [implying that as an anthropologist . . .]," and I answered that I was running a session on Tourism. He asked again, "Tourism? Why tourism?" to which I answered, "You know, tourism as a metaphor of postmodernity." "Oh yes, brilliant, brilliant!" he replied.

I have been very fortunate to join the community of scholars studying tourism by participating in a number of institutions, some led by Jafar Jafari, such as an associate editorship of *Annals of Tourism Research* (since 1980) and the International Academy for the Study of Tourism (since 1988). I have also been active in the Research Committee on Tourism (RC-50) of the International Sociological Association (ISA), led by Krzysztof Przeclawski and Marie-Françoise Lanfant. These activities have also facilitated two of my long-term professional goals and given me and my wife a network of friendships lasting nearly two decades. My two professional, but also very personal goals are to foster (a) interdisciplinary scholarship on tourism and (b) the establishment of centers of research and scholarship in non-Western societies. I try to envisage a series of tourist studies allowing one to move seamlessly through social, cultural, psychological, economic, religious, historical, and environmental aspects of tourism.

When Jafar Jafari and I co-edited the special issue of *Annals* on Tourism Social Sciences (1991), we concluded that it was much easier for tourism scholars to move across disciplines than to cross language barriers to understand others' works. Though I have tried to overcome these barriers, especially in my work with René Baretje, the Thurots, and Marie-Françoise Lanfant in France, and with Ishimori, Yamashita, Zhang Xiaoping, Yang Hui, and Peng Zhoarong in Asia, language barriers still remain an impediment, especially for those of us in the English-speaking world.

At Berkeley, I have taught the evolving graduate seminar "Tourism, Art and Modernity" since 1990 and find that without a conscious aim, we read and discuss works and theories without stopping to think whether they are anthropological, sociological, psychological, historical, or merely cultural studies. The seminar is always attended by graduate students from a number of disciplines, particularly architecture, comparative literature, and ethnic studies. The major barrier we find is the divide between quantitative and qualitative research.

Growing centers of research and scholarship outside of European and North American academia have involved international networks such as those to be found in teaching at Berkeley. Both the IAST and the Research Committee on Tourism have made efforts to expand their meeting venues and to include more non-Western members and participants, though progress is slow. Concomitantly, many senior and junior scholars have come to Berkeley—either as visitors or students, and they take part in the "Tourism, Art and Modernity" seminar. Recently, scholars have come from Jordan, Indonesia, Malaysia, China, Japan, Zululand (S. Africa), and S. Korea, as well as a number of Western European countries. Many of these scholars have returned home to found or expand centers for the study of tourism in their own universities.

Most importantly, the study of tourism has increased my own enjoyment of living, traveling, and friendship. Some people have remarked: "How sad that you have made an academic task out of experiences that most people just enjoy for the moment." But I reply, "No! I get a double enjoyment, not only of the place and the experience, but also thinking about the analytical aspects of these." The works of former student Nancy Frey (1998) and colleague Julia Harrison (2003) have raised my consciousness about the inner journeys that a tourist undertakes, as in an exhausting night time ascent of 7240-foot Gebel Musa (Mount Moses) in the Sinai Peninsula to see the sun rise over the Arabian Peninsula in December of 1998.

There it was, a small oval disk, brilliant and growing, and as it grew we became aware of the whole earlier unseen world around us—the tops of all the other mountains glowing gold and the depths of all the valleys between them becoming visible; and we found ourselves perched on the summit of a steep mountain overlooking all the others in the range. I looked back toward the sun, half of which was plainly visible, threatening to burn our eyes. We stood still in the cold, muscles stiffening up, focusing on the light. I thought to myself, why did I make this extraordinary, exhausting, and exhilarating midnight climb with these people, most of whom less then half my age? Twenty-four hours before, I had never heard of this climb and never knew of its import until I was there on top. Then as we "oohed and aahed" at the rising and warming sun, I said to myself: "I am here to welcome the rising **sun**—to welcome the new **son!**" And then it became clear to me: that my first grandson, Noel Kenzo Graburn Alves Martins, had been born early that same morning in Lisbon, some 2000 kilometers to the west. The climb and the reward were, for me, a grandparental form of *couvade*, which any anthropologists will tell you, refers to the empathetic feelings felt by a husband or other close male relative, when a woman gives birth.

Jafar Jafari (1942–) is a faculty member of the University of Wisconsin-Stout Department of Hospitality and Tourism, Menomonie WI 54751, USA (e-mail:jafari@uwstout.edu), where he teaches undergraduate and graduate courses dealing with tourism as a sociocultural phenomenon and as a world-wide field of operations. He is Founder and Editor-in-Chief of *Annals of Tourism Research: A Social Sciences Journal* and *Annals of Tourism Research en Español*, Editor-Chief of the *Tourism Social Science Series* (in which this volume is included), and the *Encyclopedia of Tourism* (2000). He also has been a Founder and President of the International Academy for the Study of Tourism.

ENTRY INTO A NEW FIELD OF STUDY
Leaving a Footprint

Like other fields, the study of tourism has its own beginning, and Dennison Nash has captured a vista of that beginning in this *Tourism Social Science Series* volume. To do so, he has invited a number of anthropologists and sociologists to submit accounts of their involvement in the study of tourism: to tell how they "discovered" this sociocultural phenomenon, to mark their entrance into the field, to note challenges faced, to identify bridges crossed or built, to cite contributions made, to name research niches filled, or, in general, to detail their journeys through the then unmarked and hardly charted landscape of knowledge about tourism. By its very nature, such a "personal history" needs to be told in the first person: a style that does not come naturally to me; but I'm going to give it a try.

This paper traces how and why tourism became an important industry, and later a multidisciplinary field of investigation. Published elsewhere (Jafari 1990a), but added here mainly for those not familiar with this transformation, this recapitulation constitutes a backdrop for the rest of the paper, which is a more personal pastiche of my academic journey.

Setting the Stage

Tourism as an *industry* has a long and considerable history, evolving from its early days when a privileged few traveled once in a lifetime, to when this practice grew relatively more popular due to improved economic conditions and increased knowledge of other peoples and places, to when technology (particularly transportation) took its many small and giant leaps, and to the present times when mass tourism is experienced in practically all countries, either as generating markets, receiving destinations, or both. Nowadays, according to the World Tourism Organization and as cited elsewhere in this volume, tourism has turned into a mega-industry. Together, internal and international tourism represent well established traditions, and despite unprecedented events such as the September 11 and SARS scares, have not experienced irreparable setbacks. Today tourism is institutionalized almost everywhere, deeply rooted enough to withstand major turbulence of a variety of types.

The gradual evolution of tourism from an assortment of fragmented businesses to a seemingly integrated industry over many centuries eventually led to the view of it as a field or a phenomenon to be studied and understood. This development became more evident after World War II, when many countries (re)discovered the "new" industry as a tool for rebuilding and re-energizing their tired and exhausted economies. During the postwar years, particularly in the '60s, studies championed tourism chiefly for its economic properties, such as its contribution to growth and development, its ability to generate jobs, and its "natural" disposition to earn foreign exchange, which was badly needed for the import of goods and services, and for economic diversification. Based on my review of the literature, I have called this monodisciplinary treatment and somewhat business-driven boosterism the "advocacy platform" for an industry, which broadcasts all that is considered good about tourism and advocates its worldwide development and expansion. Early financial support by the World Bank for development efforts in the Third World and elsewhere helped reinforce this platform.

This one-sided economic position was followed by what I have termed the "cautionary platform," representing views and studies arguing that tourism is not all benefit, but on the contrary, comes with many unwanted sociocultural and economic costs. This position, which certainly is familiar to participants in this volume, resulted in many publications, which mainly focused on the "dark side" of the industry and cautioned host or destination countries against tourism's perhaps unanticipated costs and undesirable consequences. In retrospect, I see that this aspect of my academic journey began in the 1970s, about which, more later.

After the advocacy and cautionary voices had been heard, the attention of many researchers was drawn to different or alternative forms of tourism development, arguing that all are not equal and, indeed, that some are more appropriate than others. This view turned into an "adaptancy platform" that favored alternative forms of tourism. Its loudest pitch was during the '80s. Associated writings argued for agritourism, cultural tourism, ecotourism, rural tourism, small-scale tourism, and, later, sustainable tourism, among others. Of course, there was one other option, mass tourism, which was almost universally considered as bad by tourism scholars.

The advocacy, cautionary, and adaptancy voices—at times heard simultaneously, both then and today—were followed by the development of a "knowledge-based platform" in the '90s. This development marks the beginning of a more informed and scientific view of tourism that was derived from the various initiatives of the preceding decades. This fourth voice has favored—and still favors—a multidisciplinary, holistic treatment and understanding of tourism. It seeks to discover tourism's structures and functions, to formulate concepts or theories accounting for it, to apply research tools and methods that best reveal its nature and substance, and to articulate its dependence on, and relationships with systems outside itself, and more.

This intellectual journey, involving the creation of pathways into uncharted landscapes, marking and mapping its fields, and naming and celebrating its achievements, has been carried out by a developing group of mostly academic researchers (a community to which I belong). They are heading in every which way, but all intend to expand frontiers of knowledge in tourism study and further the scientific investigation of the subject. This journey was aided by insights from a number of related fields that were "imported" into tourism study, thus making progress in the study of tourism a multidisciplinary enterprise.

This is a much simplified backdrop for my views on the early development of tourism study (see also Jafari 2001). Now what can be said about the new decade, the 2000s, which is only a few years old? Several colleagues have already asked what I might be calling the platform for viewing the subject now. Initially I did not have the slightest clue, as no pronounced character seemed apparent. One could, of course, note the progress of the knowledge-based thrust. But as recently as May 2003, two distinct developments have increased public attention to the fact of tourism.

So far, the biggest event of the twenty-first century has been that of September 11, 1991, which has been felt worldwide and with consequences still unfolding, and this followed by dangerous epidemics that have influenced tourism movement everywhere. In these instances, high-profile institutions and individuals throughout the world came to the "rescue" of tourism with statements about its importance and various helpful actions.

There was also a third development, very different in nature yet quite significant, that focused world attention on tourism. In December 2003, at its 58th session, the United Nations General Assembly unanimously made the World Tourism Organization (WTO) a full-fledged UN agency. Significantly, this heightened WTO position enables it to work with the UN General Assembly, Economic and Social Council, and the Security Council. It also gives to the WTO a status within the system equal to such institutions as UNIDO (UN Industrial Development Organization), UNESCO (UN Educational, Scientific, and Cultural Organization), ILO (International Labor Organization), FAO (Food and

Agriculture Organization), and WHO (World Health Organization). This provides WTO—through the UN system of organizations—an additional public platform, from which its influence can reach afield.

These separate developments suggest that tourism—because of two unfortunate circumstances, plus its new UN connections—has become better known and more influential. In contrast to the past, tourism is now spoken of by people, groups, and institutions outside of what used to be its normal areas of operation; and citizens of destination areas, as well as public agencies have gradually taken "ownership" of it ("the tourism industry" now becoming "*our* tourism industry"), and in doing so, have begun to accept responsibility for its development, which has been especially evident during the SARS crises.

Recognizing that the decade is too young to be characterized in a restrictive way, I see that this may be a wish on my part: for tourism to occupy a "public platform" as its fifth phase, which calls for the formation of a badly needed public standing that will help it assume its legitimate position—side by side with other industries and institutions, in both local and global circles—and enjoy the support it deserves, including when it is blamed, perhaps mistakenly, for this or that consequence. Such a public platform, actually a call for its nurturing during the remaining years of the decade, needs to purposefully influence our research agendas and action plans, both in the academic community and in the industry itself. If measures are not introduced in favor of turning this momentum into a platform, then this opportunity will be lost. This call makes sense too, and would get support from those who think that a trend can be managed. Tourism is too important to be left to the industry alone, to a mainly internal voice still hardly heard beyond its immediate circles and captive audiences. Sooner or later, tourism should opt for the public platform—as its *modus vivendi* and *modus operandi*—a position for which I recently argued (Jafari 2005) in a UNESCO seminar held in Cuba.

Entering the Field of Tourism Study

Those with many years of residency in the field of tourism study have come to it through different "back doors," as the personal histories published in this volume suggest. In my case, the tourism vista opened not through an academic door, but through my first job as a tour guide. I had no training for this position as a culture broker, my only qualification being that I could speak English, which I spoke as a college student at the University of Isfahan, Iran.

As a tour guide, one sees various sectors of the industry interactively. This experience, in itself, suggested the big picture and the possibility of understanding it at university level. In the mid-60s, despite the fact that tourism had gained a strong advocacy voice in that decade, no US universities offered degrees in this field. Finding my way to Cornell University, where I pursued a BS degree in Hotel Management, I soon found out that the day-to-day operational aspects of this business did not appeal to me. In my last undergraduate year, I decided that graduate school was my game. Not knowing how I could find entrance to fields broader than hotel management, I started searching for avenues leading to a broader, multidisciplinary perspective on tourism.

Facing the realities of time and the unseated position of tourism on US university campuses, I decided to pursue an MS in Hotel Administration at the same institution, but with the intent of reaching out beyond the academic confines of the program—something that my advisor (Professor Paul Broten, may God bless his soul) enthusiastically endorsed. I selected International Relations as my minor and informally worked with Davydd Greenwood, a cultural anthropologist at Cornell, who introduced me to many social science vistas. These provided an "unofficial" outreach beyond the program in which I was actually registered. Occasional calculated outreaches of this kind were used in writing my thesis on The *Role of Tourism in the Socioeconomic Transformation of Developing Countries* (Jafari 1973).

Here, to capture the general attitude of the time, a couple of anecdotes may be added. One relates to the trivial image held of tourism then (and still by many today), let alone the study of it at the university level. I recall how amusing it was for graduate students in my campus residential hall to hear that I was doing research on tourism for my thesis. There were fellow dormmates who were writing theses (some at the PhD level) on flies and insects, how birds mate, how bats fly in the dark, etc., none of which were suspect academically.

One might wonder, for example, why birds' seasonal migration would do for serious research, but not peoples' temporary migration, why the flying patterns of geese would do, but not tourists' travel patterns, and why birds' choices of migration destinations would do, but not those of tourists. In other words, why was studying how the human species chooses to go away or stay put in their usual habitat be suspect or unimportant at that time. Also suspect was some of the nonordinary touristic behavior at destinations, their unusual appetites during their sojourns, and their sometimes immense impacts on nature, culture, politics, and more—all of which raised questions about the legitimacy of the subject of tourism.

Why then did I have to defend my choice of thesis topic, particularly in the university atmosphere traditionally known for promoting the culture of research and scholarship on anything and everything, and for sometimes carrying on what seemed to be research for its own sake. Why would tourism—such a giant worldwide industry (then and now) and such a ubiquitous phenomenon—be considered trivial, and not deserving serious research attention. Perhaps it is tourism itself, this very giant industry, which has failed to make its presence and significance known beyond its own immediate circle, also by not nesting in institutions of higher education. Perhaps tourism owes it to itself to go public and make room for the outside voices for (or even against) it. Such questions and issues about how things can be changed in favor of tourism: how it can go public, etc., fall outside the parameters of this paper, but still remain important. We all need to do our share in bringing tourism to the forefront of public and academic consideration.

Back to my situation in graduate school: in order to reduce the need to justify the importance of my academic journey, I put a name card on my dormitory door, which playfully indicated that I was studying "Hotopology" ("ho" for hotel, "to" from tourism, followed with "pology," suggesting "the study of"). Though I did this mostly as a teaser, it still says something about the way tourism has been viewed as an academic subject.

Upon graduation from Cornell, I decided I might contribute to the tourism industry by entering the tourism education field. Thus, I joined the University of Wisconsin-Stout, whose Hotel and Restaurant Management program was five years old at the time. I was attracted to this campus because of its willingness to feature tourism in its curriculum. The program started offering a single course in tourism as soon as I joined the faculty, and additional ones followed soon, with the initial name of the program changed to Hospitality and Tourism Management a few years later.

My graduate studies at Cornell had already frustrated me with the single-minded advocacy voices on tourism, which I had discussed in a chapter of my MS thesis dealing with the then rarely discussed negative consequences of tourism. Such writing was regarded as antitouristic from the point of view of the advocacy platform. Such an intolerant attitude bothered me and led me to feel that a new medium was needed to foster a variety of perspectives on tourism, positive or negative, especially from a non-economic point of view. Could a new academic journal help to meet this need? The result of my deliberations was the creation of *Annals of Tourism Research* (1973–) shortly after beginning teaching at Stout.

As expected, the advocacy-oriented players of the time did not receive the journal sympathetically. But critical voices were gaining momentum and *Annals* started receiving increasing attention within a small, mostly academic circle. After five years, in order to encourage input of theories and methods from the social sciences, I added the subtitle "*A Social Sciences Journal*." With an obvious tendency to favor research for the sake of research, with or without immediate applications in the industry, *Annals* parted ways from the mainstreams of the time; and with a definite commitment to the formation of knowledge as its *raison d'etre*, the journal was on its own. The then-favored quantitative research methods that were often used in economic contributions to tourism research began to give way in *Annals* to the qualitative treatment of the subject as a sociocultural phenomenon.

In the beginning, *Annals* had to face its own moments of doubt and challenge. One early question I was often asked was whether there would be an adequate number and continuous flow of submissions—issue after issue. *Annals* had already become a mission for me, and the road ahead seemed promising; but I must confess that there were moments when doubts mounted up. With perseverance (some say this being one of my fortes), however, bumps in the road were overcome by an overflow of submissions. Still, I recall the early lonely days on this road, and some reactionary, advocacy-oriented letters during the first two or three years of *Annals*. One in particular comes to mind, which considered the articles in *Annals* as antitouristic "rubbish." Those involved in tourism should either speak favorably for it or get out. Such a general position was taken by Robert Lonati, the first Secretary-General of IUOTO (International Union of Official Travel Organizations, the predecessor of WTO), who, having read the critical chapter on tourism in my thesis, said how displeased he was with it. But to his credit, he soon wrote back: to tell me that he had read the thesis in its entirety, congratulated me on my work, and invited me to visit him in Geneva (where the headquarters of IUOTO was located), which I did in 1975. He received me warmly and even presented me with an "Outstanding Contribution to Tourism Research" award.

As should be clear by now, since *Annals* did not want to project an advocacy voice, it started with a cautionary tendency, which rather quickly became a knowledge-based platform (almost bypassing adaptancy articles). During its formative years, I also managed to finally complete my doctoral studies in cultural anthropology, a discipline that inspired and nourished the journal's early development.

In the '70s there were no PhDs in tourism. But even if there had been, I would still not have opted for them. I did not believe that tourism study had sufficiently matured in substance to offer a doctorate in its own name (an opinion which I still hold today). My idea was to enter a well-established field, to make it my intellectual home, and there in well-founded and fertile grounds, to plant touristic roots. This is precisely what I did and I still recommend a similar approach to those who want to study tourism at a doctoral level.

Parenthetically, it was during my tour-guide years, as a culture broker that despite the view that all tourists are the same, I noticed how the tourist cultures of different peoples varied, depending on their country of origin. I could easily see that each nationality practiced tourism differently, viewed local people and their culture and patrimony differently, looked for experiences and shopped differently, bargained differently, joked and laughed differently, tipped differently, and even looked for different snapshots. It was years later that I could connect these different behaviors to their so-called national characters, which may have played a role in studying cultural anthropology for my PhD.

After I was admitted to a graduate program in anthropology, all I needed to do was to find a professor who knew something about tourism and who was willing to supervise an anthropological study of it. Professor Luther Gerlach of the University of Minnesota enthusiastically received my research ideas and later acted as my PhD advisor, guiding me all the way through my successful dissertation defense. He even took upon himself the task of educating other members of my PhD committee about tourism and its connection to anthropology, which helped me get their support for my dissertation topic. Both he and I had to argue with the committee that the concept of Culture has broader meanings in modern times, and thus allowances needed to be made for different cultures. One of the committee members remained unconvinced, refusing to downgrade Culture to cultures, but at the end he reluctantly went along with the will of the committee as a whole.

Some aspects of my dissertation later appeared in a journal article (1987), arguing that in tourism there are more than two cultures of hosts and the guests. It went on to assert that there actually may be more than one tourist culture This in turn can be discerned as having two sides: one which we may still call the tourist culture (what all tourists, regardless of their origin, have in common) and a residual culture (what each national group brings along as its carry-on baggage to the destination, detectable as a version of the national culture manifested away from home). Further, I argued that in this multicultural arena of tourism, one will still have to account for the presence of corporate tourism cultures: one being local and one imposed by foreign tourism businesses. In essence, the study argued that tourism reflects certain tendencies derived from home, that it operates within its own nonordinary world, and that the concepts of play, ludic animation, and antistructure mostly characterize tourist culture. It was further argued that tourism, in its holistic sense, connects together the worlds of the ordinary (home) and nonordinary (destination), with the latter contributing to the maintenance of the former, thus making tourism a necessary ingredient of on-going socioeconomic life. I owe much to Professor Gerlach for his role in shaping my academic position and outlook and for supporting my tourism research theme in a traditional anthropology department; and thus I wish to humbly dedicate this personal history to him.

Looking back, now that I can call myself a cultural anthropologist, I remember a situation from my tour-guide days with particular pleasure. I had the amazing good fortune of being the guide of the famous anthropologist Margaret Mead in Isfahan. But, unfortunately, at that time I had no idea who she was (nor did I know her travel companion, anthropologist Geoffrey Gorer). Upon her departure, Margaret Mead presented me with an autographed copy of her edited book, *Cultural Patterns and Technical Change* (1955), and Geoffrey Gorer, a copy of his, *The American People, A Study in National Character* (1948). Many years later, when on the faculty at the University of Wisconsin-Stout, I gave Margaret Mead a call. To my surprise, she remembered me quite well. She recalled places I had taken her during her four-day stay in Isfahan, details I had shared with her, and more. It is funny how one serendipitously meets "gods" in the field, yet not knowing it at the time.

Back to *Annals*: it turned 30 years old in 2003 and is today recognized as the leading journal in the field, with some 100 editors from over 30 countries, representing diverse disciplines, who together have lifted it to its present landmark position. Its 25th *Silver Anniversary Supplement* (Swain, Brent and Long 1998) featured its 1973–1998 subject index, as well as a complete list of thousands of authors and referees who, with the editors, represented a dedicated army of explorers in this field. The contribution of this growing group is updated in the 30th anniversary subject index of *Annals* (Swain and Xiao 2003).

The story of *Annals* somewhat reflects processes at work in tourism research. Its efforts to be multidisciplinary are many: having editors with a representative geographic and disciplinary spread; seeking contributions from various fields of study; encouraging submissions by those whose mother tongues are not English; publishing article abstracts in French to signal its recognition that tourism research is also lodged and nurtured in many languages; being the only tourism journal also appearing in Spanish (*Annals en Español, 1999–*); initiating publication of thematic special issues and popularizing the idea in the field; publishing comprehensive annual subject indices, etc. These few examples simply illustrate the challenge and transformative processes at work, whose details do not belong to this paper.

In the meantime, many new tourism journals have appeared, with each pushing the frontiers in different directions, resulting in the fast-growing knowledge-based landscape of the '90s platform. Presently, over 50 English-language journals are engaged in this scientification journey, reinforced with an exponential growth in the number of tourism books. For example, in the early '70s, there were only two or three tourism textbooks such as that of Robert McIntosh (1972; now in its 10th edition under the authorship of Charles Goeldner and Brent Ritchie, 2006), which clearly suggested the bright academic future awaiting tourism. Friendship with Bob McIntosh has continued to help and guide my professional growth years after the single semester I spent with him at Michigan State University doing research for my MS thesis. Today, practically every week new tourism books appear, produced by publishing houses around the world (the numbers are much larger if one accounts for books and journals published in other languages).

In addition, other forces have been present and pushing the knowledge frontiers outward. Initially, tourism associations were doing their part in contributing to applied research. But I always felt that there was a need for a group exclusively committed to the advancement of knowledge in this field, without necessarily being concerned with immediate applications or obligations to please (business-minded) audiences. I also felt that tourism—in the journey of scientification—needed to fashion itself after other established fields. Thus, in the early '80s, I started thinking about the formation of a scholarly institution that would become an academy of tourism. After consultation with a small number of recognized tourism scholars (particularly Abraham Pizam of University of Central Florida, a friend and colleague since our days at Cornell University), a process which took about three years, the Charter meeting of the International Academy for the Study of Tourism was finally held in Santander (Spain) in 1988, made possible with the aid of Julio Aremberri, a colleague and friend (now at Drexel University) of many years.

As per the Academy's mission and bylaws, admission to membership is judged on the basis of one's scholarly contributions to the advancement of tourism knowledge, a process which begins by being nominated and seconded by Academy members and continues when a candidate is voted on by the entire membership, with successful ones inducted into the Academy at the next biennial meeting. With its quota of 75 members, the Academy is presently very close to reaching is full capacity. Its biennial meetings, each held in a different country and open only to members and their invited guests, have already resulted in several scholarly books, the first of which, *Tourism Alternatives: Potentials and Problems in the Development of Tourism*, was edited by Valene Smith and William Eadington (1992). The former, of California State University-Chico, who also is a friend and colleague of a number of years, has been a strong supporter of the Academy and *Annals,* and she *is,* in my mind, the one who, through her many contributions to an anthropology of tourism, starting in the early '70s (the decade of the cautionary platform) has done the most to introduce the social sciences and tourism to one another. Much of the multidisciplinary strength in tourism research we witness today is due to her pathmaking initiatives.

Another example of the maturation of tourism studies (and again fashioning things after other established fields' practices) is the production of reference books, with the academic encyclopedia being one type. After discussing this need with a couple of publishers in the mid-90s, I made the commitment to produce such a reference volume, acting as its Chief Editor. With the efforts of some 25 Associate Editors, and 300 authors from around the world contributing to the making and shaping of its contents—a process that took about five years—the *Encyclopedia of Tourism* appeared in 2000. Its 1200 plus entries provide snapshots of the building blocks of knowledge on which our field of research is based.

Some years earlier, the same social science orientation that had shaped *Annals* and the Encyclopedia, and the very thought that good ideas should be borrowed from well-established academic fields, also led me to start a book series. Its name, *Tourism Social Science Series* (1996–) captures the nature of the field very well. So far it has featured several tourism social science books, with a few, including this volume, in the making.

In a different vein, but still concerning the expanding landscape of knowledge in the field of tourism, during the advocacy era of the '60s, only a handful of colleges and universities in the United States and elsewhere offered predominantly hotel management programs. Then suddenly came a shift in favor of combined hotel/tourism curricula and later freestanding tourism programs. These now offer BS, MS, and PhD programs and research opportunities, all acting as academic fountains and rivers of knowledge, together irrigating multidisciplinary fields, with rewarding harvests. The pattern is international and its development is especially striking when compared with the popularity and growth of other fields. Speaking of my own professional beginning, when I joined my university, I helped in bringing courses in tourism to students in Hotel and Restaurant Management; and in the '80s I helped establish a graduate program in Hospitality and Tourism Management, the naming of which now agrees with the ongoing trend in the field.

As an example of another of my educational missions, I have assisted in designing a Master's and a PhD program in Tourism and Environmental Economics at Universitat de les Illes Balears, Spain (where I spent my 1997–1998 sabbatical leave and where *Annals en Español* is being published). Scheduled to begun in October 2004, this postgraduate program will have a number of faculty members, mostly from other countries, teaching modular courses. I feel comfortable with this design, as the PhD is not a tourism degree as such. It will also be an environmental/economics degree program, an adaptation that agrees with my position that tourism is not ready to offer its own freestanding doctorate degree. Because it is located in the faculty of economics, the program in Spain is not as multidisciplinary as I would wish, but its boundaries are left open, accommodating and actually encouraging research outings to other fields, particularly for students seeking additional expertise. Here, another personal acknowledgement is in order. My recent entrance to, and sojourn in Spain was greatly aided by another friend and colleague Eduardo Fayos-Sola who has now managed to firmly lodge tourism research and education in the structure of the World Tourism Organization, with the WTO Education Council decisively in place and performing the tasks assigned to it.

To bring out still a different point, because of my past work experience and academic training, I continue to believe that tourism is first and foremost a sociocultural phenomenon, now institutionalized worldwide, and thus anyone in this field must be a cosmopolitan in thought and action. Minimal ingredients of cosmopolitanism are the knowledge of other cultures, the ability to cross cultural boundaries, the feeling of being comfortable across the lines, and openness to and respect for what stands as the norm there. In addition, the ability to speak a foreign language as integral to the cosmopolitan notion, as is membership in the global community, to which tourism belongs and in which it functions. It is with this in mind that even the aforementioned PhD degree in Tourism and Environmental Economics features at least one required sociocultural course intended to bring these cosmopolitan notions to the forefront of thinking and planning (the programs will also produce multilingual graduates). This belief, originating in my years as a tour-guide, and today, having deep-seated roots, has received its confirmation during my education in cultural anthropology, followed by many years of professional engagements in some 100 countries.

The Road Ahead

On the basis of what has been said here, is it possible to predict where tourism study is headed? As already noted, the rapid growth and development of the industry has received plenty of attention. Its occasional slow-downs in some parts of the world, and even such exceptions as the recent incidents of the World Trade Center, the Iraq War, and SARS, may amount to "short-term pains for long-term gains," especially when one considers that governments, policymakers, and citizens of the world are recognizing tourism's global importance. This view is reinforced by my many years of continuous or occasional work with the World Tourism Organization, UNESCO, United Nations Development Program, Inter-American Development Program, national tourism authorities, and national masterplans, which point in the direction of the very public platform that I hope will become a major thrust of the present decade. A discussion of tourism as an *industry*—both its present shape and future prospects—belongs to another paper, and so does its full institutionalization in the everyday lives of peoples, and in its ubiquitous practice everywhere. Here, I am mainly considering tourism *as a field of study and scholarship*, as well as my involvement in it.

But how do we look ahead within the already established and outlying academic parameters? To me, this forward movement and solidification will continue, even more enthusiastically than before, with a better sense of direction and informed vision. I see more scholarly journals taking their debuts in years ahead, each wanting to carve out and contribute to a niche for itself and each trying to compete with the others—a necessary academic exercise that should expedite the scientific study of tourism. The number of university programs committing to the study of tourism—hopefully not in isolation from other disciplines that contribute to it—will continue to grow, with many accommodating basic, rather than strictly applied research on the subject.

Various disciplines, especially in the social sciences, will more openly adopt tourism as a research area, both on campuses and in various disciplinary associations (a development which is already under way). Other fields or disciplines will (re)discover tourism in new ways. For example, the rather neglected relationship of tourism to health and space voyaging will be explored and possibly "exploited" within this decade. In a different vein, tourism study, already a regular importer of knowledge from other fields to form its own multidisciplinary building blocks, will more readily export knowledge to the very fields from which it has been productively borrowing. All tourism scholars can help this happen. In this respect, it is important that we also publish our research findings in establishment journals of our native disciplines much more frequently than we do today.

Furthermore, our research community should make it more evident to governments that tourism is not just a trade or an industry, but a sociocultural phenomenon that must be studied and understood; and its applications should not be limited to economic affairs. With this recognition, government tourism offices (whether called Ministry, Secretary, or Board of Tourism) will have to employ people who have studied tourism and understand it both as an industry and a sociocultural phenomenon—a development that would be a drastic departure from the profile of their present personnel. The industry itself will have to finally sit with its academic partner—which it has hardly noticed all these years—to begin offering substantial and ongoing energizing support for its maintenance and the fueling of its forward mission, including financing graduate students in this field, funding additional endowed chairs, and building on the foundation that tourism studies have already provided.

In my view, the boosterism approach of the past—chiefly belonging to the still very strong advocacy platform—may get tourism going, but it will take the means and ways of the knowledge-based platform and the public platform to make it prosper. This all speaks of a process to which colleagues around the world have contributed, with examples of those from anthropology and sociology included in this volume of the *Tourism Social Science Series*. As the editor-in-chief of the series, it has been my intent to feature similar volumes from other disciplines in the series, which will register the personal accounts of pioneers in other fields.

While such accounts will tell us about past initiatives, the future of our field is open before us. An informed visionary mission for tourism—as a field of both study and practice—must be opened up among past and present students for moving ahead. It may not be apparent from this personal history that I also have been preoccupied in teaching tourism courses at my university (the University of Wisconsin-Stout is primarily a teaching institution). Also, during recent years, I have been participating (during sabbaticals summer leaves, , and other breaks) in educational give and take at other institutions. Those of us in the field of education can take satisfaction in having contributed to this process in its formative years; and as our students come to occupy lead positions in the field, we will know that the journey is well on its way.

In closing, I would like to emphasize that tourism—both as an industry and a sociocultural field of study, with a strong national and international economic position and with the firm foothold on major university campuses worldwide—is here to stay; and past achievements will soon seem meager to scholars like those in this book who were here during the beginning and the early development of the field. There will be many occasions to celebrate advances in this fast-expanding, and fascinating field of knowledge. Fortunately, we come from different fields and have had different experiences, making tourism a truly multidisciplinary field of study. We are also well rooted in a knowledge-based platform based in the social sciences. It only remains for us to adopt a public orientation in order to progress further.

Marie-Françoise Lanfant (1932–)   15 rue Rollin, Paris-7500, France (e-mail: marie-francoise.lanfant@wanadoo.fr), is Directeur de Recherche Honoraire, Centre National de Recherche Scientifique (CNRS) where she has developed a Sociology and Anthropology of World Tourism and created a network of international research. During her career at the CNRS and Sorbonne, she has concentrated on Gender Studies, Volunteers, Cultural Policies, Leisure, and International Tourism. Although retired, she has continued to deepen her interest in these matters, especially on tourism as a "total social phenomenon." Among her publications are *Les Theories de Loisir: Sociologies and Ideologies* (1972) and (with John Allcock and Edward Bruner) *International Tourism: Identities and Change* (1995). She initiated the Committee on International Tourism of the International Sociological Association, of which she has been Vice President and President, and she also is a Founding Member of the International Academy for the Study of Tourism.

CONSTRUCTING A RESEARCH PROJECT
From Past Definite to Future Perfect

> Verrai-je de vents s'accorder
> Et calmement mon navire aborder
> Comme il soulait au havre de sa grace.
> – Pierre de Ronsard, *Les amours.*

When I began research in the Sociology of Tourism, I had little understanding of where it would lead me.

The Decisive Moment

I have often spoken of the reasons that led me onto this career path. For me, the whole thing began around the beginning of the 1960s. I was then associated with the Sociology of Leisure Research Team at the National Center for Scientific Research (CNRS), and because of that work, I was destined to introduce a new teaching field in sociology at the Centre d'Etudes Supérieures du Tourisme (CEST) at the Sorbonne. CEST, which had been created as part of the Institut de Géographie, offered a multidisciplinary education for advanced students seeking to specialize in some area that would allow them to become professionally active in the field of tourism. This type of education is rare, if not unique, in the French university system.

From the end of World War II, with the aid of the Marshall Plan, tourism began an uninterrupted course of development in France. Such development along the

Mediterranean coast was beginning to produce saturation problems. In the Alps region, with the aid of the latest innovations, ski resorts were flourishing. The Hexagon (France) was receiving more and more foreign tourists. On the other hand, the overall view of tourism in France, where it existed, was not well developed. The French seem to have been unaware of political options involved in transforming national territory into leisure and vacation zones. And when a high-level decision was made to convert Languedoc into a tourist region, it was derived from a broad plan full of international implications. Local populations were worried—even more so when a good many were asked to move in order to make space for tourism; and when local identities were disturbed in regions having strong attachments to their language and autonomy (perhaps where regionalist movements were already active), people began to react. In the face of such opposition to tourism development, those in charge of such projects began to wonder if they had not embarked on an impossible mission.

I taught at CEST from 1964 to 1973 along with my research activities at the CNRS. This experience was a real lever in my decision to undertake research in the sociology of international tourism, in which I sensed the importance of thinking about tourism on a global level in terms of exchange. Over the course of those years I saw students from many countries in Africa; the Mediterranean basin, North, South, and Central America, the Asian continent, and all parts of Europe. In 1972, there were as many as 28 different nationalities in my classes.

In my teaching, I used what was an unusual pedagogy for the French university system at the time. I invited the students to speak. I encouraged them to choose thesis subjects in relation to their backgrounds and present situations, and from the beginning, I found them to be really interested. There in front of me, I had French students, convinced of the value of free time and leisure (even more so among those with legitimate professions in view), and students from the Third World for whom the words *free time* and *leisure* had no place in their vocabulary, but who were nonetheless looking for the meanings associated with the power they sought to acquire. These last spoke of their countries and of themselves as confronted by the challenge involved in the penetration by international tourism. They spoke of the circumstances in which they lived—of their home communities, which in some cases still had rudimentary conditions of existence. They spoke of their religious beliefs, held together by sacred rites, which some no longer believed in. They spoke of their families that were still attached to the old traditions. And they spoke of themselves in the face of touristic intrusions. I can testify to troubling exchanges between French students and foreign students with different points of view that created a split in the class. It came to the point where there were disputes provoked by racist sentiments. In this class the question of the Other rose to the surface with all its psychological force, and I was taken aback.

At this point, I thought about the limits of my specialty in the sociology of leisure. Its conceptual apparatus had been forged in an industrial context in which people were freeing themselves from often difficult and painful work. Faced with students coming from numerous under-developed, nonindustrialized countries, I became aware that the criteria on which our sociology was founded were not pertinent in the process of international development. I was able to assess concretely the effects of the Western ideal of leisure associated with the expansion of the richer societies over the poorer.

Through the spontaneous remarks of these students, I discovered a whole series of discouraging facts: the implantation of ghetto-like tourist enclaves suggested massive expropriations; the intrusion of foreign multinational firms, controlled by great banks that acted with no regard for local or national powers; police surveillance, often in the hands of private militias; the creation of segregation, repression, and exclusion for certain ethnic and marginal groups; violation of norms of sacred places; the ruination of local arts and crafts; and systematic organization of the prostitution of women, including adolescents and young children. The list is long, but I refused to take a pessimistic view. Is it not the job of the sociologist to analyze the processes of destructuring/structuring which are always at work in a society?

In the face of facts like these about the world, and particularly France, research on the subject was practically non-existent, and the sources of information on which I could base my teaching were not available. Certainly, numerous works on tourism had already been produced by studies in geography, economy, history, sociology, etc., but these works furnished mostly local or limited facts which provided a fragmented image of a tourism that seemed ripe for ideological explanations. The best works were those of isolated authors, who more often than not, condemned tourism in elitist terms. Official research was under the auspices of tourist organizations that distorted the facts and provided results favoring their vision of profitability and social control. So in 1970, I decided to explore this domain myself according to the usual norms of scientific research, which implied a team of researchers, financial support, and an appropriate institutional framework. So began my struggle.

Antecedents

In order to situate the research orientations, with which I began, it is necessary to briefly go back along the road that led me into this field of study. My method of approaching problems owes much to my education, and this education is, of course, linked to a personal history, which began with my birth in 1932 in Le Havre, Normandy, where I spent my early childhood. At that time, Le Havre was an Atlantic port city, ranked among the most modern in France and Europe, a place where superb ocean liners arrived and departed for New York. By 1944, because of the war, Le Havre had been almost completely ruined. As a little girl, I witnessed the blows that struck our region, like so many others in the world where the Second World War was waged: bombardment, exodus, extortion, enemy occupation of our homes.

Our family took refuge in a small seaside resort on the Normandy coast, which was well known for its monumental cliffs, that was inviting to artists—Manet, Courbet, Monet, Maupassant, Massenet, Offenbach, among them. But from that time on, that place was laced with barbed wire, flanked by blockhouses, and filled with mines. In March of 1944, our family was expelled and our house was burned and razed by decision of the Komandatur. On June 6, 1944 came the Normandy invasion at Sainte-Mère-l'Eglise-Arromanches- 100 kilometers as the crow flies from the place where we are living. These events were burned into my memory, and this is undoubtedly why I felt compelled to consider the facts of social life; and from the beginning of adulthood, I have been involved—at a modest level, it is true—in studying the evolution of French society.

In 1945 in Paris, I returned to my studies, which had been seriously upset during those years of anguish during the war; and I was extremely lucky to be able to begin my post-secondary studies at the University of the Sorbonne a few years later. There, I was instructed by distinguished professors who had made their mark on contemporary thought; and from 1951 to 1957, I obtained my teaching license in three disciplines: philosophy, sociology, and psychology.

In these post-war years, intellectual and university life in Paris was very exciting. It was the era of the great existentialist debates introduced by Jean-Paul Sartre, of disputes over psychoanalysis created by the views of Jacques Lacan, and of the development of structural analysis by Claude Levi-Strauss in anthropology and Roland Barthes in literature. At the same time, positivist currents took hold in the social sciences—in economics and sociology with the introduction of mathematical and statistical models, and in psychology with behaviorism. But one should emphasize the impact of the work of Marx on intellectual life of that time. References to Marx—whether those of Marxists, Marxians or Marxologues—were everywhere in written work and lectures. This was in sharp contrast to what was taking place in the US at the same time where citing Marx was at least imprudent, if not forbidden.

I was immersed in this intellectual universe, more so because I was an active participant in student life through a group of psychology and philosophy students, one very much attached to the teaching of Jean Piaget who was teaching at the Sorbonne at the time, and the other which invited Jacques Lacan to discuss his views of psychoanalysis. There was a good deal of political ferment among the students, with many students attracted by communism and nearly as many by the extreme right. This was the context in which I became a delegate to the Polish Festival of Youth in August 1955, which for me became an important initiation into the social and political context in which I was involved.

Certainly, I am not a Communist, but I was curious about what was happening behind the Iron Curtain. I wanted to see for myself, and I seized the opportunity to undertake this trip, which attracted me also because I could travel with a friend. Over the course of two weeks, I attended numerous lectures and visited many places that were shown to us as propaganda. And I visited Auchwitz.

The moment came to make some choices about my life. Putting the past behind me, I turned away from my earlier education in my family and looked elsewhere. I wanted to be a professional researcher. In 1957, I became a candidate for the CNRS, which was a rather lofty ambition. I knew that positions there were rare and much sought-after. The CNRS includes almost all the scientific disciplines and is the most prestigious basic research organization in France. Entry to the CNRS represents quite a feat in itself. It is necessary to go through a procedure filled with obstacles. Admission is subject to a vote by a Commission of some twenty scholars representing a discipline, who come from a variety of venues. The candidate must make himself known to each of them by a research proposal, written according to the rules of his or her discipline. His proposal is presented to the Commission by *a rapporteur*, not chosen by himself or herself. With many candidates and with the limited positions available, it is very rare for young applicants to be admitted as early as the first year.

My candidacy involved a research project on the condition of women. I did not obtain the position of *research attaché,* for which I had applied, but was offered instead a post of *research assistant,* which I accepted. From 1956 to 1961, years that might be considered probationary, I worked on questions concerning the feminine condition, during which time I was invited to participate in a debate about sexual biases in UNESCO, after which I worked two years with Henri Lefebvre, an important Marxist and libertarian philosopher and one of the masters of critical sociological thought. But I had already made the acquaintance of a man who was going to have a great influence on my later life: Joffre Dumazedier. I was then twenty-three years old.

Joffre Dumazedier was not an ordinary man. At the age of 40, his name was well-known. He had distinguished himself in the French Resistance during the War, after which he and some comrades from Liberation days founded the adult education movement *People and Culture,* which would play an important role in defining cultural politics in France in the '60s. In 1953, at the request of Georges Friedmann, he created a team at the CNRS to study leisure. Using the developing city of Annecy as a field site, he began an ambitious investigation of leisure activities in an urban milieu, which was based on the model that Robert Lynd had used 20 years before in Middletown, USA.

Joffre Dumazedier was an engaged sociologist. For him, there was a close association between his duties as president of *People and Culture* and his involvement in the Sociology of Leisure at the CNRS. From our first meetings, he led me into this double involvement, and I followed him with conviction. We had a very close collaboration over many years and were linked by a profound friendship. In 1961, at his request, I was transferred to his research team by the CNRS and put in charge of a study in the Moselle region on the role of volunteer associations in the cultural development of local collectives. This study, which had developed over some twelve years, was a great sociological enterprise. Thanks to this investigation, which I directed from start to finish, I acquired a vast experience in research practice. The context was favorable for the emergence of difficult problems posed by the distribution of culture in a democracy. At that time, a Ministry of Culture was created in France; and at about the same time, a Commission of Cultural Development was instituted. Our team was much sought-after, and we were asked to give our views at meetings, in which decisions with nationwide significance were taken. We were enthusiastic. Our work contributed to a conception of the cultural politics of the nation.

In these pioneer years, the influence of the CNRS's leisure team continued to grow outside of France. Dumazedier was president of the International Committee on Leisure of the International Sociological Association. He supported research teams investigating leisure that were forming in various other countries. Beginning in 1965, I accompanied him in his inquiries. Even before being transferred to his laboratory by the CNRS, I was closely associated with his projects. In 1959–1960, I accompanied him to the International Conference of Meina-Stresa where the first meetings of the Committee on Leisure Research took place. During those days in Meina, we looked for a definition of leisure that could serve as a common denominator for international comparisons. When J.D. asked me to do a synthesis of the papers and the debates., I encountered my first problems with the concept of leisure that was to give me so many personal difficulties later on; and indeed, it was because of this concept that differences began to emerge between us.

Joffre Dumazedier played a determining role, that is certain—give to Caesar what is Caesar's. Without him, I would not have gotten into the Sociology of International Tourism. However, it is necessary to understand that from the moment I become a professor and was confronted with the problems mentioned earlier, my problematic took another direction. This divergence was largely created by teaching problems I encountered in trying to connect facts about international tourism with the Sociology of Leisure. I soon found myself at odds with my own convictions, and because, at the outset, my discourse was inextricably linked to that of J. Dumazedier, I examined more closely the reasons for my disagreement. This is where my *Les théories du loisir* (1972) originated. In this work, I introduced a methodological procedure and a questioning of sociological epistemology that raised a series of embarrassing questions for so-called leisure sociology, of which Joffre Dumazedier was the best-known representative My methodology took the form of a radical critique. Looking back, I can say now that this was an important fork in my scientific itinerary. The conclusions that I reached became the platform for future research in the sociology of international tourism.

The book did not propose a theory of leisure but it questioned the procedure that sought to make leisure a scientific concept in sociology. I noted that the word had origins in antiquity: Greco-Latin and Judeo-Christian, for example. I also recalled significant moments of its history. Thinking about leisure has always taken the form of some kind of moral, philosophical, or political connotation, and it is no different in our contemporary world. After being condemned as a kind of plague by most theoreticians of nineteenth century industrial society, *leisure* began to acquire a more positive meaning in the twentieth century. For me, the most important development was in this transition, in which there was a reversal of values between work and leisure.

In the nineteenth century, the sociological conception of leisure was tied into the analysis of industrial society and its work. (I made reference to works by Saint-Simon, Marx, Veblen, and a few others in the book). But the modern conception which emerged in the twentieth century puts leisure in opposition to work, and little by little, this break takes the form of a clear separation between the two. The result was a reality *sui generis*, in which leisure acquired its own justification and finality.

In the 1950s and '60s, discussions of these questions were very lively in the Leisure Research Committee of the ISA, in which I was a member. Having access to documentation from many different sources, I was able to undertake a systematic comparison of liberal and Marxist conceptions of free time and leisure that were proposed by sociologists working in radically opposed sociopolitical contexts of North America and Western Europe and the controlled economies of the popular democracies of Eastern Europe and the USSR. In this work, I relied on numerous references, including works in English.

The main concepts involved were free time and leisure. These concepts were at the center of the political analyses dealing with the respective merits of the powerful capitalist and socialist systems that aimed at the domination of the world stage from the two sides of the Iron Curtain. These words, which symbolize states of future happiness promised to the masses, on one side or the other, are strongly imbued with ideology. In the two blocs, there was a valuation of free time or of leisure, which was related to internal crises that determined, one after the other, alternating positions of optimism and pessimism. Leisure and free time, involving the triumph over alienation, class conflicts, and scarcity, were a part of everyone's fantasy life. The sociology of leisure had to deal with anxiety-ridden questions about the end result of capitalist or socialist industrial production.

However, in the 1960s when I wrote my book, contacts were being established between the East and the West. Points of view were converging, and I noted that the Marxist and liberal problematics of free time and leisure, distinct at the beginning and issuing from different orientations, tended to fuse. It became necessary to question the reasons for and the consequences of this reconciliation; and I inquired into the cognitive processes by which such conceptions were transformed into theoretical structures.

This economic theory held my attention particularly because it inspired one of the works that was and remains for me most stimulating in my efforts to understand the significance of tourism at the heart of modernity. This work by the German-speaking Swiss economist Kurt Krapf, entitled *La consommation touristique: Contribution à une théorie de la consommation touristique* (Krapf 1964)—the same author, who later as an expert for the World Bank, sought to help developing countries open themselves to international tourism (Krapf 1961). Kurt Krapf was apparently well-informed about the new ideas of the Vienna School and its marginalist economic theory, from which we derive our notion of *homo turisticus*.

Krapf had a really far-sighted vision at the time when mass tourism had begun to spread. He understood that mass tourism stimulates the process of consumption at its roots by mobilizing our deeply repressed desires. For him, touristic consumption became an exemplary case of the consumption process that the marginalists referred to as "final consumption," which involves pure pleasure. (I proposed a new reading of Krapf's thesis in my *International Tourism Reconsidered*, Lanfant 1992b).

Beginning of Research on International Tourism: Methodological Orientations

The arrival in bookstores of *Theories of Leisure* made my relationship with Joffre Dumazedier rather delicate. I found myself entangled in a paradoxical situation. As a research assistant, I was under his tutelage. How then to pursue research in a new direction, which made me a dissident in his laboratory? The year 1970 marked the beginning of a new course. I became obsessed with the preoccupation of freeing myself from Dumazedier's Leisure Team and creating one of my own.

To do that, I had to change my institutional classification, i.e., apply for the title of *chargée de recherche*. This would be complicated, but it was with this goal in mind that I prepared a research project for presentation to the CNRS Commission. (My initial project, entitled *Le Tourisme international: un cas de mobilité sociale et culturelle: Répercussions dans la sphère du temps libre et du loisir*, already contained the basic orientation for my future research.)

My first concern was to construct a methodology that permitted me to grasp the phenomenon in its global sense over and above the various representations in ordinary social discourse. To do this, I proposed at the outset to approach tourism, using the principles of systemic analysis, as an "international phenomenon." Following these principles, it was no longer a question of reasoning on the basis of selective studies or national references, but of defining at the outset the socio-logical object as a phenomenon of interaction and interrelation that transcended national or local limits. Situating the project in this perspective meant breaking with all the dominant approaches that look at the development of tourism as a consequence—read: a consecration—of a leisure demand emanating from postin-dustrial societies. At the same time, I was trying to overcome the existing dis-junctions between studies and research done separately in countries sending foreign tourists (for the most part Western societies) and the societies called upon to receive them (for the most part underdeveloped societies). This separation existed de facto and is created by the compartmentalization of research depart-ments by discipline—analysis of the demand being most specifically attributed to sociology (leisure sociology in particular) and analysis of destination milieus falling into the domain of anthropology—from which results the difficulty of understanding the phenomenon as a whole.

From this perspective, the fundamental anthropological concept of "exchange" took precedence. The hypothesis was that through the growing movement of tourists around the world, new types of exchange emerged between different groups and affected their patterns of socialization, which in turn transformed the ways in which the people involved thought of themselves and their relations with the Other. Finally, I proposed to introduce the touristic phenomenon as a total social fact, which was not an affirmation of reality of the phenomenon, but a methodological choice for approaching the study in a multidimensional way while, at the same time, recognizing the confusing and polymorphic nature of the word "tourism." In adopting this terminology, I connected the premises of this field of research with the anthropology of Marcel Mauss, whose book *l'Essai sur le don* (1923), is a funda-mental text. In this domain, the working hypotheses, which freed any explanation of touristic facts from the Western ideal of leisure in favor of a symmetrical view in terms of exchange, would turn out to be the ultimate determinant.

Toward an Official Recognition of the Field within the CNRS

My research project, held over from the first round of selections, was approved in 1972 by the CNRS. In my view, this moment was very important because it opened up a field of research, against which there was so much prejudice among intellectuals, into a great scientific institution of basic research. But unfortunately, budget restrictions, which are endemic in the CNRS, prevented the immediate realization of the project. Still, I took every opportunity to deepen the research problem and assemble the widely scattered documentation for it. All of my travels were transformed into study trips. I visited numerous countries in Africa, in Western and Eastern Europe, and in the Americas. I attended colloquia like those of the International Association of Scientific Experts of Tourism where I was able to personally gather information about the politics of tourism and meet the important people in the field. I visited the head-quarters of several international organizations (the International Union of Official Tourist Organizations [IUOTO] in Turin and Geneva, which would, in a few months, become the World Tourism Organization [WTO]) There, I learned about the beginnings of promotion of international tourism. I explored centers of documentation, etc. At the same time, I brought together some young researchers, barely out of university, who found in their collaboration with a CNRS researcher a way to strengthen their own projects. So began what would later, in 1976, be called URESTI (Unit for Research on the Sociology of International Tourism).

In 1975, after five years of waiting, I received confirmation of the title I had been seeking: *chargée de recherche*, which allowed me, finally, to think about the creation of a research team that was officially recognized in the CNRS. But from then on, it was up to me to establish the significance of the new field of research. Now, the real difficulties began. The budget allowed by the CNRS was very modest, and therefore insufficient. This meant that I had to find other sources of funding, which involved approaching various organizations support-ing research, writing a lot of proposals that satisfied administrative require-ments, and spending a lot of time making the case for a cause that at first seemed suspicious (because of the word "tourism") in an institution of scien-tific excellence. I felt that I had to transform myself into an advocate of the sub-ject, and I did not hesitate to exhort influential people to become interested in the consequences of tourism in contemporary societies. My discourse took a high line. Finally, in 1975, I secured a first contract with the Center for International Relations to finance my research and to compensate the researchers who were working with me.

Early Results: International Tourism in the Logic of World Integration

Taking a view opposed to the theory that makes "demand" (in the economic sense of the term) the cause of tourist migrations, our first investigations focussed on the national and international decision-making centers that promote tourism throughout the world. For this largely unexplored domain, the questions were simple: Who are the agents? What are the places of intervention? What are the strategies?

The methodological approach, on the other hand, was more rigorous. I began this analysis by relying on Graph Theory, as well as the sociological conception of (subjective) actors. I used the concept of network for analyzing the relationships between the different agents of tourist action. It was not a *network* in the common sense of the term, but, rather, mathematical, which permitted one to bring out the structural characteristics of a system of relationships. But it was on the discourse of the subjects located in the network that I based my analysis of strategies. First, it was necessary to locate the agents of tourism promotion who acted at different levels of intervention: local, regional, national, and international; second, to assemble the texts and the discourses produced in the different locations, that is, from different international organizations, the reports of experts, and all other documents, which would help establish the roles played by the great multinational and transnational tourism organizations such as the World Tourism Organization, the World Bank, etc. These documents would be analyzed by content analysis based on structuralist principles (already used successfully in my previous work), and it would permit me to work out the conceptual scheme common to all the discourses of the actors involved.

This scheme functioned on the basis of a plan of observation associating paired receiving and sending societies. Using it, studies were done in thirteen developed and developing societies. Investigations were done in thirteen countries: developed countries/developing countries and Western Europe under liberal regimes/Eastern Europe under centralized regimes with controlled economies. Assignments were divided among the four members of the URESTI according to their knowledge of the selected countries and their languages: England, Belgium, Morocco, Tunisia, Romania, Bulgaria, Senegal, Spain, Italy, France, Indonesia, Poland, and West Germany.

The result of our research was a real discovery. It brought to light the existence of a tourist power, which was establishing itself internationally. This power depended on a network of agents with various subsidiary powers who were beginning to coordinate themselves at various levels. So we were witness to the formation of a central decision-making system having a variety of ramifications at all levels.

Our conclusions were far-reaching: for the international realm, the politics of tourism followed a model of development that brought together the apparently contradictory goals of increased leisure and increased economic development—an arrangement that could be found in the logic of a new world order. So the study of tourism, which many had thought was a futile undertaking, now had become a key element in understanding the world economic system and the globalization of exchange, which would serve as a background for the research that followed (see Lanfant 1980).

In 1975, 250 copies of our initial report on the results of this first research were published in the form of a report entitled *International Tourism, social fact and act* and distributed by me in spheres of tourism politics and development. Its effects were quickly noticeable. Several organizations invited me to present our conclusions: in France, in the Ministries of Tourism, Local Development, Youth and Sport, etc., and at UNESCO. I learned that the Secretary General of the WTO had the report and that he was reading it to prepare for the Manila Conference on sociocultural values. This was an opportunity to argue for more support for the sponsors of our young field of research and its developmental needs. They listened. From 1976 to 1980, URESTI received subsidies from the Ministry of Local Development, from the General Delegation of Scientific Research, from the Research Mission, and from UNESCO; and we prepared ourselves to undertake a much more ambitious research program.

1978–1985: Local Implications and Processes of Internationalization

In 1978, with my URESTI colleagues, I began a large study on the local implications of international tourism, the goal of which was to study simultaneously regions situated far from one another so as to better understand the processes by which the tourism phenomenon was being generalized on a world scale and the stakes involved in this process. Here, I deliberately adopted a methodological approach that broke with the problematic of the sociocultural *impact* of tourism, that is, as a system of action striking a locality from outside (see Lanfant 1987). This was because, what interested us, as sociologists, were the norms by which the local milieu appropriates to itself touristic functions.

The field studies were carried out by the researchers of URESTI for the duration of our inquiry of more than 10 years—on the island of Ibiza (Danielle Rozenberg), on the island of Bali (Michel Picard), in France (Dordogne by Claude Bazin and Côte Varoise by Jacques de Weerdt, and myself). To these regions, which we studied personally, were added numerous other studies from people associated with our team: Pierre Aisner in Peru, Christine Plüss in the Maldives, Anath Ariel de Vidas in the Andes Mountains, Marc Laplante in Montreal, etc. Local data were collected and studied by our group in long discussions. I pushed the researchers to analyze their own investment in the object of research: tourism. And, because in our little group each person analyzes the symbolic content of the word "tourism" and the unconscious desires that its discourse reveals according to their own personal experience, we were able to arrive at very sensitive questions. For my part, it was undoubtedly because of this non-academic way of working that the idea of what tourism represents in contemporary subjectivity began to form in my head: what kind of civilization does it represent? That was certainly a question for current consideration.

This study opened up new paths of research on different aspects of the subject: thematic, methodological, epistemological. It found points of connection through the publications of my collaborators and associated members—the most remarkable being the work of Michel Picard, *Tourisme culturel et culture touristique a Bali (1992)*, for which I wrote an Introduction. It would serve to fit the early part of our research into the framework of the 1990 World Congress of Sociology in Madrid, which opened with *International Tourism: Identity and Change*, edited by myself, John Allcock, and Edward Bruner (Lanfant et al, eds. 1995), a book which is an important step in the evolution of our field of research.

Patrimony, Identity, Memory, and World Tourism

In the globalization of exchange, our approach offers something special: to know that a prospective receiving society will not only be called upon to open its borders and its homes to foreign visitors, but to engage in a special kind of business, which involves the commoditization of culture, patrimony, traditions, social identity, certain population groups (e.g., in sexual tourism), and finally, to turn life itself into a tourist product. Everywhere in the world where there is touristic exploitation of societies, we are witness to a fantastic exhibition of signs of identity: historic sites, the heritage of traditional societies, special knowledge, historic monuments, ethnological, and natural patrimony that are considered as things to be converted into touristic products. It is in this way that the touristic Power intervenes, directly or indirectly, into emblems and markers of social and cultural identity (Lanfant 1992a). And this connects us with a series of fundamental questions.

In my introduction to the work just mentioned, I try to shed some theoretical light on the identity crisis with which our societies are confronted because of their touristic functions. A second work, *Heritage, Identity, Memory, and World Tourism*, prepared in collaboration with Nelson Graburn, which is being revised at the moment, emphasizes the conversion of the Human Patrimony into a touristic product.

Struggle for Institutional Recognition: International Expansion of Research

The years 1975–1985 were really fertile and productive. However, when I think about this period and I look over my career at that time I say to myself that it was also the most destructive time that I ever went through. Our research team, URESTI, was created in the CNRS at a moment when the institution decides to put some order in the management of its research. In the 1970s, the Direction of the CNRS required reforms in the laboratories. URESTI, a newly created research unit with a small number of researchers, was most affected. In 1978, the team I had formed with much patience over time and which had just received official recognition was dismantled. The research credits were frozen by an administrative decision. For several months in the 1980s, I would not even have an office in which to work and to meet with my colleagues. I had a difficult time maintaining a certain cohesion not only among the members of our young team, but in the flow of my thoughts. I thought seriously about ending this adventure. But, surprise! In 1985, just when I had abandoned all hope of continuing, I received the title of research director that I had been awaiting for seven years. And we were off again on a new adventure.

I had been trying for a long time to create an International Committee of Research that would offer researchers from around the world a place for dialogue and information. It is an indispensable methodological tool for studying the touristic phenomenon worldwide. So, as soon as I was promoted to Research Director of the CNRS, I felt I had the authority to move forward with this project. Once more, I argued our cause before organizations and individuals likely to support it; and in 1986, with the help of the Ministry of Research and the CNRS, URESTI organized at Marly-le-Roi a Round Table entitled *The Social and Cultural Impact of International Tourism: interdisciplinary questions and responses*. At this meeting, there were some thirty carefully selected foreign and French researchers, the majority of whom favored the idea of creating an international research network (see Lanfant 1987).

Just after this conference, I went to the World Sociology Conference in New Delhi with the idea of inserting our network as a Research Committee into the International Sociological Association (ISA), which includes sociologists from all over the world. We had to conform to certain requirements: getting the signatures of at least fifty researchers—university professors from different nationalities, submitting a well-argued request that justified the vitality and scientific value of the international network we were forming, organizing an international colloquium, and agreeing to having sessions in at the World Sociology Congress that meets every four years.

From 1988 to 1998, I personally directed this process all the way to its end while my CNRS team slowly deteriorated. I must say in my defense that I received a lot of encouragement and support from my foreign colleagues during this time and that my French colleagues did not abandon me. In 1990, we obtained the right to hold sessions in the 12th World Sociology Congress as a working group (ISA/WG5). We seriously prepared for this conference and were successful! From this moment, the procedure followed its course, but not without some misadventures that made me fear the worst. The worst now is over, and today, relief is assured. Thanks to internationalization of our research, data and questions spring from everywhere. It turns out that this field in the sociology of international tourism is really a privileged domain for studying the great challenges with which contemporary societies are confronted.

Conclusion: An Unfinished Task

Today, when I think about the questions that haunted me at the beginning of my research and at certain fecund moments along the way, I feel obliged to state that I have not finished the task I took on at the outset. I have continually put off writing the book that I had proposed at the end of the 1970s, in which I intended to construct the research object from the subject in question—a crucial point in sociological epistemology. The practice that I have been forced to adopt to meet the requirements of the present work, which is to lay out my personal investment in the study of tourism as a total social phenomenon, has re-started that project. I have meticulously gone over my career by systematically rereading my archives and my reports on various activities and forcing myself into the work of reminiscence that has been painful at times. And now as I look back over this long journey, I am surprised at my perseverance in pursuing this enterprise. Even today, it is an enigma for me. This remembering, now fixed on paper, brings to mind a good deal of confusion about my choices and the meaning of my involvement in this research. But the story is not yet finished. There is more to come.

Trans: Dennison Nash and Bambi Billman

Dean MacCannell (1940–) is Professor of Environmental Design and Landscape Architecture, University of California, Davis, 1 Sheilds Ave, Davis CA 95616, USA (e-mail: edmaccannell@ucdavis.edu), where along with administrative duties, he has taught graduate and undergraduate courses on landscape and memory, research methods, and postmodern landscapes. Besides work on tourism, art, landscape, myth and modernity, tradition, and conservation, and rural and urban differences, he is author of *The Tourist: A New Theory of the Leisure Class* (1976/1999) and *Empty Meeting Grounds: The Tourist Papers* (1992), as well as studies of communities of farmworkers and the homeless. He was a founding member of the International Academy for the Study of Tourism.

ANTHROPOLOGY FOR ALL THE WRONG REASONS

This is the second time I have been asked to reflect in print on my research and writing (MacCannell 1990) and the first time to comment on how I became interested in tourism. It is somewhat daunting to try to look back beyond the 29 years since my first publication on tourism. But challenges interest me and I will try to respond to this generous invitation with the seriousness it deserves and as much clarity as I can muster. Going through my files in preparation to write this piece I made a lucky discovery: my first proposal to study tourism. It was written when I was half-way through my graduate study at Cornell. It is dated November 20, 1966, 10 years before publication of *The Tourist* (1976). It provides some answers to the questions Dennison Nash asked, and I have reproduced it, in part, below.

First, I want to state that I have always been under the influence of anthropology, more so than any other discipline, but I have not presumed to call *The Tourist*, or anything else I wrote, an "anthropological" study. My modest grasp of anthropology is based on my 1963 undergraduate (AB Anthropology) degree from Berkeley and postdoctoral attendance at Lévi-Strauss's course on "Myth" at the Collège de France in 1968. I have never held an appointment in an anthropology department or taught an anthropology course. Although I can now see from my files that this was not for lack of serious efforts, especially from Ed Bruner, to recruit me.

As an undergraduate I studied anthropology for all the wrong reasons. My mother graduated from college and my father finished his PhD while I was in high school. I couldn't help but note that they had more "homework" to do than I did. At the time, this put me off any thought that I might pursue an academic career. In Seattle I built and raced cars, climbed mountains, and chased girls.

When I was 17, my family moved to San Diego for my father's first academic appointment as assistant professor of sociology at San Diego State. Within a few weeks of our arrival we made a family trip to Tijuana. I fell in love with my first taco and with the "anything goes" border town morality, which seemed to be in a death grip with traditional Catholic values; the Spanish language, which I immediately began studying; peasant serapes and sandals with tire tread soles; and the brilliant colors. In short, I fell in love with everything that was different from the culture I had grown up in. Immediately I began crisscrossing the border without my family.

For the next two years, I spent almost every vacation and weekend in Tijuana, or further south in Ensenada or San Felipe, or climbing in the San Pedro Martir. I explored the palm canyons along the western edge of Laguna Salada, was in one of the early groups to ascend Picacho del Diablo, and made rare contact with the Pai Pai Indians who had a winter village at the southern end of the Laguna. I led climbing parties from Mehlings Ranch and made friends with the United States Border Patrol agents who smuggled pre-Colombian artifacts and stashed them in the Anza Borrego desert for future pickup on the U.S. side of the line. One of my best friends was eaten by a shark. There was no highway patrol in Baja, or speed limits, and we could race flat out for hours on some of the nastiest roads in the world with anyone who would rise to the challenge. I loved tequila and the fact that four years short of the US legal age, I could buy a drink in any bar. And I especially loved the strip clubs with no ban on total nudity.

Before satellite imagery, Baja California south of Ensenada was a white spot on the map. No one had documented what was down there. I drew crude maps of the canyons and streams on the eastern approach to Picacho del Diablo and shared them with other climbers in Southern California. This was what I did for fun. Today, when I am told what teenaged boys in the United States do for fun I become depressed. In Baja, I learned to take personal responsibility for my actions, especially for my most irresponsible actions, which were manifold. My experience during these late teen years was the basis for my eventual decision to study anthropology (and tourism).

I enjoyed being known as the person who could carry the heaviest pack, climb without resting, and hike the farthest in a day. My best friend and mentor at the time was Baja expert, mountaineer, and heroic rescuer of lost climbers, Edward Douglas ("Bud") Bernard. In my research, I have stubbornly refused to accept the distinction "traveler versus tourist," perhaps because the tourists my colleagues call "travelers" don't quite measure up to the travelers I have known.

When my anthropology professors at Berkeley heard I was involved in expeditionary mountaineering they told me that this would be good preparation for the rigors of field work. I loved and devoured classic ethnography, but never once entertained the notion that I would be able to follow in the footsteps of Mead or Bateson, or Malinowski. The "cultural isolate" my professors were so fond of speaking about seemed to me to be an unsustainable fiction.

The Pai Pai Indians' main village is near the ruins of Santa Caterina Mission, which they destroyed in an uprising in the eighteenth century, killing all the missionaries and soldiers. They are classified as Hokan, Esselen-Yuman, Yuman Pai. By the time I made my first visit, they had persevered for 200 years in self-imposed isolation. They caught and trained wild horses, hunted small game, and raised some corn. Only two or three of them spoke Spanish with any fluency. They had no electricity, no telephone, radio, or even a road to the outside world. Nevertheless, on my unexpected arrival on foot in their upper village at Santa Caterina, the chief demanded a detailed technical explanation of the Sputnik satellite, which had appeared in the sky a few months before. He told me that there was something new in the night sky and he believed my people put it there. We talked half the night about it and many other things. He knew exactly when Sputnik would fly past and was delighted to hear about rocket propulsion, orbital physics, and wireless radio transmission. His questioning tested my grasp of western science and technology.

This was how I came to experience the beginning of the age of global communication and interpenetration—concretely, intimately, late at night on a high desert plateau in conversation with a 70-year-old Indian who hadn't seen another white man since he was 20. This is how it happened that a year before I decided to go to college, I lost any illusion about eventually doing fieldwork among "primitive" peoples. The "primitive/modern" antinomy dissolved in that conversation. I had friends in high school in San Diego who were more "primitive" than the Pai Pai chief. We were all tourists in each others' worlds.

Ten years later, hanging out with anthropology graduate students at Cornell, a drunken conversation began, "Why do we do anthropology?" After several slurred attempts at philosophical answers, someone ended it saying, "Cut the crap! We're in it for the bone through the nose." I had never been in it for the bone through the nose. Anthropology held me with its impossible drive to write holistic descriptions of cultures, i.e., to totalize its subject matter. Today, this is a very much discredited impulse. We now study cultural fragments and collage, and hybridized cultural forms. The easy confidence with which anthropologists once treated "total" societies, cultures at degree zero, and "total" social facts, has gone the way of structuralism. And yet, totalization continues to haunt the discipline if only in the energy expended to discredit it. And, of course, there are always embarrassing questions, "Fragments of what?" "Hybrids of what?"

I eventually conceived *The Tourist* as enmeshed in this dialectic: system/fragments. There is no longer such a thing as a "cultural totality" or a "cultural isolate," if there ever was. Every human being on the face of the earth is more or less "out of place," either shoved out of place by global movements of capital, or propelled out of place by tourism. All our lives are shaped by our encounters with others, or even "otherness." There is no border or boundary that has not already been crossed in both directions. This much I understood before beginning my anthropological studies. But I still felt a deep need to understand cultural forms *as totalities*. If cultures are nothing but fragments, I wanted to know "Why?" And if there is no longer any functional logic to the ways the fragments fit together, I still wanted to discover patterns and look for reasons. In other words, I conceived of *The Tourist* as an impossible project but also as necessary in the drive for the kind of understanding I always took to be anthropology's true genius.

I decided to study tourism because of my discovery that there was no precise definition, boundary, or limit to the things tourists travel to see. George Washington's bed, moon rocks, sewers and slaughterhouses, the Great Barrier Reef, Lenin's Tomb, Auschwitz, and the Barbie Doll Museum are all on tourist itineraries. Indeed, tourists will very often go so far as to see nothing—as in "on this spot once stood the . . . ." Sightseeing was a singular activity that defied the global fragmentation of human existence. My selection of the figure of the tourist as a focus for inquiry was motivated out of concern for the dilemmas humanity and the human sciences were facing as new kinds of cultural arrangements were coming into being. I viewed reactionary political forms and the retreat into religious orthodoxy as responses to the same global forces. But I had no stomach for sustained study of conservative political or religious movements, which in any event seemed more limited and limiting as modes of understanding than tourism. Frankly, I was not especially interested in the tourists either. As a temporary class or category, I didn't like them very much. But they were definitely the lesser of three evils, and more interesting. For the duration of my research, I tried to remember my anthropological lessons and treat the tourists with neutrality and respect, and without prejudice.

As an undergraduate at Berkeley, I took a course on the Middle East from Laura Nader when she was still an assistant professor. She was smart and beautiful, and I got a crush on her. I took courses on Meso-American archaeology from Rene Millon; on Indians of North America from Robert Heizer; on European peasants from May Diaz; Africa North of the Sahara from Robert Murphy; linguistics from Del Hymes; and physical anthropology from Theodore McGowan. My sociology professor was Erving Goffman.

Heizer always treated me with a respect that went beyond what Berkeley undergraduates of that era were used to. His encouragement was sustaining, and I acknowledged my debt to him in a recent article I wrote about Heizer versus Kroeber on the drawing of American Indian territorial boundaries (MacCannell 2002b). The next time I saw Laura Nader was several years later at a party after a talk I gave at Berkeley. She was still smart and beautiful, but our reunion was marred by an unfortunate parapraxis. When I told her that the course of hers I took was "unforgettable," she heard me to say "unforgivable." The conversation Goffman and I started after his Sociology 1 class in 1962 lasted until his death. One of the saddest tasks I had to do was to prepare Goffman's intellectual necrology for *Semiotica* (MacCannell 1983).

Pre-Free Speech Movement study at Berkeley was more like a war than an education. There were always more students in the classes than there were seats. Fights for space in the classrooms often became physical. We were graded on a strict curve in every class: an equal number of As and Fs; an equal number of Bs and Ds. Half the freshmen class flunked out at the end of the first year. Half of those who survived the first year were gone before graduation. Soon after I arrived, the university installed plate glass on the Campanile observation deck because so many students had jumped to their death during finals.

The anthropology department had adopted a bizarre method of "undergraduate advising." We didn't actually meet our faculty advisors face to face until our final semester. Until then we would come to "office hours" to get our course lists approved, but the professor's door would remained locked. We inserted our forms under the door. We would hear file drawers opening and closing. After a few moments our form would come back out from under the door. It would either be signed or accompanied by a note, e.g., "Mr. MacCannell, you cannot take 100 level anthropology courses until you have completed Italian 3." The last semester before graduation, the door would swing open and the professor would invite you in.

The overall quality of my Berkeley experience notwithstanding, I believe that my eventual focus on the symbolic in tourism, on cultural production and ritual, on the ways that sightseeing mythologizes work, and on the neo-totemic aspect of the attraction, constitute a return to what are essentially anthropological questions, the questions I first learned to ask at Berkeley.

In 1963, I applied for graduate study at Cornell because of its reputation for excellence in "applied anthropology" and international development. I was admitted with full support, so I piled everything into a half-dead 1946 GMC pickup truck and drove across the United States. At Cornell, I changed fields to rural sociology, but still did much of my work in the Anthropology Department. My major professor was Frank W. Young, who was then in the process of transferring his appointment from anthropology to rural sociology. I also studied with Victor Turner, John Roberts, Robert Asher, Bernd Lambert, and others, maintaining anthropology and archaeology as minor specializations through to the PhD degree. In my personal statement for my Cornell graduate application, I expressed interest in the study of border towns, hybridized cultural arrangements, and other border and boundary phenomena. At the time, these were deemed to be sociological, not anthropological subjects.

Juliet Flower came to Cornell to study Comparative Literature at the beginning of my second year. She was the most beautiful graduate student, and the smartest; and she had a perfect character except that she was (and is) incapable of even the smallest deception. From the first moment I saw her, I pursued her romantically and have done so continuously for 40 years. Starting on our first date, we have discussed everything we think and write about. My mind would certainly not have been as open, or my approach as free, without Juliet's intense interest and unwavering intellectual support.

Erving Goffman allowed me to keep up a correspondence with him while I was at Cornell. He sent me several of his manuscripts to read, and generously footnoted my suggestions when he incorporated them in the published versions. He also continued to give me comments on my student work and this is how it I happened to send him my PhD dissertation proposal either before or at the same time I submitted it to my committee. Here it is as recently found in my files:

MEMO
TO: Erving Goffman
FROM: Dean MacCannell
RE: Proposed European Tourism Study
DATE: November 20, 1966

Certain areas of the world possess reputations in broader geographical and social contexts than their situation seems to warrant. Nations' capitals and sites of conflict have traditionally been in the news in terms of "history in the making." But the dramatic action of current affairs does not explain the reputations, or the long-term image consistency of international tourist destinations such as those found in the Alps, along the Rhine and on the Riviera. In addition to sharing the news with capitals and battlefields, these tourist destinations also share a common social plight: namely the organization of large populations that enter and leave for other than the biological reasons of birth and death. Rapid mobility through a total social context—one in which people eat, sleep, work, and play—implies a high degree of structuring. This structuring is especially important when the activities of peoples from different cultures and social positions must be organized for short periods of time, and under conditions of minimal initiation. These conditions appear to be on the increase in many parts of the world today, and warrant analytical attention. The case of the tourist region has been chosen over other obvious "laboratory" settings such as the college campus or the military camp. In addition to providing a broader analytic context, the tourist region exhibits more rapid seasonal mobility than the campus, and the tour director does not ordinarily enjoy the control advantages of the military drill sergeant.

Returning to an earlier theme, the precision of definition that allows stereotyping of international tourist regions by people in other cultural contexts, even those who may never actually visit such places, is probably an artifact of structuring for high visitation. At least the two seem to be related when one observes the fascination for military, recreational, hospital, and campus settings in modern western mythology.

The immediate purpose here is to understand the regions that host high visitation. Regional organization, and the mobilization of public symbolism in these contexts might teach us much about the future plight of nearly all areas of the world as visitation increases, as it appears to be doing, quite dramatically, today.

The definition of the unit of study and the main variables: The tourist region is conceived as a matrix of communities, which by virtue of their systematic interrelations, form a regional unit. The tourist region will undoubtedly share many characteristics with its non-recreational neighbors. One such characteristic would be a hierarchy of communication, along which the communities can be arrayed. One of the communities will have highest access to all the others in terms of its position in the pattern of transportation and communication ties in the total region. The pattern of internal contacts can be used to specify the position of communities in the overall matrix and its general structure, including its boundaries, established by "border" communities which have the lowest centrality index possible in the matrix, without having a higher centrality index in a neighboring region.

It is hypothesized that as communities increase in communicational distance from the regional center they will be increasingly specialized in their expressive attributes. Thus, around the more generalized central community one will find smaller villages and hamlets which possess the necessary "special attractions" which contribute to the diversity of the image of the total region. It is in these smaller communities that the beaches, ski-lifts, yacht harbors, architectural ruins, race tracks, and wineries appear in their local specificity. The border communities contribute specialized information displays to the overall image of the region. Following

Cassirer, information is here conceived as being polarized. Specific forms—language, myth, law, religion, propaganda, etc.— tend toward either specific or concrete, or general and abstract symbolism. All complex social entities must be able to process general and abstract information. This is most evidently apparent in the elaborate, abstract legal symbolism underlying the functioning of modern nation states. Guy Swanson in *Birth of the Gods* indirectly makes the same point for religion when he brings evidence in support of his hypothesis that the presence of three or more sovereign groups in a society is associated with monotheism, while fewer than three sovereign groups is associated with polytheism, or—in the present context—more concrete symbolism.
[. . . .]

Concrete symbolism does not unify information, but rather fragments, specifies, and intensifies it. As such, it is antithetical to general legal and bureaucratic order. The tourist destination has a special problem. It must possess general, abstract, legal, and bureaucratic organization. And it must project "mythic" imagery if it is to successfully compete with other destinations for attention on the stage of world appearances. The fringe communities in tourist regions are the logical location of this type of imagery, given the framework that has just been laid out. It is therefore expected that the "stuff" of mythic constancy from which intense stereotyping and apparent reputational information is extracted— i.e., the "quaint" customs of local behavior and dress, the colorful festivals, the strange sounds, sights, and tastes of cultivated unfamiliarity. All these will be found at an "appropriate" remove from the central community. The distinction between concrete and abstract symbolism will array itself along the community centrality continuum, and the region will also exhibit elaborate strategies of making public, maintaining and projecting, the concrete symbolism at its borders.

While this phenomenon is not well documented in writings about social and cultural organization, it is rather thoroughly apparent in our image of travelers. The key factor which distinguishes the adventuresome traveler from the mere tourist is his store of quaint anecdotes, and avoidance of what would, in this context, be called central communities. More effort is needed to elaborate the structural corollaries of this phenomenon. [It is hypothesized] that ordinary tourist visitation statistically begins in the more differentiated and articulated central communities. In so far as these communities are participant in generalized "international" culture they may serve as settings for basic initiation into esoteric local variation.

[. . . .]

Given the above definitions, the tourist region is expected to differ from other social regions along the following dimensions: (1) The entire area will exhibit refined development of highly staged and organized "back region" and "underlife" activities. (2) As opposed to other regions, the component communities will exhibit greater division of labor in terms of what types or kinds of people and activities can be hosted by them. (3) Public symbolism, as embodied in local dress, place names, ceremonies, etc. will be more concrete, specific and intense in the border communities of tourist regions than would be the case for similarly positioned communities in other regional contexts. (4) The overall structure of the tourist region will be more flexible and less subject to rapid change than would be the case for other regions.

Discussion: In an earlier study of a co-educational preparatory school in which I used the paradigm from "The Underlife of a Public Institution," I noticed something which appears to be relevant for the study of tourism. The boarding school I studied was in the delicate position of not being able to over-control its underlife lest it lose customers. Similarly, the spa is situationally bound to non or semi-official forms of social expression by its visitors. It must organize its workaday activities so as not to interfere overmuch with the appearance of gaiety, light interpersonal intrigues, spontaneity of expression and so forth, which superficially at least, mark the culture of those away from home. Since this type of expression is usually reserved for back regions, the host area has a special regional management problem which—if effectively met—will be evidenced in its social structure. Specifically, the successful tourist area will open its back regions to transient participation, or stage a second "back region" which provides an effective setting for the culture of recreation without up-setting "real" back region activities requisite for expressive and organizational stability. The former strategy (i.e., opening up an existing back region) probably marks early stages of tourist development, which the latter (i.e., creating fake back region intimacy and familiarity) would be the case for mature or institutionalized high visitation. The image of the "ugly American," or the boorish tourist, may result, in part, from the absence of sufficient back region staging.

A common practice that illustrates this kind of back "region staging" at the level of the tourist encounter may be seen in restaurants that are more than "eateries." In these establishments—which are themselves stages for recreation—at certain points in the preparation of food, the round of activities that ordinarily takes place behind closed doors is loaded onto a cart—a kind of mobile micro-region—and rolled into the dining room so that the visitor might both give and have the impression of actual participation in the mixing of a salad, or choosing a cut of meat, a desert, etc.

[. . . .]

A theme that unifies the rather diverse efforts of Georg Simmel in "The Secret Society," Tom Pynchon in *The Crying of Lot 49*, and *Entropy*, and Thomas Kuhn in *The Structure of Scientific Revolutions*, is the idea that overt structuring of society is delicately balanced by "non establishment" variation. The flexibility or constancy of official definitions appear to be directly related to the degree to which they can penetrate and control underlife activities. The strategy of control that is highly developed in tourist regions contains lessons that may be of value to some university officials and other self-styled counter-revolutionaries.

Several of the themes I would eventually develop in *The Tourist* are outlined here: the attraction, staged authenticity, and the symbolic work that is accomplished in tourist settings. I didn't follow up on other themes, especially the emphasis on the ways in which tourist regions maintain representational focus and image consistency. Interestingly, this latter set of questions is currently being pursued by other researchers, especially those who study tourism geography.

What was the eventual fate of my 1966 proposal? Goffman invited me to visit him at his sabbatical residence in Cambridge on Christmas Day, 1966. He was at Harvard's Center for International Studies for the year. He made many helpful suggestions and encouraged me to go forward. But my proposal was rejected by my Cornell thesis committee. They said it was "unprecedented" and probably "undoable". They told me they didn't want me hanging around in graduate school for the next ten years working on such an unwieldy project. So I set tourism aside while I gathered data and wrote my dissertation, an empirical study of the social impacts of differences in civil rights laws in 48 states (1968; Young and MacCannell 1979).

Both Goffman and Juliet were angry that I was forced by my committee to pursue a different topic. I was more accepting because I didn't plan to spend much time on the fall-back thesis. It took me four months to gather the data, three months to build scales and do the analysis on the computer, and four more months to write. My level of effort and energy was high, but the time spent was minimal; i.e., under a year. The speed of my work apparently did not degrade its quality. My dissertation, "Structural Differentiation and Rigidity in Forty-Eight States of the United States" (MacCannell 1968) was awarded the American Rural Sociological Society's annual dissertation award.

I was 27 years old and ready to take on the bigger tourism project. Nor can I say that my large-scale structural comparison was a step backward in my preparation to study tourism. When I first assembled all my tables, correlations, and tests of hypotheses, I remember sitting for several days without writing a single word and complaining to Juliet, "I'm sorry, but I am just too young to write about the entire continental United States." I soon realized that getting beyond this moment was crucial preparation for dealing with the eventual scale and scope of *The Tourist*.

My initial appointment was at Cornell, but the first academic positions Juliet and I were able to get in the same city were in Philadelphia, mine at Temple and Juliet's at Haverford College, 1969–1970. Philadelphia was (and is) an excellent site for tourism research. My initial approach was to gather site descriptions. Whenever I found a tourist marker, I stopped and wrote down the information, photographed and described the object and the behaviors of the other people who had stopped by. When my students went on vacations, I asked them to fill out a form containing questions about how the place was marked, landscaped, the behavior of the other tourists, etc. I collected old guide books, travelers' accounts, and newspaper travel section stories about local and far-flung attractions. My notes and clippings in cardboard boxes eventually overflowed my study. I made futile attempts to create typologies of attractions.

In the end, the only principle I could adhere to was the absence of redundancy. "Here is a nineteenth-century description of an English woman's visit to an Italian garden: I don't have one of those yet. I'll keep it." Some of my categories grew large and filled several boxes: e.g., "famous and not so famous mountains." I observed, read, and collected until I got to the point that I already had examples of virtually everything I encountered. This took five years. Then I re-entered my files and made selections within each category of attraction. I selected material for my final working "data set" based on the tone of the descriptions, the telling detail, and averages and extremes internal to the category. A European reviewer of *The Tourist* complained about its "excessive empiricism." I was happy when I read that.

Eventually, I winnowed the roomful of data down to one large box. In late summer of 1970, Juliet Flower MacCannell, pregnant with our first son, Daniel, and I with my large box of data, moved to Paris. I kept the box in our cabin on the *S.S. France*, intending to work out of it between bouts of sea-sickness. On our second day at sea, we returned to our cabin and found the box missing. I called Antoine, our cabin steward, and asked if he had seen it. Yes, he had seen it. He thought it was garbage and waste-paper and had thrown it away for us. Until that moment, it had not entered my mind, but the box *did* look exactly like garbage with paper clips and hand-written notes. "And so, Antoine," we asked, "when you throw out 'garbage' on the *S.S. France*, where does it go?" "Overboard. Out to sea," he said. "Directly?," we asked. "Or does it go somewhere before it is dumped in the ocean?" "Yes, it goes into the garbage bay and is bull-dozed off the stern every couple of hours." Antoine was beginning to understand the seriousness of the situation as we told him to run as fast as he could to the garbage bay with me in hot pursuit. He may have feared for his life at that point. It was a pit the size of a basket-ball court and perhaps eight feet deep. I was greatly relieved to find it almost full and jumped in. Antoine dived in after me and together we found all (perhaps not quite all) of my data in several damp clumps. Almost everything we retrieved that afternoon is now preserved between the covers of *The Tourist*.

Although I have not been a constant contributor to it, I have enjoyed watching tourism research grow over the years. I have learned a great deal from the contributions of others, especially from Nelson Graburn, Eric Cohen, Ed Bruner, Shuzo Ishimori, Marie Françoise Lanfant, Barbara Kirshenblatt Gimblett, and younger scholars, including Sylvia Rodriguez and Sharon Gmelch.

What Has Changed?

Given the number of years I have been at this, I am asked with increasing frequency: what has changed? What has happened? Where do you stand now? I tried to answer some of these questions in the "Epilogue" to the most recent edition of *The Tourist* (1999). Here I want to note what has not changed. I still regard "public space" (the space of the attraction) in our emergent culture as the masterwork of the symbolic order, the locus of credible fictions that sustain life in common. It is also the locus of dereliction, the dispossessed, the neglected and forgotten, and other evidence of our collective failure to renew the symbolic. Public space, occupied by the tourists, the derelict, the homeless, and the domain of landscape architecture, remains my primary concern.

While on sabbatical at Santa Cruz in 1994, I decided it was time for me to move my academic appointment from the social sciences to a field where my colleagues would be actively involved in planning, designing, and constructing the built environment. After some heated discussion, the administrators in my college and on my campus agreed that my research and teaching fit into Environmental Design and Landscape Architecture, and they approved a "voluntary internal transfer." My new colleagues share my fascination for the small and large objects and behaviors that struggle to give fleeting definition to the space between the inside and the outside, the one and the other, male and female, Arab, Gentile, and Jew. I teach a graduate seminar on "Landscape and Memory" and a popular upper division studio titled "Postmodern Landscapes." The change in program gives me new freedom to explore the questions that now animate my research and my growing collaboration with public artists. In her recent study of the artist Sophie Calle's experimental interventions in public space, Juliet Flower MacCannell comments:

> Her art is made up for the exchange of signs, of recognition, and a love that alters all discourse—a force of love that pries apart what divides private from public space. Modestly, without invoking the shamefully visible, she stubbornly resists how *the between* of self and other has been mapped out . . . . (J. F. MacCannell 2002:71)

If this is precisely opposite to the way most tourist attractions are constructed, it also represents the pure potential of future attractions and the landscape, a potential I would like to see realized.

Eric Cohen and I first met in Spain at a gathering of people Jafar Jafari invited to help put together the charter for the International Academy for the Study of Tourism. I had admired Cohen's work for years and we had long and lively discussions during the breaks from our work on the Academy. After a couple of days, Eric confessed to me that he didn't believe that he could comprehend my writing until we had met and spoken. "Now that I have heard your voice," he explained, "I know everything you say and write must be understood as lightly ironic." Until that moment I had hoped that my "lightly ironic" tone came through in the writing and didn't require actually knowing me for it to be heard.

Cohen (2002:110) has recently published some kind remarks about my contribution to Valene Smith's new volume, *Hosts and Guests Revisited* (Smith and Brent, eds. 2001). In it he asks if I am not changing my position to be closer to that of Boorstin, who I criticized in my first published writing? I have changed my position on many things, but not on Boorstin. Here, I want to disagree with the numerous efforts to sloganize *The Tourist* by saying that I "believe in the structural binary authentic-inauthentic" and that I reduce the tourists' quest to a "search for authenticity". (For my extended response to Urry, see MacCannell 2001b) Yes, it is about a search. But it is a search for understanding of who we moderns are and how we fit into the world and try to make sense of it.

The authenticity chapter, which many readers seem to get hung up on, was intended to describe an ironic double movement of *Gesellschaft*: as social relations in the modern world become increasingly rational and impersonal and people become nostalgic for the putative simplicity, intimacy, and authenticity of traditional cultural arrangements. It is perfectly predictable, within the framework of what Max Weber liked to call the "progressive rationality of the Western world," that this nostalgia for putatively simpler times would be met by the manufacture and sale of "staged authenticity." I was angry at Boorstin for blaming an acceptance of the "inauthentic" in tourist settings on the intellectual shallowness of tourists. It seemed evident to me that the development of increasingly elaborate and sophisticated staging of "authenticity" in tourist settings was historical and structural (for an earlier discussion of these issues, see MacCannell 1973). Most tourists see through the elaborate constructions that have been created for their consumption, but are reasonably satisfied with the show.

In *The Tourist*, I wrote as clearly as I could, "None of the accounts in my collection support Boorstin's contention that tourists want superficial, contrived experience" (1976:104). This is followed by several examples of tourists (today I guess they would be called "post-tourists") who laughed about the stage-managing of their experiences and enjoyed themselves nevertheless. At the time I was convinced, and remain so today, that "authenticity" is a terminally corrupt concept. There is no "authentic-inauthentic binary" because there is no cultural possibility of authenticity in some pure form. Analysis of *authenticity*-as-such should only be attempted by the smallest minds able to work with no evidence. On the other hand, abundant evidence for a pretentious elaboration of fake authenticity can be found everywhere. All we can ever hope to discover via observation are increasingly clever fictions of authenticity, and varying human responses to them. My chapter is about "staged authenticity," which on the face of it, is about "*not* authenticity."

What has changed in the last 35 years is not the tourist. It is a new intensity in the drive by global capital to manufacture and sell tourist experiences. The original system of attractions is now overlaid with malls that entertain, amusement parks, virtual environments, indoor plastic rain forests, replicas of the pyramids, the Eiffel Tower, San Francisco, heaven and hell, and entire communities built by Disney and Dreamworks. I think that tourists are still capable of fighting their way through this crap and trying to connect with something that might help them construct a meaningful sense of themselves and the world. But it is becoming more difficult. Increasingly, my attention is turning to the ways the original tourist project falters in the face of the obstacles to it that are being erected everywhere by big capital (MacCannell 1999, 2000, 2001a, 2002a).

Eric Cohen (2002:110) suggests that my most recent work "heralds a dismal future for tourism." As with almost everything I have written, I deeply hope that I am wrong, that the people, the tourists, might be able to wrest some control of their experience away from the global corporations that seek to shape it. What hasn't changed in the past 35 years is my commitment to understanding modern cultural arrangements. When I am mentioned in their books and articles, most anthropologists write "sociologist of tourism, Dean MacCannell . . ." I have no problem with that, but at this late date, I seriously doubt that sociology would be willing to reclaim me. There is understandable bewilderment about my proper placement in an academic field or discipline. My PhD in Rural Sociology, Cornell, 1968 is not quite "sociology." To add to the confusion, Cornell changed the name "Rural Sociology" to "Development Sociology". My early research and teaching appointments were in the Center for International Studies at Cornell, Temple University Sociology Department, the Center for Peace Studies at Haverford College, and the American Studies program at American College in Paris. I came to the University of California at Davis in 1975 to teach in an interdisciplinary applied social science program in the College of Agriculture. In 1995, I transferred my appointment to the Department of Environmental Design and Landscape Architecture in the college now named "Agriculture and Environmental Sciences."

My current appointment is as Professor of Environmental Design and Research Rural Sociologist and Landscape Architect in the California Experiment Station. Recently, I finished a five-year term as Chair of Landscape Architecture, and co-chair of the graduate program in Geography. I have just returned from a visiting appointment in the Graduate Architecture program at City College in New York. I have always been connected to the core humanities, theory and criticism through Juliet, and recently to other fields and disciplines through our sons. Daniel is a film writer and director in Hollywood; and Jason, a gifted writer of fiction, is finishing his PhD in geography and collaborates with me on our current studies of homelessness.

When a professor on the east coast, who had been one of my graduate students at Temple, heard that I had left my old department to become head of "landscape architecture," she wrote me to ask how I decided to leave academia and start a business. Until I explained it to her, she was unaware that landscape architecture is taught in universities. With apologies for the seeming paradox, I think I have been able to move between disciplines because my method and approach have remained steadfast. Probably I would have been more harried by changing intellectual fashions if I had experienced the paroxysms of the past four decades inside anthropology departments.

The flexibility my colleagues have so kindly extended to me on the matter of my academic appointments was also based, in part, on the fact that no field or discipline has effectively claimed tourism as its exclusive domain. At the moment, the question of getting beyond current architecture, planning, and landscape design for tourism is intellectually cutting edge (MacCannell 2001d).

There is one final matter I would like to address here, which is why I write at all. My understanding of my own motives was clarified by an incident ten years ago. In 1993, I was invited to spend three months in residence at Headlands Center for the Arts in Sausalito, California. It was the first artist residency awarded by the Headlands Board to a writer of nonfiction. Juliet Flower MacCannell joined me. Before my three months were over, she had so fascinated the other residents and staff that *she* was invited for a residency when mine ended, and I joined her. So we were both able to spend a wonderful six months living with artists in the woods at Baker Beach on the Pacific where Headlands Center for the Arts is located.

Juliet had another obligation, so I spent the first four or five days at Headlands without her. The artists were suspicious and unfriendly toward me. I sensed a deep prejudice but didn't know where it might be coming from. On the second or third day I encountered Bob Johnson, a painter from South Carolina and fellow resident, on a trail. He came directly to the point. "So you're the professor?" I could tell from the way he said "the professor" that he was not happy about a prized residency being awarded to the likes of me. It was clear from his tone that he would have disapproved even if I had been a professor of art. Before I could answer him, Johnson followed up with, "Publish or perish, huh?" His voice was flat and derisive. I answered. "Yeah, we have to publish. We have to publish a lot." Then there was a silence which I filled with a spontaneous (and truthful) observation: "But I have never sat down to write anything with the university's publication requirement weighing on my mind." Johnson's attitude change was immediate. He helped me out. "Oh. OK. You're one of us. The reason you work comes from your own desire. You don't work just because someone tells you to. Right?" I hadn't thought of it in those terms before, but he was exactly right. From that moment, I was no longer "the professor." Juliet and I were welcomed into the community of artists who remain among our closest friends to this day.

In 1995, Juliet, Bernie Lubell, an extraordinary sculptor, and I created an artist tour of San Francisco for Headlands (Lubell, MacCannell and MacCannell 1998). We put 50 collaborators on a bus and together produced an extraordinary meta-touristic experience. We went to the places tourists visit to see them with a critical, analytic, and artist's eye. But mainly, we went to places tourists would never visit to discover the city that is missing from the touristic consciousness. This was the first of several recent collaborations with artists, arts organizations, and museums intended to push the tourist experience off its benumbing coordinates (MacCannell 2001c, 2001d).

Thus, my greatest happiness is also my greatest professional defect (MacCannell 2002a). My talent and desire for academic scheming are zero. I have never gone anyplace uninvited, not even to an academic conference, and I have never studied and written about anything for strategic reasons. I have not cultivated beneficial relationships, "power," or prestigious invitations; nor do I try to market my ideas or create and control a "niche" for them. I study and write only because the subject intrigues or puzzles me. If I can't figure out something new to say, I fall silent. When I finish a piece I usually give it to the first editor who is kind enough to express interest in it, and after that it is on its own. When something I write fetches me a new friend or enemy, I am delighted, but I have no expectations in this regard. Let me be the first to say that this is not a smart way to manage an academic career, and I specifically do not recommend it: kids should not try this at home. My colleagues at the University of California have been mainly tolerant of my idiosyncrasy and I owe them gratitude. Mostly, I have been supported by the extraordinary creative and intellectual strengths of Juliet Flower MacCannell and Daniel and Jason. If everything else disappeared, our family conversations would sustain me. OK, go ahead and try it at home, if you are fortunate enough to have the kind of home that I do.

Dennison Nash (1924–) is Emeritus Professor of Anthropology, (U-2176), University of Connecticut, Storrs, Ct. 06269, USA (e-mail: dennison.nash@ uconn.edu) where he has taught undergraduate and graduate courses in sociology and anthropology over most of his academic career. Since formal retirement, he has continued teaching a course in ethnographic fieldwork. The author of many publications, of which *A Little Anthropology—Third Edition* (1999) and *Anthropology of Tourism* (1996) are recent examples, his research interests have covered subjects such as tourism, religion, ethnographic fieldwork, wine production in Burgundy, American and Japanese expatriates, and strangers generally. He is a founding member of the International Academy for the Study of Tourism and an Associate Editor of *Annals of Tourism Research*.

A NATURAL PROGRESSION

Background

As I look back over a career in anthropology and sociology, it seems that my discovery of tourism as a subject to be investigated scientifically came about in an entirely natural way. As I now see it, my inclination to look into tourism seems to have sprung from a long scholarly interest in various kinds of outsiders or marginal people and a personal history as one of the same. I was never a "bad boy," delinquent, political radical, or seriously out of step with my middle-class peers, but I have always been conscious of being somewhat out of the ordinary, which is, I suppose, a reflection of my parents' admonition to "be different" and my status as an only child. In this regard, my background seems to be not unlike those anthropologists studied by the clinical psychologist, Anne Roe, some years ago. She found that her subjects had had a significant parental loss in their childhoods, which suggests some kind of alienation. This, Michael Agar thinks, is one of the two fundamental prerequisites for students' interest in anthropology—the other being childhood experience in a multicultural environment.

This background seems to be related to my doctoral thesis in sociology undertaken at the University of Pennsylvania, which dealt with contemporary American composers of serious music and their adaptation in a largely unresponsive world. Subsequent empirical studies of strangers, informed by the theoretical work of Georg Simmel and Alfred Schutz, in the laboratory (Nash and Heiss 1967) and real world (Japanese immigrants in Cuba, Americans in Spain, American students in France) followed. And there even was a more theoretically oriented publication (Nash 1963) that looked at ethnographic anthropologists as strangers whose activities in the field reflected a kind of alienated condition.

What was the nature of the social context in which all of this work was carried out? From 1953 to 1956, I was an instructor at Middlebury College where I had a great deal of freedom to expand my range of competence and fields of interest. This was accompanied by a good deal of pressure associated with teaching six undergraduate courses, advising up to sixty undergraduates, and finishing my PhD dissertation at the University of Pennsylvania where I had majored in sociology with undeclared minors in anthropology and psychology (The dissertation was finished during my first year at the Vermont School, and I remember getting a raise of $100 for that accomplishment.). At Middlebury, I was an enthusiastic young faculty member with a gratifying student following, and I was eager to take on the numerous responsibilities that came my way. Though I did undertake some research, it was teaching and interaction with students and other faculty, especially Alvin Wolfe, an anthropologist fresh from Africa, and his wife that tended to preoccupy me. But after three years, during which I had a bout of what I now believe to have been a stress-related illness, I had had enough of the pressure, the snow (even in May), and a routine, which while rewarding in many ways, had too little socializing with like-minded colleagues, and I left Middlebury without another job in hand.

With only minimal financial support, I began to explore the possibility of studying a small group of Japanese immigrants in Cuba who I had come to know about during a brief, stress-reducing vacation from Middlebury. Such a project, I thought, would give me greater anthropological legitimacy. Very quickly, the focus of the research, which was carried out in several field trips, turned to the psychological adaptation of these immigrant-strangers in a foreign culture, a project very much in tune with the interests of one of my advisors at Penn, A. I. Hallowell, an important figure in the Personality and Culture field, whose studies of the psychological aspects of acculturation of Ojibwa Indians already were well-known.

In seriously reduced financial circumstances and while getting to know the Japanese, I received an invitation from Melford Spiro, my friend and former MA advisor at Washington University, St. Louis, to take over his position at the University of Connecticut the following year when he would be on leave. When I agreed, he recommended me as his replacement in a post that turned into a tenure-track appointment in sociology and anthropology when Spiro took a permanent position at another school. My research with strangers was to continue at UConn where I, at first, found the colleagueship I had been looking for and (under department head, Jim Barnett) all the academic freedom I desired. Teaching large numbers of undergraduates was still my forte, but I was also able to create a smaller, upper-level course on Americans abroad, which I continued to teach throughout my career at Connecticut.

All did not go well with me at UConn, however. Once again, I began to experience what I thought were psychosomatic symptoms (this time there was a woman involved in the pressures), which began to seriously hinder my teaching and research; and knowing something about such matters, I sought psychological counseling, which eventually turned into serious psychotherapy with genuine psychiatrists over a number of years. This therapy was successful in that it reopened the door to creative work. I was not without problems, but I began to fathom what was going on and make better choices in terms of new orientations, all of which seems to have increased my appreciation for personal agency in human action. In the end, I have come to function reasonably well without therapeutic support; but I do recognize that it is always possible to do better.

As UConn grew and PhD programs multiplied, more graduate students came on board, new faculty in both sociology and anthropology arrived, and new department heads appeared, some of whom had to deal with a group of radical faculty and students, whose activities in an outside of class reflected the social unrest of American youth in those days. Such activities continued as the department was split in two (anthropology and sociology), a scheme that the administration had been considering for some time. Though I was to maintain a joint appointment in sociology, I decided to be primarily involved with anthropology, where, as it turned out, the real political action was to be.

A new Head of Anthropology and faculty members he brought on board, turned out to be heavily committed to issues of social development in the Third World, with which I could easily identify (I tended to give such developmental issues a psychological twist in line with the work of my mentors, Spiro and Hallowell). But I had trouble with the political agenda of the new arrivals, which involved the creation of a "progressively" organized department in which graduate students and even undergraduates had a good deal of say. Their views were at first interesting to me, but as time went by, it became clear that they were not simply concerned with voicing their views in the interest of a more democratic regime, but in dominating the department; and as more and more students were drawn into their ideologically driven camp and conflict emerged between them and others in and beyond the department, particularly the biologically oriented faculty and students in physical and medical anthropology, the department became a difficult place in which to work. Indeed, I found myself spending a good deal of time coping with political matters, and I was increasingly aware of colleagues talking in offices behind closed doors. Sometimes I had the taste of gall in my mouth, which after years of therapy, I recognized as an indication that all was not well within me. The pressures were hardly lessened by my being in the middle of the fight between combatants, which involved those (mostly Marxists) increasingly radicalized by the Vietnam war, and the biologically oriented wing of the department and their associates.

Eventually, despite "in-house" attempts to resolve the department's difficulties by reorganizing it from within so that there was adequate protection for the rights of all, the exasperated administration put the Department of Anthropology into what amounted to receivership with a biocultural side in one building and the socioculturalists (including the Marxists and some more moderate others like myself) in another. This arrangement prevailed until the late '70s when the department was made whole again under the acting headship of one of us moderates, Seth Leacock, who was backed up by a toughened Administration that had had enough of our bickering and let it be known that the two sides, now in separate buildings, were to get along if anthropology was to receive administrative support. The split in the department had not healed entirely however, and signs of it are still evident several decades later in a department that has been reunited in one building. By now, of course, the principal combatants have retired or moved elsewhere, but conflict over issues, some of which are clearly continuations from the past, has once again made an appearance in the hands of others.

It is difficult to say how much I was influenced by these historical developments. Certainly, my interest in acculturation and development was strengthened; but though I felt entirely comfortable in dealing with these subjects, I never entered the Marxist camp, which in our department, had a know-it-all line and an aggressive political posture that I found difficult to swallow. Working on department committees in which radical faculty and students often were pushing some political line was not a pleasant experience. In our department, I was a somewhat left-of-center liberal who tended to think positively of historic figures such as Max Weber, a position which was hardly acceptable to the Marxists among us; but when I associated with students and faculty in other departments such as psychology or political science, I often found myself feeling like a radical.

I took sparingly from the Marxist view of things and struggled to remain autonomous in a departmental atmosphere that was a far cry from the one which I had encountered initially under Jim Barnett. Social communion was not easy to find even with the few faculty who shared my view on intellectual freedom and colleagueship. Unlike what I had been led to expect about college life, there were few rounds of invitations among us. This meant that alone and without family, I had to find my social life elsewhere.

So it went for me in the Department of Anthropology at the University of Connecticut. I could teach pretty much what I wanted on the undergraduate level (large introductory courses, culture and religion, personality and culture, anthropological theory, and Americans abroad), but not too much to grad students who tended to gravitate to the political poles of the department. As far as publication was concerned, the door was open, but there wasn't a great deal of support from colleagues. Despite its absence within our department, I managed to lead an active social life. I traveled, attended meetings, was involved with interesting women, including graduate and undergraduate students (not mine at the time), was active in sports, and did a lot of outdoor work at the vineyard in the Hudson River Valley, with which I became associated in 1977, or cutting and splitting wood for my home stove. The life I led certainly had many gratifying aspects; but the academic home I had been looking for hardly existed at Connecticut.

Into Tourism

My study of tourism evolved in a most natural way. I had been interested in various kinds of strangers and the psychological consequences of their experience in that role. Though this was not the focus of the burgeoning acculturation and development literature of the time (which was concerned mostly with the consequences of Western contact with less developed, Third World peoples), it was invigorating for me to be adding something special to this increasingly popular line of research. Very few anthropologists or sociologists (but see Eric Cohen in this volume) were interested, as I was, in the empirical study of the stranger's role and the consequences for those who were playing it, all of which was crystallized in my study of a group of American expatriates in Spain (Nash 1970), an ethnographic study carried out on a year's sabbatical leave and break from psychotherapy. This first real book of mine developed very well, and I am still pleased with how it turned out.

As I saw it, the Americans in Spain, were agents of American imperialism in a particular situation of culture contact in which they (and I) had to work out some kind of adaptation. The problem, of course, went against the grain of acculturation research where the focus had been on the powerless rather than the powerful. But it turned out that the Americans I studied had more than their share of problems in a great city with many proud inhabitants. With a combination of careful selection and plenty of luck, I had managed to select a group of expatriates who were really struggling with their adaptation. Without significant institutional support such as on an American military base abroad, most of these people had to do much of their adapting by themselves or through nuclear families, which involved more than usual personal difficulties for them.

In living with these Americans (as well as our hosts) for an extended period, I came to be intimately acquainted with their lives and the problems they encountered. On my side, as I went through many of the same problems, worked out an adaptation to them, and began to function more like our hosts, I gradually (but not without difficulties) acquired a sense of personal well-being that exceeded anything I had experienced in a long time; and the resulting enthusiasm could have had something to do with my continuation on this line of research. Before returning home, I made a side trip to Stockholm to study Americans there for comparative purposes, after which I got busy working on the book, which practically wrote itself.

Shortly after completing *A Community in Limbo*, I happened on a notice in the Newsletter of the American Anthropological Association from Valene Smith asking for papers on tourism to be presented at the 1974 meeting of the American Anthropological Association in Mexico City. Considering my intellectual state at the time, it took hardly any effort to prepare a contribution on tourism as a form of imperialism, which was published in Valene's first edition of *Hosts and Guests* (1977) and later in a second edition. About the meeting, I recall only vaguely that we met in a small suite following the interesting session, and after some discussion, chose Valene to be the editor of a volume of articles, the substance of much of which had just been presented in our session on tourism. As Valene no doubt will remind us, publication of this volume did not come about easily, but it turned out to be the first of several works in which she and I have collaborated. I hope that she and others will give a much fuller account of those first deliberations and developments, which have receded from my memory, but some of which she had helped me to recover.

I remember better my thoughts as I went about preparing the paper for the session. As in my work on Americans in Spain, I saw that tourists were involved in a historical process that could be called imperialism, which I thought of then simply as an extension of various interests of national centers of power, as say with the British empire, into less powerful places abroad and the subsequent course of relations between them. Like the Marxists in our department, I saw imperialism linked to production, but for me, touristic imperialism was conceived as specifically involving the production of leisure and travel, which I took to be at the core of the touristic phenomenon (grand economic schemes being beyond me at the time). This specific view, I thought, would help comprehend tourism wherever it could be identified, which I was beginning to think, extended beyond the Western, and indeed the contemporary world. I went on in the article to deal with the specific nature of intercultural transactions in tourism, its consequences for the people involved, and the development of touristic systems—all of this flowing from my pen in the easiest possible way.

Now it looks as if I may not have made my views on imperialism entirely clear. The position I took in the article seems to have been, in part, the result of my "debate" with the Marxists in the Department of Anthropology at UConn. I had taken what I wanted from them and their mentors and discarded what amounted to the core of their position. I have been somewhat chagrined, therefore, to encounter people who refer to this work as Marxist. This, of course, ignores my struggle over Marxism—a struggle that, however, seems to have preoccupied me less and less as the departmental fracas quieted down and I came to appreciate the work of enlightened Marxists such as Wolf, Godelier, Mintz, and Roseberry, the last of whom had been a respected graduate student in our department.

As I have said elsewhere (Nash 1996:1), those of us who were lucky enough to be among the first to discover tourism found "the air of discovery and sense of freedom associated with being on the frontier enormously exciting;" and I myself became increasingly preoccupied with the subject. I also came into greater and greater contact with scholars from a number of disciplines who were similarly interested. The atmosphere among us was alive with the new subject, and some of us even entertained the naive notion that we could nail down the true nature of tourism and find out what made it tick. Only gradually did I come to realize how multifarious this subject was and the variety of points of view from which it could be studied. The multidisciplinary *Annals of Tourism Research*, created by Jafar Jafari in 1973, became a natural place to publish social scientific articles on tourism, and I later was to become a member of its editorial board.

Support from the anthropological establishment was forthcoming in the form of cooperation in the scheduling of conferences of one sort or another such as had taken place in Mexico City. I also profited from residence at René Baretje's multidisciplinary Centre des Hautes Études Touristiques in Aix-en-Provence where I had an opportunity to explore enormous archival resources and participate in graduate seminars such as one led by Joffre Dumazedier. Here, tourism research seemed to be a valued and entirely normal field of study. I did work at the Centre during several productive stays at the Camargo Foundation in Cassis, which was only a short distance away, and I shall always be grateful for the hospitality and resources extended to me at both institutions. The publication by the Centre of my "Tourism in Pre-Industrial Societies" (1979) was a direct result of one sojourn there.

At home in America, however, I sometimes encountered puzzlement or even outright dismissal of my interest in tourism. By this time, I was used to people in public, who when informed that I was an anthropologist, began asking about ruins or fossils. Now I was encountering misunderstandings and even rejection, not only from the public, but from colleagues. At one party I recall, people from an elite American university (I think they were specializing in kinship) began to snicker when I mentioned tourism as a specialty, and I had to endure a spate of hostile joking about fieldwork vacations, etc. Responses like this, as well as my own timidity about broaching the subject, though possibly confirming my identity as an outsider, did not dissuade me, however, from the exploration of an exhilarating field.

The culmination of what I consider to have been an initial, exploratory phase in my study of tourism was the acceptance of an article "Tourism as an Anthropological Subject" in the prestigious *Current Anthropology* (1981). This article, which was first refereed and then subjected to rejoinders by a number of interested readers, gave me an opportunity to test my views against a broader spectrum or colleagues. In it, I established tourism as a transcultural, historically conditioned kind of leisure activity that involves the generation of tourists, their travel to or through various destinations, and their dealings with touristically involved people along the way. I also suggested lines of research over all of what I thought was best conceived as a social process or even social system. With few exceptions, the views I expressed in that article have persisted up to the present, an indication of which is given by the friendly arguments that Eric Cohen (an interlocutor for the article) and I continue to have over touristic fundamentals, as well as the broader subject of expatriates. On the whole, the response to this article has been gratifying from the beginning.

The publication of one of the first articles on tourism in a leading anthropological journal, may have had something to do with establishing the legitimacy of the subject in the discipline, but it really seemed to be taking a long time for the study of tourism in anthropology and other social scientific disciplines to get off the ground. An oft-noted mark of progress, publication in mainline disciplinary journals, which certainly increased, still was not especially noteworthy at the time. Lett's notion (1989) that there was an "explosion" of publications on tourism in that period seems to me to be an overstatement.

Looking back now on my exploratory phase in tourism study, I would say that I received all the support I needed for continuing my research; and the negative feedback there was did not dissuade me from continuing. I certainly was aware that what I was doing was not mainstream anthropological or sociological research; and the notion of its seminal importance never entered my mind; but such study contributed to the satisfaction I was finding in a career that included research on strangers of various kinds, wine producers in Burgundy (where I put to work the fruits of my association with America's oldest surviving vineyard), and religion. I continued to profit from anthropology, sociology, and neighboring social scientific disciplines in a rather free-wheeling and often invigorating investigation of tourism; and I tried to keep abreast of developments in relevant fields, which was aided by contacts with a wider and wider circle of colleagues.

Further Progress

From the vantage point of the present, it looks as though my subsequent intellectual career to formal retirement and beyond was established early on in my history as a tourism scholar. The fundamentals of my approach to tourism seem to have become well-established then, and further progress in such study was mostly a matter of making minor adjustments. There have been no major creative sallies (until possibly in this book), only a gradual evolution. All of this took place in a context of associations with institutions and like-minded colleagues, which was generally supportive of my work, and which may have taken on a special significance because I never married, and since the death of my mother in the early '80s, have had no relatives of any significance.

The first of these associations occurred during my ongoing visits with two psychiatrists, who though differing in their approach, provided real support for a growing autonomy. The last of these psychiatrists sometimes suggested that what we were doing was having an afternoon chat now and then; but it is hard to over-estimate the effect of those "chats," which sometimes plumbed emotional depths even while maintaining the general character of a conversation between adults—something of which is conveyed by a response of mine during our last session together. When informed by this psychiatrist that he had terminal cancer, I exploded with "What a crock!" After that, it was goodbye to psychiatry. I have not felt the need to return; but of course, there might be circumstances which could draw me back for a little chat, or even more.

The second significant association has been a continuing involvement of almost half a century with the University of Connecticut, where even after my formal retirement in 1991, I have taught a course in anthropological fieldwork and carried on research with the aid of infrastructural arrangements such as a hide-a-way study and a shared office in the Anthropology department, as well as informal contacts with friends and other working scholars. These arrangements, which are exemplary, make it possible for productive scholars to continue in residence, contribute directly to, and profit from the intellectual life of the university. There is little formal emphasis on tourism in the curriculum at UConn, and there are only one or two other faculty at all involved in such study; but the association I have managed to develop at and beyond this university seems to have provided more than enough stimulation and support to make up for the lack of specialization in tourism research at the university.

Third, the association with tourism scholars around the world, a testament of which has been the ease with which I have gathered together participating informants for this book, was aided by my becoming a Founding Member of the International Academy for the Study of Tourism (in 1988), a group of social scientific scholars organized by Jafar Jafari, that continues still. In this group, I have had an opportunity to associate with a multinational, multidisciplinary group of people whose interests in tourism have often surpassed my own. Relations within this group have not always been easy. Indeed, disagreements are not unusual, and emotions sometimes do boil over among us. Further, a few members have become disaffected with the intellectual orientation of the group and the lack of serious participation of some members. Business meetings are not much fun either.

But so far, we have managed to overcome what seem to be perennial problems. Now that I am an Emeritus member with fewer responsibilities and have acquired a somewhat more distant relationship to this group, I feel freer to pick and choose my involvements with the Academy, some of which have been truly rewarding. Besides the intellectual side, I have taken on the role of sommelier at the wine and cheese functions that mark the installation of new members at our biennial meetings. Though illness had prevented me from performing this role recently, I did manage to make it to our 2004 meeting in Savonlinna, Finland where Steve Smith (University of Waterloo) and I officiated.

A fourth association that has been important to my work in tourism came about with my accession in 1987 to the editorial board of *Annals of Tourism Research*, where I have had a coordinating editor's duty of reviewing submitted papers that coincide with my expertise. Besides helping me to keep abreast of the field, this job has sharpened up my editorial acumen, which as the editor-in-chief, Jafari, regularly reminds me, tends to be rather severe. In the beginning, he often responded to my outright rejections and refusal to send papers out to reviewers by reminding me that "We should be gate openers, not closers." My adaptation to this editorial position has included a good deal of fuming and fussing, as well as a decision to spend considerable time with some authors to get papers into reviewable shape, an alternative in which I have had mixed success. At the same time, the editor-in-chief has adapted by agreeing to limiting the papers I review in terms of my other obligations.

Of course, some of the papers I have received have gone out to reviewers immediately, and some are a pleasure to read again from time to time. I have also gotten into the habit of writing more than my share of critical "Rejoinders" to articles that seem to call out for them. All of this plus other reviewing, as well as comments from other editors, has raised questions in my mind about the general quality of tourism research and the competence of its authors. Recently (see, e.g., Nash 2000), I have indicated that though there has, indeed, been an expanding interest in the field of tourism study, the quality of research has not always kept pace with that expansion. There continue to be problems with fundamentals, some of which Graham Dann, Philip Pearce, and I (1988) addressed some time ago. People I talk to generally complain about the lack of theoretical underpinning, which is surprising considering the array of thinkers drawn on in our early days. The names of Leach, Eliade, Victor Turner, Levi-Strauss, Barthes, Gunder Frank, Said, Huizinga, Simmel, Schutz, Hobsbawn, Goffman, Veblen, Urbain, Marx, Weber, and Mauss are some of those who come to mind.

What of the methodological competence of such research, which Dann, Pearce, and I argued, should balance the theoretical contribution? Too often, in anthropology, for example, it has involved not very rigorous impressionistic, ethnographically oriented description of single cases, which do not provide the kind of foundation we need to build on. One had hopes that progress would come about as researchers jettisoned their value-laden baggage regarding the consequences of tourism; but a wave of new entries in the field suggest that that may not be the case. Consider, for example, Cultural Studies, from which emanates the distinctive smell of Marxism, to which I am so sensitive, as well as a tendency toward not very rigorous impressionistic observation and grand speculation. It may have something to teach us about approaching sociocultural phenomena (see, e.g., Storey 1996; Wade, ed. 1997) in an interpretivist mode. Unfortunately, its practitioners, it seems to me, have so far not done very much to add to our understanding of touristic phenomena. Nor, excepting some few outstanding examples, have the proponents of qualitative research generally (see, e.g., Phillimore and Goodson, eds. 2004), which is closely associated with the ethnographic method, produced anything so far to remind me of any error of my ways during an anthropological career that has included both qualitative and quantitative approaches as needed. It may have contributed to a developing reflexivity of self in methodological matters, however.

On the whole then, I do not feel that we tourism researchers have progressed very much in the fundamentals for studying our subject. A few theoretical "traditions" and accompanying terminology have made an appearance, but unfortunately these "traditions" often require clarification and lack adequate methodological support and follow-through in their application. An example is MacCannell's (1976) notion of an authenticity motive in Western tourism, which derives from his analysis of inauthenticity in Western culture. This hypothesis, which has been widely attended to over the years, has only slowly been clarified and has yet to be put to an adequate test (see his comments in this volume). Another example is the notion of commoditization of local culture as the result of Western-inspired touristic development, which is closely associated with the work of Davydd Greenwood (1989) on the transformation of a Basque festival. This study, which certainly illuminated an aspect of tourism's consequences and which, like MacCannell's work came to be very popular, has since been criticized by others, as well as its author in the second edition of *Hosts and Guests* (Smith, ed. 1989), which gave authors an opportunity to critically review their contribution in the first edition, written more than a decade earlier.

What has been my own orientation in the study of sociocultural phenomena? So far, it has been that of a scientific humanist who favors the recognition of personal agency in the consideration of human action, which I see as having mental, emotional, and behavioral aspects. That position, as developed in Chapter 4, has a good deal in common with the one put forth recently by Frederick Barth. My research attitude is basically empirical, but not naively so in that it insists that knowledge must be gotten from a real world by procedures that require continuous reflexive monitoring.

As far as tourism is concerned, my approach is built around a notion of a tourism field inhabited by various actors, including tourists, host personnel, travel agents, etc. This field is conceived as a probably universal acculturative process extending from the production of tourists through their various involvements to their accommodation and reception abroad, and ultimately to their return home. Research on any aspect of this process can be carried out from a variety of theoretical points of view and involve both quantitative or qualitative approaches, provided that the fundamentals of research, mentioned earlier, are observed. I am not one of those grand theoreticians, but lean toward theories that can be put to some empirical test, as in the critical work of Edward Bruner (see, e.g., 1994, 2005), Handler and Gable (1997), and Benita Howell (1994), all of whom have used ethnography in their studies of tourism. These authors emphasize social contestation in their studies, which doesn't always go down easily for a person with my functionalist background (see, e.g., Merton 1968), but which I now see as essential for viewing the problems involved.

Unlike these and other ethnographic studies of tourism, most of which have focussed on the reception or destination end of the touristic process, I have felt free from early on to attend to other of its aspects, in particular, the tourist generating situation. Such a change in orientation in studies of development was called for more than 30 years ago by Laura Nader who advocated that we move our attention from the powerless at the periphery to the powerful in Western metropolitan societies and begin to seriously "study up," an argument that seems also to apply to the study of tourism when conceived in acculturative or developmental terms (see Nash 2004). Though the application of ethnography in this area, of course, cannot easily be accomplished by social scientists, the potential for learning about the ultimate forces that drive tourism—say in the deliberations of boards of directors of some corporation engaged in tourism development—is inviting and has the potential to provide more adequate information about the production of tourism (certainly a key question in tourism research) than the so far few somewhat speculative investigations of tourism generating forces in Western societies making use of discourse analysis on advertisements. The example of Handler and Gable in their Williamsburg study, mentioned earlier, should encourage us to move forward in getting the necessary cooperation and prepare us for what would seem to be the inevitable difficulties involved.

It would seem that while I still have much to learn about anthropology and other social sciences, I have found something like a home in tourism studies and a good deal of freedom in seeking out and carrying through various approaches, which comes from being at a distance from disciplinary mainstreams, which as

I write this, have been significantly influenced by postmodernism. As with Marxism, I have been particularly sensitive to this development in anthropology and other social sciences and have struggled to situate myself while hoping that it would go away; and as with Marxism, it seems that even as postmodernism has become a part of our disciplinary landscapes, I have found myself, consciously or not, internalizing some of its postulates (which some of my friends in psychology might refer to as an "identification with the aggressor"). As an example of this development, I note that I have become something of what some people refer to as a critical realist, which often is associated with a (moderate) postmodern outlook. I recognize that I am not an omnipotent observer, but one who is moved by the same kinds of forces that move my subjects. However, I feel that when push comes to shove, I am capable of understanding a sociocultural phenomenon better than the people involved in it.

Keeping in touch with a number of substantive fields of study in anthropology, sociology, and related disciplines, I have also had an opportunity to explore a number of aspects of the tourism field from different points of view. It still appears to me to be a fruitful field of study, and I feel that we tourism researchers are fortunate to be involved in it. There now is something of a tradition in the social scientific study of the subject. Indeed, there have been several decades of serious inquiry by basic and applied researchers, a good deal of which can serve as a foundation for developing research, which looks promising from time to time. There are days though, when the latest issue of *Annals* doesn't offer me much to gnaw on, and I am less optimistic. It will be interesting to see how I locate myself in relation to the developments in our field after writing the concluding chapters of this book.

Michel Picard (1946–) is Chargé de Recherche de 1ère Classe at the French Centre National de Recherche Scientifique (CNRS), where he is Director of the Laboratoire Asie du Sud-Est et Monde Austronésien (LASEMA), CNRS - UPR 297 Centre A.G. Haudricourt, 7, Rue Guy-Môquet, Campus CNRS, B.P. 894801, Villejuif Cedex, France (e-mail: mpicard@vjf.cnrs.fr). His principal areas of interest have been in Indonesia, especially Bali, where, besides tourism, he has been concerned with a variety of aspects of Balinese culture within a context that extends to a global world. Besides many articles, he is the author of *Bali: Cultural Tourism and Touristic Culture* (1996), co-editor (with R. Wood) of *Tourism, Ethnicity, and the State in Asian and Pacific Societies* (1997), and co-editor (with J. Michaud) of *Tourisme et Sociétés Locales en Asie Orientale* (Picard and Michaud 2001).

FROM TURKEY TO BALI
Cultural Identity as Tourist Attraction

How Did I Come to be Involved in the Study of Tourism?

Besides the usual mix of deliberation and serendipity, my involvement in the study of tourism is the result of two intertwined developments in my personal history, intellectual as well as existential. One thread led me from the critique of economics to the anthropology of tourism, by means of the sociology of leisure. Another, seemingly unrelated one, brought me from an early attraction to the Orient to an involvement in Balinese studies by way of a discovery of culture.

As far as I can remember, I have always been a xenophile. But my first meaningful encounter with otherness happened in the summer of 1964, after I had graduated from college, when I drove through Turkey with a group of friends. Since then, I had been looking forward to going further East, with a view to discovering other ways of being human.

Meanwhile, the events of May 1968 in Paris had changed my world outlook rather drastically. I was studying economics, and at 22, I was neither interested in politics nor much inclined to intellectual endeavour. In retrospect, I can say that I experienced that period of turmoil as a revolt against economic rationality and the pretensions of its proponents to command life in society. Feverishly reading Marx and Althusser, as well as Debord and Baudrillard, I started apprehending economics as the ideology of modernity, and viewing *homo economicus* as a trivialized and serialized individual, alienated and reified.

Thanks to the intellectual effervescence of the day, I began to take an active interest in philosophy, history, sociology, and anthropology, which I started studying in earnest at the newly opened University of Vincennes, where so many of the most famous intellectual luminaries of the time were teaching—such as Foucault, Deleuze, Lyotard, and Bourdieu, to name but a few. Yet, all the while, I was painfully aware of a feeling of discrepancy, of a difficulty in fully identifying myself with the intellectual cum political milieu of which I had apparently become so much a part. If economics was clearly opposed to real life, I did not know yet where to look for it.

Not too keen to start on a professional career as an economist once I had graduated from university, in 1972 I went to join some friends in New York City. After several months of doing menial jobs, I hitch-hiked through the United States all the way to the West coast. The time I spent in communes along the way, enjoying a carefree life of hippy counterculture, managed to unsettle for good my Parisian leftist intellectual references.

A year later, my visa having expired, I returned to France. In need of money, I approached a friend from my student days, who had acquired an important position in one of the leading advertising agencies. Among various studies done as a freelance consultant, I was commissioned to write a report on the changing attitudes among French people towards leisure and tourism (Picard 1973). Acquainting myself with the literature on the subject, I fell upon Marie-Françoise Lanfant's book on "The Theories of Leisure" (1972), which was to have a decisive influence on my approach on several counts: her analysis struck a discordant chord on the rather uninspiring conventional views of the sociology of leisure; it challenged the idea of individual freedom convened by the ideology of leisure; and above all, it denounced the conceptual grip of economic rationality upon the theoretical apparatus of the sociology of leisure.

With some money in my pocket, I finally decided to embark upon a journey to Asia, which I had been dreaming of since I had had my first taste of Turkish exoticism, almost a decade previously. Nine months later, in April 1974, I found myself in Bali. The journey had been both exhilarating and disappointing. Looking for a more meaningful life, my wanderings had in fact boiled down to a series of repetitive cycles: departing, moving, feeling weary, stopping, resting, becoming bored, departing, and so on. My dominant impression of the countries I had gone through was that of a décor, the reality of which was not very firmly established in my eyes.

Bali happened to be another story, not only due to the exceptional appeal of this island and its people but also because it was the end of the road. Beyond its shores was the dreaded perspective, inescapable given the rapid exhaustion of my meager savings, to have to look for work in Australia. I kept putting off this perspective as long as I could manage to by hanging about, in Bali as well as in Java, which imbued these places with a more meaningful reality in my eyes. After having spent six months in Australia, working mostly as a scaffolder on a building site, I decided to go back to Indonesia.

During my second stay in Indonesia, I started taking a keen interest in traditional theater, Balinese and even more so, Javanese. Something happened then, quite unexpectedly, akin to a revelation, as if these theatrical traditions, of which I knew nothing and which were completely alien to me, had become a personal concern of mine. In retrospect, I realized that through my encounter with these traditional cultural expressions, I had eventually found the missing term of the relation which had led me to rise against economics. Culture was indeed the locus of real life that I had been looking for all these years; and it had to be defended against the ever expanding encroachment of economic rationality.

Back in Paris in 1975 after two years spent in the East, I felt rather disorientated. Not really knowing what to do, I went back to the academic fold and registered in post-graduate studies in anthropology with the idea of doing research on Javanese theater. With this purpose in mind, and after having acquired a working knowledge of the Indonesian language, I returned for three months to Java and Bali the following year and wrote a paper on one of the most popular forms of Javanese theater, the *Wayang Wong*. It was only then that I began wondering about the fate of traditional cultural performances once they started being staged specifically for tourist audiences. The fact is that until then I had tended to perceive these performances as an immutable tradition, assuming implicitly that they had always been there and would always remain so, as if only waiting for me to take notice of them.

As I was getting more concerned with the predicament of Javanese and Balinese traditional theater and the likely consequences of their staging as a tourist attraction, I was contacted by a former friend of mine, who was in charge of prospective studies at the French Department of Tourism. He had found my earlier report interesting and asked me to write another one on the demand for leisure and tourism (Picard 1976). On that occasion, I decided to approach Marie-Françoise Lanfant, who shortly afterward invited me to join the research team that she was establishing within the French National Centre of Scientific Research (CNRS)—the "Unité de Recherche en Sociologie du Tourisme International" (URESTI).

Surrounded by a group of young and enthusiastic sociologists, M.-F. Lanfant was then busy designing a conceptual and methodological scheme capable of comprehending tourism in the "process of internationalization" (Lanfant 1980). However, there had been a slight *malentendu* from the start, as she had hired me because of my qualification as an economist. In fact, I was determined to engage in more sociologically oriented pursuits. Be that as it may, under the stimulating intellectual leadership of M.-F. Lanfant, I was able to carry through my own critical analysis of the sociology of leisure by investigating its conceptual borrowings from the neo-classical school of economics. My point was that the advent of the sociology of leisure, which was claiming that there is something akin to a free choice when individuals behave in conformity with the normative model of *homo economicus*, reveals the grip of economic rationality upon the activities filling so-called "free time" (Picard 1980).

How Did I Go about Studying Tourism?

Until then, my dealings with tourism had been under the heading of leisure, as if tourism was but a leisure occupation among others. But working with M.-F. Lanfant convinced me that there was much more to tourism than what was commonly thought at the time. Rather than being an activity to be studied in order to improve its consequences, be they for the tourists themselves or for their hosts, tourism appeared to me as a phenomenon which gives insight into the relationship people have with their own society as well as with societies other than their own. With tourism, we are not only faced with people travelling in search of otherness, but with a reframing of nature, history, and tradition, which is progressively reshaping cultural identities.

Accordingly, instead of considering tourism as a circumscribed field, noticeable by the presence of tourists and the amenities designed to accommodate them, one should approach it as a "total social fact"—to borrow Mauss's felicitous concept—touching all levels of society, spreading to all areas of the world, and establishing between them new social ties. In that perspective, far from being an object empirically given in experience, which would be present immediately in the intelligibility of its manifestations, tourism required the construction of a methodology based on a corpus of hypotheses grounded in a system of concepts. This perspective required that it would no longer be possible to dissociate the study of tourism developments from the institutional as well as scientific conditions of such a study. Specifically, researchers had to reflect on their own relationship to their object of study.

Besides being based on these epistemological elaborations, the way I approached tourism was closely linked to my initial perception of this social phenomenon, which in turn resulted from the twofold development previously mentioned. The first thread led me to view tourism, in a Marxian fashion, as an extension of monetary value to various domains that had until then remained out of its reach—heritage, customs, ceremonies, landscape, local colour, and so forth—in short, as a generalized commoditization (Greenwood 1977, 1989). As for the second thread, in line with Debord and Baudrillard, it brought me to see in tourism an expansion of simulacrum and a staging of authenticity (MacCannell 1976), bordering on falsification—in brief, as a generalized spectacularization.

I was going to test these assumptions within the framework of a comparative research launched by the URESTI on the local implications of international tourism. Bali appeared then to me as the most appropriate locus of observation, and I went back to conduct research on the island in 1978–1979 (Lanfant, Picard and De Weerdt 1982). Stimulated by the results of my initial investigations, I determined to pursue my fieldwork in 1980–1982, with the idea of using my findings to write a doctoral dissertation (Picard 1984). Meanwhile, I had the good fortune of being admitted as a fully-fledged *Chargé de Recherche* at the prestigious CNRS.

Today, one has to make an effort to remember that it was far from obvious in the 1970s to study the local implications of international tourism; and my intention to go to Bali in order to elucidate what happens to a society that turns its cultural identity into a tourist attraction gave rise to a number of misunderstandings. For the direction of the CNRS, tourism was certainly not (yet) an anthropological—nor even a sociological—subject, and it was out of the question that a researcher could go and bask on a tropical beach at the expense of this venerable institution. As for my fellow countrymen, it was clear that my purpose could only be of interest to the tourist industry, or else if need be, to the French government. In short, there was very little evidence of any academic interest in my project.

Such a lack of interest was not really surprising, given the shortcomings of most studies that dealt then with the local implications of international tourism. In my opinion, the problem with these studies, other than the inadequacy of their conceptual framework (on which more below), was twofold: either they were a by-product of research conducted by anthropologists interested in other topics, or they were the work of tourism specialists who had only a superficial knowledge of the society in which they were doing research. This is the reason why I decided early on to acquire a serious knowledge of Balinese society, which explains both the length of my fieldwork and my longtime involvement in Indonesian studies. This in turn allowed me to take a diachronic view of the development of tourism in Bali, as I have been doing by going back to the island every year since completion of my fieldwork in 1982.

Once in the field, my initial idea had been to adopt the localized approach favoured by most anthropologists. It was indeed tempting to merge into the Balinese milieu, if only in order to distance myself from the tourists and thus avoid incurring the risk of being taken for one of them. But that attempt turned out to be ineffective, as I realized that the Balinese looked upon me as a tourist studying tourism. Besides, the misapprehension I had encountered back in Paris did not vanish once I set foot on Bali. Indeed, my interlocutors there seemed to be mainly concerned to enlist my expertise in the service of the tourist promotion of their island. Thus, after having attempted in vain to explain what I intended to do, I decided to keep a low profile, and whenever asked, simply declared that I was studying "Balinese culture", which appeared to be good enough for my local informants.

In any case, after having considered conducting a comparative ethnographic study in two villages, Kuta and Ubud, undergoing markedly different tourism development, I chose instead a macro-sociological approach that addressed the whole island of Bali as the relevant level of analysis for my research. This stance, I have to admit, did not fail to bring criticism on the part of some fellow anthropologists, who thought that my research was insufficiently grounded on ethnographic evidence. But I had not embarked on such study without having equipped myself with substantial conceptual tools beforehand. Indeed, my first study of tourism with my colleagues of the URESTI had consisted in an epistemological elucidation of the way researchers from various disciplinary backgrounds in the social sciences approach the issues involved in the opening up of a society to international tourism.

The Problematic of the Social and Cultural Impacts of Tourism

As is by now well known, concern about the impacts of tourism arose rather belatedly. In the 1960s, international tourism was generally recognized as particularly useful in the economic development of Third World countries that were well-endowed with natural or cultural resources. During the 1970s, however, the doctrine of development through tourism came under critical fire, when it was found that economic benefits expected from tourism development projects had been overestimated and that their related costs had not been taken into account. Far from being a factor of development, international tourism was, to the contrary, considered by some observers to be a transfer of the riches from countries receiving tourists toward those generating them—a form of imperialism perpetuating the dependence of the Third World on the developed countries (Nash 1977, 1989). At the same time, the idea that tourism would help conserve cultural heritages by inscribing them into the economic market was challenged by a number of authors, who denounced the damage wrought by the commercialization of indigenous cultural traditions converted into tourist attractions (Turner and Ash 1975).

This critical reassessment was to find its official consecration in 1976, with the holding of a "Seminar on the Social and Cultural Impacts of Tourism," jointly convened by the World Bank and UNESCO in Washington (DeKadt, ed. 1979). Given the significance of this seminar, the URESTI conducted an analysis of its proceedings on behalf of UNESCO (Picard 1979). Our analysis revealed that the very terms of the debate implied an implicit representation of the way societies are thought to be affected by their opening up to international tourism. Indeed, the mere fact of talking about the "impact" of tourism entailed something of a ballistic vision, that led to perceiving the so-called host society as a target struck by a projectile, like an inert object passively subjected to external factors of change, which experts were expected to assess by means of a cost–benefit analysis, involving some sort of trade-off between cultural and economic values.

This way of tackling the problem appeared to be structurally determined by a recurrent set of oppositions: on the one hand, an opposition between local societies and international tourism expressed in terms of "inside" and "outside"; and on the other hand, an opposition between "cultural" and "economic" values. The resolution of these oppositions rested on the capacity of tourism to open the inside toward the outside, by helping transmute cultural values into economic values. Consequently, if it was indeed necessary to challenge the problematic of impact, it was because by dissociating tourism from society, it did not permit an understanding of the process in which a society becomes a tourist product.

Cultural Tourism

At the same time as it was stressing the social and cultural costs of tourism, the problematic of impact led to the quest for a kind of tourism whose benefits would override its costs. This beneficial tourism was the so-called cultural tourism, which promotes the cultural identity of a local population as a tourist attraction. In the opinion of its proponents, cultural tourism, far from degrading indigenous cultures, would contribute to safeguarding them to the very extent that it benefits from it. Looking over the literature on the social and cultural impacts of tourism, I noticed that Bali was depicted as a model example of cultural tourism. Indeed, for most observers, this island appeared as a destination where tourism had contributed to the preservation and regeneration of the traditional cultural heritage. Nonetheless, in spite of these favorable views, there was no lack of authors who cited Bali among the destinations where tourism had corrupted the indigenous culture. For me, these contradictory statements were sufficient to challenge as misleading the very question they addressed. And indeed, even though the answers differed, the question remained the same. Hampered by a normative approach and wondering whether tourism was beneficial or detrimental to a culture, one was forced to ask when Balinese culture could withstand the impact of tourism.

Consequently, instead of trying in my turn to assess whether or not Balinese culture had proved to be capable of withstanding the impact of tourism, I set about investigating how tourism has contributed to the advent of the very notion of a "Balinese culture" (*kebudayaan Bali*). In doing so, I was not so much concerned with what has been described—by anthropologists and travel writers alike—as the culture of the Balinese people, as with the dialogical fashion in which a certain touristic image of their culture came to be used by the Balinese themselves as an identity marker.

In order to conduct my research, I put into perspective the presentation of their culture that the Balinese offer to tourists and the representation of their culture that they make to themselves when they speak of tourism. Specifically, I examined how some Balinese "cultural performances," first among them their famous dances, were turned into tourist attractions, while simultaneously analyzing the discourses held by the Balinese authorities on "cultural tourism."

Following Foucault and Bourdieu, as I understand it, a discourse is both a body of cultural assumptions about reality and a set of social practices that establish and maintain that reality. Accordingly, those whom I call the Balinese authorities are not limited to the personnel of the Indonesian state apparatus on the island, but include those among the Balinese authorized to speak in the name of their society and who are thus in a position to monopolize legitimate discourse about Bali. These opinion-leaders are the actively culture-producing people who formulate, propagate and explain contemporary issues and emerging ideas to the rest of the population. So it is to the members of this local intelligentsia that I refer here when I speak of "the Balinese" without further qualification.

Cultural Tourism in Bali   While the island of Bali has been famed as a tourist destination since the 1920s, it was only in the early 1970s that tourists started landing on its shores in significant numbers. This was the result of a decision taken in 1969 by the Indonesian government to open up the country to international tourism. Banking on Bali's prestigious image as a tourist paradise, the government decided to make this island the showcase of Indonesia. Between 1970 and 1980, the number of foreign visitors to Bali multiplied from fewer than 30,000 to around 300,000 a year, while hotel capacity increased from less than 500 to about 4000 rooms.

From the start, the Balinese authorities had an ambivalent attitude toward tourism, which they perceived as being both fraught with danger and rich in the promise of prosperity. On the one hand, the artistic and religious traditions that had made Bali famous worldwide provided its main attraction in the eyes of tourists, thus turning Balinese culture into the most valuable asset for the island's economic development. But on the other hand, the invasion of Bali by foreign visitors was seen as a threat of "cultural pollution." To prevent such a fatal outcome, the Balinese authorities devised a policy of "cultural tourism" (*pariwisata budaya*), which was intended to develop tourism (without debasing Balinese culture) by using culture to attract tourists and tourism revenue to promote it.

By thus attributing the success of their island as a tourist destination to the alluring attraction of its cultural manifestations, the Balinese were led to link the fate of their culture to that of tourism. Not content with offering their visitors contrived attractions staged only for their benefit, they invited them to participate in "authentic" cultural performances. These performances were festivities and celebrations of all sorts, such as temple festivals, rites of passage, processions and cremations, that provided occasions for those exotic pageants for which their island was renowned.

But cultural tourism was not only a way of responding to the expectations of tourists in quest of authentic cultural manifestations, it was also, above all, a means of protecting Balinese cultural integrity. Hence the necessity of deciding to what extent Balinese culture may be put to the service of tourism, by issuing directives permitting the local people to know what they are authorized to sell to tourists and what must not under any circumstances be commercialized. In cases where they were unable to differentiate between what they did for themselves and what they did to please their visitors, the Balinese people incurred the risk of no longer being able to distinguish between their own values and those propagated by the tourists. And if this were the case, Balinese culture would become a "touristic culture" (*budaya pariwisata*)—defined as a state of axiological confusion between that which pertains to tourism and that which belongs to culture.

This concern for discrimination was never so pressing than when faced with a threat of "profanation." In this respect, the subject most bitterly debated, which caused the greatest confusion and raised the thorniest problems, was the performance of "sacred" dances for tourists. Indeed, these celebrated dances that have done so much for Bali's fame are not only a spectacle to be enjoyed, but also a ritual to be enacted. As long as their dances were being performed in their traditional contexts, the Balinese had no need to ask themselves where ritual ended and where spectacle began. But the arrival of the tourists, by confronting them with an unprecedented situation of having to interpret their culture before a foreign audience, would compel them to mark a boundary between that which belongs to religion and that which pertains to art. These two dimensions were to prove difficult to differentiate for the Balinese, as testified by their inability to dissociate "sacred" from "profane" dances (Picard 1990).

Cultural Tourism and Touristic Culture

When I arrived in Bali to conduct my fieldwork in 1978, the attitude of the Balinese authorities was undergoing a striking change. The fears initially aroused by the coming of tourists were giving way to expressions of undisguised complaisance. Accused earlier of being a vehicle of "cultural pollution," tourism was now extolled as a factor of "cultural renaissance." According to the Balinese authorities, the money brought in by tourists had stimulated the interest of the Balinese for their cultural traditions, while the admiration of foreigners for their culture had reinforced their sense of identity and their pride in being Balinese. So much so that by becoming the patron of Balinese culture, tourism—to the extent that it had turned culture into a source of both profit and prestige—was said to have contributed to its preservation, and even revival.

In the change from the threat of a "cultural pollution" to the claim of a "cultural renaissance," the meaning of Balinese culture had undergone a revealing shift. When tourism was accused of corrupting Balinese culture, what was at stake was the desacralization of temples, the profanation of religious ceremonies, the monetization of social relations, the weakening of communal ties, or else the relaxing of moral standards and the rise of mercantile attitudes. From then on, the issue was about what could be presented and marketed to the tourists, in which culture was treated as artistic. From being lived through as a process, culture was being designed as a product.

In order to understand how the initial conflict of interests between culture and tourism had been defused by the doctrine of cultural tourism, I conducted an analysis of Balinese discourse involving representations of the relationship between the signifiers "tourism" and "culture." Inspired by a stucturalist approach in both anthropology and linguistics, which was still holding strong in French academia in those years, this analysis led me to conclude that what the Balinese authorities were celebrating as a "cultural renaissance" was simply the logical outcome of what they formerly denounced as a "touristic culture." By becoming Bali's brand image, that is, something which distinguishes its tourist product in a highly competitive international market, culture had become an identity marker for the Balinese, which was used to define and recognize themselves.

It seemed to me that one could speak of a touristic culture once the Balinese came to confuse the two uses of the term, when that by which the tourists identified them became that by which they identified themselves, that is, when the imperatives of the touristic promotion of their culture informed the considerations that motivated their will to preserve it; in which case the Balinese ended up taking the brand image of their tourist product for the marker of their cultural identity.

The Process of Touristification

By the beginning of the 1980s, sociologists and anthropologists alike had started challenging the problematic of the impact of tourism. They rejected both the conception of international tourism as an external factor of change and the assessment of its local implications in terms of costs and benefits (see, e.g., Cohen 1979a; Nash 1981; Thurot 1981). Actively involved in these debates, URESTI organized an international seminar in Marly-le-Roi in 1986, bringing field researchers together to take a fresh look at the issues raised a decade earlier by the "Seminar on the Social and Cultural Impacts of Tourism."

The outcome of our debates confirmed that the dichotomy between the "inside" and the "outside" remained the major obstacle in understanding the local implications of international tourism. This meant that one ought to push critical assessment further so as to break out of the harness of the dominant frame of observation and the conceptual scheme on which it is based. It is only then that one would be able to apprehend tourism and society in the same process. And in order to do this, rather than speaking of tourism and its impacts on a receiving milieu, I deemed it preferable to speak henceforth of "touristification" to designate the process through which a society becomes a tourist product.

This conceptual recasting was fully endorsed by my experience in the field. I was able to test both the grip of the problematic of impact on the local actors and their resulting inability to confront its consequences. Perceiving tourism as a threat coming from beyond their shores, the Balinese authorities attempted to set up protective barriers against the foreign invasion in order to put their most "sacred" values out of reach of the threat of such touristic "profanation." This attempt failed, as may be seen in the manifest inability of the Balinese to maintain a boundary between their religious ceremonies and the commercial performances derived from them, that is, to keep what belongs to culture separate from what belongs to tourism. In hindsight, one could say that the Balinese attempt was doomed to fail, for it was based on a illusory vision of their culture as insulated, precisely bounded, and clearly identifiable.

Thus, following the example of tourists and the discourse of international tourism promotion, one notices that the touristified peoples have borrowed from anthropologists an ontological vision of culture, conceived as a substance with precisely defined characteristics, even as this view began to change in the development of a constructivist approach (Bruner 1996; Wood 1993). The analysis of the Balinese strategy and the reasons for its failure allowed me to understand that far from being an external force striking a society from without, the touristification of a society proceeds from within by blurring the boundaries between the inside and the outside, between what is "ours" and what is "theirs," between that which belongs to culture and that which pertains to tourism. This implies that tourism cannot be conceived of outside culture and is inevitably bound up in an ongoing process of cultural construction.

Balinese Identity and the Challenge of Tourism

In the late 1980s, the development of tourism on Bali shifted into high gear, with a sharp upsurge in visitor arrivals that was associated with an even more rapid rise in hotel investment and other tourism-related facilities. The number of foreign visitors reached about 1 million in 1990 and was hovering around 2 million for 2000—this, without taking into account Indonesian tourists, for whom estimates diverge widely. During the same period, hotel capacity jumped to 20,000 in 1990 and up to over 40,000 rooms in 2000.

While tourism has boosted the economic growth of Bali, the uneven distribution of economic benefits within the population and throughout the island, as well as the growing encroachment of foreign interests, had become a matter of serious concern. At the same time, the physical environment was becoming inexorably degraded as the rice fields and beaches were covered with concrete, and the anarchic proliferation of hotels and souvenir shops ravaged the beauty of the landscape for which Bali was once renowned.

The fact is that the Balinese were beginning to worry about the future of tourism on their island. And indeed, there was a widening gap between what the tourists were supposedly seeking in Bali—unspoiled landscapes and an authentic culture—and that which they actually found there. Hence the insistant rumour that Bali was becoming too touristic; and in an attempt to restore an already tattered authenticity, influential spokespersons for Balinese tourism then came to propose that certain villages, considered to be especially picturesque, should be conserved in their traditional state for the tourists. With this initiative, one was witnessing yet another reversal in the relationship between tourism and culture. Formerly, the Balinese had perceived their culture as a living tradition that ran the risk of being corrupted by tourist commercialization. Now, however, tourism was called on to "revitalize" a traditional culture threatened by the homogenizing perils of modernity. The Balinese authorities' change of attitude toward sacred dances is significant in this regard. Whereas not long ago, the concern was to prevent their profanation by restricting their performance to ritual use only, it had become a matter of saving them from obsolescence by tapping them to inspire new dances that in turn could regenerate tourist performances.

Such a reversal met with some criticism on the island. Thus, one would find recurrent allusions in the local press accusing the Balinese of holding ever more spectacular ceremonies with the intention of impressing the tourists rather than pleasing the gods. But there were more radical accusations such as the debate that stirred up the Balinese intelligentsia in 1989, following the publication in the main newspaper on the island of an article entitled "The Balinese are losing their Balineseness" (*Kebalian*). The author accused his fellow countrymen of being intoxicated with the prestige of their touristic reputation abroad and unaware that the authenticity of their cultural identity was being seriously compromised. A survey among the newspaper's readers was taken on this occasion, showing that while 40 percent of the persons interviewed attributed the erosion of "Balineseness" to the influence of tourists, there were 60 percent who thought that to the contrary, the increasing number of tourist arrivals in Bali was the best proof of the enduring cultural authenticity of the island.

Thus, called upon to conform to their image, the Balinese not only were required to be Balinese, but they had to be worthy representatives of "Balineseness"—they must become signs of themselves; and for all their attempts to assert their identity, they were continually reacting to this injunction, from which they are unable to extricate themselves. They have appropriated the touristic vision of their culture while at the same time trying to prise themselves free of its grip. Such is the challenge of tourism for the Balinese. They have been enjoined to preserve and promote their cultural identity as the outside world sees them, which is to say that the Balinese have come to search for confirmation of their "Balineseness" in the mirror held up to them by the tourists (Picard 1996).

The Dialogic Construction of a Balinese Identity

At the end of my study, it was clear that tourism had neither "polluted" Balinese culture nor promoted its "renaissance," but simply contributed to its "preservation"—to use terms employed in the debates involved. What happened is that their focus on "cultural" tourism had rendered the Balinese self-conscious about the thing they possess called culture. It was as if the interests of the tourists, as well as the money at stake with their arrival, had convinced the Balinese that they "have a culture," which was taken to mean something precious and perishable that is at once a heritage to be protected and capital to be exploited for a profit. And so it is that their culture became reified and externalized in their own eyes, turning into an object that could be detached from themselves in order to be displayed and marketed for others, and also something of which they could be dispossessed.

As it was being manipulated and appropriated by the tourism industry, their culture became not only a source of profit and pride, but also a cause of anxiety for the Balinese, who started wondering whether they were still authentically Balinese. Thus, the touristic emphasis on culture provoked an overriding concern about their identity. This is the issue I decided to tackle, by shifting the focus of my investigation from the challenge of tourism to the role of tourism in its construction of Balinese identity. The issue of identity has become pervasive in discourses on tourism during the 1990s (Lanfant, Allcock and Bruner 1995), as the paradigm of "globalization"—with its corollary, "localization"—tended to establish itself in academic parlance. This paradigm now informs both Balinese and tourism studies alike. And in this respect, it appears that the authors who address international tourism as an agent of globalization for local societies are prone to taking a view that is opposite to the problematic of impact. Far from viewing the host society as a powerless victim of tourism, they stress the ability of the local people in tourist destinations to localize global processes by appropriating tourism and turning it to their own advantage.

Such a view has been gaining ground in Bali where, along with the rise of an affluent native middle class, a new generation of public intellectuals has emerged. Mediating between the global and the local, and well informed about current intellectual trends, they confidently discuss matters with foreign specialists, even to the point of challenging their conclusions. I found myself involved in these discussions because my views on the touristification of Balinese culture have become a hotly debated issue among the Balinese intelligentsia. So much so, that it is now difficult for me to proceed to the analysis of the Balinese discourse the way I had been able to do it in the 1970s (as if over the shoulder of their authors without them knowing it).

These Balinese intellectuals appear to have a better grasp of what is happening on their island. In particular, they have come to understand that tourism is not an exogenous phenomenon striking Bali from abroad, but that it has become an integral part of their own society. And even if some of them persist in denouncing tourism for the degradation of their culture and the erosion of their identity, there are many who claim, on the contrary, that the Balinese people have been able to take advantage of tourism in strengthening their "Balineseness." According to these authors, the touristification of their island has led the Balinese to reflect on their identity and assert it in a movement which they call "Balinization" (*Balinisasi*). This movement has gained momentum since the downfall of President Suharto and the demise of the régime in 1998, which thawed the political situation while releasing centrifugal forces in the regions. Denouncing the plundering of their natural and cultural resources by foreign capital and Jakarta's elite, the Balinese authorities claimed the prerogative of promoting their own views on a tourism policy that was appropriate for their island and beneficial to its population. At the same time, the growing presence of Javanese Muslim migrant workers, attracted by job opportunities offered by tourism, has triggered social, ethnic, and religious strife on Bali, the population of which is becoming more and more heterogeneous. So it appears that, in this period of instability, the affirmation of Balinese identity has led to political claims—the more so since the hotel bombing of November 12, 2002, which cost the lives of 202 people, not to mention the collapse of an economy based on tourism, and other social crises.

If tourism is indeed part and parcel of the so-called Balinization movement, it is not its only, nor probably even its main factor, in the sense that the promotion of tourism may serve as an inspiration for initiatives with very different goals. And as I was beginning to contextualize the part taken by tourism in the contemporary transformation of Bali, it dawned upon me that I had embarked on the study, with the implicit assumption of Balinese cultural identity, instead of seeing it as an ongoing process of identification that was relational, politically contested, and historically constructed. By the same token, I had tended to assume that what defined the Balinese to outsiders was more important than what divided them internally. Consequently, I needed not only to reconstruct the process of ethnogenesis, in which the Balinese have come to view themselves as a people sharing a common identity, but also to investigate the significant internal cleavages among them.

Meanwhile, intellectual trends had undergone a significant shift, and I found myself influenced less by structuralism and more by so-called poststructuralism, not to mention "postmodernism" and "postcolonialism." Thus, while becoming acquainted with the interpretive anthropology of Geertz and Sahlins, I looked for theoretical references less to Althusser or Lévi-Strauss, and more to Hobsbawm ("invented traditions") and Anderson ("imagined communities"), Appadurai ("public culture") and Clifford ("traveling cultures"), Hannerz ("global ecumene"), and Robertson ("glocalization").

As I was taking a constructionist-cum-interactionist perspective on culture and identity, I started to realize that the Balinese concern with their identity did not date from the coming en masse of tourists during the 1970s. In fact, it went back to the military conquest of their island at the beginning of the twentieth century and to its subsequent incorporation within the colonial empire of the Dutch East Indies. And it was revived after the independence of Indonesia, when the Balinese had become citizens of the new nationstate.

So I was led, by the very logic of the issues I was pursuing, to enter further into the study of Balinese society, all the while widening my field of investigation to the multiethnic national ensemble of which Bali is but a part. And with the purpose of carrying this research through, it appeared more appropriate to join a pluridisciplinary team composed of Indonesianists. It is with this intention that in 1991 I became a member of the "Laboratoire Asie du Sud-Est et Monde Austronésien" (LASEMA) at the CNRS. My decision was not always understood by colleagues involved in the study of tourism—and certainly not by M.-F. Lanfant, who had done so much to convince me of the importance of tourism for the study of identity. She found it rather surprising that after having been a party to the pioneering work conducted in the 1970s, I would distance myself from tourism precisely at the time when this social fact was finally becoming acknowledged by the academic milieu as a respectable field of research.

As a matter of fact, I was not so much distancing myself from tourism research as approaching tourism from a different perspective. Whereas I had started studying tourism as a challenging contemporary social phenomenon, and then had chosen the island of Bali as an appropriate research site for a case study of the local implications of international tourism, I was now firmly locating myself in Bali and considering the part played by tourism in the construction of a Balinese identity.

In 1994, I took the opportunity of the 13th World Congress of Sociology, held by the International Sociological Association in Bielefeld, to convene a session entitled "Tourism, the State, and Ethnicity" under the auspices of the Research Committee on International Tourism. Following the congress, I co-edited with the American sociologist Robert Wood a volume of essays dealing with the interplay between international tourism, state policies, and ethnic identities in Asian and Pacific societies (Picard and Wood 1997). We wanted to investigate how, in such multiethnic societies where the promotion of tourism focuses explicitly on ethnic minorities, the development of tourism interferes with the already complex task of reconciling nationhood and ethnicity. While on the one hand, tourism presents a rationale for increased state intervention in cultural practices; on the other hand, it provides new leverage for certain ethnic groups to use the state to further their own ends.

My own contribution in that volume has suggested that tourism development—specifically cultural tourism—has supported the Indonesian state's attempt to domesticate ethnic identities by enlisting them in the process of nation-building: first, by confining the realm of ethnic culture to artistic display and, second, by turning the archipelago's ethnic cultures into so-called regional cultures. With a view to building an Indonesian national culture, the government has been aiming to induce in each of the country's provinces a distinctive homogeneous provincial identity, grounded on a single set of unique cultural features, at the expense of the diverse ethnic cultures enclosed within their boundaries. As a regional culture among others, "Balinese culture" was thus placed in a similar position with respect to both tourism and Indonesia, that is, as a resource whose function is to contribute to the development of international tourism in Indonesia as well as to the fostering of the Indonesian national culture. For this to be feasible, though, Balinese culture had first to be divested of its anthropological singularity, in order to become commensurable to the other regional cultures of Indonesia, as well as to the other tourist destinations with which it competes (Picard 1997).

Subsequently, in order to better understand how the Balinese have come to conceive their cultural identity, I engaged with their own reflexive thinking. Specifically, I set about reconstructing their ethnogenesis by investigating the transcultural dialogues they have been engaged in with their different interlocutors, in a context defined by the growing integration of their island within the overlapping networks of the international tourism industry, the state apparatus, colonial as well as postcolonial, and with tourists, artists, and all those who had contributed to the formation of Bali's image.

While this was rendering the Balinese conscious of their "Balineseness," such a confrontation with significant others impelled them to formulate what it meant to be Balinese in terms comprehensible to non-Balinese. Thus, the same process that prompted the Balinese to question their identity by thinking in foreign categories, dispossessed them of their own voice. Consequently, far from expressing a primordial essence, as they would have it, the Balinese conception of their "Balineseness" proved to be the outcome of a process of semantic borrowing and conceptual recasting that they have had to make in response to the colonization, the Indonesianization, as well as the touristification of their island (Picard 2002).

In retrospect, it seems to me that by shifting the focus of my investigation from the challenge of tourism to the Balinese identity to the role of tourism in the construction of a Balinese identity—thus by conducting a research at once diachronic, contextual, and emic—I put myself in a better position to elucidate the set of constraints, within which tourism is being used by local actors to further their own position in ongoing cultural politics. This is because tourism is inextricably bound up with prevalent processes of change—global, national, and local—to such an extent that I have come to think that it is the complex ways tourism enters and becomes implicated in these other processes that has to engage the researcher's focus, rather than any illusory belief that its so-called impacts could be isolated and identified.

Valene Smith (1926–) is Emeritus Professor of Anthropology, Department of Anthropology, California State University, Chico CA. 05020-0400 (e-mail: csuchico.edu) where she has taught courses in anthropology and tourism. She is also a frequent and far-flung traveler and an organizer of colloquia involving applied aspects of tourism study, in which she is deeply involved. Her publications include articles on many aspects of tourism as well as editorships of *Hosts and Guests: The Anthropology of Tourism* (first and second Editions, 1977 and 1989) and (with Maryann Brent) *Hosts and Guests Revisited: Tourism Issues of the 21ˢᵗ Century* (2001). She is a founding member of the International Academy for the Study of Tourism and currently an editor of a series of books on tourism dynamics.

STUDYING TOURISM? 1974 AND BEYOND!

Travel has unquestionably contributed more to human knowledge of our planet than any other single activity. Travel is a form of migration, and decisions to settle depend on understanding a resource base and its ability to support a resident population. Human groups were moving across formidable physical frontiers and sharing information long before writing appeared. They also studied the planets, recognized their cyclical patterns and devised thoughtful explanations. They learned to use celestial navigation to chart their courses across oceans and deserts. They also developed that knowledge to create sun calendars that were helpful in agriculture, in world areas as diverse as the American Southwest and in Hunza, in the Himalayas.

As universities were founded and the academic traditions established, scholars organized their data into bodies of related information, or scientific disciplines. Discoveries led to mapping, and geography and recorded legends became history. The art of careful comparative observations helped spawn biology, botany, and anthropology—all of which have a base in astute observation and travel. It was also travel that stimulated the inquiring minds of Alfred Russell Wallace and Charles Darwin. Their parallel interests in evolutionary theory took place in different milieux, but both were meticulous observers. Their awareness of changing phenomena and their delay in publication of their research have analogies with the founding of tourism as a subject of scholarly interest. Both Wallace and Darwin, were aware that colleagues, as well as the public, would be skeptical of their research. They stood alone without much literature to cite.

The Founding of Tourism as a Subject of Study

In 1965 when I was a new doctoral candidate at the University of Utah, I proposed a dissertation topic that involved study of the effects of tourism on the Eskimo culture of Kotzebue, Alaska (NB. Eskimo became Inuit in 1971 under the Alaska Native Claims Settlement Act). I had already traveled widely on six continents and recognized the consequences of tourism for culture change over much of the Western world. It seemed to me that this was an appropriate topic for anthropologists to investigate. I had 1950 and 1963 data from Kotzebue, with which to initiate formal fieldwork. My PhD committee listened politely but refused to accept my proposal because, in their words, "there is no literature to cite." But they suggested that with degree in hand, I might wish to pursue this idea independently.

There was so much to consider, and I delayed for nine years before getting down to work. Behind my back, campus colleagues were snickering, for surely I was less a scholar than they, who were involved in the currently correct topics of the day—women, homelessness, and drugs, for example. Finally, with the assurance of a degree and tenure in hand, in 1974 I inserted a notice in the Newsletter of the American Anthropological Association, which asked in essence, " Is anyone else interested in the study of tourism?" The rest is history. I personally lay no claim to any exceptional role in the events that followed, other than the initiative to call for research papers and organize a first tourism symposium.

Within days after publication of the notice, there were 28 replies, followed by immediate phone calls to determine how many respondents could attend the forthcoming AAA meetings in Mexico City where their papers would be presented. In those days, we could not depend on such things as e-mail or FAX, so there was quite a rush with airmail and special delivery letters to get in abstracts and fees. We barely met submission deadlines, but with a favorable response from the referees, our proposal for this new topic was accepted!

Mexico City 1974—AAA Meeting

The Meeting took place at the Maria Isabel Sheraton Hotel in the Embassy district of Mexico City. The assigned room for our presentations was a small auditorium with tiered seats. Attendance varied by presenter, but the audience averaged 50 to 75; and because of the Mexican venue, it included a good Hispanic representation. The papers continued through the day, but by early afternoon, we began to sense that this would be no ordinary occasion. My husband Ed Golay had anticipated our needs and had reserved a small suite and invited the presenters for a post-session cocktail. Everyone seemed to feel that we, in one day, had opened the door to a new field of research with vast implications. The spirit of innovation, almost magical in form, filled the air. If my memory serves me correctly, it was Nelson Graburn who first articulated that sense of drama. In his inimitable style, he said "we have really done something important."

The discussion almost immediately turned to "what next?", and the answer was inevitable: "a book." All eyes turned to me, with the obvious expectation that I was the one who should edit the "book." I was stunned, for I was never to become a wordsmith, and at that time I had never edited a paper. I know I gulped hard, then murmured, "what is the title?" Theron Nuñez immediately responded with "Hosts and Guests," whereupon we added "The Anthropology of Tourism," and the project took off.

Progression of the Book

The authors of the papers were so enthusiastic about our newfound topic that the symposium papers were rather quickly rewritten and forwarded to me. In the meantime, I had been looking for editorial models. The need for an introduction with some analysis of the subject was essential. That, I assumed, would be my responsibility. For the summary I turned to Nuñez whose *Weekendismo* article (1963) was one of the first to be published on the subject.

Soon after the Meeting in Mexico City, Nelson Graburn came to Chico where we sat on my patio facing the mountains and just "visited" about tourism. We laughed about our picnic lunch, and using Graburn nomenclature, referred to it as an "out of the ordinary" touristic event. As we subsequently wrote our individual chapters, elements of that Chico discussion emerged in each. It had been a very fruitful afternoon.

In my view, two points would be central in the Introduction: (1) a definition of tourism, and (2) a classification of types of tourists. There had to be three elements in the definition, which I formulated as follows:

Tourism = leisure time + discretionary income + positive social sanctions.

Time and money are easily understood, but positive social sanctions—the sense that it was appropriate to travel for pleasure—seemed not to have been recognized as a factor in tourism. My family had personally experienced negative travel sanctions when we began to travel overseas in 1951, at a time when the USA was still dominated by the Puritan ethic that honored work and denounced idleness. My 70-year-old father who, like many of his generation, had finished only the fifth grade in school, worked for a minimum wage in a wholesale hardware store. When he traveled to Europe for a two week vacation with me, his coworkers sharply criticized his extravagance as "squandering his retirement savings." But he so enjoyed the experience that he continued traveling every year while working full-time to the age of 78.

A Classification of Tourist Types

The 1977 edition of *Hosts and Guests* pioneered a chart of tourist types, primarily identified in terms of their numbers, their adaptation to, and effect on local host cultures. They ranged from the minimally present Explorers, to Elite, Off-Beat,

Unusual, Incipient Mass, and (a category then typical of tourism) Charter. I created the terms mostly on the basis of my experience as a travel agent or tour escort. Here, the reader should understand that mass tourism did not truly begin until the early 1970s, and when the first edition of the book went to press in 1976, we were only beginning to realize the magnitude and importance of vastly increased tourism for both land and culture. Indeed, terms such as "carrying capacity" and "sustainability" were not even indexed in the second (1989) edition. However, most of the classificatory terms, especially mass tourism, were quickly adopted, and mass tourism is still a term in widespread use. As an early book on tourism, I was adamant that the book must include the best possible bibliography. Several students, notably Phyllis Quinn who became a lecturer in our department, gave their time to comb the available literature. A number of reviewers expressed their appreciation for this effort as a valuable contribution to the development of tourism research.

Publication

The final effort was to find a publisher. Being naïve, I broke every convention in the publishing process and wrote a generic letter offering the manuscript, and sent it out broadcast to all known university presses and other potential publishers—some 80 in all. The letter read: "There is something NEW in anthropology besides women and drugs—TOURISM." A week later, I received a reply from the Acquisitions Editor at the University of Pennsylvania Press, expressing his great interest in the topic and asking for the manuscript. No other reply was ever received.

In the process of publication, the issue of royalties arose, which if adopted, would have added an additional US$10 per copy to the sales price. Because I thought that it was more important to make the volume available to the widest possible audience, especially to students and colleagues in developing countries, I rejected this alternative, and all the authors agreed with me. The volume was widely read and cited, and publication rights were sold to the British firm Blackwell to more easily serve the European market.

The Second Edition

The research on which the first edition (Smith 1977) was based had been carried out as much as five years earlier. By 1987, several major symposia as well as articles in leading tourism journals suggested a changing perception of tourism. The economic and scholarly mood was shifting from concern about the impacts of culture change—the so-called Cautionary approach put forward by Jafar Jafari—to a new principle of tourism as a tool for economic development, which corresponded to his "Advocacy" approach (see Jafari 1987). The World Bank and international businesses offered and gained economic advantages for their support in the development of tourism in the then-termed Third World areas (a process now involving globalization). I believed the authors of the *Hosts and Guests* 1977 first edition could make an important further contribution to tourism research through some time-depth analysis, a field technique that is often overlooked or impossible. Each author of a field study was asked to reconsider her/his chapter and, where possible, to return to the field to re-evaluate the role of tourism in local sociocultural change. Only one author was eliminated on this second go-round, and almost all of them wrote an addendum concerning the consequences of tourism for the cultures studied in the intervening years.

It was clearer now to most of the authors that what they may have considered simply as Westernization had become an increasingly global process in which tourism had come to play an important role. We were less tentative about what we were doing and rejected implications that as scholars we were defending some sort of anthropological zoo for our own research interests. As Institutes of Tourism study opened up on university campuses and students and faculty obtained grants for research on the subject, there was less finger pointing and ridicule about our projects as simply presenting vacations as research.

The second edition of *Hosts and Guests* was translated into Spanish and Japanese, which is an indication of the general expansion of the field of tourism research. A later version in Chinese also appeared. Some people were critical of my not having rewritten the Introduction, which in truth I had. What they may have sensed was my reluctance to make major changes. The future modes of tourism were still unclear to me. The implications of the generational shift in travel styles between the cost-conscious "Depression kids" and their self-indulgent children, the "baby boomers," was still not clear. It seemed better to say nothing than to make potentially false projections.

Hosts and Guests Revisited: Tourism Issues of the 21st Century (Smith and Brent 2001)

In 1999, 10 years after the appearance of the second edition, students in my classes were complaining that there still was still no textbook that brought together the sociocultural elements of tourism, as did some texts on tourism business management. Their observation was valid. Nothing combined theory with case studies, and in many institutions, the library did not subscribe to, or have complete runs of major tourism journals. Further, many community colleges offered tourism programs in which only a little theory was combined with application to fill broad educational needs. Maryann Brent (a former student) and I sought to counter this trend by including theoretical sections, each of which was illustrated by case study material. And we included new research topics—e.g., war and terrorism—and their impact on tourism, space tourism, the role of governments as culture brokers, advances of much-discussed sustainability, and ecotourism. At Nelson Graburn's request, we retained the Inuit data, but not as a case study. Instead, because I have long believed that indigenous people also engaged in tourism in response to the same motivations as modern travelers—visiting family and friends, attending special events, shopping, vacationing in a new place, and engaging in new activities—we chose to use Inuit activities as an indigenous example of those concepts.

The reviews of this book were complimentary, but it has not been widely used. In retrospect, the title was unfortunate, especially inasmuch as the publisher chose to market the book as a third edition of *Hosts and Guests*. To my knowledge, many colleagues presumed that this new book would be a rehash of old data; and who buys a third edition, except to require it of their students for the royalties it will generate? So it turned out to be a disappointing endeavor, involving a lot of effort, to create a text that would assist students to more quickly grasp the sweeping implications of an industry as complex as tourism.

Milestones

The volume for which this personal history is written is unique, offering to each author three unusual opportunities for self-appraisal. Anthropologists have traditionally considered an autobiography as a window through which to view themselves and their associated culture. The initial avenue here is the set of pathways and processes that first awakened our individual awareness of tourism as a topic for investigation. The second is the opportunity for a personal critique of our contributions to the topic. The third, an opportunity to give our ideas on the future of tourism research. Let me begin with the important milestones in my life leading up to the Symposium in Mexico City.

1947   With a BA in geography in hand, my teaching career began at Los Angeles City College. In my first class, all students were male veterans of World War II studying under the GI Bill. They had traveled all over the world and had many skills. I knew the US well, thanks to several summers spent driving to all of the (then) 48 states while studying US geography. After class on the first night, I vowed to see the rest of the world. 58 years later, I am still a peripatetic scholar engaged in the study of tourism.

1948   The Department Chair asked me to teach a course in Cultural Anthropology (a "first" in California, outside of Berkeley and UCLA). I read a good deal of anthropology!

1950 June (with MA in geography in hand), in Seattle. My mother and I put our car aboard an Alaska Steamship (my first cruise) and disembarked at Valdez. We drove over every road in Alaska, and back on the Alcan Highway. In Fairbanks, when Alaska Airlines offered a tour to Kotzebue and Nome; we signed on for the opportunity to see the Arctic in my first tour and first plane ride The Eskimo came out to the dirt airstrip to see "the tourists," noting especially our camera straps and gear. There were eight of us tourists who watched a few Eskimos dancing that night, for which we each paid $1, which was considered a good income for them and a good introduction to tour pricing for me. We overnighted in a dormitory owned by the airlines. The only earned income for the Eskimo came from dance money and craft sales, partly of archaeologic items excavated from a 1400 AD beach site.

1951 My first trip to Europe: 9000 miles in 12 weeks, in a little Renault filled with textbooks to study and museums and archaeologic sites to visit, including Lascaux.

1952 Back to Europe, armed with books and maps for a drive to India. Turned back in Amman, Jordan because of Iranian coup; shipped the car to Egypt, then back to Europe, and sold it. Learned about people, places, and politics in the Middle East!

1953 Was awarded a Fulbright grant to teach at the University of Peshawar, Pakistan. Bought a used car in Paris and headed East. Turned back again in Amman due to Iranian coup. Shipped the car to Karachi and flew. Drove 10,000 miles that year in Pakistan and India. Learned to read an Official Airlines Guide to plan our routing east. University MA classes filled with mullahs and women in burkas!

1954 In the Fall, our Department Chair asked me to teach a new course on how to travel for Los Angeles school personnel who needed units for advancement. Some 200 people enrolled. Title: "Be a Traveler, Not a Tourist"—"Understand, not rubberneck!"

1955 Department Chair asked me to take a student tour to Europe with 46 students. Somehow I survived 63 days in 17 countries with two buses, during which I learned that Europe was not ready for tours—every night we were in two or three hotels. Price? US$1275 from Los Angeles. We parted friends, and 8 of us will share a 50th reunion in 2005. I was learning something about tourism as an industry.

1956   Back to Europe with a tour party: one bus, 30 people in First Class!

1957   First Sabbatical Leave. Escorted Tour party of 16, "Around the World in 80 Days." (This was the most expensive tour American Express had ever operated, and it was filled with much information about tourism.) Routing: Honolulu, Tokyo, Kyoto, Hong Kong, Taipei; Manila, Singapore, Bangkok, Nepal, Delhi, Udaipur, Jaipur, Agra, Lahore, Peshawar, Karachi, Baghdad. Amman, Damascus, Beirut, Ankara, Istanbul, Athens, Greek Island Cruise, Rome. All flights were still in propeller planes. Everywhere we went in Asia, our tour group was photographed and appeared on the front page of the leading newspaper. We were questioned on radio, "How do you find our country?" We were school teachers on sabbatical, not business tycoons or diplomats. But we were one of the first of Group Tours to visit there. In Taipei, Mme Chiang Kai Chek, as First Lady, invited us to lunch at the Palace and for a tour of some of her favorite charities! We were the first tour into Nepal, arriving by DC3. There was no hotel in Katmandu, but American Express had found an American nurse who operated an orphanage and agreed to take us in. We slept on army cots, and she fed us. His Majesty was so thrilled to have tourists that he loaned us his three cars that had been carried in pieces by porters up the trail into Katmandu, and we used them for our sightseeing. There were no drugs nor hippies then. All of this, when compared with the situation today, gives some idea of the rapid growth of tourism over half a century.

1959   I went into partnership with a Swiss employee of American Express, and opened Jet-Age Travel Service in North Hollywood, honoring the first year of jet air service. For the next 20 years, I was a co-owner, or later, owner/manager of the agency, working and teaching full-time. We continued to sell escorted tours.

1965   Sabbatical leave, during which I temporarily moved to Utah to complete my PhD in anthropology, which as a discipline, seemed to offer the broadest interpretations of human behavior, as well as the opportunity to continue the study of tourism and its impact on indigenous peoples.

1966   Relocated to Chico State to teach and moved the agency to Chico.

1974   By the time of my AAA call for a tourism symposium, at the meetings in Mexico City, I had been an active travel agency owner/manager for 15 years. I had written itineraries, operated international travel from our office, and escorted 12 group tours on 6 continents. I understood accounting, marketing, personnel issues (salary, benefits), and real estate investments. I had taught principles of tourism for 10 years and done some writing. To me, the evidence of tourism impacts and culture change were overwhelming. It seemed time for academia to put its analytical skills to use, and to develop research methods and theory.

As we know, when Darwin and Wallace communicated, they discovered they were on the same intellectual track, but someone has to start. When I made the announcement of the Symposium, I found that there were 28 fellow anthropologists, as well as geographers, sociologists, and economists who agreed that it was time to talk tourism! We soon learned also that Charles Goeldner had started the Journal of Travel Research, Jafar Jafari was pioneering *Annals of Tourism Research* and Tej Vir Singh was preparing to launch *Tourism Recreation Research*. Together, we had taken important steps in founding a field.

Academic Development

As a geographer (with a geology minor), I found Carl Sauer's work on the morphology of landscape important for areal interpretation. While an undergraduate, I continued with my high school French and added German, both of which have proved useful in travel as well as necessary for meeting the doctoral language requirements. As I moved into anthropology, my perception of world culture was influenced by British archaeologist V. Gordon Childe who divided human history into cycles based on the dominant form of energy—the Paleolithic as a time of human muscle power; the Neolithic with animal power; and a third, the Technic, with the use of various kinds of resources ranging from the non-renewable, such as oil and coal, to renewable, such as wind, water, and the sun. Transitioning between the different phases of use has been marked by social disruptions of various kinds.

Tourism can be related to this format. Indigenous people walked and backpacked possessions until they had dog traction, horses, travois, and boats. Generations later, globalization is reterritorializing culture, and the world population is consuming planetary resources at an unprecedented rate. The Neotechnic is upon us, with uncertainties about employment and confusion about future job skills. Uncertainty and stress leads to lawlessness. Government is less effective in leadership and the maintenance of social order.

This last paragraph can serve as a preface to my belief that I have lived in the freest nation in the world during one of the best half centuries in history. During this time, tourism developed at an unprecedented rate, opening new markets and developments around the world. In the 1950s, the world was essentially at peace. Americans were global heroes, and there were good economic opportunities everywhere. According to my experience, a woman could walk alone or drive at night without fear; even in the city, no one locked their house. Your handshake was your honor, and your word was your bond. Ordinary citizens like me could dream of driving from Paris to India, or from Cairo to Cape town, and some of my peers realized such dreams.

To travel—while learning first-hand about cultural diversity and differences in land use—is a personal obsession, and a lifelong passion for me. To know the USA thoroughly was an important first step, and while I was on a Fulbright in Peshawar, Pakistan in 1953–1954 I began to be concerned with the geographical basis of US power and how it was being squandered.

As I traveled in Europe and elsewhere, I found that the quality of touristic training was generally impressive. But such training appeared to be nonexistent in the USA. Ever the pragmatist, I developed a survey instrument and asked for information from 104 countries which had certified programs of guide training. Most responded promptly. The Japanese even forwarded copies of their written examination (in English). The USSR did not respond, so I cashed an annuity and paid for the trip to Moscow, where I spent a pleasant two hours with the Director of Intourist (the survey results served as the basis for my first professional publication). In 2005, I am still campaigning without success for a national guide training program in the USA comparable to that enacted by the EU.

The 1974 symposium in Mexico stimulated an interest in more such meetings. Especially notable was the first tourism symposium held in conjunction with the Society for Applied Anthropology at its meeting in Merida in 1977. There, with considerable fanfare, the Government of Mexico honored Dr. Vila Rojas for his work with Robert Redfield in the study of acculturation in the Mayan village of Chan Kom. The meeting was a singularly appropriate venue to discuss tourism, and it included a field trip to Chan Kom. The day ended on an unusual note. As we boarded our bus to return to Merida, a dozen gaily dressed Maya women also boarded, and demanded that we drive them to the Governor's office and request some new sewing machines. We replied that we had no influence. They retorted, "If one anthropologist can come to Chan Kom and change our lives, fifty anthropologists can get us new sewing machines." Regrettably, those ladies were disappointed.

In 1993, tourism study gained further international recognition with a full day session at the International Congress of Anthropological and Ethnographic Sciences (ICAES) meeting in Mexico City. In 1994, the Society for Applied Anthropology again met in Mexico, this time at Cancun, where papers on tourism and indigenous people were presented to an interested audience that included not only foreign scholars, but "locals" of varying ethnicity.

At that meeting, anthropologist, Robert ("Van") Kemper urged that we move ahead during the next five years toward establishing a Commission on Tourism within the ICAES, which could provide both a platform for discussion and a source of various publications. I sent out the call for papers for the next meeting, which was to be held in 1998 at William and Mary College in Williamsburg,

Virginia. The tourism sessions, which were among the best attended, included four full days, 48 papers, and representation from 18 nations. Thanks to the strength of this program, our request for a Commission on Tourism was approved. In this regard, it would seem appropriate to offer a special acknowledgment to Dennison Nash who not only developed an interesting opening session, but remained throughout the four days as a commentator and critical presence.

Publication

In a good many of my publications, which have covered considerable touristic ground, I have been editor—either on my own or with someone else. The various versions of *Hosts and Guests*, which have already been mentioned, included two publications on tourism development in less developed societies in a series called "Studies in Third World Societies," from the William and Mary Press (Smith, ed. 1978a,b). In *Annals of Tourism Research*, I shared editorship with Dennison Nash for an article on Tourism and Anthropology in an issue on *Tourism Social Science* (1991). I edited issues on *Pilgrimage and Tourism* (1992) and with Steve Wanhill (Smith and Wanhill, eds. 1986) on Domestic Tourism and John Splettstoesser (Smith and Splettstoesser, eds. 1994) on Antarctic Tourism, *Tourism in Antarctica* (1993), which was the first issue on a regional topic among 26 Special Issues of *Annals*. The isolation of the land mass, the hardship of living in cold and darkness, and loneliness are daunting personal issues that could be relevant as far as space tourism is concerned. Issues concerning governance and the protection of cosmic matter also could be relevant.

The issue of sustainable tourism research has also preoccupied me and others in the International Academy for the Study of Tourism. Indeed, much of our first published work, *Tourism Alternatives*, edited by Bill Eadington and myself (1992) was concerned with issues related to the famous Brundtland Report. The philosophy of "sustainability" expressed by the Bruntland Commission (WCED 1987) generated a significant literature supportive of local, small-scale, and sustainable development, in which authors extolled the virtues of self-operated, small home-stay enterprises as a source of personal—or familial—independence and "grass roots" income; but my observations suggested that hotel employees frequently enjoyed a higher standard of living with more certain pay and an easier workload than the much-touted self-employed.

The issues discussed in *Privatization in the Third World: Small-Scale Tourism Enterprises* (Smith 1994) now reach far beyond the original home-stay theme. Tourism has become increasingly complex along with numbers of tourists; and sanitation problems abound. Many villages in the developing world have no sewer systems, and houses have no septic tanks. Local drinking water is highly suspect, as in home-stays in now-popular Bhutan. In Polynesia, the supposedly pristine lagoons are polluted in heavily touristed islands such as Moorea and Bora

Bora, where new private homes and small rental properties are virtually contiguous at the water's edge. Swimmers and snorkelers use the beaches at personal peril. On a 2004 journey across the Pacific, we were cautious about snorkeling inside the reefs and near the outflow channels.

During the 1990s I was back in the Arctic several times, and in visits to Inuit communities, was disconcerted by the widespread discussion of the positive benefits of ecotourism. Some contract specialists seemed to have very little understanding of the Arctic and failed to realize that many tourists had only a short-term interest in "seeing" the Arctic. Most were far more interested in the wildlife (especially whales and polar bears) than in Westernized Inuit culture. Some cruise ships actually cancelled scheduled visits to a third or fourth Inuit village because of passenger boredom. People said, "when you've seen one, you've seen 'em ALL." Given the extreme seasonality and very high costs for construction and maintenance, the Arctic alone is not a truly viable tourism market. While in the North, I developed a set of criteria or markers with which to quickly measure and understand tourism potential, as for example, in an Arctic environment. This scheme eventually became the "4 Hs of Tourism—Habitat, History, Heritage, and Handicraft"—and I continue to use it as a quick assessment in every community new to me, whether in Russia's Commander Islands or a Micronesian village on Yap.

War has been real to me since World War II, and I have become involved in its touristic aspects during my travels that included two visits to Vietnam during that engagement. What really surprised me was the magnitude of tourism markers related to war, especially those commemorating some event or other. It seems to me that the amount of tourism research on the subject, in which I am involved, does not match the possibilities available.

The 1990s generated a rash of new publications on tourism, mostly from the UK, which were so expensive that students and US libraries could not afford them. That issue prompted me to seek a publication outlet, and I developed a series on Tourism Dynamics for Cognizant Communication Corporation in Elmford, NY, which may have had some effect on UK marketing strategists. In any case, their books seem now to be more competitively priced.

A Futurist Perspective

Americans may have discovered tourism recently. But as a human activity it is as old as the species itself. There are a number of prehistorically based popular works that deal with the travels of Neanderthal and Cro-Magnon peoples, including their summer gatherings that were the aboriginal equivalent of our summer resorts and shopping malls. Thirty years (1974–2004) of concentrated analysis by tourism specialists from many fields have generated a vast body of data, theories, methodologies, and so-called best practices, which suggests that the basics of tourism have been largely identified and described. I finally retired in 1997 after 51 years in university classrooms, during which I was directly involved in teaching and writing about tourism. During that time, I also developed itineraries for, and escorted 82 tours, earning at least US$50,000 in revenue for the sponsoring charitable organizations. It has been a privilege to meet and get to know hundreds of true "travelers," for whom I tried to provide a pleasurable learning experience. I continue to attend conferences, travel extensively, and monitor new tourism niches such as in the currently popular adventure tourism.

In the near future, outbound tourism from the West may decline somewhat because of terrorism, epidemics such as SARS, and the fears they generate. But on the other hand, there could be a significant increase in Asian tourism as well as domestic travel in the West and elsewhere. In all of this, there would seem to be no shortage of problems for applied researchers to address. For example, the greater emphasis on adventure and outdoor tourism may pose an increasing threat to the environment. How to deal with that?

Space tourism is now a certainty thanks to the successful test in 1995 of SpaceShipOne and the award of the Ansari US$10 million X-prize. More prizes will reward further research, and space tourists are expected to be airborne before the end of this decade, traveling perhaps on Brannon's Virgin Galactic Space Voyages. Faculty at the International Space University in Strasbourg predict that earth-based colonies will be established soon in space; and the development of the mineral resources there will mark the beginning of the Neotechnic stage of human culture. Millions of potential space travelers (including me) want to get orbital, and have a look down at our planet from a height of 70 miles. To paraphrase Carl Sagan, we earthlings live on an island, and island people have always visited their neighbors. Islanders have gone on trading expeditions, and so shall we to obtain the minerals on the Moon and Mars. As island populations have grown beyond the carrying capacity of their land, members of their societies have relocated on other islands, and so shall we. In this process, augmented by various technological innovations, tourism will increase in both size and complexity. Tourism researchers must be aware of these trends and give thought to the new dimensions of hospitality that space travel will require; and, of course, the notion that tourism can be a passport to peace will have new implications in an era of space travel.

Margaret Byrne Swain (1948–) is Adjunct Professor of Anthropology, Director of the Center for Gender and Global Issues, and Co-Director of the Women's Resources and Research Center, University of California, Davis, CA 95616, USA (e-mail: mbswain@ucdavis.edu), where she teaches Gender and Globalization, Ethnic Minorities of China, and Feminist Ethics. A continuing feminist interest in minority indigenous people, missionaries, and tourists, as well as global, environmental and population issues forms her current work in Southwestern China. Other recent works include (edited with Janet Momsen) *Gender/Tourism/Fun?* (2002) and the edited Gender and Tourism for *Annals of Tourism Research* (1995). Her research is usually gender oriented in an active, applied way.

ON THE ROAD TO A FEMINIST TOURISM STUDIES

Introduction

In 1991, I made a strategic choice that became a defining moment for my engagement in Tourism Studies. I chose to pursue the study of gender in tourism in order to reclaim a place for myself in the field. It soon became apparent that I was one of several tourism researchers who had simultaneously had the idea of stimulating new scholarship by looking into issues of gender in tourism. I promoted this agenda in the US (Swain 1995), while Vivian Kinnaird and Derek Hall (1994) worked together in the UK. In both cases, our immediate goal was to produce a collection of articles demonstrating the utility and significance of gender analysis in Tourism Studies. Hearty responses to our separate calls for papers provided encouraging evidence that we were on to something, and we followed this up with correspondence and collaboration over the years. This project revitalized my interests, and gave me an identity as a tourism researcher. Studying gender drew on my training in anthropology and continued my earliest work on tourism (1977) in ways that could produce new, usable scholarship.

Let me begin this personal history by first discussing what in my career led into this project and how my interest in the issues involved have continued to grow since then. I hope it will show that though I have been on the margins of academia, I have found community in tourism studies.

Toward a Feminist Tourism Studies

Before I became engaged in Tourism Studies, I was a feminist, and consequently my understanding of tourism is permeated with gender analysis. For me, being a feminist means believing that sexism, prejudice, and associated inequalities between men and women must be eliminated in order to provide equity for everyone; and understanding cultural constructs of gender is the key to revealing sexist hierarchies of power. As an adolescent, when I was beginning to seriously contemplate such issues, I happened to read the novel *Orlando* by Virginia Woolf, which changed my life. It tended to corroborate earlier experiences when our family had lived in various racially segregated and class stratified communities around the United States. So by the time of adolescence, I had been exposed to the three basic "food groups' of feminist thinking: gender, race, and class. International travel, which I first experienced in 1964 when my father took a Summer job in India, was another major ingredient in my academic future, as was a 1966 Beloit College anthropology seminar in Taiwan. I was blown away by the experience of distinct Asian cultures. It was all fascinating—the landscapes, peasants, elites, urban workers, indigenous peoples, languages, cultural ideals, and aesthetics. With this experience, the die was cast for my future course of study.

Just before entering graduate school in Anthropology at the University of Washington in 1969, I had chosen to go with my father on a visit to Iran, where I learned something about life in the Middle East. It was filled with sexism. There, I was harassed, proposed to, and even stoned (literally, with rocks), none of which would have happened if I had been a man.

When I started graduate school, many things interested me, but I kept coming back to focus on what we then called sex roles, which are now referred to as gender relations. My intellectual framework for explaining what I experienced is rooted in the perception that the personal is political. I thought about the double messages from my own society that women were best in the domestic sphere, yet they can and should do anything. Being a young American woman in the 1970s was empowering in terms of second-wave feminism, as intellectuals and working women made alliances to push for the basics—still not fully secured more than thirty years later—such as an equal rights amendment. Female suffrage is great, but hardly enough. My political education was also deeply influenced by an increasing awareness of the fact of modern imperialisms- both at home and abroad- acquired not only in the classroom, but as an active protester against, for example, the war in Vietnam.

Discovering the Study of Tourism

I had just started graduate school, when another travel opportunity lured me away—this time to Panama, where I married Walt Swain and became an army wife. But my housebound days were numbered when Walt politely suggested that I get a life by volunteering at a local museum. I ended up at the *Museo Nacional*, becoming the staff's pet *gringa,* with useful skills in English and museum techniques. It was a fantastic move, getting me out into the city, interacting with Panamanians, and learning about Latin American history, society and culture. One topic that really intrigued me was the culture and political history of the Kuna Indians who live in the San Blas Islands off the Atlantic side of Panama.

When finally free of the army, Walt and I chose to go back to the University of Washington. For my PhD dissertation project in Anthropology I later decided to return to Panama to work with the Kuna, who interested me because of their matrilocal society and their ritual celebration for women's coming of age. This was hot stuff for a nascent feminist anthropologist, tying directly into my training at Washington. From my encounters with Kuna people and my studies in Euro-American ethnography, I knew that women's position in Kuna society was a good research topic. But I would need a new angle to make it exciting scholarship. How was the status of women changing in contemporary society? Tourism was one source of economic and social "development" in their homeland, a series of coconut palm–dotted islands along the Caribbean side of Panama. I was intrigued by the fact that women's position in Kuna society was heavily used in Panamanian and international tourism promotion. Iconographic images of Kuna women in face paint, gold nose rings and intricately sewn *mola* blouses were exotic and alluring. Kuna women's *mola* handiwork was the ubiquitous souvenir from Panama, and the images of Kuna women were used to "sell" Panama as a tourist destination. I was drawn to the study of tourism through my interest in this particular people, who happened to be involved in tourism. It was a topic ripe for investigation. Or so I thought.

I had innocently assumed that tourism was a legitimate and respected topic of study, given Valene Smith's call in the *American Anthropology Association (AAA) Newsletter,* for participants in a session on tourism at the 1974 annual meeting to be held in Mexico City. Though no one on my faculty at the University of Washington knew a thing about tourism, here was proof that someone did. I soon noticed that there was very little scholarly work on the subject, but then maybe I was not looking in the right places. Only later on did I learn about Pierre van den Berghe in Sociology at Washington, whose research project in Peru during the 1970s included tourism issues.

I began my involvement with Tourism Studies by inquiring about the AAA session being organized by Valene Smith on tourism in Mexico City. I sent in my abstract, which was based on my dissertation proposal, and it was accepted for presentation. Very exciting, it was also the beginning of a defining relationship between Valene and myself, in which she became a mentor, impossible role model, and ultimately a friend. Her AAA session, which arguably marked a beginning for Tourism Studies, also coincided with the beginnings of my own academic career. I was one of a small group of graduate students fortunate enough to be included in what was to become Valene's publishing project that was to be based on presentations delivered in that session. The timing was perfect. I was just starting my research in Panama, and Walt and I decided to drive there from Seattle. On the way, we stopped in Berkeley to drop off a draft of my paper for Nelson Graburn, a discussant for the tourism session, who I met for the first time. Then on to San Blas for some months.

I returned to Mexico City for the AAA meetings, and it was a heady experience being part of what was clearly a path-breaking group. I remember the excitement after our session had gone so well, talking late into the night with the other graduate students, and being very impressed with the more seasoned professors amongst us. The unusual fact was that our meeting was being held outside the US, which added transnational flavor to our discussions. This meeting also exposed me to many different ways of thinking about tourism, and I could see clear links between my feminist project and those viewing tourism as economic development, cultural commoditization, or imperialism. My focus was, on the people receiving tourists, or the "hosts" in Valene Smith's terms. Thinking about the "guests" or tourists was interesting to me in terms of how they interacted with the locals, but I was not concerned about tourist identities, experiences, or markets per se. While seeing the tourist as a topic of great importance, I was little engaged with this aspect of Tourism Studies. Rather, I was primarily concerned with studying the impacts of tourism and how the host populations reacted to them.

First Tourism Research Experiences

From this energizing start of the AAA session, I thought that my research would be tightly focused on tourism, but soon discovered that political realities in Panama and the Canal Zone would force me to become more oblique. There were various impediments to my project, including armed revolt in San Blas over control of tourism sites and the activities or missionaries with the Southern Baptist Foreign Mission who were trying to restructure local communities. Life in the field was filled with drama outside of my personal circumstances and routine ethnographic chores. Volatile conflict between the state of Panama and the Kuna Reserve governments over who would control San Blas tourism development, combined with tensions in the community of Ailigandi (where I was located) over control of a Baptist missionary hospital. Ailigandi was both a significant tourism destination and a long-time mission town, and it soon became abundantly clear that tourism was a hot topic, with indigenous Kuna people ejecting outside entrepreneurs and Kuna orators taking on Panamanian representatives. Eventually, the state backed down from their grand plan for a theme park in San Blas, but hostile sentiments remained high.

In 1975, mid-way through my fieldwork, I decided to change my focus from tourism to women's identity issues. I was still taking notes, but no longer asking direct questions. But even so, the questions I was asking Kuna women generated some difficulties with the newly arrived Southern Baptist missionaries from the United States.

One of the reasons I had settled on Ailigandi instead of some other island experiencing the impact of tourism was that Walt and I could clearly give something back to the community there by working in the local hospital, which we did. Early on in our stay, the hospital changed hands, and what had been an excellent working relationship with the resident missionary doctor and his staff soon soured under a new regime which thought that I had been stirring up dissent over womens' roles. Indeed, my anthropological investigation was perceived to be at direct odds with the missionary ideas about female domestic modernity; and my Kuna field assistant was challenging Kuna and Baptist values by her questions and behavior.

We asked women about changes going on in Ailigandi and to think critically about their lives. For example, one of the mission's major development projects had been to pipe in fresh water from a river source on the nearby mainland. This greatly eased the task of securing fresh water, and was a real boon to the resident missionaries, anthropologists, and visiting tourists. But when we asked about this development, the local women said that they missed going together upriver by canoe to wash and fetch water. As one woman put it, *"somos como las palomas,"* that is that they had become like the caged doves kept on the island with little chance to get off. Consequences such as this tended to reinforce my skepticism of externally dictated developmental projects—from missionary works to tourism schemes. Fortunately, when the missionaries were removed from the island by local leadership, Kuna control was effectively reasserted in all areas, including tourism.

Another challenge for me was my simultaneous engagement in the emerging fields of tourism studies and feminist studies. Either field was new territory at the time, and trying to combine the two proved difficult without some sort of "map," which I needed to draw for myself. When I started my fieldwork I had limited theoretical underpinnings in both literatures, which were just beginning to be pursued by anthropologists. But when I was writing up my ethnography there was an explosion of publishing activity in both Tourism and Feminist Studies that helped me a great deal in my dissertation, but was too late for my first article in *Hosts and Guests,* which combined the two fields.

By the time I was back in Seattle and beginning to work on my dissertation, Valene Smith had the book *Host and Guests* (1977), which was derived from the session in Mexico City, well on its way. It was a huge honor to have my article on the Kuna included. Almost all the twelve case-studies in the book were authored by new scholars in the field of tourism studies, some of us still in graduate school. The theoretical work by Smith, Graburn, Nash, and Nuñez in the book framed our reports from the field. When I look at my chapter some twenty five years later I am struck by how descriptive it was, with all the theory informing it almost totally implicit. I was interested in portraying how I saw women's roles in tourism production, but did not press the case for what it meant in terms of the big picture of gender equity, and human relations. In my dissertation, tourism became one section in a community study of continuity and change in gendered ethnic identity.

The next several years of my life were a blur of finishing my PhD, producing two babies, teaching, writing, and ultimately disappearing from academia for an extended period of time. I practiced a radical kind of feminism by dropping out of paid employment for a while, a decision I was privileged to make because of income from a supportive husband and the very limited opportunities for women all around us. I put most of my energies into mothering, a task in which I was not particularly good; and I was certainly a domestic nightmare; but being there for my daughters took high priority. While living in Colorado, I worked part-time and started to entertain ideas about China. I wanted to learn the language, go to the mainland and learn about a culture I had just begun to appreciate in Taiwan years before. The Kuna had become a part of me, but they did not particularly need me in building their relationships with the world at large. New opportunities to practice my own kind of anthropological craft could open up in this direction.

Walt's work moved our family to California in late 1985, and I really began to learn about China at the University of California, Davis where I took courses in Chinese. Then just as I was becoming immersed, a letter from Valene Smith arrived, in which she asked those who had originally written chapters in *Hosts and Guests* to consider participating in a second edition. Again, the timing was perfect for me. I was newly engaged in an academic setting, and now I had this chance to think about my research again. It had been more than ten years since I had finished my dissertation in 1978, and I had no idea what had been happening in tourism research; but when I went to the library, I discovered that people were actually citing me—a person who had only a tiny scholarly reputation based on a few publications in the field. And besides Valene's encouragement, there was Dean MacCannell who taught at Davis and was willing to talk with me. With their inspiration, I started to write again, and do research, the first publication from which was a revisit to my Kuna work for the second edition of *Host and Guests*

(1989a). Here I named "indigenous tourism" as a particular type of production by indigenous people, which became a research topic for other researchers in the 1990s; and I also graduated into gender studies as an enduring way of thinking about women and men. My chapter, which also received heartening feedback from Kuna researchers, was a step into gender studies—a more enduring way of thinking about women and men.

During this same time I also eased back into the academic conference circuit, attending anthropology meetings and my first tourism meeting, that astounding intellectual who's who gathering in 1988 in Vancouver at the "Tourism as a Vital Force for Peace" conference. Valene encouraged me to contribute, and she soon had me involved in a long-term project as Index Editor for *Annals of Tourism Research*. This was another gift from Valene—an entrée into the world of *Annals* and (with editor Jafar Jafari) various related publishing projects.

A Change of Sites

My article in the second edition of *Hosts and Guests* (1989) was the latest thing I have written on the Kuna. Late in the 1980s, I started teaching an occasional anthropology course at UC Davis and began to develop a new research site in Yunnan, China, a fantastically ethnically diverse part of the world where a few minority indigenous groups, including the Sani of Stone Forest, were beginning to get involved in tourism. I traveled to Kunming, Yunnan for the first time with a summer abroad student group in 1987. Situated outside our hotel, a band of Sani women were selling their embroidered handicrafts to tourists and doing a brisk trade exchanging currency on the black market. This seemed remarkably like what I had experienced with the Kuna, raising familiar questions about indigenous tourism and gender issues. So I spent as much time as I could that Summer sitting on the sidewalk talking with them and looking like some sort of tourist.

My first publication on the Sani came out in *Tourism Recreation Research* (Swain 1989b). This was followed by a piece in *Cultural Survival* (Swain 1990) about ethnic/indigenous tourism in Southwest China, which was quickly translated into Chinese for the Yunnan Academy of Social Sciences journal. It is important to me that at least some of what I write reaches the people that I am writing about. Getting to my peers in Yunnan was a first step in engaging with Sani communities. In the early 1990s, in preparing for developing a grant proposal, I researched Sani history, focusing on a period when they were under French colonial domination (1888–1930s) and the Chinese communist revolutionary era.

In 1993, I was successful in obtaining a year of funding from a National Academy of Sciences program for China. My project focused on intersections of gender and ethnicity hierarchies in contemporary Sani communities, with some attention given to tourism development. What transpired in the course of the research was quite ironic in that it duplicated what had happened with the Kuna in Panama twenty years before. Due to armed conflict and the intervention of the State in matters of birth control, I found that I could not focus on tourism as I had planned. So in accord with my feminist-touristic inclinations, I focused on the role of women in certain touristic activities, which state officials seemed to think was much less controversial.

The Sani are a Yi ethnic minority group living in the Stone Forest region, a place highly exploited for tourism based on natural scenic attractions and, more recently, Sani culture. The Han majority population of China colonized the Sani many generations ago. In Sani eyes the Han have often been the Other who were feared, distrusted, and stereotyped. I, myself, did not sense any hostility from the Sani in racial, ethnic, or national terms. And because the issue of my female gender was not a problem for these people, I felt quite comfortable among them. It is not too surprising, I guess, that I have chosen to work in two societies, the Kuna and the Sani, where the issue of gender inequality does not exist.

However, I did have problems with the Chinese majority and State officials who tended to curtail my freedom of action in living arrangements and research activities. It was said, for example, that I was a woman and in need of protection. This kind of thing gave me something to complain about with my Sani friends who readily saw some fellow-victimhood in how I had been treated. The Sani view of gender relations is one significant distinction they have in Chinese society, which in the late twentieth century was reverting to precommunist era hierarchies; and it would seem to affect how they as a group respond to tourism development—dealing with everything from control of sexual services to souvenir production. My access to the responses of Sani in various aspects of such development was, naturally, uneven. For example, after months of observation only (and always being careful about asking questions), as I was about to get on the bus and leave for the year, a group of women decided to give me their opinions about the local sex trade. Their concern was that I understood that they knew about the sex workers living among them and the organized prostitution going on in Stone Forest. What they wanted me to be sure about was that the sex workers were from the outside and that local Sani women were not participating in sex tourism. What I gained from observation was that this was, perhaps, true for the women who were talking, but perhaps not for other Sani. In any case, it said something about trust and community image control among these people.

Besides practicalities, as with the Kuna, I found myself deeply concerned about asking too much while inserting myself into peoples' daily routines in the course of fieldwork. I continue to write about this, as well as about ways to give a bit back to one's hosts (Swain 2002). For example, one of my more creative moves led me to a collaborate in the creation of new tourism souvenirs for my Sani companions to sell little cloth dolls produced I must say, by both women and men.

1993 in Kunming, China, was my year of living dangerously, far away from my family for months at a time. In the summer, I traveled to Mexico City—returning 19 years after the first AAA session on tourism, this time for the International Congress of Ethnological Sciences (IUAES) meeting. There, I worked with Valene on tourism sessions, and this provided me with opportunities to meet new colleagues in the clearly growing field of Tourism Studies. In 1994, I was back in the US and became immersed in a UC Davis Feminist Studies project, Gender and Global Issues, which I still direct; and began serious work on my edited *Special Issue* of *Annals of Tourism Research* on *Gender in Tourism* (Swain 1995).

Theoretical Issues for Gender in Tourism

I started this piece by noting that I had reclaimed my place in Tourism Studies in the early 1990s. I did this in two distinct ways: through ethnographic research, mentioned earlier, and by pursuing theoretical issues of gender in tourism. At about the same time that I began to refocus my ethnographic work on China, I began to concern myself increasingly with feminist theory. While I was writing grant proposals to get myself funded for fieldwork, I was also developing a prospectus for a collection on gender in tourism; and after talking with Valene Smith I wrote a letter of inquiry to Jafar Jafari, in which I asked him to consider my proposal for a special issue of *Annals of Tourism Research* on Gender. He responded with his renowned care and thoroughness, raising many questions while also encouraging me to follow through. He sent me articles that he found as he checked on the legitimacy of this focus, and ultimately we agreed to go ahead with it. By November 1991, we had a call for papers that was ready to go out in the 1992 issues of *Annals*, with an abstract deadline of August 1993, and full papers due in January 1994. I mention these dates because I ended up doing much of the preliminary work while still in China, and delved into the manuscripts as soon as I was back in the US. Among more than thirty submissions, I chose twelve articles and four research notes that explored gender in terms of consumption practices, perceptions of tourism development, identities, sexuality and nationalism, the political economy of tourism, relations between tourism providers and consumers, and the changing of ideologies through tourism leisure practice.

In early 1992, Jafar had put me in touch with Vivian Kinnaird on gender analysis of tourism, and soon I was in direct contact with Vivian about our respective projects. For a while I planned to contribute a chapter to the book, which she and Derek Hall were putting together (Kinnaird and Hall 1994), but found that to be impossible while working in China. Her suggestion that she submit an article to the *Annals* collection had to be ruled out because it was too late. But the fact that her book with Hall came out first gave me something to respond to in my *Annals* project.

Our efforts were the first systematic attempts to combine the focuses of Tourism and Feminist Studies. My work on the *Annals* issue was an important step personally, signaling a progression from specific ethnography to general theorizing. To increase my base in Tourism Studies, I wrote reviews of other people's work, published articles, and participated in conferences, all the usual things to become established in an academic community. At the same time I developed connections in Chinese Ethnic Minority Studies that also sustains me. In my research on tourism, gender issues (identity, work roles, relations) have been primary themes, whether in Latin America, Asia, or my own back yard; and I found out that a number of other researchers were interested in these combined matters as well.

In the *Annals* collection, there was no mention of sexual difference, disabilities, or age differences in tourism. The fact that I did not think to write about these aspects of the body in the Introduction was reinforced at the time by the lack of submissions about them for the *Special Issue*. Over the following years, we have begun to see more inclusive scholarship in Tourism Studies as evidenced by current research that takes into consideration multiple points a of view and life experiences. Evolving perspectives on gender and sexuality were clearly articulated in the "Gender/Tourism/ Fun(?)" conference that I organized at UC Davis in the fall of 1997 with Janet Momsen and Dean MacCannell. This turned out to be an international gathering of energetic scholars. About half of the original conference papers were revised and published in a collection that I edited with Janet Momsen (Swain and Momsen, eds. 2002). Some of these authors pushed Tourism Studies research to engage in constructivism and embodiment theory, while others stayed clear of such postmodern talk. There has been a growing range of approaches to the study of gender in tourism. One trend has been for researchers to write in their own voice, rather than the usual disembodied type of "scientific" analysis." The other perspective involves a researcher who is mindful of his or her own embodiment and enriches any qualitatively oriented project. I saw this collection as a direct continuation of my work with the *Annals* project, which continued with a small jointly edited collection with Derek Hall and Vivian Kinnaird for *Tourism Recreation Research* (Hall et al, eds. 2003).

In terms of my ongoing focus on gender in tourism, I sneak in material whenever I teach. I had the luxury in 2002 at UC Berkeley to teach a class specifically about gender in tourism, using the *Gender/Tourism/Fun?* text of course, and it was a great vehicle to address both questions in tourism studies and the issues of gender equity, exploitation, and pleasure. One of the issues that came out during the class is that Feminist Studies literature on travel and tourism and Tourism Studies literature on gender and sexuality issues have very few connections, which is a waste of scholarship, and one that I try to address by promoting dialogue of these two fields of study.

Developing Tourism Studies

When I was not thinking about gender issues in Tourism Studies, I had another task with *Annals*, which was to do with the index editing job I had inherited from Valene. The biggest project I encountered was the 25-year cumulative index, a project I could not begin without significant help. With Valene's help, I recruited two other of her proteges, Maryann Brent and Veronica Long (1998). Other primary help was provided by Jafar Jafari, who cared deeply about the outcome of our work, which involved the creation of a computerized master index and an immense amount of time by us and others. What resulted was a work in progress, which continues to grow as a primary reference tool in Tourism Studies. After a few more years of working on the annual index, I left the editing job, which was taken over by the new editor, Honggen Xiao in 2002–2003.

Another way that I have been engaged in Tourism Studies has been through work with a small group at UC Davis who have talked for a number of years about building a program in tourism on our campus. Dean McCannell, Janet Momsen, and I called in the expertise of our regional California colleagues Valene Smith and Nelson Graburn to help with this work. It has been a difficult task, but we are beginning to see some future possibilities in connections with a graduate group in Geography. It remains a conundrum that social science based Tourism Studies programs remain few and very far between in the United States while they can flourish elsewhere, as with the exemplary program at the University of North London in England with which Tom Selwyn is associated. We hope that a growing awareness of tourism as an aspect of society will make it possible to build an academic niche for its study at UC Davis.

My own connection with these efforts has been strained by the fact that I am an adjunct professor—someone who is not salaried to develop academic programs, but rather is paid by the course we teach. Despite this, I function as a "regular" professor, advising a small herd of graduate students gratis. While I may have had a bit more time than my colleagues to pursue the establishment of Tourism Studies, I literally have had no established position to work from. I was and continue to be an outsider in the extremely hierarchical world of the university, and I often feel that, despite my accomplishments, I am not really accepted in academia. Just in case I sound too pathetic here, I need to distinguish between my research communities and my academic institution. As Valene Smith recently reminded me, my idol, the anthropologist Margaret Mead, never held a full-time academic appointment, paid for much of her own fieldwork, and only occasionally gave a seminar.

In 2003 GRITS, the Gender Researchers in Tourism Studies Network, was formed by Irena Ateljevic to support researchers exploring the interplay between tourism, identities, genders, races, sexualities, and embodiment. It has sent out a call, with the New Zealand Tourism Research Institute, the Welsh Centre for Tourism Research, and the Institute for Tourism, Zagreb, for an international conference in 2005 where Derek Hall and I spoke. Gender in tourism research has arrived as an organized, international presence, and I am currently focusing my own research on cosmopolitanism as a gender-embodied phenomenon in the contemporary global tourism industry. This interest has grown out of my fieldwork in China, as well as asking theoretical questions about how humans combine mobility with cultural exchange. I am interested in the embodiment and positionality of tourism researchers as well (Swain 2004). My ultimate concerns have to do with how we as researchers can increase human understanding and affect lives for the greater good of human beings everywhere.

Conclusion

While completing my doctorate, I was among the first to publish on gender (or sex roles as we said back in the 1970s) in the Tourism Studies literature (Swain 1977). When that article was revised (Swain 1989a), it marked my re-entry into the field after more than a decade away, but it was not until I edited the Special Issue of *Annals of Tourism Research* (1995) that I truly claimed my place as a Tourism Researcher. My trajectory from graduate student to author of a body of work on gender in tourism developed out of my life experience and my positioning outside of the academy. In the ensuing years, I moved from empirical research to theorizing about gender in tourism from a feminist perspective (Swain 1995; Swain and Momsen 2002). I grew to believe that we should be concerned about gender for the very basic reason that tourism includes interactions among women and men. Tourism is a human activity that mirrors ideas about gender relations and identities from all cultures. The push and pull between local and global norms provides constant material for analysis. It is significant to me that tourism practice has the potential of promoting either gender hierarchy or equity. My hope is for increased equality in this world. Like many other tourism researchers, I believe that tourism can be a vehicle for the common good of humankind, but we have a long way to go.

I have only named a few of my colleagues in this chapter, but many people have encouraged my work along the way, and I thank them all, especially Dennison Nash who has cajoled and prodded me to think about how I have done what I have done. Through this challenging process, I came to realize that my ambivalence about academia and my place in it is more than balanced out by my being involved in the field of Tourism Studies.

Pierre L. van den Berghe (1933–) is Professor Emeritus of Sociology and Anthropology at the University of Washington, Seattle, WA 98195-3340. USA (e-mail:plvdb@u.washington.edu) where he continues to teach a course on ethnic tourism. Over four decades, his field work, mostly on race and ethnic relations, and since 1980, on tourism, took him to South Africa, Kenya, Nigeria, Mexico, Guatemala, and Peru. Among his books are *Human Family Systems* (1979), *The Ethnic Phenomenon* (1981), and *The Quest for the Other: Ethnic Tourism in San Cristóbal, Mexico*.

TOURISM AND ETHNIC RELATIONS
The Obvious Connection

If all anthropology is, at some level, autobiography, we must try to make as explicit as we can how one's origins and circumstances influenced what we said about what we studied. This, I tried to do in both chapter and a book-length accounts (van den Berghe 1989, 1990) from which I will borrow here, with a much narrower focus on how I came to study tourism.

First, my social origins. Mine is not a morality tale of overcoming daunting obstacles through diligence and determination. As a product of what the Germans aptly call the *Bildungsbuergertum* (the "educated" as distinguished from the "moneyed" bourgeoisie) of early twentieth century Western Europe, I was heir to a good deal of privilege. I was born, in the then Belgian Congo, on January 30, 1933, the very day Hitler became Reich Chancellor. On the paternal side, a dynasty of physicians practiced medicine in the Flemish city of Ghent, Belgium. My Belgian father, Louis, a physician as well, taught tropical medicine in Antwerp, and did research in tropical parasitology, in the Congo, which explains my African birth. My French mother, Denise, was the daughter of an eminent biologist, Maurice Caullery, professor at the Sorbonne and President of the French Academy of Sciences.

Academia was, thus, almost a caste occupation for me. The only questions were where and in what field. The location was my father's choice. As the Congo had no university when I graduated in 1950 from a Jesuit secondary school in Bukavu, I had to go abroad for further studies. My father, a great fan of the United States and a visiting professor of Tropical Medicine at Tulane University, picked Stanford for me. Soon after graduating from Stanford, the US Army drafted me during the Korean War, and sent me to Germany, where I met my German wife and soon became a US citizen. That is roughly the point at which my own decisions began to shape my future life and career. After being demobilized in Germany, I spent a year at the Sorbonne, and then went on to get a PhD (van den Berghe 1960) in the Department of Social Relations at Harvard.

Why and how did I become an anthropologist and what kind of anthropologist did I become? My turning away from a biological and medical ancestry was due to a combination of factors. First, I wanted to do something different from my father, with whom I had a tense relationship during my late adolescence and young adulthood. Second, the Jesuits, while giving me a solid classical education in Latin and Greek, also communicated to me a stupid disdain for mathematics and the hard sciences. Third, there was an African colonial experience. My father's acquaintance with the Mwami of Rwanda, and perhaps most of all, my observation of Jacques Maquet doing fieldwork among the Tuzi wetted my appetite for learning more about African cultures. I was also intrigued by the ethnic, racial, and linguistic conflicts I had experienced in bilingual Belgium, during the Nazi occupation of the Second World War, and in the colonial setting of the Congo in the late 1940s.

Even so, my path to anthropology was somewhat crooked. My double undergraduate major in Stanford was in Political Science and Sociology, but I had taken a graduate seminar with George Spindler. My Stanford MA was in Sociology, but based on urban fieldwork and interviewing. My year at the Sorbonne consisted of a mixture of anthropology (with Lévi-Strauss and Dieterlen), sociology (with Gurvitch and Balandier), and "Social Psychiatry" (with Bastide). What was clear to us graduate students, however, was that the labels "sociology" and "anthropology" did not clearly differentiate where and how people worked. This was especially evident in the approach of Balandier, Mercier, and other Africanists who labeled themselves sociologists but did fieldwork in rural Africa just as did anthropologists who called themselves "ethnologists."

The same message of the fundamental unity, in both subject matter and methodology of sociology and anthropology, was also the basic creed of the Department of Social Relations at Harvard where I next found myself in 1957–1960. I studied with all three members of the ruling triumvirate of Parsons, Kluckhohn, and Allport, as well as with Homans, Sorokin, Barrington Moore, and Evon Vogt. Basically, I had the choice of label for my PhD, and opted for "Sociology" out of what I saw as political expediency. At that time, when I intended to specialize in Africa, and, in "African Studies," anthropology was associated with colonialism. Many African intellectuals argued that whether one labeled oneself an anthropologist or a sociologist was determined principally by the skin pigmentation of the people one studied. For a young Africanist, "sociologist" was the politically correct label. Most new African universities, for instance, only had departments of sociology, staffed mostly by anthropologists!

Because my trade union ticket was in Sociology, my main academic appointments, first at the State University of New York at Buffalo, and, since 1965, at the University of Washington, have been in sociology departments, with an Adjunct position in Anthropology. Most of my courses have been cross-listed, and most of my career has been spent trying to make my colleagues in Sociology somewhat less ethnocentric, and to expose Sociology undergraduate students to at least a smattering of material from non-Western societies and associated methods of fieldwork. As for graduate students, I attracted mostly non-mainstream types and foreign students doing "nonquantitative" theses.

My rejection of a meaningful distinction between Sociology and Anthropology made me somewhat marginal in both fields. This marginality increased even further when, starting in the early 1970s, I perceived the social constructionist paradigm of the social science mainstream as beginning to spring serious leaks. Increasingly, I saw the necessity of incorporating the social and cultural evolution of our species into neo-Darwinian theory. We, humans, were clearly on a double, intertwined evolutionary track: biological and cultural. The central agenda of anthropology, as I now saw it, was to understand the interplay of biology and culture. I began to acquire literacy in primatology, human paleontology, and evolutionary ecology, and to associate myself with the emerging approach of human sociobiology. Even though the issue of the role of biological evolution in human behavior has split anthropology more deeply than ever before, anthropology and psychology were the only behavioral and social sciences that addressed the issue seriously. Once more, I found myself solidly on the anthropological side of the fence, proposing nothing short of a unified anthropology as *the* general science of human evolution, behavioral ecology, and culture.

During the 1970s and 1980s, I largely applied the "new synthesis" of human sociobiology to the two fields of anthropology that had interested me most, namely, kinship and marriage, and race and ethnicity. In my *Human Family Systems* (van den Berghe 1979) and in various articles, I looked at the conventional anthropology of kinship and marriage through the sociobiological lenses of kin selection and reproductive success. Then, in my *The Ethnic Phenomenon* (van den Berghe 1981), I took the leap from kinship to ethnicity, viewing the latter as extended nepotism. It was probably the experience of living in a lineage and clan society (the Yoruba of Western Nigeria) which made me realize that the vast web of nepotism extended from ego through a continuous series of concentric circles. There was a seamless continuity from nuclear and extended family, to lineage, to clan, to local sub-ethnicity, to the larger ethnic groupings. Kinship and ethnicity are nested phenomena, the later being simply an extension of the former. Only in industrial societies with bilateral descent and fragmentary extended family ties does there appear to be a discontinuity between kinship and ethnicity. The biology of nepotism or kin selection was a parsimonious explanation of two universal phenomena: preference for kin and ethnocentrism. One directly extended into the other. Two fields that had hitherto diverged into two discrete specialties, now neatly converged into one.

Having summarized my meandering in the morass of the social sciences in general, and anthropology in particular, I now come to my "discovery" of tourism as a largely neglected topic and one of both huge practical import and theoretical interest. I clearly came to it through my long-standing interest in ethnicity, and approached it primarily as a special type of ethnic relations. An additional incentive in turning to tourism as a field of study is that it is generally regarded as nonsensitive (and nonserious), and, thus, widely open to fieldwork in Latin America (which, by then, had become my principal area of research). Perhaps as an aging field worker somewhat traumatized by two decades of studying sensitive topics (e.g. race relations in South Africa), I was at last looking for a comfortable topic relatively free of suspicious political associations and encounters with the police. Indeed, tourism was a "natural" for participant observation. The anthropologist shares with the ethnic tourist a quest for the exotic other. Thus, the line between the anthropologist as a professional tourist, and the ethnic tourist as an amateur anthropologist is very blurred. At the limit, the anthropologist does not even have to *pose* as a tourist. He *is* one. With a camera around one's neck, the disguise is perfect, the mimicry uncanny.

My moment of revelation came as an afterthought of my 1972–1973 Peruvian fieldwork, when I had been doing a fairly conventional study of "Social Inequality in the Peruvian Andes." During my fieldwork on ethnic and class relations in and around Cuzco, I was, of course, acutely aware of the presence of tourists. Indeed, I was encountering them daily, sometimes engaging them in conversation, or even inviting them home for tea or coffee when I found them particularly simpatico. (They were, for the most part, North American and European backpackers of the long-term-low-budget type.) Many pumped me for information, which in turn, made me aware of a large overlap in our interests. Common themes, for example, were a search for continuity between the Inca past and the ethnographic present, and a concern for mestizo-indigene relations. We differed mostly in the intensity, duration, and depth of our search for the "other", but I might easily have hired them as my assistants.

Yet, as I now look at the main monograph my student George P. Primov and I published out of that study, references to tourism appear only in three different spots (van den Berghe and Primov 1977). On p. 18, there is a brief reference to tourism being the only major "export" of the Department of Cuzco, and to 37,683 visitors spending $2.8 million in 1971. On pp. 113–115, there is a somewhat more extensive account of tourism, covering two pages. We briefly discuss the only "major industry" in the Department, besides the wool trade, tracing it back to the "discovery" of Machu Picchu by Hiram Bingham in 1911, describing the behavior of the foreign tourists, and assessing the impact of tourism on the total economy. Finally, on pp. 221–222, we treat the reception of a small group of transient "hippies" by the locals in the small community of Chinchero, and refer to the fact that they are treated as an ethnic category.

In short, we recognized the local impact of tourism, but we certainly did not make it the focus of our study. I only developed a sense of a missed opportunity when, in 1977, I revisited my very first fieldwork site, the town of San Cristóbal de las Casas, in the Mexican State of Chiapas. There too, in 1959, I had been studying ethnic relations between indigenes and mestizos with my friend and colleague, Benjamin N. Colby (Colby and van den Berghe 1961). The tourist presence back in 1959 was still minimal, so we can be excused for ignoring it, but, by the late 1970s, San Cristóbal was definitely on the backpackers' circuit.

Indeed, I found the town transformed by tourism. Local town mestizos were quickly converting the quaint colonial houses around the main square into scores of restaurants, cafes, bars, hotels, pensions, boutiques, travel agencies, and so on, catering to foreign tourists. Where the existing stock of colonial buildings did not suffice, they built neocolonial ones. Besides the local produce market that had at least quadrupled in size, and which had itself become a tourist site and fertile ground for pickpockets, an open artisanal market and several galleries catering to tourists had sprung up around a shady plaza dominated by two lovely colonial churches. What an exciting place to study tourism, I told myself. Surely, I must return, and I finally did, but not until 1990 (van den Berghe 1994).

More than any other single experience, it was the vision of how tourism had transformed San Cristóbal which reoriented my research efforts. I had only recently published my Peruvian fieldwork, but I now looked at my field notes again, especially at the great annual series of rituals around the Catholic feast of Corpus Christi and the re-enactment of the Inti Raymi, the Inca winter solstice festival, on June 21 (van den Berghe 1980). Here was a deliberate attempt by the local Cuzco bourgeoisie to foster tourism by combining the Inca revivalism of the Inti Raymi pageantry with the no less spectacular processions of Corpus Christi into the vast show of the Semana del Cuzco. An entire neo-Inca theatrical performance was invented for the purpose, and staged in the Inca "citadel" of Sacsayhuaman overlooking the city of Cuzco, with hundreds of performers and tens of thousands of spectators, mostly locals, but also national and international tourists (van den Berghe 1980).

Two things became clear to me at this stage, although it took me a few more years to bring them out into print. One was that tourism was, almost by definition, a type of ethnic relations, since it generally brought together "hosts" and "guests" of different ethnicity. Thus, tourism was squarely within the purview of what had been my main theoretical interest and fieldwork focus for a quarter century—of considering race and ethnic relations. This explains why I approach tourism primarily from the angle of ethnic relations, and why I am principally interested in ethnic tourism, that is, the kind of tourism where the cultural exoticism of the "other" is the main tourist attraction.

The other revelation of reanalyzing my Cuzco data from the early 1970s was that tourism, far from being the destroyer of local culture, the imperialistic pollution of hitherto pristine societies that it is frequently portrayed to be, can, and often is, a catalyst for the invention of new cultural products, or the revival of moribund traditions (Graburn 1976). Even though some of these newly created cultural products were initially aimed at tourist consumption, they can acquire a vitality of their own, and become incorporated into a new self-image of the local culture. Staged authenticity (MacCannell 1973), in short, can become "real." New inventions can quickly become "tradition." To view tourism as the great destroyer of authenticity is a narrow and prejudiced perspective. To be sure, tourism can be destructive, but it can also be a great ferment for cultural change and florescence, as was the case in Cuzco (van den Berghe and Flores Ochoa 2000).

Meanwhile, back in Seattle, my friend and colleague Charles ("Biff") Keyes and I were both active participants in an on-going University of Washington seminar on the "Comparative Study of Ethnicity and Nationalism" (which also included sociologists like Michael Hechter and political scientists like Paul Brass, as well as other anthropologists like Simon Ottenberg). We started exchanging experiences, he on Chiang Mai, Thailand, and I on Cuzco. We applied for a National Science Foundation grant to do a comparative study of the impact of tourism in the two settings, but we were turned down, despite generally favorable assessments of the proposal. We were, of course, disappointed, but as a consolation move, we decided to organize our annual ethnicity seminar for 1981 on the theme of "Tourism and Ethnicity," subsequently publishing the papers in the 1984 Special Issue of the *Annals of Tourism Research* (Volume 11, Number 3). In our Introduction thereto, we formulated what we saw as the special features of tourism as a form of ethnic relations, and of ethnic tourism as a special kind of tourism (van den Berghe and Keyes 1984). We were especially intrigued by the role of intermediaries in the tourist trade, by the conversion of natives into "tourees" (i.e., targets of tourist curiosity who consequently modify their behavior), by the transientness and nonrepeatability of tourist–touree interactions that encourage "cheating", and by the complementary asymmetries of assets between tourists and tourees (the tourists being privileged in wealth and leisure, but ignorant of local conditions, the tourees being materially poorer but well-informed of local prices and conditions).

By now, I was eager to return to the field, both to San Cristóbal and to Cuzco, but in the absence of outside funding, this had to wait on my sabbaticals. Be it noted here in passing that on my return from my NIMH-funded research in Peru in 1972–1973, Senator Proxmire awarded me one of his notorious "Golden Fleece Awards," for, in his view, wasting taxpayers' money on trivial subjects. All my attempts to get outside funding for my research have since proven fruitless, but I must say I enjoyed the freedom and independence of not having a paymaster. In 1990, I finally returned to San Cristóbal to conduct a general study of ethnic tourism (van den Berghe 1994, 1995). My research was greatly enhanced by the perspective of having known the town for thirty years. Through half-a-dozen short visits at roughly five or six years' intervals, I had followed its astonishing transformation from a provincial backwater town of some 20,000 inhabitants to a bustling tourist mecca of 150,000. One of the striking changes was the liberalization of indigene-mestizo relations, and the valorization of indigenous culture in good part because of the tourist interest in "living Mayas." From a despised, discriminated-against minority, "Indians" had been turned into a highly marketable commodity (van den Berghe 1995). Hotels and restaurants assumed Maya names and decorated their rooms and patios with local pottery, weavings, and hats. The walls of the municipal tourist offices were covered with posters of both Maya ruins and local "living Mayas."

Just four years after my fieldwork there, San Cristóbal hit the world stage by becoming the epicenter of Zapatista revolutionary theater and the venue of the inconclusive negotiations that followed. In book reviews of my 1994 monograph, I was taken to task by not having seen the Zapatistas coming, but, of course, the movement was located in the lowlands of Chiapas, not in the highlands of which San Cristóbal is the center. The highland communities of Tzotzil and Tzeltal speakers were only peripherally affected. The tourist trade, however, responded very quickly. Hordes of journalists and political tourists descended on San Cristóbal, jokingly referred to locally as "el tercer ejercito" (the third army). Soon San Cristóbal tourist stalls filled with t-shirts of Sub-Comandante Marcos, Zapatista dolls in ski-masks, and even expensive amber carvings of the new saints in the revolutionary pantheon. As for the statue of the local conquistador, Diego de Mazariegos, it had already been smashed to bits in a 1992 march to "celebrate" the 500th anniversary of Spanish arrival in the Western Hemisphere.

My return to Cuzco to conduct a similar study had to wait until 1996 (van den Berghe 2001; van den Berghe and Flores 2000). There also, I had the benefit of a quarter century from which to mark change, and of excellent local contacts, especially with local anthropologists Jorge Flores Ochoa and Abraham Valencia and my former assistant Gladys Becerra. Another former assistant, Narciso Ccohuana Ccohuana had recycled himself as an Inca curandero taking "mystical tourists" on remote (and expensive) jaunts to worship the mountain spirits.

The overwhelming impression that Cuzco left me with in 1996 was that tourism had only a peripheral effect on the countryside. Most tourists do not wander past the well-defined circuit circumscribed by the city of Cuzco, the ruins of Machu Picchu and the "Sacred Valley of the Incas" that links the two. The hinterland is still only superficially touched by tourism, and, if anything, even more pauperized than it was in the early 1970s. Small towns, even close to Cuzco, offer virtually no tourist facilities or even crafts for sale, unless they are, like Pisac, on the main tourist loop of the "Sacred Valley." Land reform of that era had a clear negative impact on agriculture and pastoralism, and the homespun weaving industry for which the area was justly famous went into a tailspin. Quechua peasants now largely dress in discarded second-hand Western clothes, except the few in the tourist spots who pose for photographs by tourists for a fee.

The city of Cuzco, however, presents an entirely different picture. It not only thrives from tourism, with several hundred establishments (travel agencies, hotels, restaurants, curio shops, and bars) catering almost exclusively to them. Tourism is virtually the only game in town, apart from the local subsistence economy which has not changed much. Unlike that of San Cristóbal, the central produce market of Cuzco, for instance, has not grown much in a quarter century. But cultural production of crafts of all kinds has increased enormously. Hundreds of urban artists and craftsmen now produce artifacts ranging form neocolonial paintings in the famous Cuzco style, to Nativity scenes in ceramics, wood and plaster, to weavings, woolen sweaters, hats, leather goods, jewelry, dolls, and countless other objects that inundate hundreds of small shops and stalls in the center of town. This vast economy of crafts is obviously stimulated and patronized by tourists, both foreign and domestic, but it is well integrated into local, urban, mestizo culture. The local bourgeoisie also buys some of these crafts, and local trade fairs, such as the Christmas market on the Plaza de Armas, are clearly dominated by locals.

The same can be said of large communal rituals such as Holy Week, Corpus Christi, and the Inti Raymi, which attract many tourists, to be sure, but are nevertheless totally integrated in the local culture and define the identity and self-image of Cuzco as a great ritual and artistic center. All these events, while both boosting tourism and being boosted by tourism, are totally "real," much as, say, their counterparts are in Pamplona or Santiago de Compostela in contemporary Spain. Tourism, in Cuzco as elsewhere, can be a major catalyst in the continuous "invention of tradition" (Hobsbawn and Ranger, eds. 1983), but the new traditions acquire a life of their own, quite distinct from the initial impetus of tourism.

Perhaps I should say something about my methodology of tourism research. I have followed very conventional anthropological fieldwork methods of participant observation, and unstructured or semistructured interviews with a limited number of nonrandomly selected informants, supplemented by whatever archival or statistical information was already available. There are, however, a few characteristics of the tourist scene which uniquely affect methodology, and I have already touched on the first one, namely, the ease with which the anthropologist can mimic the tourist and blend in as a participant observer. In no other situation is participant observation so absurdly easy. Indeed, as I suggested earlier, the identification is so easy because, at the limit, anthropologist and tourist are one. The anthropologist is a professional tourist; the tourist an amateur anthropologist. Ethnic tourists are so often engrossed in their own observation that they can, in turn, be unobtrusively observed. They are so used to regard the ethnic "other" as an object of interest that few conceive of themselves as targets of curiosity, and when so revealed by the anthropologist, their reaction is often one of amusement rather than irritation.

A second feature of tourism that affects methodology is the transience and multi-ethnicity of tourists. Studying tourees and middlemen does not differ much from other fieldwork situations in that one deals with a relatively stable population and often one of limited ethnic diversity. Tourists, however, turn over quickly, often by 80% or more per week, and come from almost everywhere. The rapid turnover means that one cannot rely on repeated interviews with a limited number of informants, as in conventional ethnography. Furthermore, the extraordinary diversity of tourists poses linguistic problems in interviewing, and requires a large enough sample to represent that diversity of class, ethnicity, nationality, and so on. One of the factors that greatly facilitated my field work in tourism was the lucky circumstance of my fluency in four common European languages (English, French, German, and Spanish). Between them, I could interview the vast majority of tourists, either in their home language, or, at least, in their best second language.

Third, the issue of reciprocity is made relatively easy in studying tourists. Many anthropologists agonize over their inability to reciprocate adequately the help they received from their hosts. In interviewing tourists, however, the anthropologist is in a unique position to reciprocate by being in possession of information valuable to tourists (about local conditions, schedules, prices, facilities, artifacts, etc.). At the conclusion of every interview with tourists, I would offer to answer any questions they might have. Not uncommonly, this started a second, more informal, conversation that became, in effect, a second level of interviewing. The tourists' questions were often as informative about them as their answers to my questions had been. Thus, I was simultaneously reciprocating and eliciting more information.

A technique I used frequently was to observe and follow a tourist for a half-hour or so, and then interview him or her. I also joined bus tours, either as an ostensible client, or with the knowledge and consent of the tour guide, sometimes for an entire day. During or at the end of the tour, I would interview two or three members of the groups, as well as—often—the tour leader.

As for photography, I generally walked about with a 35-mm camera equipped with a large 35–200-mm zoom lens. The camera enables me not only to blend in more easily, but also to record information and illustrate situations, with the triple use of helping me in writing up my data, of illustrating my later publications, and of accompanying my public lectures and slide shows. In fact, I still teach an undergraduate seminar in ethnic tourism at the University of Washington, notwithstanding my formal "retirement."

The issue of institutional support for tourism research may be of some interest. Of my colleagues in two departments, anthropologists tended to show more interest and understanding than sociologists, although the majority of both seemed to view tourism as a peripheral subject, indeed not a very serious one. Several joked that it was a good ploy to deduct one's vacations from one's income taxes. That said, I encountered interest and encouragement from a few, benevolent amusement from most, and sporadic attendance at my periodic slide shows. Nobody ever discouraged me or my students from pursuing research in the field, and, indeed, the Sociology Department even hired one of my PhD students (Susan Pitchford) as an Assistant Professor, though not because of her specialty in tourism. To my knowledge, none of my students in tourism has experienced career difficulties. It is clear, however, that neither in anthropology nor in sociology, is tourism an established mainstream specialty, and that job candidates had better market themselves as competent in other fields as well.

Regarding institutional support for tourism research, it is fair to say that, apart from sabbaticals, I received none, as previously mentioned. I made two grant applications for tourism research, one with Charles Keyes, one by myself. Both received quite favorable reviews, and both were turned down with the standard "regret" letter indicating that many more worthwhile projects were received than could be funded. But the proposal by myself was the more informative one. It received such favorable evaluations that I was informally told over the telephone to expect formal approval within days. But the letter I received said that I had been turned down.

Although I cannot prove it, I strongly suspect political intervention there. It was probably connected with the 1973 "Golden Fleece Award" from Senator Proxmire, mentioned earlier. That "award" was made for research connected with sex, not tourism, but I suspect it gave me the reputation of not doing serious work, and, thus, it dissuaded government funding agencies from supporting me for fear of attracting political censure on themselves.

Conclusion

In conclusion, I would like to situate myself in the field of "tourism studies," and more specifically, at the anthropological end of it. There is much in the tourism literature both to titillate and irritate. The field is fertile ground for postmodernists and social constructionists of all ilks. Much of tourism is a stage for the recreation of the self and of the other, and much of tourism interaction rests on "working misunderstandings" and on mutual misperceptions between strangers. The social construction of "reality" in tourism is all the more obvious for its being self-conscious. Deceit is not only rampant, but expected. Yet, tourism is perhaps the least conflict-ridden form of interethnic relations. Tourism generally presupposes a minimum of peace and security to develop, but, once there, it ranks remarkably low as a generator of hostility.

This is the great paradox in tourism. Relying largely on transient, non-repeated interactions between total strangers, tourism should foster cheating, deceit, and conflict. Those are the very conditions that produce crime in large cities, for instance. The sharp ethnic boundary between tourist and touree should only exacerbate this state of anomie. Yet, amazingly, tourism works remarkably well, to the mutual satisfaction of most concerned. In my field studies in Cuzco and San Cristóbal, both tourists and locals expressed a preponderance of positive reactions to their interactions, by a margin of at least ten to one.

To be sure, I have been accused of presenting too sanguine a view of the effects of tourism, and this may be due to the fact that ethnic tourism, my main concern, in one of the more benign forms of the phenomenon. It may also be attributable to an alleged conservative bias on my part, even though my politics are close to the anarchic end of the spectrum. However, by the acid test that the native is always right, my relatively benign view of ethnic tourism is validated by the positive response one gets from the vast majority of natives in the host societies. Except for occasional complaints that tourism causes inflation, represents cultural imperialism, or corrupts the youth, most natives simply welcome tourism because it brings in money. In the field, one hears but faint echoes of the litany of ills associated with tourism in the minds of First World intellectuals, not least among them, anthropologists (DeKadt, ed. 1979; Smith 1977).

Why, then, does tourism "work," as well as it does, despite possessing many of the characteristics favoring anomie, deceit, mistrust, and conflict? The answer, I think, lies in a materialist, "rational choice" model of human behavior. At the risk of drawing a caricature, many anthropologists (and ethnic tourists) see the tourees in Third World countries as powerless, exploited victims of a capitalist world order, who had lived in harmony with their natural environment until the depredations of Western slavery, colonialism, and "development" (DeKadt, ed. 1979; Smith 1977). Without in any way denying the devastation of pandemics, genocides, slavery, deforestation, and other catastrophes that frequently accompanied the expansion of the capitalist world system between the late fifteenth and the twentieth centuries, this romantic vision of the noble savage has one capital flaw. It reduces history to a morality play that not only vilifies the West, but also reduces the "other" to a passive victim. In so doing, it negates the common humanity of conqueror and conquered, and creates two distinct species of brutal victors and noble vanquished. It basically denies the equal aptitude of both to be nasty to one another and to destroy their environment, as countless non-Western societies have repeatedly demonstrated.

The only significant difference between the West and the "rest" is that industrial technology has greatly accelerated the scale and rate of destruction. The machine gun kills more and better than the spear; the chain saw can deforest faster than the stone axe. Put that modern technology into the hands of "natives," however, and they quickly show an equal ability and eagerness to destroy one another and their habitat. The common denominator of humanity is that we are selfish maximizers endowed with a creative adaptive capacity to make the most of new situations, and to earn a living with the least effort.

Seen in the light of such a model, the general success of tourism becomes easily understandable. Middlemen, craftsmen, artists, and tourees are all part of a vast, complex enterprise where the "hosts" quickly adapt with incredible ingenuity to satisfy tourist demand for services and experiences in order to maximize their income. They quickly produce anything that sells. They reinvent "tradition," stage performances, offer new services, create new objects, and modify their behavior and their dress, if these new products attract the tourist gaze and dollar. To be sure, the economic benefits of tourism are very unequally distributed, and are often accompanied by high costs, but this is true of any complex system of exchange. Sometimes, tourism creates new forms of exploitation and misery, e.g., the sale of young peasant girls and the spread of HIV in the flourishing Thai sex tourism industry.

Overall, however, tourism is no different from any other economic transaction that is relatively free of coercion. A transaction only takes place if both parties feel that they have gained by it. The issue, then, is not how "just," "equitable," or "exploitative" the tourist–touree interaction is, but how free it is from external constraints. To be sure, tourism is often a high-risk industry, beyond local control. Tourist demand is highly elastic and responsive to conditions such as political unrest, crime, terrorism, and natural disasters. The tourist has an ample array of alternative destinations, and freak events can devastate local tourist economies. Volatility is one of the major risks in the tourist industry.

However, hosts can, and often do, have considerable control over their guests. Local states can impose severe restrictions on visas, currency exchange, forbidden zones, choice of guides, and so on. Communist countries, notably China and Cuba, have been extreme cases of a supply-driven, state-controlled, tourist trade, which even survives in post-Communist countries such as Russia. Local peasant communities can and often do control and restrict access or behavior (e.g., forbidding photography). Not uncommonly, they create "front stages" for tourist gaze while keeping tourists out of the "backstage." Vendors can fix prices and restrict the flow of information. Finally, the tourist trade is replete with deception, fraud, and petty theft. Tourists are frequently cheated, but generally on a scale that is sufficiently small relative to their resources as to be fairly inconsequential for their subsequent behavior.

In short, tourism is best understood as a complex set of interactions and behaviors in which all parties actively adapt to each other in order to maximize their respective outcomes: satisfaction with the tourism experience for tourists (and tourists often spend lavishly, and, by local standards, stupidly, to gain "unique" experiences); monetary gain for the hosts. There are many asymmetries of wealth, leisure, knowledge, experience, background, class, and ethnicity between hosts and guests which sometimes make transactions appear irrational, but in the end most participants on both sides are satisfied with the outcome most of the time. Or else, the system breaks down (e.g., after a terrorist incident).

What many might see as my overly sanguine view of tourism has, in the last analysis, to do with ethnicity. By its very nature, tourism is a form of ethnic relations. True, these relations are often superficial and transient, but they are massive in scale. Nearly a billion people a year—one sixth of humanity—travels internationally each year. At their destination, they encounter several times that number of locals. Probably three fourths of humanity encounter or, at least, observe tourists many times a year. Exoticism has been almost totally globalized. Yet, compared to other forms of ethnic relations with which modern societies are sadly familiar, tourism is astonishingly peaceful. Every year, a few tourists get killed or raped by bandits, kidnapped by guerilleros or imprisoned by governments. Freak misunderstandings can have lethal outcomes, as when a few tourists in Guatemala were killed because they were wrongly suspected of abducting children to trade their organs. But these episodes are widely publicized and generally quickly suppressed by governments eager not to jeopardize their tourist trade. For every tourist killed in anger, thousands of people perish in civil wars, genocides, race riots, and the epidemics, famines and other disasters caused by ethnic conflicts. For all its downsides, tourism is probably the best opportunity we have for getting to know and for liking the "other" better.

Chapter 4

The Emergence of a New Field of Study

Tourism Study as a Social Fact

That tourism is a social fact for most of us is something that is generally taken for granted. There is little doubt about its existence; and people in the Western world and beyond have referred for some time to one or more aspects of this subject with only a minimum of quibbling. Even academics, who are accustomed to disputing over definitions, have come to recognize it as an aspect of the social reality in which we and others exist. One has to be puzzled, however, that considering the magnitude of the social fact before them, and assuming normal curiosity about various aspects of social reality, it took the academics dealt with in this book and other scholars so long to put the subject of tourism under scientific scrutiny.

In this chapter, we will be looking into the emerging social fact of tourism study, which with a few earlier exceptions, began to emerge in the disciplines of anthropology and sociology shortly after the middle of the twentieth century. Such study, which had earlier been carried out in a fragmentary way by a few scholars, was not all that enthusiastically greeted in academia and beyond, but in fits and starts, it came to develop a history of its own. In Chapter 1, we introduced some grounds for getting on with the study of that history; in Chapter 2, we showed how it has been carried out; and in Chapter 3, the personal histories of the participants in this study were laid out.

Having established the existence of a discipline-related practice that has studied tourism, and having perused the personal histories of those anthropological and sociological scholars who were on the ground early and who have become our principal informants, now we are in a position to embark on a consideration (with the help of their personal histories) in some depth of the beginnings of such study and to trace its early development. In order to do that, let us follow up our inclination to consider the anthropological/sociological study of tourism as a pursuit of a certain kind of knowledge, which can be studied in the same general way as other academic subjects such as physics, religion, art, molecular biology, or botany—all of them considered as forms of sociocultural activity created and developed by human beings.

Our approach in this study has involved "cracking" the taken-for-granted notion of knowledge as simply a corpus of substantive assertions and ideas about aspects of the world as, for example, relativity in physics, the double helix form of DNA in biology, the twelve-tone row in music, biological evolution, Theravada Buddhism, or graphic artistic traditions in whatever culture(s). This purely idealistic notion of knowledge as an aspect of sociocultural reality overlooks the fact that it is, according to Bourdieu (1977:xvii), "indivisible from the conditions of its production," and according to Geertz (1974:4), from its "instruments and encasements." Barth (2002) elaborates on this, by taking all knowledge to have an idealistic aspect that is everywhere expressed and transmitted in certain media and produced and distributed among networks of socioculturally constrained actors. And Pickering (1993:14), pointing to what appears to be a growing consensus in the social study of scientific knowledge, speaks of how various elements of scientific culture—"social, institutional, conceptual, material"— evolve in a dialectical relationship with one another.

Without insisting definitively on the priority of one of the various aspects of knowledge that have been suggested, we can nevertheless venture the opinion that early ideas and practices that helped to make up our comprehension of tourism appeared in certain social settings to certain people with dispositions to look at, and communicate about the subject in anthropological or sociological ways; and their early formulations would seem to have established a range of possibilities for the development of those ideas and practices. What can be said about the early social and personal conditions that contributed to the development of such a configuration in anthropology and sociology?

In the Beginning

At the time of their "discovery" of tourism, however conceived, the anthropologists and sociologists participating in this study already were more or less socialized creatures of established disciplines who were situated in certain academic locii— departments, schools, research centers and the like (loosely referred to here as academic), which were directly or indirectly associated with the study of anthropology, sociology, or both. One should be careful, however, about tying a participant too closely to a particular institutional locus. First of all, the editor is aware of at least one legitimate tourism scholar, who though having anthropological or sociological credentials, was working in a non-academic milieu. Also, disciplinary connections were not always clear (the editor of this volume, for example, was in a period of transition from an academically defined sociologist to anthropologist at the time), and several participants vacillated in their identifications. There were also a few with connections to several other disciplines. Nevertheless, it may be of some use to know that six of our participants tended to think of themselves primarily as sociologists and seven as anthropologists at the time they were getting into the study of tourism.

The academic institutions with which our scholars were affiliated and in which they had been trained operated in a familiar Western academic way, the main tenets of which had a considerable history. Scholars in departments or schools were organized in terms of a more or less specific production and dissemination of certain kinds of knowledge, which took the form of teaching, research, or both. As Barth (2002:9) points out, "The ideological and organizational visions of knowledge in such institutions were most clearly epitomized in the Humboldtan university concept." In this arrangement, the production of knowledge came to be seen as involving scientific research by "autonomously driven scholars," who in a pattern established by von Humboldt at the University of Berlin in the early nineteenth century, were "free" to teach or do research as they wished.

Such freedom, however, had certain qualifications. True, an element of personal freedom is involved in Western academic pursuits, but this usually is considered to be freedom from non-academic constraints while engaging in such pursuits. However, academics are certainly subject to disciplinary constraints, as pointed out by Finkelstein (1984:221), who in speaking about the American academic profession, says, "In at least one fundamental respect, professors are a world apart from most other workers: their on-the-job performance is determined to an extraordinary degree by their professional values and standards." Such standards, of course, have included institutional regulations, and for some, would extend further into the non-academic world in various sorts of arrangements, including those for applied research (Bourdieu 1987).

In applied research, scholarly work is put at the service of public or private sponsors. So in speaking about the applied aspects of the work of some scholars in one of the disciplines being considered here, Kuper (2004:53) points out that "applied anthropology was initially conceived as an aid to colonial administration;" and on the sociological side, Rossides (1978) reminds us that sociologists worked (consciously or unconsciously) to provide information that might help to reduce certain social problems of Western industrial societies. But despite the existence of applied research with its acknowledged constraints derived from the practical needs of sponsors, the ideal of autonomously driven scholarship within disciplinary confines, continues to pervade academic scholarship.

At the time they were becoming involved in the study of tourism as a scientific subject, all of the participants in this study were positioned in Western academic institutions, which provided them with support and (more or less) direction; also, some of them participated in formal or informal supra-institutional discipline-related associations such as the American Sociological Society, the American Anthropological Association, or the French CNRS (none of them relating directly to tourism, however), which performed similar functions. Though some of these scholars may have been academically marginal in certain respects, there were no academic isolates among them. Professions of personal independence or lack of institutional support to the contrary, all of our participants were in some degree structurally constrained in their discipline-related pursuit of knowledge, a fact that ought to be kept in mind in any reconstruction of their developing involvement with the subject of tourism.

It would be fair to say, however, that taken as a whole, our participants at the outset had little, if any, discipline-related support or direction for their developing interest in tourism. It is hard to find any academic positions for such study in the disciplines involved; nor was there much in the way of support in anthropology and sociology for studying leisure-related subjects (of which tourism may be taken as one). According to Rojek (1989:69), most university departments and nearly all the leading journals having to do with leisure and recreation were founded in the 1970s and early 1980s. And as far as the great anthropological/sociological scholars mentioned in Chapter 1 are concerned—those who established a good part of the theoretical groundwork available to our participants—such subjects never occupied more than a peripheral position in their thinking (Rojek 1985:1–4). In sum, therefore, Nuñez' (1989:265) comments about the lack of respect for the subject of tourism in anthropology would seem to warrant expansion to the social sciences in general, to leisure studies, and even beyond in academe (Jackson and Burton 1989:11), in which case, Cooper's comment (Cooper 1989:50) of a decade or more ago is relevant to our consideration of tourism study. At that time, he said, "The very idea of a serious study of leisure, not to mention a science of leisure, is intellectually suspect."

Going beyond academic institutions to the whole of Western culture in the period we are considering, therefore, we can take note of certain historic stirrings that would ultimately make themselves felt throughout academe. MacCannell (1976:5), in an aside, speaks of the increasing social significance of leisure (as opposed to work) for the period associated with the beginnings of academic interest in the subject by anthropologists and sociologists; and Rojek (1985:2) points out that by the fifth decade of the twentieth century there had been a shift from a work-centered to a more leisure-oriented culture in the Western world, a natural effect of advanced industrialization.

Dramatic manifestations of such historic stirrings had already been demonstrated toward the end of the nineteenth century in England by the appearance of phenomena such as the tours of Thomas Cook, and in France after 1936, the institution of a government-decreed vacation with pay. As indicated earlier, such manifestations seem to have been thought worthy of attention by certain national and international agencies as, for example, the United Nations, the World Bank, and Swiss Research Institutes, which kept track of acknowledged or unacknowledged touristic activity in various ways, but mostly in the form of straightforward demographic analyses. A somewhat deeper and more personal indication of the nature of the beginnings of such touring is to be found among those engaged in tourism itself, i.e., the tourists. McCabe (2002:64–69), in discussing MacCannell's earlier leisure-related observation on tourism, as well as his own work, emphasizes what appears to be a persisting ambivalence about touristic practice even among tourists themselves, which, from the beginning, has included a "resistance" to being called a tourist.

Such was the situational nexus of our participating scholars who had been trained in anthropology, sociology, or both, and variously socialized before that. (Any search for earlier common socializing experiences such as childhood travel or personality manifestations was doomed to disappointment before it had begun.) All of them were more or less embarked on academic careers within the framework of these disciplines when they "discovered" the possibility of studying tourism scientifically; but to engage in such study was to undertake something out of the ordinary—not in any disciplinary mainstream.

There is a good deal of evidence in our sample of participants for a (perceived) lack of social support or the rejection of early ventures in tourism research—negative implications that were, perhaps, balanced for those involved by some sense of freedom and excitement derived from being in a peripheral, but nevertheless somewhat legitimate, academic situation. In describing the experience of anthropologists who were developing an interest in tourism, Nash (1996:vii) says elsewhere, "Being on the margin of our professional cultures, with all the looseness of social ties that this implies, we have had an opportunity for adventure which may be even greater than that which is routine among anthropologists who are well-known for their adventurous natures." One would expect, therefore, that any of our scholars who began to focus on the subject of tourism would display, among other traits, qualities of independence necessary for negotiating what significant others may have considered questionable or even forbidden academic territory; and from the evidence available, this appears to be so. At a minimum, our participants experienced a lack of social confirmation of their interest in tourism, as well as an enlarged sense of freedom associated with sociocultural distance from their academic establishments.

Consider participant Eric Cohen as an example. In his personal history, he says that in his fledgling days at the Hebrew University, the sociology department was conducting various studies of developing towns, in which he participated. According to him, these studies were being carried on mostly within a theoretical framework dominated by Parsonian functionalism (discussed earlier in Chapter 1), with which he appea`rs not to have been terribly sympathetic, especially with "disturbing" tourists muddling up the research scene. In trying to make sense of the tourism-related facts he had encountered in his research, he says that he felt forced to go it alone theoretically, and possibly put his academic career at risk. An interest in religious studies, as well as an acquired penchant for phenomeno-logical analysis derived from Mircea Eliade and the sociologist Alfred Schuetz, among others (with whom he had become familiar in his academic socialization), were the master theoretical tools he used for developing an alternative theoretical path for his investigations.

Dann and Crick, having chosen academic positions on the outskirts of a declining British empire, had an opportunity to create new teaching programs on their own within a framework of what appears to have been—at least at the out-set—minimal institutional intervention. This freedom, combined with Dann's location in a well-known tourist destination, Barbados, helped him to create some hands-on tourism research for his students and himself. Crick, though apparently lacking institutional and personal support that Dann was able to cultivate on his own, made his way into the field without much in the way of help from confreres. As is apparent in his personal history, he also reveals qualities of independence that enabled him to negotiate a rather unorthodox (touristic) career path. Both of these scholars reveal an ability to go their own way, especially with regard to their touristic interests.

Lanfant conveys a profound sense of self-reliance before and during her aca-demic life, even in the face of authority figures with whom she disagreed, or who raised questions about her choice of subject matter. So one cannot help but recognize her persistence in personal initiatives regarding leisure and (interna-tional) tourism. Nash struggles a bit with developing his own viewpoint in the face of local partisans of culturally oriented Marxist and biologically based views in his department at Connecticut. Boissevain, a solid empiricist, found himself some-what at odds with popular dependency theories of "underdevelopment" in his stud-ies of tourism and development in Malta and elsewhere in the third world. On the basis of a personal history, which fairly bristles with the go-it-aloneness that has marked Van den Berghe's academic career since the beginning, one is hard put to imagine this already well-established scholar requiring permission or direction from anyone to carry out research on anything (see also his personal history in Bennett Berger, ed. 1990). And from the beginning, Swain appears set to bring her feminist slant to the study of tourism regardless of obstacles encountered.

And to conclude this by no means all-inclusive, but fairly representative survey of our group of independently oriented scholars, there is the declaration of independence by Dean MacCannell at the end of the personal history written for this volume, which confirms and extends a quality revealed earlier in his autobiographical contribution to the Berger (1990) book. It can be taken as a somewhat extreme, but nevertheless representative statement by the kind of person who broke ground for the study of tourism in anthropology and sociology—one who was capable of going against the grain of existing institutional and disciplinary norms, and even profiting from such a situation.

So, it is apparent that the general impression from our sample does not disappoint expectations that early anthropological and sociological inquirers into the subject of tourism had qualities of independence that one would expect of people in the forefront of any new field of study. How different they were from colleagues in their own disciplines, which have some reputation for their cultivation of independence and tolerance of personal freedom, is difficult to determine, and of course, subject to further inquiry. Indeed, how much they stand out in an academic culture oriented around the Humboldtan ideals of freedom, cannot be definitively decided here. But the editor's own research experience with certain independent-minded creative artists could suggest that we are on the right track in emphasizing this personality trait among our tourism researchers.

Indeed, a good many of our participants brought to mind a certain kind of composer of serious music, with whom Nash (1954) was concerned in an earlier study. This kind of composer-type, labeled as "Ivory Tower," was absolutely insistent in going his or her own way in the production of music, regardless of the views of significant others such as conductors, publishers, instrumentalists, etc. Of course, such comparisons are difficult to make, but the fact that such artists, studied by the same author, have come to mind here should give us a further reason for suggesting the salience of this personality trait among our early tourism scholars and to argue for the importance of personal independence as a factor in the creation of the (then) new field of tourism studies. But that there also were enabling social factors, such as the general spawning of new specialties in the disciplines involved, as well as the increasing valuation of leisure-related activity, should not be forgotten.

Perhaps, a final caveat about linking qualities of personality with the social conditions of particular social roles is warranted here. Experience suggests that any such attempt should be undertaken with caution and that a variety of kinds of people can function in specific social conditions. In general, the more narrowly those conditions are defined, the more likely is there to be some connection, but even then the prospects are not good for discovering any one-to-one connection. However, where confreres are lacking, the linking of qualities of self-involvement and independence with performance in an apparently ambiguous or anomic situation is not exactly unexpected (Nash and Heiss 1967).

Getting Involved

How did these people get involved with the subject of tourism? As Cohen's account suggests, the recognition of some aspects of that subject (e.g., tourists, relationships between tourists and hosts) and the act of putting it under scientific scrutiny are not identical. Cohen's personal history shows that the transition from the former to the latter, when it occurs, does not necessarily happen immediately. Indeed with him (and unlike some other participants), it took a number of years. Assuming that our participants had come to recognize tourism in one way or another as a fact of everyday life before they began their careers as anthropologists and sociologists, it was only later, after having acquired some experience in anthropology, sociology, or other disciplines, that they could see the subject in disciplinary terms. This path to "discovery" seems never to have come about through some kind of rational planning. So, for example, Cohen, who devotes much attention to this process, noted that there are some others who he had come to recognize as tourists in his research field, but who at the outset, though recognizable, were not yet (for him) conceived as objects that fit into some line of anthropological/sociological inquiry.

Though a variety of psychological factors seem to have been at work among our participants in the transformation of tourism into a scientific subject, most, if not all, of these academics would probably agree with Nuñez (1989:265), who in speaking about anthropological discoverers of tourism, says that the process of discovery was dominated by accident or serendipity. Referring especially to early anthropologists getting on to the tourism track, he says that they "have gone abroad to study other things or other people, and almost everywhere have discovered tourism." But, further, according to him, they were delayed in bringing their discovery into scientific light by what amounts to a discipline-wide tabu against any serious study of the subject. The evidence for such a tabu is not entirely clear from our participants' personal histories. Was it directed specifically at the study of tourism, something more inclusive such as leisure, or as Crick suggests, some broader deviation from academic norms? Unfortunately, our evidence is inadequate in this regard.

Nevertheless, the evidence for some kind of social situation that—partially, at least—worked against their study of tourism is widespread in the accounts of our participants. Cohen refers to what he fears might be negative attitudes of departmental peers and preceptors. Lanfant and Picard mention what appears to have been a latent, non-supportive culture in the CNRS, which seems to have been activated after they showed their touristic inclinations. Lanfant mentions comments by one sympathetic reviewer who, in discussing her application for tourism study, says that should she persist in her project (to study international tourism), she would most likely have to rely on herself alone. Jafari mentions his own "protests" (e.g., signs on his dormitory door) against those others who would denigrate the choice of tourism as a subject of inquiry; and he puts his well-known perseverance to work in finding a path into the field. Graburn speaks of academic or bureaucratic resistance to a proposed course on tourism and his difficulties in getting some early tourism research published. Smith (1977) mentions numerous difficulties experienced by colleagues and serious problems of her own in finding a publishing outlet for *Hosts and Guests: The Anthropology of Tourism*, which has been widely considered as establishing a path into the field. Swain raises the possibility that her study of tourism may have obstructed her professional progress. And Nash speaks of low-level opposition from some other academics in the form of smiles, smirks, or jokes, suggesting that one could not possibly be serious about such a subject, not to mention an almost total lack of encouragement from local colleagues.

Of course, any perceived opposition to a person's desire for tourism study varied. In his account, Van den Berghe reveals none, which may have something to do with the lateness of his discovery (and, therefore, increased acceptability) of the subject. Whatever opposition there was appears to have been disregarded by him as his interest in touristic phenomena developed. Dann seems to have been able to go his own way with a subject that had some applied relevance for the Caribbean island of Barbados where he had begun his career. (He also appears to have made up for a lack of local intellectual input for his tourism interests by assiduously cultivating selected contacts outside.) And Boissevain makes it clear that he did not experience any of the "guilt by association" (Nash 1996:1), in which his identity as an anthropologist was questioned by his choice of subject matter—in this case tourism. The evidence thus points largely to the lack of social support or negative pressures from colleagues, administrators, publishers, and possibly even the proverbial people-in-the street against our participants' efforts to study tourism; but such social conditions obviously were not enough to dissuade them from studying the subject. Therefore, the Nuñez notion that there was some kind of disciplinary tabu against the study of tourism seems to be on the right track, but as we shall see, requires refinement and, perhaps, some toying with the notion of ambivalence rather than tabu.

All of this would seem to be consistent with an understanding that there was an increasing tolerance for serious consideration of leisure-related subjects such as tourism after the mid-twentieth century—enough for seriously concerned, independent-minded scholars to gain some social support for a sustained interest in tourism. Indeed, the evidence from our group of anthropological and sociological pioneers appears to conform to this view.

Tourism Study as a Cultural Innovation

Anthropologist Homer Barnett (1953:188) argues that any cultural innovation, an example of which is the scientific recognition and study of tourism, involves an "hybridization or cross-referencing of existing configurations." This leads us to consider, first, the conceptual resources tapped by our participants for their notions about tourism. What were the "existing configurations" in anthropology and sociology? Speaking for sociology as well as anthropology, which have been considered here *en bloc*, one of our participants, Eric Cohen (1984), suggests four principal issue areas that were tapped for the early study of tourism by practitioners in those disciplines: characteristics of the tourist, relations between tourists and locals, the structure and functioning of the tourist system, and the consequences of tourism (for some host society)—the last of which seems to have dominated in social scientific research generally since its beginnings (Cohen 1984:79; Swain, Brent and Long, eds. 1998:996–1002).

Cohen's categories, while perhaps not exhaustive, offer us a point of entry for comprehending research areas that attracted early students of tourism in anthropology and sociology and provide examples of the kind of early research that was conducted in each. For example, concerning the "tourist," which according to Böröcz (1996:42) is the oldest tourism-related concept in Anglo-European languages (the term "tourism" appeared in dictionaries a few years later), Cohen refers to early studies that deal primarily with demographic characteristics of tourists, tourist motivations, and tourist behavior; and in a separate, more theoretically oriented paper (Cohen 1979b), by way of emphasizing his view that tourists constitute a key concept in the study of tourism, he uses a phenomenological point of view to propose a range of attitudinal postures adopted by tourists in their touring.

Cohen's early and continuing insistence that tourists pursue different modes of experience in their touring continues to inform a good deal of work on this aspect of tourism, including (as his personal history suggests) his own (see also Smith 1977:8–13). He also mentions the early theoretically informed work of Dean MacCannell (1973, 1976), another of our participants, whose consideration of tourist motivation serves as a basis for a critical analysis of modern Western society. The tourist also is one of the focii in early studies by another participant, Nelson Graburn (1977), who like the others just mentioned, is indebted to the view of tourism as something like a religious pilgrimage (see Smith, ed. 1992).

Again, keeping in mind that we are bent primarily on exploring early ventures in tourism study and not in categorizing our participants in terms of their fields of interest, it is nevertheless useful to get some idea of the weight of early anthropological/sociological interests in the various aspects of tourism. What of the issue area identified by Cohen as concerning the relationship between tourists and locals? As Nuñez (1989:267) suggests for anthropology, research on socio-cultural change at the time when the study of tourism was beginning was often carried out (especially in America) from an acculturation perspective (SSRC 1954), which stresses the encounter and interaction between people from different cultures and the consequences for change (and persistence) among those involved. The nature of this encounter, however, was not often the focal point of research. As Cohen (1984:379) is at pains to tell us for early research on tourism in anthropology and sociology, "Few studies deal specifically ... with the nature and dynamics of the tourist-local relationship;" and indeed, the distribution of interests of our participants—only two of whom appear to have settled on this issue area in their early work on tourism—is consistent with his view. In this regard, Nash's (1977) first work on tourism, "Tourism as a Form of Imperialism," is unambiguously concerned in part with the nature of the social relationship between tourists and their hosts wherever it occurs—a relationship that, because of the inevitable dominance of the tourists involved, is inherently imperialistic. Another of our participants, Pierre Van den Berghe, immediately saw the relationship between what he refers to as tourists and tourees (hosts) as a special type of ethnic relationship (Van den Berghe and Keyes 1984). In the case of ethnic tourism, this can involve ethnic relationships of greater complexity; and as his personal history shows, this view, given an economic cast, has continued to inform his subsequent work on tourism.

As mentioned above, the most frequent aim of research in early tourism study and later on has concerned tourism's consequences for locals (or hosts) in the less developed parts of the world; and among our participants, at least five appear to have been particularly taken by this aspect of tourism at the beginning of their interest in the subject. There, the concepts of acculturation and development, then prevalent in social scientific discourse, were adapted for tourism study (Nash 1996:19–38). For example, in her early study of gender roles in tourism development among the Kuna, Swain (1977) speaks of one measure of development, namely, "the role opportunities tourism generates for women and men;" and in so doing, she reveals how gender differences appear to affect such development.

Another example from the early work of Jeremy Boissevain considers the neo-Marxian issue of "underdevelopment" (Frank 1972) in Malta, which has concerned him over a considerable part of his career. At first, he found that, in contrast to what was frequently maintained in the "Cautionary" thought of the time, there was not much evidence for negative developmental consequences from Western touristic contact in Malta, a positive view of tourism's consequences that he shared with others who would seem to have held views comprising what

Jafari, in his personal history for this volume and elsewhere, refers to as the Advocacy Platform (see Cohen 1979a; Hermans 1981; Moon 1989; Preister 1986; Pye and Lin 1983); but later, after studying the situation over time, as his personal history attests, he began to find increasing evidence of what some of the "under-developers," whether theoretically oriented or not, had been talking about, e.g., greater dependence on the outside, economic leakage, structural inequalities, resentment (and worse) among the increasingly dependent hosts, skewed economic development, etc. (Farver 1984; Harrell-Bond 1978; Jurdao Arrones 1990; Kottak 1966; Lee 1978; Rosenberg 1988).

Inasmuch as Marie-Françoise Lanfant provides perhaps the best example from among our participants of an early and continued concern with the structure and functioning of a tourist system (MacCannell, Graburn, as well as some others, also delve into this issue-area), it would seem that her case should merit some special consideration not only because it is exceptional, but also because of its theoretical significance. Reflecting French structuralism, as well as Marxism, her work on international tourism is also significant as an early indication of increasing attention to the dominance of multinational systems of control in the contemporary world—a research theme that has continued to inform her career, as well as the careers of a small research group of colleagues, including another of our participants, Michel Picard.

Collaborating with the same research team (URESTI) of like-minded scholars that Lanfant has managed to put together under the aegis of the CNRS, and sharing the same views on the nature of an international touristic system, but with different points of attack, these two, have increased our understanding of how even the simplest touristic actions of people anywhere in the world can be shaped by an international context.

Social Scientific Understanding in Tourism Study

So, at the time of their discovery of tourism, early representatives of tourism research in our sample seem to have been drawn to various issue areas in the anthropology/sociology of tourism identified by Cohen, but more to some (especially that concerning tourism's consequences) than others. In the preceding section, we learned something about the different aspects of tourism that tended to preoccupy them at the outset of their tourism studies. How, then, did they go about their investigations of tourism? One could, of course, simply say that these were social scientists who used social scientific procedures for carrying out their investigations, but as pointed out earlier in the book, such a generalization tends to mask a variety of research approaches in anthropology and sociology that were in place at the time when tourism study was beginning. It is probably true that the bottom line for their approach would be that like that of other social scientists, that is, their science had to have some empirical basis, which is to say that, even for the more humanistically oriented, some objective, experience-based view of the world had to be involved. But a variety of scientific approaches are still possible; and ultimately, the subjective worlds of actors studied pose problems not encountered by natural scientists. Such problems are especially acute for the cross-culturally oriented researchers who comprise much, if not all of our sample.

In referring to research approaches in the social sciences, Seale (2001 :1363) seems to be referring especially to anthropology and sociology when he says that there are methodological differences among these researchers, all of whom claim to be scientists. For example, there are differences between adherents of the hermeneutic or interpretivist tradition and the positivist, the literary and the scientific, and the ideographic and the nomothetic, an all-embracing statement which seems consistent with Merton's (1996:25) comment about the situational nexus of the social sciences as falling somewhere between the natural sciences and the humanities, and what Denzin and Lincoln (1993) see as a continuum extending between "quantitative" and "qualitative" science. Indeed, it would seem that anthropologists and sociologists are particularly subject to methodological pressures associated with the ambiguous research location of their disciplines.

Whether they were aware of this problem or not, most of our researchers seem to have followed scientific procedures that came "naturally" to them from their training—procedures that later critical analysis would reveal as falling into one methodological camp or another. In fact, not unlike a number of other disciplinary colleagues, most of those who chose the subject of tourism for study were not very self-conscious methodologically. Though there are some acute comments from our participants from time to time, methodological acumen and reflexivity appear not to have been strong points in their work. Of course, one might argue that they were not asked specifically about such matters; but Dann and his colleagues (1988) provide confirmation of methodological inadequacies among early tourism researchers generally in their discussion of the subject. In fact, their analysis of tourism articles published in *Annals of Tourism Research* and the *Journal of Leisure Research* reveals that in the earliest period analyzed (1978–1980), the majority of published articles were comparatively naive as to methodological issues.

According to Riley and Love (2000:180), who used one overlapping journal (*Annals of Tourism Research*) among the four used in their study for analyses, there were a variety of research approaches in early studies of tourism, but "there is little doubt that the dominant paradigm in early tourism research was positivistic," which though perhaps naïve methodologically, was oriented toward the style favored by the natural sciences. Riley and Love point out that the results of such research, though informative, were often of rather limited interest. But they would probably agree with Cohen (1988:30), who, elsewhere, was able to find research initiatives employing a "loose qualitative methodology," which "despite a lack of methodological rigor," were the point of departure for several fertile research "traditions" in tourism study.

On the basis of direct experience and existing analyses, therefore, one cannot be impressed with the methodological acumen or rigor of early tourism research. Most of the articles published tended to be of an explorative character as early researchers explored the new terrain of tourism much as those in the Chicago School of American sociology explored different aspects of the Chicago social landscape. Positivism, involving some kind of not terribly sophisticated quantitative approach, was the preferred method for doing this exploration; but some of the few qualitative contributions, which were more likely to be found in anthropology and sociology than in other social sciences, turned out to be rather fruitful for further research development.

In order to provide greater depth for this discussion, a brief excursus might help us to better understand a frequent methodological failure in early positivistically oriented tourism research. It concerns the consequences of outside-inspired tourism development for certain peoples, which as has been pointed out, has been the most frequent kind of research problem chosen by early scholars of tourism, anthropologists, and sociologists included. Often, a researcher, noting sociocultural changes associated with tourism development, simply assumed them as its consequences. But as all scientists are supposed to know, any demonstration of the consequences of tourism development requires the use of some kind of control in the research operation—either in the laboratory or the real world (i.e., using some variety of the experimental Method of Difference). Though associated sociocultural changes often were noted, a causal connection between tourism development and one or more sociocultural changes usually had not been established; and further, as Smith (1989) notes, the tourism component (as opposed to, say, the development of an extractive industry such as mining) might not have been the principal driving force involved. Without necessary controls, it was impossible to tell what role tourism was playing in that development. Fortunately, not all early tourism researchers investigating this problem failed to deal (consciously or unconsciously) with the control issue (see, e.g., Jurdao 1990; Schlechten 1988 for more successful examples). From such examples in similar situations, comparisons between touristic and non-touristic consequences are possible, and we can come to firmer conclusions about the causal or functional relationships involved.

Dann and his colleagues also point out the general lack of theoretically informed research in early tourism studies; but they do find some early studies, whether methodologically competent or not, that were theoretically oriented. A number of contributions from our participants in one or more early writings are noteworthy for their theoretical acumen, which was activated in their tourism studies in the way that Barnett suggests. For example, the indebtedness of Lanfant (1980) to structuralism and Marxism in her analyses of international tourism is evident; and so too are the views of Durkheim and Weber, which inform Dann's early writings on tourist motivation (Dann 1981). Then there are MacCannell, with his reliance on Marx and Durkheim, the American sociologist Irving Goffman (1959) and various semioticians; Graburn with his indebtedness to Durkheim, Mauss, Leach, and Victor Turner (Graburn 1977, 1983a); Cohen with his reliance on the phenomenologist and religious historian, Mircea Eliade (see, eg., 1974), Alfred Schuetz (1944, 1964), as well as others (see Cohen 1972); and Nash (1977, 1981) with an orientation derived from Simmel, Schuetz, American social psychology, and acculturation theory.

Dann and his colleagues also entertain a notion of ideal social scientific research, which in their view, involves some kind of "correct" balance of methodological competence and theoretical sophistication (within what appears to be an unstated positivistic frame of reference). Examples of this are few and far between in early tourism research; and their analysis contains an implicit notion of yet unrealized progress toward that ideal. Another "progressive" scheme for the hoped-for development of tourism research is to be found in Jafari's (1987) view of movement toward a "knowledge-based platform," which involves what appears to be a somewhat broadly defined scientific (perhaps positivistic) attitude toward subject matter, i.e., tourism is intrinsically neither good nor bad and can be studied objectively—a viewpoint that is amply elaborated in his personal history. Jafari wanted early tourism researchers to divest themselves of any personal bias toward the subject of tourism. This meant that in studies of tourism development, one did not begin with biases (pro or con) about the consequences of tourism input, which is consonant with his "scientification" of tourism research.

Enough of such utopian visions, all of which have their flaws, as we are learning in our discussion of the development of tourism research in anthropology and sociology. By way of concluding our consideration of the beginnings of such research on tourism, it might be useful to sketch out in summary fashion the nature of the originating situation in which our participants acted. Of course, that situation, like all social situations, must be conceived as having a history, which is intraculturally and interculturally variable; and for purposes of this study we have oriented it around the participant-actors whose burgeoning interest in the subject of tourism we are investigating.

With their developing interest in the newfound subject of tourism, our participants may be seen to have been involved in a changing sociocultural world. Central to our consideration of that change has been the relative value of work and leisure at the time when tourism research was emerging. Toward the middle of the twentieth century, more frequent manifestations of leisure activities such as tourism have suggested the increasing importance of leisure (as compared to work) to people in the Western world and beyond. Though the "drive" to work, discussed so eloquently for its various manifestations by Weber (1958, 1967), continued, its primacy was being eroded, and increasingly prevalent leisure activities, spurred on perhaps by developmental necessities (Krippendorf 1986), had begun to be taken as legitimate. But reservations about accepting them as significant social phenomena continued; and in academia, which was to be the main venue for anthropological and sociological, as well as other social scientific research on tourism, any serious consideration of subject and other leisure-related subjects was dogged with questions about their academic respectability. So one suspects that serious consideration of tourism, which had become an increasingly obvious sociocultural phenomenon, was delayed by something generally unacceptable about it.

Our participants, who were in fact among the pioneers in tourism research, had been trained in Western academic institutions to investigate sociocultural phenomena scientifically; and their personal histories reveal that they had developed a variety of research interests in the multifarious affairs of the world. In their work as social scientists, they had learned to follow up these interests in ways that were called scientific. We suppose that at some point in their academic development, something happened that attracted their scholarly attention to tourism. Some of the personal histories provide interesting examples. It could have been a chance encounter in the real world such as that of Cohen in Acre, a lecture by an important French professor for MacCannell, a chance "aside" by a Maltese official concerned with developmental issues to Boissevain, being surrounded by tourists in Barbados for Dann, an invitation to a Conference for Nash, and so on. For these researchers, sooner or later, tourism eventually became a scientific subject to be studied like other scientific subjects that were routinely investigated by other practitioners in their disciplines.

Coming from different backgrounds and being variously motivated, our participants had began to study aspects of tourism and include it in the course of their academic work. In this "touristic undertaking," they were largely alone without much in the way of sociocultural support from colleagues, administrators or the general public—an essentially anomic situation, which for some like Van den Berghe may have been experienced as little more than a bump in their academic road; but for others, like Jafari, with his "theses" fixed on the dormitory door, it was a more disturbing encounter, which threatened certain "inalienable" rights of a scientific investigator. And for all, there could be the excitement if breaking ground to new vistas, which has always been important in scientific inquiry, not to mention other fields.

In order to cope with the various aspects of a situation that had been at least partially generated by their interest in tourism, these neophytes were initially thrown back on themselves and whatever strategies they could muster to continue their research. Having coped more or less successfully with such a situation, one would expect that these tourism researchers would reveal in their personal histories qualities of personal independence, which would have enabled them to function and move forward with their somewhat academically questionable touristic interests; and indeed, this trait seems to have been adequately demonstrated for all of our informants.

Development of a New Field

Gradually, the tendency among our participants to go it alone in their path-breaking endeavors was complemented by the social connections they and others managed to establish among like-minded researchers. Individuals began to recognize through contacts of various kinds that they were not alone in their "touristic" endeavors. There were, in fact, other similarly interested academics who might be contacted—in books and journals, or more directly, in person—to profit from an exchange of ideas. Dann, for example (with the benefit of special financial aid), made a special effort to travel about; and in the course of working on various projects, he invited other tourism researchers to visit him and his wife in Barbados, a not entirely unattractive proposition. Nash, who had been finishing up some research on American expatriates in Europe at a foundation in the south of France, profited from nearby archival materials and discussions with other interested parties, especially at the Centre des Hautes Études Touristiques in Aix, then directed by René Baretje, but also in a visit to the Danns in Barbados; Swain reveals the wonder of it all—that there were tourism-interested others like her who could be contacted for help if necessary; and Crick, who obviously suffered the most from the lack of direct contact with other tourism researchers, may have made up for this with his diligent and exhaustive use of published sources on the subject. These are only some of the instances of reaching out for contact with like-minded others that began the process of institutionalization of the field of tourism knowledge.

What does the study of the reaching out process among our participants reveal about early compatibilities of disciplines with which anthropological and sociological practitioners came to be involved? What were the disciplinary orientations of other scholars who could help them in their investigation of the new subject. One thinks first, of course, of exchanges between scholars from anthropology and sociology. Nash and Smith (1991:13) point out that not only was there borrowing within those disciplines, but between them (Cohen 1979b; Graburn 1983a); and borrowing from scholars in other social sciences was not unusual. Consider for starters the work of the historian Daniel Boorstin (1964), whose views about tourists have been extensively criticized by Dean MacCannell (1976), Nash's (1979) use of the views of a variety of other historians in developing his anthropological approach to tourism, and Dann's work with the geographer Potter, which is recounted in his personal history.

Some of this cross-disciplinary activity could have been the natural result of early explorations into a new subject when any study of tourism was attractive for satisfying exploratory urges. But such activity had its limits, and some disciplines were more likely to be mined than others. A look through the personal histories of our participants reveals—not surprisingly—that when extradisciplinary borrowing or collaboration occurred, it was more likely to occur between disciplines that were more compatible in their research orientations. Assuming that anthropology and sociology are among what some might call the "softer" social sciences, it is not surprising that work from "harder," more quantitatively oriented disciplines is less frequently mentioned than that from the "softer" ones. Over and over among anthropologists, one heard of the value of economic research on tourism, but they made comparatively little use of it in their work. One reason for that might be that economists studying tourism seem to have been more inclined toward the "Advocacy" mode as compared to the "Cautionary" mode of anthropologists and sociologists. Another might have been the dominant research style in the disciplines considered.

Institutionalization

The process of institutionalization of a scientific field, of course, begins with the establishment of more stable social arrangements around a particular subject—a process that Lewenstein (1995:866) alludes to in a book review about the emerging, but questionable field of cold fusion. He (Lewenstein) says that "… five years after the saga began (i.e., involving the alleged discovery of the phenomenon), cold fusion looks like many other scientific subspecialties, with its own publication patterns, international conferences, funding sources, and internal disputes." Lewenstein here is referring to the emergence of a particular scientific institution that he calls a "sub-specialty," the kind of thing that we have had in our sights throughout this book. His comments, as well as the extended discussion of the process by the sociologist Merton (1996:267–336), can be brought to bear on early tourism study in the social sciences.

In the reaching out process involved in institutionalization, one ought not forget the give-and-take involved in the teaching of students in early courses dealing with tourism, which might be seen as a kind of proto-institutionalization. One is reminded here of a range extending from the small, somewhat informal teaching-research situations, reported by Dann and Lanfant in their personal histories, to the larger, more formal teaching arrangements at Berkeley that is reported by Graburn. This, of course, was not the reaching out to academic peers that has been discussed above, but the give-and-take involved would seem also to have been a significant element in the establishment of the more stable social relationships that were involved in the institutionalization of tourism study.

Other early steps in this direction were conferences such as the one sponsored by the International Union of Travel Organizations in 1963 and others like it, which were designed to get the emerging facts about contemporary tourism on the table, so to speak. They tended to be little more than that, however. A more academically oriented, self-generating step in that process, in which a number of our participants were involved, occurred during the 1974 Meeting of the American Anthropological Association in Mexico City. There, a session devoted to the Anthropology of Tourism, organized by one of our participants, Valene Smith, was scheduled. That session, which is mentioned by Smith herself and other contributors to this book, produced various discussions about the opening up of a new field and the eventual publication of *Hosts and Guests: The Anthropology of Tourism* (Smith, ed. 1977), the first edition of the book derived from selected presentations in the session. This development, details of which are provided in a number of our personal histories, came after a period of minimal, scattered tourism research and is often mentioned as a landmark in the field. Subsequent international symposia in the late 1970s such as those sponsored by UNESCO (DeKadt, ed. 1979), the World Bank, Le Centre d'Études des Caraïbes, and the World Tourism Organization resulted in similar publications on the subject.

At approximately the same time (1973) Jafar Jafari, another of our participants, took a further self-generated, institutionalizing step for tourism research by creating a multidisciplinary, international journal of tourism research, *Annals of Tourism Research*, in which representatives of various disciplines, including anthropology and sociology were to function as editors and contributors, and for specialized issues such as those dealing with the sociology of tourism (Cohen), the anthropology of tourism (Graburn), the geography of tourism, the economics of tourism, and tourism social science. Other relevant journals or publications, such as *The Journal of Leisure Research, Leisure*

Studies, the Journal of Travel Research, and Tourism Management, began to appear; and there were early spin-offs of *Annals* that followed, such as the Polish *Problemy Turystyki,* the Spanish *Annals en Español,* the Indian *Tourism Recreation Research,* etc. Such publications, in the English language alone, now number well over 50 (Goeldner 2003).

Considering the early difficulties some of our participants faced with finding publication outlets for their early research (as well as the questionable quality of some of that research on the subject (Dann et al, eds. 1988), the establishment of journals with reasonably rigorous standards (as well as receptive editorial boards), more or less devoted to the subject, was a significant step in the development of the field. Also there were the small, but growing numbers—more than 150 by the year 2000 (Baretje 2003)—of publishers specializing in tourism, including multinational agencies like the World Tourism Organization and tourism research centers such as the one at the University of Berne. The publication trajectory of early tourism researchers might begin with an article in some tourism-oriented journal such as *Annals* or a compendium such as *Hosts and Guests,* the editors of which were, presumably, more receptive to such things; but publication in broader, discipline-oriented journals or reviews such as the *American Journal of Sociology, Sociology,* the *International Social Science Journal,* the *Annual Reviews of Sociology* or *Anthropology,* or *Human Organization,* which may have been less receptive to early tourism research, was also a possibility realized by a few of our participants. Certainly, as with any new field, editors had to face the issue of quality versus novelty, which is revealed in Jafari's activities as editor of *Annals.*

Perhaps the most important development in the institutionalization of the study of tourism was the establishment of various academic research centers, which according to Baretje (2003), now number more than 550 in 86 countries, a good example of which was the European Centre for the Coordination of Social Science Research and Documentation in Vienna, which sponsored the huge multinational comparative project "Economic and Sociological Problems of Tourism in Europe" under the co-direction of a Polish informant, Kryztopf Przeclawski. Perhaps an even more important Center for tourism research was the Centre des Hautes Études Touristiques at the Université d'Aix-Marseille and its later spin-off, the Centre International de Recherches et d'Études Touristiques (which has become a more specialized, heavily computerized archival center), begun in 1959 under the direction of René Baretje with the aid of his mother, the archivist, Alice Baretje Keller, and the University of Aix-Marseille. Originally, this institution carried out research, some of it contracted by outside organizations such as UNESCO, doctoral teaching, provided various venues for publication (by, e.g., authors such as participants Graburn and Nash), hospitality for visiting scholars, the development and continual updating of a tourism library, and some other minor functions. Several of our participants, as well as other colleagues, have benefited from its hospitality.

Following a spate of University politics involving the issue of autonomy, Baretje, with the aid of Jean and Gaetane Thurot, formed the spin-off (CIRET), which has brought the latest advances in computer technology into its operations. The aim, however, according to Baretje in a personal communication, continues to be to prevent the tourism research community from continually "reinventing the wheel."

Still another indication of institutionalization of tourism study was the establishment in 1988 by Jafar Jafari and other scholars of the elite International Academy for the Study of Tourism (IAST), which was to provide an opportunity for social scientific researchers on tourism to discuss tourism research, to publish transactions of meeting presentations, and to provide applied assistance to host nations, which continue to offer venues for Academy meetings, such as in Beijing (2005). With a membership of elite tourism researchers from a variety of social scientific disciplines, this organization with a limit of 75 members, among whom (in 1998–1999) the disciplines of geography, economics, sociology, business and management, and anthropology were the most frequently represented (see Appendix C). It also provided some indication of a developing stratification within the tourism research community. In it, anthropologists and sociologists have been active participants in all of its operations; and they clearly have profited from the multidisciplinary exchanges involved. Indeed, the field of tourism study has shared many of the developments of other emerging scientific disciplines, as Lewenstein (1995:145) suggests even for the somewhat questionable field of cold fusion.

Lewenstein suggests that all sciences develop intradisciplinary conflicts, and these have begun to emerge in the IAST. For example, there have been disputes regarding the fundamental issue of membership in the academy, ultimately resolved in favor of those with expertise and accomplishment in tourism study rather than in their primary disciplines or endeavors. In some cases, this may have meant some sacrifice of overall academic expertise for an identification with the field of tourism. The implications for the comparative status in the field of the two orientations remain unclear, but some indication of how it is being played out is given in the next chapter.

A number of more discipline-oriented organizations for the discussion and publication of tourism matters among anthropologists and sociologists have also appeared. For example, there is the International Sociological Association with its self-generated Committee on Tourism Research, in which a number of our more qualitatively oriented participants—both sociologists and anthropologists, are involved. It has a publishing program on topics of interest to its various committees, which has resulted in path-breaking works (Dann, ed. 2002; Lanfant et al, eds. 1995) on tourism. A similar entity, the Commission on the Anthropology of Tourism, which is a part of the International Union of Anthropological and Ethnological Sciences, arose somewhat later mainly through the efforts of participant Valene Smith (see her personal history) and some other anthropologically oriented researchers.

Finally, it should be mentioned that in the early institutionalization of the field there were certain passionately involved anthropologists and sociologists who have became conscious or unconscious proseletizers for tourism study. While it is obvious that Jafar Jafari was an important institution builder in this mode, there were others like Valene Smith, Nelson Graburn, Marie-Françoise Lanfant, Eric Cohen, and later in England, Tom Selwyn and his Roehampton Institute (later at London Metropolitan University) who affected students and associates with their passion and expertise on the subject of tourism. And our participants have mentioned still others who have been active in this form of recruitment.

The Component of Meaning

Some readers might feel that we have been concerning ourselves too much with what some might feel are secondary aspects of knowledge and not what Barth (2002:3) refers to as the "corpus of assertions and ideas" produced about certain aspects of the (in this case) touristic world. Of course, the anthropological and sociological practitioners, who constitute the base of this study, are actors who have been primarily (if not exclusively) involved in mental actions that seek to make some scientific sense of the newly discovered world of tourism. It is, indeed, in such mental actions as working out meaningful scientific definitions of this subject that primarily distinguishes them in their work.

Definitions

As we have maintained throughout, following Crick's (1989) oft-quoted view, tourism is a "multifaceted phenomenon" with different aspects to consider. The geographer Richard Butler (1993:151), for example, has said that "while tourism has finally begun to be accepted as a major phenomenon with economic, social, and environmental ramifications, the great diversity of tourism has rarely been recognized." Indeed, as we have suggested earlier and will elaborate later, researchers have taken it to be a kind of pilgrimage, a fact of international exchange, a special kind of social relationship, a variety of activity (e.g., play, traveling), etc. Recognizing this and the numerous sub-categories of tourism that have appeared in the literature, the umbrella-like definition of tourism as a somewhat loosely conceived social process used in this book has aimed at being as inclusive as possible, while still maintaining a necessary internal coherence.

The matter of what tourism is provides us with an opportunity to open up our consideration of how the issue of meaning has been handled by tourism researchers, some of whom think that definitional matters have been too infrequently discussed in this scientific field (Pearce 1993:2). On an early occasion involving anthropologists and sociologists, the discussion around a "forum" article in *Current Anthropology* (by Nash 1981) included a number of references to definitional issues, which throw some light on this matter. As was suggested in that give-and-take, the notion of tourism as a kind of sightseeing, begun several centuries ago with the practice of "educational" touring through Europe by young aristocrats and their tutors, had become well established among interested parties (Adler 1989; Boyer 1972) by the time of the forum discussion. But in their comments concerning this definitional issue, Nash and some of his mainly anthropological and sociological interlocutors seem to have been more comfortable with deeper, less ethnocentric, and more generalizable notions of the tourists involved. The definitional positions in this multinational discussion tended to crystallize into two camps: Either tourists were a certain kind of traveler, i.e., temporary, voluntary, non-recurrent, etc. (Cohen 1974; Dann and Cohen 1991:158), or a person in a state of leisure, with traveling (Nash 1981) and possibly other attributes (Smith 1989:1–4) as qualifiers.

In the CA article and the associated give-and-take around it, as well as later discussion at the first (Zakopane) meeting of the IAST, there were also suggestions that definitions are related to disciplinary or theoretical agendas, which tends to relativize, if not minimize them. In any case, though there have been a number of definitions of the subject, though leisure-oriented definitions have tended to prevail, and though the whole notion of leisure travel needs to be continually discussed because of, among other things, leisure's historically mutable relation to work, the definitional issue has generally not been heavily debated in the field of tourism studies (but see Dann et al 1988; Graburn and Jafari, eds. 1991; Lanfant's personal history, as well as her treatise on the subject of leisure (Lanfant 1972)).

All of this would seem to raise some questions about the scientific credibility of the field in the face of historical change, especially in an era of heightened reflexivity (Giddens 1995:276–277), in which discussion of researchers, as well as their operations, has become increasingly *de rigeur*. So far, this issue appears not to have impeded research progress, which according to Dann (2002:13–14), includes a continuing generation of new metaphors for tourism in an increasingly fluid and mobile society. Simply put, different viewpoints about tourism have tended to be a *modus vivendi* for the developing field, and (perhaps because there has been so much overlapping) they have not prevented researchers in it from communicating with each other and moving forward scientifically. The lack of an agreed-upon definition undoubtedly is associated with the multifarious nature of the field, but it is for some a sign of scientific immaturity. There may, indeed, be no agreed-upon definition of tourism by tourism researchers, but at the very least, this calls more than ever for some associational statement between the scientific question being investigated and the definition employed at the beginning of every presentation.

Some Meaningful Traditions

Consider some of the more fertile assertions about the touristic world that have been produced by our anthropologists and sociologists, as well as others, during the early days of tourism research. But before doing so, it might be wise here to point out that we are not searching primarily for some veridical assertions or "truth" about the subject that researchers have produced—things that most researchers probably think are the overriding point of their work. Rather, we intend to deal mainly with some of the more influential assertions—true or not—about tourism made by those researchers in the early days of the field—a simple indication of which could be the number of times they have been mentioned in some cumulative index in the library. Whatever their veridical status, these concepts do, however, represent a good deal of "academic capital" (Bourdieu 1987) for tourism research. Whether or not the assertions about tourism are acceptable according to some scientific standard is regarded here as less important than their nature, the conditions of their production, and their propagation—our ultimate aim being to attain some understanding of the science of tourism study as it has been conceived and practiced in anthropology and sociology, not of the nature of tourism itself (Barnes, Bloor and Henry 1996:viii).

The assertions about tourism we will be considering have had some "life" to them in the form of popularity, longevity, etc. They may be seen to amount to what Cohen (1988) refers to as "traditions" in scientific inquiry. One might also use the term "perspective" or "ideology" for them, but perhaps not anything so grand as a "paradigm," an ultimate example of which, according to Thomas Kuhn, whose name is often associated with the word, would be the notion of biological evolution. Evolutionary theory, derived from the work of Darwin and Wallace, has evolved a good deal over the years, but in many ways, has remained true to the views of its founders. Moreover, it currently appears to be the dominant theory in the life sciences. We certainly will not be considering anything quite so grand or all-encompassing as that, but something like the theory of Evolution provides a kind of ideal-typical example of what most researchers have been—consciously or unconsciously—striving after.

Further, if we accept the fact that in any mature science, there must be some optimal combination of theory and method, we should take note of Dann and his colleagues' comment (1988:4) that "in the relatively new sphere of tourism research ... there was an unfortunate tendency to gloss over questions of theory and method, and a concomitant failure to acknowledge their interrelationship." The authors of this statement were especially critical of the great number of "impressionistic" case studies which had been done; they also criticized studies that were theoretically oriented, but had methodological deficiencies. Indeed, the harmonious blend of theoretical sophistication and methodological competence they were looking for as evidence of mature scientific work was hard to find.

Besides questions about theory and method, a preliminary concern might be with the social location or context of our participants, which is a key issue in studying the production of knowledge. It helps us to know where scientific discourse is coming from. All of our participants and most of our other informants are located in Western academia, and they have significant reference groups in Western anthropology and sociology. Further, though some of these academics have been more concerned with practical issues, the position of most of them suggests that they are not encumbered by practical concerns, which would seem to have some consequence for their approach to the subject of tourism. We are reminded of this by an article on policy issues facing the tourism industry in the 1990s by Brent Ritchie, a Canadian tourism scholar. He (Ritchie 1993:206) says that "academics, in contrast to applied researchers ... often have an interest in more fundamental or basic research about major issues with medium or long term implications." And in a comment that recalls Jafari's Cautionary Platform, Butler (1993:138) points out that, in their studies of tourism development, academics have tended to carry out their work after the fact and concentrate on the negative or undesirable consequences of such development. Such comments remind us that in our discussion of the production of the meaningful component of scientific knowledge, the social context in which ideas are produced also is a factor that shapes them.

Some Fertile Conceptual Traditions

What have been some of the significant conceptions of tourism put forth by our participants and some other anthropologists and sociologists in the early development of the field of tourism study? No attempt will be made here to cover the field exhaustively, but as Dann's (1996) more systematic view of tourism from a sociolinguistic perspective demonstrates, a variety of conceptual traditions have emerged.

First, consider the notion of *Tourism as Pilgrimage* which has occupied a prime position in tourism study since its inception, and in one form or another continues still (Smith, ed. 1992). Obviously, there are compelling similarities between pilgrimage and tourism; for example, in an early article, Dean MacCannell (1973:593) says that "the motive behind a pilgrimage is similar to that behind a tour." Smith (1992:3) says that "the superficial relationship between tourists and pilgrims have been recognized for several decades;" Cohen (1984) points out that "Graburn's (1977) paper, identifying tourism as a form of "sacred journey," brings the study of tourism even closer to that of pilgrimage;" and Graburn (1983a:17), himself, says that "... it is not claimed that all kinds (of tourism) have the quality of prototypical pilgrimages, but the possibility cannot be ruled out for any particular occasion or person." Despite their similarities, the two concepts, as used by tourism researchers, have not been identical. Cohen (1979c:18) says that pilgrimages and modern tourism "are ... predicated on different social conceptions of space and contrary views concerning the kind of destinations worth visiting and of their location in socially constructed space." Smith (1992:1–17) thinks they are closer than that, and in the introduction to an issue of *Annals* dealing with the subject, she formulates a continuum extending between pilgrimage and tourism, saying that "individual belief or world view ... would appear to be the single most important criterion to distinguish pilgrims from tourists." What feature of the belief of the tourist distinguishes it from that of the pilgrim? According to Smith (1992:4), the sacred (religious)-secular (non-religious) distinction, used earlier by Durkheim in various works would appear to apply, with a mixture of the two somewhere in the middle of her continuum (to accommodate the "fun and games," say, of those on pilgrimage).

Considering Nelson Graburn's notion of tourism as a "sacred journey" away from the ordinary (mundane) experience of daily life at home to some kind of extraordinary experience abroad, which he has formulated in terms of Victor and Edith Turner's (1978) concepts of *liminas* and *communitas*, we are led to his conclusion that these constitute extraordinary, even desirable experiences that function to "recreate" tourists (see especially Graburn 1977, 1989, 2001; but see also Nash 1984). Unfortunately, after more than three decades of use, it is still difficult to nail down the specific meanings involved here. Nevertheless, there is something about Graburn's notion that speaks to the heart of potential tourists who are "buried" in some kind of dull routine at home and looking for relief.

However, the promising notions of "ritual inversion" or "recreation," also offered by Graburn (1983a:21–23) to refer to touristic experiences in which rules of ordinary behavior are "changed, held in abeyance, or even reversed," may be no easier to grasp rationally today even after years of use by so many students and scholars.

MacCannell sees tourism as a ritual of modern peoples, in which they "scour the world" looking for some kind of *authenticity*, a quality which many think is lacking in modern social life; and in this intention they are aided by hosts who attempt to "stage" it for them in their touristic presentations (MacCannell 1973, 1976, 1992, 2001a). This notion, which MacCannell, himself, feels has often been misconstrued (see his personal history, as well as his 2001b), has been criticized by a number of scholars (Cohen 1988, 2004:2–5; McCabe 2002) for both theoretical and empirical inadequacies. But even with its faults, it continues to fascinate with its substantial theoretical depth (from Marx, Durkheim, Goffman, not to mention various semioticians), as well as his critically oriented analysis of modern society and its inhabitants; it certainly has functioned, at least, as an important heuristic device, and it even has received sporadic support from some fairly well controlled research (Waller and Lea 1999). But Cohen (2004:5) feels that it is no longer applicable in a post-modern era where "the craving for enjoyment and fun become a culturally sufficient justification" for touring.

It does not take long to sense where MacCannell is coming from in his critique of modern society, if not its individual inhabitants, about whom he seems to remain optimistic. Basically, he feels that modern social life, with all of its deceits and impersonality, is preventing people from realizing what might be said to be their true selves—a lamentable destiny according to any number of critical thinkers. Not being able to realize ourselves fully at home, we moderns have been using tourism as a means of redress, and touristic hosts have been cooperating to satisfy this need—even while thwarting it—by staging spectacles of *false authenticity*. From his stance as a critical theorist on the side of the socially alienated at home and abroad, MacCannell uses tourism to analyse the social situation in which they are embedded; and readers are invited to use his personal history, as well as his writings, to see how all of this works out according to the agenda of social action that pervades this book. They should also be reminded that, in MacCannell's case, the agenda extends beyond normal academic action into a world containing not only his family, but also his own brand of self-generated tours.

Again, as with Graburn, we wonder who are the tourists MacCannell is talking about. For both of these authors, they are people who seem to be experiencing a kind of alienation in their lives, for which they are seeking some kind of compensation—people, say, for whom the high point of their existence is some tour or other, the nature of which (accompanied by photographs) they will be happy to tell you about. One suspects that they have many of the alleged qualities of the Western middle class, who according to Berger, Berger and Kellner (1973:85), as well as others, are not entirely accepting of existing social arrangements; and one cannot help but think of the critical work of Krippendorf (1986, 1987) on tourism in industrial society when reading MacCannell.

It is the issue of empirical exceptions that strongly fuels Cohen's critique of Graburn and MacCannell. Though there is some empirical support for their rather broad generalizations, Cohen feels that the variety of tourist orientations ultimately raises serious questions about too much generalizing; and in pioneering, theoretically based writings that appear to have stood the test of time (Cohen 1974, 1979a), he has developed a typology of tourist intentions that apply to modern tourists and perhaps others. Ultimately, Cohen comes to the view that the positions of Graburn and MacCannell are only partially correct. Indeed, he argues that the majority of tourists probably have other orientations.

As his personal history shows, early on in his study of tourism, Cohen created a typology for the modes of touristic experience that is supposed to embrace the entire range of orientations of modern tourists—a conception which has served him (and many students and others) well throughout his career. Though the origins of this typology seem not to be quite the same as those Valene Smith (1977: 11–17) used in developing a similar scheme for the First Edition of *Hosts and Guests*, both of these participants' typologies seem to be based, more or less, on some notion of strangerhood (Smith's typology also includes the number of tourists involved and their effect on host cultures); and though the number of categories of tourists are different in the two typologies, the continua involved are similar. For Cohen, it ranges from those tourists who wish to remain close to home while experiencing mere pleasure (the *recreational mode*) to those who find meaning in some foreign Center (his *existential mode* in some *Centre out There*). For Smith on the other hand, it ranges from *Charter* types who "demand" Western amenities and who arrive *en masse* to not so numerous *explorers* who fully accept the need to adapt to host norms.

So far, our consideration of important theoretical traditions of tourism research in anthropology and sociology has been concerned mainly with tourists. As we know, there are other aspects of tourism, the most heavily researched of which concerns hosts and the societies in which they live. These studies have been mainly concerned with matters that are framed in terms of concepts such as a variety of kinds of *development*. To begin with, however, let us consider the process of *commoditization*, which has been thought to be brought about by the advances of tourism, particularly in less developed societies, in which strictly commercial values are seen to displace other values.

Informed scholars probably would agree that this commercial process is one, if not the only way of producing inauthentic, spurious, or superficial experiences. This concept, often referred to in the early literature on tourism development, had already been taken for granted by some anthropologists in their treatment of economic exchange (Appadurai 1986; Sahlins 1962) by the time that tourism study got under way. This suggests that the fact that many societies in the process of tourism development were becoming increasingly commoditized through tourism should not have come as a surprise to scholars who have learned that there probably was no society, ever, in which some commoditization was not evident.

Among the early tourism researchers who employed the term is Davydd Greenwood in his by now well-known account of the transformation of a Basque *Alarde* festival, published in the first two editions of Smith's (1977, 1989) *Hosts and Guests*. This article, which according to the author (in a personal communication), has excited a good deal of interest even though its usage has been criticized by Greenwood, himself, in the second edition. The use of this concept has gained something of a taken-for-granted quality in anthropological/sociological studies of tourism, possibly because it fits so neatly into an existing bias against tourism development, which is widespread among anthropologists and sociologists—something that Jafari has referred to as the Cautionary Platform.

Another term with similar antecedents and ramifications that has often been used in early studies of tourism and other development by anthropologists and sociologists is *imperialism*, which Nash (1977) developed out of his own notion of *acculturation*, a concept which, according to Nuñez (1989:267), supported most early anthropological studies of tourism. If the term is used in a scholarly way, say, as an indication of some kind of domination by external powers, and not as politically or ethically based criticism, it can serve a useful scientific function. But even Nash, himself, whose article in the two editions of *Hosts and Guests* (1977, 1989), like those of Greenwood, seems to have excited something of a feeding frenzy among readers, has had second thoughts on his use of the concept, which often has been applied in association with an enumeration of the negative consequences of external domination in societies undergoing Western-inspired development. Such an occurrence, which we will gloss simply as *underdevelopment*, is something which, in its various forms, Boissevain, van den Berghe, Swain, and some other of our participants have been dealing with throughout their careers.

This concept, which emerged among neo-Marxist scholars particularly (Frank 1972), has been used to suggest all that is bad with development as it has been going on in the less developed parts of the world—increasing dependency and social stratification, loss of identity, pollution, crime, etc. The notion of outside contact producing some kind of valued input for lesser developed peoples is taken as a given, but that input was seen to come with various strings attached, the effects of which for people in the less developed world are hard to overcome.

On a more positive note, the concept of *sustainable development* is a term with applied implications borrowed from the famous Brundtland Report, the document produced for the United Nations by the World Commission on Environment and Development (WCED 1987). In that report, which was later adopted by the UN, the Brundtland group expressed a concern for both the environmental depredations of development and the needs of present and future generations of the peoples involved. According to sociologist-economist Emanuel DeKadt, an expert on developmental issues, including those associated with tourism (DeKadt 1992, DeKadt ed. 1979), this may be the most productive line to take for progress in the policy area. Most tourism scholars would probably agree with this applied intention; and they also would agree that accomplishing it will not be an easy task, which is clearly illustrated by DeKadt's 1992 article. In all such studies—even those that focus on *Ecotourism*, which in its ideal form, is generally considered to be development that is small, clean, green, and above all, sustainable—the negative aspects of tourism development loom large, which does not augur well for sustainable tourism. That it sometimes appears to happen, as in experimental projects such as those reported in DeKadt's edited work for the United Nations (DeKadt, ed. 1979), provides only a glimmer of hope for anthropologists and sociologists associated with the study of development (Goldfarb 1989).

The issue of change and persistence in the social identity of the host peoples involved in internationally spawned processes of development has been dealt with recently in a theoretically informed, cross-cultural study by one of our participants, Marie-Françoise Lanfant and a number of colleagues (Lanfant et al, eds. 1995), with support from the CNRS and the International Sociological Association. This study is an indication of some progress in a field where simple impact studies had held sway since the early days of tourism research. In it, a more sophisticated point of view that gives freer reign to an interpretive approach in ethnographic work is advanced. For Lanfant, this study represents a collaborative fruition of a long and difficult research saga that is only partially revealed in her personal history. That saga has involved bringing to bear a theoretically sophisticated and methodologically competent point of view on aspects of the field, which she refers to as *international tourism*. Through this comparatively recent work, we can gain an understanding of how well she and her colleagues, not only in this study, but also in the field have done in advancing our knowledge about some developmental aspects of tourism.

Overview

If the point of tourism research may be seen to be the development of meaningful, discursive statements concerning the field of touristic action, we can see that the anthropologists and sociologists featured in this study have accomplished a good deal in the course of their careers. In considering some of the core concepts that they have developed so far in dealing with the phenomenon of tourism, we have tried to avoid criticizing them. Rather, we have maintained that our principal concern here has been to confine ourselves to a description of the scientific understandings produced, and the conditions of their production during the early development of an anthropology/sociology of tourism. Such a posture, of course, has not been easy to maintain; and we intend to give ourselves a somewhat freer reign in the Epilogue to follow, which will include some preliminary judgments about progress in the field.

Meanwhile, it might be useful to suggest what we hope to have accomplished in this chapter. It would seem that the account we have given of the early development of an anthropology/sociology of tourism suggests that the development led to an institutionalized field of study, but with blurry boundaries, especially between it and the other social sciences. Not surprisingly, perhaps, there were difficulties in creating a new opening into the world that scientists attend to—difficulties that have not been entirely overcome.

Above all, the development we have been concerned with has been seen to be a human enterprise with many features that are shared with other fields of knowledge. Its emergence occurred at a specific point in the history of the Western world for historical reasons that have been elucidated; and it has been carried forward by a group of academic men and women whose training had been largely in anthropology and sociology, which is to say that they were primarily concerned with sociocutural phenomena. Something of what they accomplished, as well as the work involved, have been discussed. Most of the scholars who "discovered" the field are still with us, and we are fortunate to have a good many of their personal histories, as well as other information, on which to base our account of what transpired. Something of what it all amounts to—for anthropology and sociology, science, and the people involved—will be discussed in the Epilogue to follow.

Chapter 5

Epilogue

Where are We Now?

Looking at the first generation of participating anthropological and sociological researchers of tourism, now late in their careers, and comparing them with themselves when they were in the process of discovering and developing the field of tourism study earlier in their lives, one naturally notices changes. Older, they are no longer alone—or mostly alone—with their newly discovered subject in the face of generally dismissive colleagues and public. Though there may have been other interested parties at the time, each individual researcher had to pretty much go it alone at first. At present, there are other known tourism researchers from a variety of disciplines and institutions engaged in the production and dissemination of touristic knowledge—something which has become somewhat more respectable as an academic pursuit, but has not yet reached the level of respect, say, of the study kinship, social stratification, or ethnic groups. Our scholars now function in a world that includes vastly increased numbers of books, articles, chapters, and discussions about tourism, which if not a discipline, certainly has become a field of study (Tribe 2004). All of this, plus the presentations and discussions at meetings, as well as grants and contracts, provides them with the capital necessary to move forward in their research on tourism, which has become in a few decades a significant aspect of their academic careers, as well as their lives.

Looking at the intellectual capital they have at their disposal, we see the subject of tourism and the theoretical concepts and methodological operations that have been created to deal with it—all of which fit, more or less, into a field of discourse, derived from their home and other disciplines, that has been continually developing to the present. Perhaps, the most important aspect of such discourse on the new subject is the theory and method that courses through their work.

The Context of Current Tourism Study: Theory and Method

As a preliminary to discussing the social context in which our scholars have operated, it might be useful to eavesdrop on academic conversations among them. In discussions of the state of their field these days, one sometimes hears these scholars lamenting the lack of theory in it. Surely, we and those in other fields, can benefit from further relevant theoretical infusions; but those lamenting scholars should be reminded that though we tourism researchers may have had more than our share of purely impressionistic/descriptive work on the subject in our groundbreaking days (Cohen 1984), though we may be lacking in theories that measure up to criteria requiring understanding, prediction, or falsifiability (Dann et al, eds. 1988), and though we have no cohesive theoretical framework for dealing with our subject such as exists in the biological sciences (Tribe 2004), we are not entirely devoid of theoretical capital to work with. Indeed, accounts of the theoretical action of our participants are available in their personal histories; and there are other theoretical contributions that have appeared from a subsequent generation of scholars such as John Urry (2002), who offers a grand theory of tourism under so-called post-modern conditions, Richard Handler (with Eric Gabel 1997), and Edward Bruner (see, e.g.,1994, 2005), who show considerable theoretical sensitivity in their investigations of the social construction of images for tourism destinations, Josepf Böröcz (1996) in a theoretically based, statistically oriented analysis of the attractiveness of certain European tourist destinations, and the works of Francisco Jurdao Arrones (1990), whose theoretically assisted analysis of what might be called the touristically induced "underdevelopment" of certain regions in Spain and the Mediterranean is quite overwhelming. We might also profit by borrowing from geography, perhaps the most compatible of the social sciences, as far as anthropology and sociology are concerned. From it, we could use the notion of "resort cycle" advanced by geographer Richard Butler (Butler 1980; Butler, ed. 2006) some years ago, but of relevance still, and a good deal of recent theoretically informed work (Lew, Hall and Williams 2004) in the same discipline. There are also ideas in the neo-Marxist-oriented offerings of scholars from the field of Cultural Studies (Storey 1996; Wade 1997), which ought to attract anthropologists, sociologists, and geographers alike. In short, putting the not-insignificant problem of translation aside, there would seem to be good deal of theory around to help us in our work.

But as Dann and his associates (1988) have made clear, theory is only one aspect of the ideological thrust of scientific knowledge—the other being methodology, which includes rules and procedures by which research is carried out and evaluated. These authors criticized the level of methodological sophistication displayed in early tourism research, a critique supported by Cohen (1984:388) in an assessment pointing out that none of the theoretical approaches used by anthropologists and sociologists had yet withstood rigorous empirical testing. This comment, of course, does not mean that the criteria of validity or truth-value involved would necessarily be those of the natural sciences, for as Barth (2002:9) reminds us, each field of scientific knowledge has its own criteria for truth.

The criticism of methodological acumen was also leveled at anthropological/sociological research on tourism more than a decade later by Nash (2000) in his evaluation of ethnographic approaches to the subject (ethnography, it will be recalled, being a technique often used in these disciplines); and one way of looking at the recent compendium put together by Jennifer Phillimore and Lisa Goodson (2004) on qualitative research in tourism study is to consider it as a critique of current methodological practice, which—everyone seems to agree—continues to be dominated by a positivist approach.

So one can say that though research is being carried out and expanding in the field, and though we have flourishing institutions devoted to the study of the subject, its methodological sophistication still may leave something to be desired. This suggests that another possible reason for the delay or rejection of submitted proposals for early tourism projects may have been not only the distaste of various "gatekeepers" for the subject matter, but the fact that in a new and peripheral field with developing standards, some researchers had not yet acquired the ability to meet normal research standards of their disciplines, perhaps because they were young and inexperienced. In any case, one has to take seriously the comment to your editor by the President of an important granting agency that early tourism proposals in anthropology were not very good and thank Jafar Jafari and other early gatekeepers for their greater receptivity to papers on tourism and insistence on developing more methodological rigor in dealing with the subject, as well as the exceptional work of some of our "beginners" in getting tourism study off the ground.

The Context of Current Tourism Study: Academic Structures

As pointed out earlier, the Humboldtan tradition in universities of original research by autonomous, discipline-oriented scholars had been well established when our participant-pioneers began to open up a new field of study concerned with tourism; and this element of our academic context has remained essentially the same for a long time. The academic disciplines of our participants then were anthropology, sociology, or both, and their administrative departments (with one or two exceptions) were similarly oriented. As university-level study expanded, there was some increase in specialization (as in the case when Nash's department of Sociology and Anthropology at Connecticut was split). Such specialization was not only administrative in nature, but also substantive, involving new fields of study such as feminism, Afro-American culture, Medical Anthropology/Sociology, Cultural Studies, and the like. So one must see the general process of specialization or diversification, which was at work in academic disciplines during the early period of tourism study, as an enabling factor in the development of the new field.

As far as administrative recognition of the subject of tourism, and leisure-related subjects more generally, in something like departments of anthropology, sociology, or both in the early days of the field, one is hard put to see any. Of course, tourism may have been cited as a part of department members' expertise, but it was rarely, if at all, an academically recognized field of study (The cases associated with Graburn at Berkeley, Cohen at Jerusalem, and Jafari at Wisconsin-Stout, where the "envelope" was more insistently and effectively pushed, are perhaps, individual-generated exceptions to this general lack of emphasis). A more recent alternative might be the establishment of a multidisciplinary department of Tourism Studies, which now is being proposed at University of California, Davis by participants MacCannell, Swain and some others, the department in England to which Graham Dann returned from Barbados at Luton, with its flock of tourism-oriented scholars, the special arrangement for Lanfant and her team at the CNRS, or the Roehampton MA in the Sociology and Anthropology of Tourism (now at London Metropolitan University), the leading spirit in which has been one of our informants, Tom Selwyn.

Finally in our discussion of the academic context of the field, we would be remiss in not noting the advance of business-oriented administrative arrangements, as for example, the so-called "Audit Culture" in England and former commonwealth countries (Shore and Wright 1999). In this, scholars are closely and specifically monitored for various aspects of their productivity, an arrangement, which seems at some remove from the basic Humboldtan model discussed earlier, in which considerable freedom from Academic surveillance (especially for scholars with something like tenure) was assumed. It appears that two of our participants, Crick and Dann, have already experienced this new British-related academic arrangement—Crick at a small institution in Australia and Dann on his return to England from Barbados. That this development could have personal implications that extend into one's academic work is clear from Crick's personal history.

There are also broader implications of this development in the monitoring of academic output. Audit Culture (Strathern, ed. 2000) is a reflection of a "neo-liberal" economic scheme put into place in Britain especially during the period of the Thatcher government. It is a form of development that may extend beyond

Britain and its immediate sphere of influence. The argument for this arrangement appears to be that any social institution, including not only businesses, but colleges, universities, etc., should operate in a business-like way; and for those of us who have acquired a view of tourism as a great world "industry," the conclusion would seem to be inescapable that not only the object, but also the study itself are affected by the culture of the world of business.

Perhaps Lanfant, in her personal history, has discussed this issue with the greatest effect. She argues that the "neo-liberal" economic view of international business, which had prevailed in many studies of development, was unacceptable for the study of international tourism phenomena which her team had put together. She argues that it had to be replaced by a more "sociological" point of view, which she and her colleagues have developed for handling their study of international tourism. Certainly, there are economic viewpoints that are acceptable to them (see, e.g., her personal history). But one wonders how they will respond to Pierre Van den Berghe's, closing argument in his personal history, which proposes what appears to be a rather straightforward, classical economic approach for analyzing touristic phenomena—a viewpoint similar to that used by a number of economically oriented students of tourism, including John Bryden (1973) in his early study of tourism development in the Caribbean. In any case, the issue of tourism as a business and its effect on touristic actors, including researchers, would seem to require continuing reflection, discussion, and even action by tourism scholars, as well as others.

The Context of Current Tourism Study: An Expanding Industry

It should not take long for those of us who have been involved with tourism study from the beginning to recognize the value of Lanfant's critique for our field. As tourism scholars, all of us have probably come to believe that we have singled out an increasingly legitimate object of investigation; and we have spent much of our careers in give-and-take with that object and the theories and methods involved in studying it. In discussions with skeptical colleagues and the public, we almost certainly have mentioned, as a kind of legitimation, the importance of the tourism industry in the world today. (Indeed, at the outset of this book, facts and predictions about international tourism were given to that end.) Early in our tourism research, we may have acquired the notion that our own careers were attached in various ways to this "industry." In short, we may have tied our own success as scholars, consciously or unconsciously, to the rising star of tourism business. Of course, there have been those of us who have adopted a critical or "cautionary" stance in our work on the subject, but generally, we have thought that if tourism flourished—whether for good or bad from whatever point of view—we, our-selves, were likely to benefit, if for no other reason than because it provided a basis for scholarly work.

In our discussion of the current field of tourism study, we have come to the conclusion that its development has followed a pattern not unlike that of other new fields of science. It can be seen for example, to have been composed of the same essential elements in any field of knowledge, which according to Frederick Barth, include assertions or beliefs, media, and some kind of social organization; and it has followed the same general path for new sciences generally, which Lewenstein (1995) discusses in his treatment of the field surrounding the ques-tionable subject of Cold Fusion. But as far as social organization is concerned, we have not yet looked seriously enough into the social processes involved, i.e., those of association and dissociation, especially the latter. Indeed, one way of looking at the development of a science has been in terms which emphasize competition or conflict (Allen 1991; Kuhn 1977)—something that, according to Lewenstein (1995:145), would appear to be inevitable, even where questionable subjects such as Cold Fusion are concerned.

As any scientific field develops, we would expect to see the emergence of sub-cultural differences and associated contestations between various social factions. So far, we have not dwelled on this aspect of the development of the field of tourism study. Perhaps this may have something to do with the existence of a kind of Ur-Myth that has hovered over us since early in our studies of tourism—a Myth, which stresses (sometimes in near-religious terms) the fact that we tourism researchers from a variety of disciplines are a somewhat heroic, multidisciplinary, multicultural lot bent on establishing the legitimacy of our subject and develop-ing a scientifically derived view of its nature. Those sharing in this myth (the edi-tor having been no exception) might have tended to minimize their disagreements in a mission in which we have preferred to see ourselves as working all together against a largely unenthusiastic world that may even include our own disciplines. With such a cooperative presentation of selves, it has helped us to have a certain degree of collaboration, if not agreement, of different scientific orientations among the social scientific researchers involved. This state of things is perhaps best expressed by the special compendium of *Annals* on Tourism Social Science, edited by Graburn and Jafari (Graburn and Jafari, eds. 1991), in which the vari-ous social scientific approaches to the study of tourism were presented together, as well as in some of the early publications of the International Academy for the Study of Tourism (IAST) (Smith and Eadington, eds. 1992).

But for one or another reason, the fact of social contentiousness may be too much to ignore, as has been indicated in some of the difficult business meetings of the IAST, of the editorial board of *Annals*, or the early "stormy" days in the

Leisure Research Symposium, mentioned by Stephen Smith (1989:130) concerning the balance between pure and applied research (despite which, according to Smith, that organization has "survived and grown"). In the face of such evidence, it would seem that Jafari's essentially ideological notion of the "scientification" of tourism study leaves out important elements of the knowledge involved. Not only does he portray the developing field mostly in ideological terms, but he also tends to minimize the potentially contentious involvement of an expanding tourism industry (acting at times through its various research and administrative representatives against certain Academic interests) that accompanies it. The argument here is that sooner or later in their research, the views of more business-oriented researchers will be shaped in some way by the "business needs" of a tourism industry, with which they are more or less associated. Looking at the matter rather loosely, one can posit a continuum extending from greater to lesser involvement in the "business" of tourism, with anthropologists and sociologists more deeply attached to a less business oriented, more academic positions, as suggested by the work of Riley and Love (2000).

Earlier, in the development of the field of tourism research, when there was more of an associative mix between business-oriented and academically oriented points of view, as in early presentations and publications of the IAST (e.g., Butler and Pearce, eds. 1995; Smith and Eadington, eds. 1992), the issue of contentiousness, if it arose, was more or less effectively suppressed on the ideological front. The prevailing view seemed to be that any information about tourism, however derived, was likely to be useful for collective research operations in the field. Speaking about the relevant social context of those days, your editor (Nash 1996:158–159) maintained that "... basic (i.e., academically oriented) and applied (i.e., business-oriented) research on tourism can go hand in hand, and each is capable of enriching the other." Such a statement was derived from a situation in which people with varying points of view could inform one another about different aspects of the field and ultimately contribute to some balanced overview of a multifarious subject.

But such a balance—if it ever existed—could be on the way to becoming seriously unsettled by the increasing success of a tourism industry and growing numbers of associated applied researchers who have taken on something of a business-oriented point of view. Earlier, statements by Butler (1993) and Ritchie (1993), both of them applied researchers of distinction, were offered to suggest the fact that applied and basic researchers have tended to differ in their approaches on the subject of tourism development. Others, despite Seale's (2001) view to the contrary for the social sciences generally, might emphasize the distinction between more quantitative (business associated) and more qualitative (academic) in methodology.

The evidence for an increasing disjunction between applied and basic researchers in tourism study is, itself, unsettling, especially to those of us who had thought that it was a non-factor for the field. But there are disquieting facts. First, the proportion of business-oriented researchers in tourism study seems to be increasing internationally, and they appear to have increasing weight in plenary institutions of the field, such as the IAST, the elite organization of tourism researchers from around the world, which has been discussed in some detail earlier. This organization is now being run—ever more expeditiously—mostly by members (and associates) from the business-oriented side of tourism research; and it has a membership that increasingly represents this orientation (see Appendix C). Second, submissions to institutional journals such as *Annals*, which is probably the most *academically* oriented of journals on tourism, are increasingly from researchers in more business- or management oriented departments (see also Appendix C). The apparent result of all this may be that, as far as any comprehensive study of tourism is concerned, the business side appears to be gaining increasing leverage in the overall tourism research agenda. In his recent comments about the development of the IAST, Eric Cohen may have summed up this aspect of the context of the field of tourism study when he (Cohen 2005:3) says "The Academy is moving from a body of academics with intellectual and theoretical concerns, to one of professionals, many in applied fields." That he thinks this is a turn for the worse is suggested by his complaint about the "problematic quality of a good number of papers presented at Academy meetings." At the very least, one can say that this changing organizational arrangement ought to affect the atmosphere in which tourism scholars work and the way in which they carry on their research.

What has been the position of anthropological and sociological researchers in the face of advances of more business-oriented research in the field? Of course, we should expect some variation. Some might be unaware of what amounts to a political situation related to the production of tourism knowledge. Others, more aware, might show indications of frustration, as in the personal histories of Dann, Crick, Nash, and Lanfant, as well as in the preceding statement by Cohen. Also, now that tourism research has become more acceptable in various academic disciplines, one would expect there to be more reaching out by anthropologists and sociologists toward confreres in more academically oriented interests and outlets, as for example, in the Research Committee on Tourism of the International Sociological Assn. and the Commission on Tourism of the International Congress of Anthropological and Ethnological Sciences—institutions in which a more discipline-oriented approach in tourism study is welcomed (A similar process is illustrated by the temporary drifting away of one of our participants, Michel Picard, from the field of International Tourism, in which he had been deeply involved, into that which might be called the field of Balinese Ethnology).

Increased publication and mention in more discipline-oriented journals like *American Anthropologist, American Sociological Review, Leisure Studies*, and books by established publishing houses, including university presses, also should be noted. Of course, there is nothing exceptional about this kind of social differentiation in the development of the sciences or any other social institution. Indeed, it has sometimes been said that the formation of different "camps" and the contention between them has a productive function for the development of a scientific field. It is only that, for better or worse, the seemingly natural and constructive give-and-take between the business oriented and the academic that was aimed at developing a field-oriented view of tourism could be lost because of the developing imbalance in its social organization.

Where are We, and Where are We Headed?

One can view the early history of tourism research as (in part) a search for legitimization, which is to say, acceptability or respect. From such a perspective, the development of tourism research by anthropologists, sociologists, and other academics was begun by academic scholars in an historical epoch when the drive to work had begun to give way to the experience of leisure in Western culture; and like all social endeavors, it required some kind of confirmation by other actors to survive and prosper. Of course, these "significant others" could be the people next door, colleagues in one's academic department, foreigners of various kinds, media gatekeepers, or international bodies awarding prizes for distinguished work in the field (notice of the last of which has been minimized in the writing of our personal histories at the editor's request).

Looking at the history of tourism research from its beginnings in terms of the personal histories included in this volume, one can see a good deal of progress in this regard. Starting out in a situation where favorable views of their "touristic activities," while occasionally forthcoming, were generally hard to find, they have come to the point where their peers in the academic community are more accepting. They have created the fundamentals of their research understandings, and indeed, have managed to establish or construct a new field of knowledge with all the earmarks of other scientific fields. Of course, as is revealed in the personal histories, there are some others who may still regard tourism research in quizzical or disparaging ways. Nevertheless, indications from participants' personal histories suggest at least some acceptance or support from significant others—publishers, academic administrators, colleagues, etc., to warrant the belief that, if not a discipline, a new field of study has been established or constructed (Tribe 2004), thanks in part to the efforts of the participants in this study, as well as pioneers in other disciplines.

The field which has been established has a considerable number of dimensions, and because of this, general statements about it are difficult to make. But they are not impossible. Indeed, this book is a testimony to the viability of an early-conceived, cross-cultural overview of the editor based on the concepts of *touristic process* and *touristic system,* as well as a fairly broad definition of tourists as *leisured travelers*—all of which suggesting a line of inquiry involving discipline-oriented questions and procedures that can accommodate the variety of scientific approaches which have been practiced by those who have produced this book.

In general, the participants in this study have had careers of approximately a quarter century in tourism research, and most have begun formal academic retirement. They continue, however, to be active in the production of tourism-related knowledge, which includes fieldwork, writing, teaching, presentations, and discussions with colleagues around the world. More or less creative, most of them appear to be satisfied with their accomplishments as students of tourism. Their field, now well into its second generation seems to be well established, but hardly fully realized. And it is not without its problems.

In truth, the field is much more complex than has been suggested by Jafari's notion of "scientification." What kind of view of science is implied? Almost everyone involved here would agree that our scientific research should not be some kind of simple, demographic enterprise (e.g., one that simply associates tourist characteristics and destination choice), which though undoubtedly useful in the past, has drawn disparaging remarks from a number of our participants. Beyond that is the kind of theoretically informed, methodologically adequate positivistic research that continues as a goal for most tourism researchers (Dann et al, eds. 1988), and is especially practiced in applied research. A smaller group—the qualitatively oriented—who, according to Riley and Love (2000), are more frequently encountered in anthropology and sociology, have always been with us, and, indeed, have established some of the more fertile research traditions from our beginnings. Suggestions by Seale (2001) and Ritchie, Burns and Palmer (2005) that we should be more flexible and less doctrinaire in our research approaches takes us further in adapting to the kind of research environment we face around the world. But what becomes essential, according to Giddens (1995:276–277), is an intensifying social reflexivity that is necessary for attaining legitimacy in a more varied and rapidly changing world—one in which everyone is a "knowledge producer" whose ways of knowing must be accounted for.

This means that we must comprehend more fully the nature of the institution we have created to study tourism, as well as the people in it who make it function—an enterprise which we have begun in a tentative, but hopefully productive way in this volume. Such a viewpoint suggests that we must understand (and declare) fully the sociocultural context in which we act, important elements of which are the tourism industry and the academic structures that shape our research operations. One can hardly say that we, here, have accomplished that. Indeed, it is a bit removed from our major concern of this volume, the main point of which was to lay out the beginnings and early development of the study of tourism (in anthropology and sociology), not the present and the future; accordingly, we have been content with raising issues rather than seeing them through. But we have seen enough to suggest that something significant is going on in shaping the structure of the research organization in which we are involved, as well as the research approaches we are employing to produce assertions about tourism. Perhaps other tourism scholars, who now are acting in a research institution that has achieved a certain degree of legitimacy, will pursue the matter further.

One cannot be too sanguine about the level of reflexiveness that has been developed by tourism researchers, but as we have seen, there have been beginnings, which give us cause for hope. The volume edited by Phillimore and Goodson (2004) presses the cause of qualitative research, but it also is a breath of fresh air to those of us who believe that increasing reflexiveness is necessary for further development of our field of knowledge. Indeed, the procedures we have developed for studying various aspects of tourism can be applied to ourselves and our operations. As Shore and Wright (1999) have shown, the resulting formulations can become the basis of actions that help us to further our research endeavors.

Like all social institutions, ours has its good and bad aspects from whatever point of view. Anyone reading this book would have to agree that the establishment and development of a new field of study has been a major accomplishment of the researchers involved. But now that institutionalization is well under way, new sorts of difficulties have emerged. What shape our scientifically derived knowledge of the subject of tourism will take, and what parts anthropological and sociological researchers will play in its development are not easily predictable; but if new researchers are recruited (from whatever discipline) who have the drive of those whose personal histories appear in this volume, if they are committed to intellectual, discipline-oriented questions, if they continue to refine their scientific approaches, if they maintain a critical stance in a reflexive mode, and if they are politically alert, significant growth should continue. What their production of knowledge will mean to relevant reference groups—to members of their disciplines (in this case, anthropology and sociology, as well as the other social sciences), others involved in the field of tourism study, and the general public—can hardly be determined in specific detail. But it would seem safe to say that tourism researchers will continue to be recruited, develop, and offer a sufficient variety of interesting assertions about their subject to chew on.

A particularly exciting example of a substantial move forward in the field was provided by the recent conclave "On Voyage" at Berkeley (October 2005). That conclave, which was largely supported academically, involved theoretically informed presentations by a variety of humanistically oriented tourism researchers chosen by Berkeley graduate students, with Nelson Graburn, one of our participants, acting as a kind of shadow coordinator.

That many-sided conclave, to which a number of participants in this study were invited, produced a kind of collective effervescence among the old and new hands attending that can only bode well for the future of the field, if for no other reasons than that it was academically oriented and enthusiastically driven. After two days in that ebullient atmosphere, even your editor was impressed and thinking positively about our future. It seemed like the old days when we were all freely breaking ground in a new field of study. Though there are institutional problems on the horizon, there seems to be no question about the relevance and viability of the field for academic study and practical application (Ahmed and Shore 1995). It looks as if the game is still afoot... .

Stay tuned!

Appendix A

Guide for Personal Histories

The aim of the proposed book is to reconstruct the emergence of a new field of study from the personal histories of pioneers in the field. People being contacted are anthropologists or sociologists who were among the first to publish on the subject of tourism. The editor (Nash), besides contributing his own personal history, will write introductory and concluding chapters that help to make some general sense out of the various contributions.

Try to remember that the aim of your personal history should be to lay out the process in which you came to grips with the subject of tourism. The essentials of this process should be covered as each author sees fit. Try to think of yourself as an informant who is conveying this information to the editor and subsequent readers. It may help you to think of this guiding question: *How did I come to be involved in the study of tourism, and How has that involvement developed since then?*

Points to cover

1. Your early academic and social background.
2. Your social (include intellectual) context at the time you became interested in studying tourism.
   a. subjects with which your were preoccupied,
   b. events of significance, and
   c. significant others.
3. Getting involved.
   a. Pros and cons and processes involved.
4. Your first works in the field and their implications.
5. Contextual pros and cons at that time.
6. Where are you now in your study of tourism, and in retrospect, how have you "progressed" in your study of the subject?
7. (If not previously answered) Where do you stand now in terms of major intellectual currents, particularly as they pertain to the study of tourism?

Note: Though your personal histories undoubtedly will differ in length, think of about 25 double-spaced typewritten pages on the average.

Editor's Explanatory Note

The aim of this Guide was to help participants tell a story of their discovery and increasing involvement with the subject of tourism. It was hoped that this would provide information about the social world around them, as well as themselves. Recall was aided by the direction to confine remarks to that aspect of a life trajectory that was immediately relevant for their study of tourism. In a study of this kind, in which interaction was reduced and most participants were beyond middle age, memories of early life experiences, especially those purportedly connected with later tourism research, were viewed with suspicion, and therefore discouraged.

The stories that participants told turned out to be more or less satisfactory for an editor, who though not always taking comments at face value, sought to steer clear of deep-seated analysis. This was made necessary by the kind of information obtained from participants, not only in their initial essays, but also after editorial interventions. An example of the constructions involved is demonstrated in the editorial conclusion that a participant was independent or independent minded, evidence for which was provided by participants' reported choice of subject matter and interpretations of it, as well as persistence in going their own way in the face of contradiction or lack of support. Fortunately for the worth of our conclusions, uncertainties about them on the part of any reader can be checked against the personal histories of our participants.

Appendix B

Serendipity

All research, like all social life, would seem to have its serendipitous aspects. But it would seem to be somewhat more so in ethnographic research, which has been a model for the methodology used in this study. Already, its operation in early tourism study in anthropology, which was largely ethnographically based, has been pointed out by the pioneer Theron Nuñez (1977) who spoke a few decades ago of anthropologists doing fieldwork and *inadvertently* discovering the fact of tourism along the way. The truth of his statement has been amply demonstrated in the personal histories of participants in this study.

Also, it can be seen in the editor's work in the present study. As already mentioned, he encountered unanticipated problems with the cooperation of some of the participants, all of whom were familiar to him, and who he tended to think of as coming from the same academic culture and presenting a minimum of translation problems (In fact, participants had been working in six different countries, all of which were more or less Westernized, at the time of this study). These problems mostly had to do with extraordinary delays or non-response of participants in the course of completing their personal histories. Some of these delays were understandable, some less understandable, and all (considering the loose time frame involved) unanticipated. That such delays took place in a research context, in which a number of other participants were able to submit acceptable personal histories in good time and without problems, made them more difficult to accept.

Though the traditional notion of the term might not seem applicable, the experience seemed to be the same as with the editor's earlier experience with culture shock in various field trips, and it appears to have had the usual dysfunctional effects such as constriction and regression (Nash 1970), which were dealt with by personal reflection, cathartic bouts, and perseverance. Fortunately, it seems that there was enough time for such adaptations to work effectively.

A further problem associated with respondent difficulties mentioned above occurred in the editorial process, where the editor may have attempted to resolve difficulties by giving up the normal give-and-take with participants and simply taking over, especially in the last "go-round," in which it was customary for the editor to make small changes on his or her own to put a piece in final order. Though the editor was aware of this problem and did everything in his power to resolve it, one cannot be sure how well he succeeded. In sum, he cannot be entirely sure that some personal histories do not include more than the usual allowable limit from the editor.

There also appears to have been a positive side to the problem of delays. Whatever their reason, they gave him a greater opportunity to consider further issues and run them to ground. Not unlike other scientists pursuing their research, he began to find out that there were facts and issues about which he was misinformed or uninformed, and thanks to participant delays and not being as quick intellectually as he once was, he found the study opening up in ways that he had not anticipated. It also helped, of course, to have a library and e-mail directly at one's disposal throughout the course of the study. But still, in other research projects, for better or for worse, he had come to a point where he was able to say with some confidence, "That's it!" or something equivalent in ending some written piece. Here, there has been a nagging uncertainty associated with the ever-expanding nature of the study and the acquisition of new knowledge along the way, tending to reduce the editor's confidence and make it more difficult to close out the writing of this book. In this regard, time and good editorial assistance have been of considerable help; but of course, I continue to feel that there is something more that could be done with the material at hand.

Appendix C

A Little Primary Research

It has become something of a tradition in tourism studies to maintain, as does Ritchie (1993:202) that the more "methodologies, concepts, energies, and disciplinary skills" brought to bear in a study of tourism, the better. But perhaps one cannot always be so optimistic about this "more is merrier" approach. One problem is that in tourism research (and presumably other research) there have emerged two distinctive forms of research-knowing, referred to by Tribe (1997:639) as "propositional knowledge," which is more likely to be encountered in academically oriented disciplines such as anthropology and sociology, and "procedural knowledge," in which research-knowing is primarily for the sake of business goals that include (again Tribe 1997:649) "the marketing of tourism, tourism corporate strategy, tourism law, and the management of tourism"—a formulation that makes one think of the general distinction between basic and applied approaches in the sciences.

For Ritchie (1993:202), tourism research should ultimately be done in an integrated, multidisciplinary fashion, in which there is a meaningful sharing of ideas and values among researchers and their supporting disciplines; and Nash (1996:141–154) has echoed this view by stating that basic and applied research ought to proceed "hand-in-hand." But as Tribe (1997:654) has pointed out, the two modes of knowing in comprehensive research undertakings have become unequal productive partners, with one being better integrated (through business-related procedural knowledge) and the other (devoted to propositional knowledge) having "no interdisciplinary framework on which to crystallize. More simply put, as Lyotard (1984:46) expresses it, profitability or performability have a greater integrating power, and because of this, we would expect that, excepting extraordinary circumstances, the business-oriented point of view to tend to "trump" the academic in the comprehensive research approach to tourism advocated by Ritchie— and even more so as the tourism industry expands and its research associates and their involvements and published contributions multiply.

Therefore, we should expect that with the expansion of the tourism industry and, however delayed, the multiplication of its research associates there would be an increase in manifestations of its power in integrated undertakings in which those associates are formally or informally involved—such manifestations including membership in elite institutions for tourism study such as the International Academy for the Study of Tourism (IAST) and publication in an elite journal for tourism research *Annals of Tourism Research*, the evidence for which is twofold:

1. Concerning membership in IAST, an elite, international organization of tourism researchers, and using department of origin as an indicator, one sees that in 1998–1999, geography headed the list for number of members, with sociology ranking third and anthropology fifth. (Researchers from business-oriented departments were hardly represented at all.) In contrast for 2002–2003, members from business-oriented departments such as marketing and management headed the list, geography was second, sociology third, and anthropology fourth. This brief secular trend for membership in the IAST, therefore, tends to be in favor of business-oriented researchers; and it is reinforced by more recent data for 2004–2005, which indicates that of seven new members for that year, five had clear business-oriented origins, and for two, such origins were probable.

2. Regarding departments of origin of authors of articles in *Annals*, perhaps the most academically oriented of all tourism journals, data for the early phase of tourism study (1974–1986), analyzed by Dann, Nash and Pearce (1988), shows geography at the head of the list for a number of publications, anthropology second, economics third, and sociology fourth. In contrast for the later period 2001–2003, analyzed by the editor (Nash), publications from departments of management headed the list, with tourism second, marketing and business third, geography fourth, sociology fifth, and anthropology sixth. The secular trend for publications in *Annals*, therefore, tends to favor those from business-oriented departments.

So, using relatively crude indications of power in the tourism research process (as measured by academic distinction and the publication rate of representatives of different disciplines), the data suggest that the power of the tourism industry in the research process has increased recently. How all this has shaped the quality of knowledge production would be important to know. For example, one might entertain the hypothesis that business-oriented quantitative research (as opposed to qualitative), already substantial according to Riley and Love (2000), would be on the upswing in recent days. Unfortunately, their analysis for the qualitative/quantitative dimension of articles was not continued for the recent period (i.e., since 1996). On the other hand, they do offer data for an earlier period (1975–1996), which, however, show that anthropology and sociology were distinguished, if not dominated by qualitatively oriented research, which is to say that they head the list for non-business-oriented research for that earlier period.

To conclude, our rather crude primary research endeavor has provided some evidence for an increase in power of more business-oriented researchers in the recent production of tourism knowledge. It has also suggested that anthropology and sociology have stood out in the qualitative orientation of their tourism research. Further, more refined efforts would help to produce more definitive results.

References

Adler, J.
1989 Origins of Sightseeing. Annals of Tourism Research 16:7–29.
Aguilar, J.
1981 Insider Research: An Ethnography of a Debate. *In* Anthropologists at Home in North America: Methods and Issues in the Study of One's Own Society, D. Messerschmidt, ed., pp. 15–28. Cambridge: Cambridge University Press.
Ahmed, A., and C. Shore, eds.
1995 The Future of Anthropology: Its Relevance for the Contemporary World. London: Athlone.
Allen, G.
1991 Essay Review. Isis 82:698–704.
Appadurai, A.
1986 Introduction: Commodities and Politics of Value. *In* The Social Life of Things: Commodities in Cultural Perspective, A. Appadurai, ed., pp. 3–63. Cambridge: Cambridge University Press.
Asad, T.
1973 Anthropology and the Colonial Encounter. New York: Humanities Press.
Bain, R., and W. Kolb
1964 Sociology. *In* A Dictionary of the Social Sciences, J. Gould and W. Kolb, eds., New York: Macmillan.
Balsdon, J.
1969 Life and Leisure in Ancient Rome. New York: McGraw-Hill.
Baretje, R.
1981 Tourisme et Histoire: Essai Bibliographique 69. Aix-en-Provence: Centre des Hautes Études Touristiques.
2003 Report of Activities 1997–2003. Aix-en-Provence: Centre International de Recherches et d'Études Touristiques.
Barnes, B., D. Bloor, and J. Henry
1996 Scientific Knowledge: A Sociological Analysis. Chicago: University of Chicago Press.
Barnett, H.
1953 Innovation: The Basis of Cultural Change. New York: McGraw-Hill.
Barth, F.
2002 An Anthropology of Knowledge. Current Anthropology 43:1–18.
Becker, W. A.
1895 Charicles (3rd ed.). London: Longman's Green.
Bee, R.
1974 Patterns and Processes. New York: The Free Press.

Bendix, R.
1962 Max Weber: An Intellectual Portrait. New York: Anchor Books.
Berger, B., ed.
1990 Authors of Their Own Lives: Intellectual Autobiographies of Twenty American Sociologists. Berkeley: University of California Press.
Berger, P., and T. Luckmann
1967 The Social Construction of Reality. Garden City: Doubleday.
Berger, P., B. Berger, and H. Kellner
1973 Modernization and Consciousness. New York: Random House.
Boas, F.
1982 [1948] Race, Language and Culture. Chicago: University of Chicago Press.
Bodio, L.
1899 Sul movimento dei forestieri en Italia e sul dendaro chi vi spendono. G. Economica 15:54–61.
Boissevain, J.
1965 Saints and Fireworks: Religion and Politics in Rural Malta (L.S.E. Monographs, no. 30). London: Athlone Press.
1974 Friends of Friends: Networks, Manipulators and Coalitions. Oxford: Basil Blackwell.
1977 Tourism and Development in Malta. Development and Change 8:523–538.
1979a The Impact of Tourism on a Dependent Island: Gozo, Malta. Annals of Tourism Research 6:76–90.
1979b Tourism and the European Periphery: The Mediterranean Case. *In* Underdeveloped Europe: Studies in Core-Periphery Relations, D. Seers, B. Schaffer, and M.-L. Kiljunen, eds., pp. 125–135. Hassocks: The Harvester Press.
1989 Tourism as Anti-Structure. *In* Cultur Anthropologisch. Eine Festschrift für Ina-Maria Greverus, C. Giordano, W. Schiffauer, H. Schilling, G. Welz, and M. Zimmermann, eds., pp. 145–159. Notizen Nr. 3O. Frankfurt: Institut für Kulturanthropologie und Europäische Ethnologie. Universität Frankfurt am Main.
1996 Ritual, Tourism and Cultural Commoditization. Culture by the Pound? *In* The Tourist Image: Myths and Myth Making in Tourism, T. Selwyn, ed., pp. 105–120. London/New York: Wiley.
2000 Changing Maltese Landscapes. From Utilitarian Space to Heritage? *In* The Maltese Islands on the Move. A Mosaic of Contributions Marking Malta's Entry into the 21st Century, C. Vella, ed., pp. 1–14. Valletta: Central Office of Statistics.
2001 Mass Tourism and the European South. *In* L' Anthropologie de la Méditerranée/Anthropology of the Mediterranean, D. Albera, A. Blok, and C. Bromberger, eds., pp 685–709. Paris: Maisonneuve et Larose.
Boissevain, J., ed.
1992 Revitalizing European Rituals. Amsterdam: University of Amsterdam.
1996 Coping with Tourists. European Reactions to Mass Tourism. Providence/Oxford: Berghahn Books.
Boissevain, J., and N. Sammut
1994 Medina: Its Residents and Cultural Tourism. Findings and Recommendations. Report of Med-Campus Euromed Sustainable Tourism Programme, University of Malta.

Boissevain, J., and P. Serracino Inglott
   1979 Tourism in Malta. *In* Tourism. Passport to Development, E. de Kadt, ed., pp. 165–284. Oxford: Oxford University Press.
Boissevain, J., and N. Theuma
   1998 Contested Space. Planners, Tourists, Developers and Environmentalists in Malta. *In* Anthropological Perspectives on Local Development, S. Abram and J. Waldren, eds., pp. 96–119. London: Routledge.
Boorstin, D.
   1964 The Image: A Guide to Pseudo Events in America. New York: Atheneum.
Böröcz, J.
   1996 Leisure Migration: A Sociological Study of Tourism. Oxford: Elsevier.
Borowsky, R.
   1994 Introduction. *In* Assessing Cultural Anthropology, R. Borowsky, ed., pp. 1–21. New York: McGraw Hill.
Bottomore, T.
   1993a Sociology. *In* Twentieth Century Social Thought, E. Outwaite and T. Bottomore, eds., pp. 632–636. Oxford: Blackwell.
   1993b Structuralism. *In* Twentieth Century Social Thought, E. Outwaite, and T. Bottomore, eds., pp. 648–649. Oxford: Blackwell.
   1993c Marxism. *In* Twentieth Century Social Thought, E. Outwaite and T. Bottomore, eds., pp.365–368. Oxford: Blackwell.
Bourdieu, P.
   1977 Outline of a Theory of Practice. Cambridge: Cambridge University Press.
   1987 Homo Academicus. Stanford: Stanford University Press.
Boyer, M.
   1972 Le Tourism. Paris: Editions du Seuil.
Bruner, E.
   1994 Abraham Lincoln as Authentic Reproduction: A Critique of Post Modernism. American Anthropologist 96:397–415.
   1996 Tourism in the Balinese Borderzone. *In* Displacement, Diaspora, and Geographies of Identity, S. Lavie and T. Swedenborg, eds., pp. 157–179. Durham: Duke University Press.
   2005 Culture on Tour: Ethnographies of Travel. Chicago: University of Chicago Press.
Bryden, J.
   1973 Tourism and Development: A Case Study of the Commonwealth Caribbean. New York: Cambridge University Press.
Butler, R.
   1980 The Concept of a Tourist Area Cycle of Evolution; Implications for Management of Resources. Canadian Geographer 24:5–12.
   1993 Pre- and Post-Impact Assessment of Tourism Development. *In* Tourism Research: Critiques and Challenges, D. Pearce and R. Butler, eds., pp. 135–155. London: Routledge.
Butler, R., ed.
   2006 The Tourism Area Life Cycle. Elmsford, N. Y: Channel View.

Butler, R., and D. Pearce, eds.

1995 Change in Tourism: People, Places, Processes. London: Routledge.

Cameron, C. M.

1997 Dilemmas of the Crossover Experience: Tourism Work in Bethlehem, Pennsylvania. *In* Tourism and Culture. An Applied Perspective, E. Chambers, ed., pp. 163–181. Albany: State University of New York Press.

Chambers, E.

2000 Native Tours: The Anthropology of Travel and Tourism. Prospect Heights, IL: Waveland Press.

Clarke, A.

1980 Growing up Stupid under the Union Jack. Havana: Casa de las Américas.

Cohen, E.

1971 Arab Boys and Tourist Girls in a Mixed Jewish-Arab Community. International Journal of Comparative Sociology 12(4):291–304.

1972 Towards a Sociology of International Tourism. Social Research 39(1):164–182.

1973 Nomads from Affluence: Notes on the Phenomenon of Drifter Tourism. International Journal of Comparative Sociology 14(1–2):89–103.

1974 Who is a Tourist? Sociological Review 22:527–553.

1979a Rethinking the Sociology of Tourism. Annals of Tourism Research 6(1):18–35.

1979b A Phenomenology of Tourist Experiences. Sociology 13:179–201.

1979c The Impact of Tourism on the Hill Tribes of Northern Thailand. Internationals Asienforum 10:5–38.

1984 The Sociology of Tourism: Approaches, Issues, and Findings. Annual Review of Sociology 10:373–92.

1988 Traditions in the Qualitative Sociology of Tourism. Annals of Tourism Research 15:29–46.

1996 Thai Tourism: Hilltribes, Islands and Open-ended Prostitution. Bangkok: White Lotus.

2000 The Commercialized Crafts of Thailand: Hill Tribes and Lowland Villages. London: Curzon Press.

2001 The Chinese Vegetarian Festival in Phuket: Religion, Ethnicity and Tourism on a Southern Thai Island. Bangkok: White Lotus.

2002 Review. Tourism Recreation Research 27:108–111.

2004 Contemporary Tourism: Diversity and Change; Collected Articles. Kidling, Oxford: Elsevier.

2005 Letter to the Editor. Newsletter of the International Academy for the Study of Tourism 15(November):3.

Cohen, S., and L. Taylor

1978 Escape Attempts. Harmondsworth: Penguin.

Colby, B., and P. van den Berghe

1961 Ethnic Relations in South-Eastern Mexico. American Anthropologist 63:772–792.

Cooper, W.

1989 Some Philosophical Aspects of Leisure Theory. *In* Understanding Leisure and Recreation: Mapping the Past, Charting the Future, E. Jackson and T. Burton, eds., pp. 49–68. State College: Venture Publishing.

Coser, L.

1971 Masters of Sociological Thought: Ideas in Historical and Social Context. New York: Harcourt Brace Jovanovich.

1993 Chicago Sociology. *In* Twentieth Century Social Thought, W. Outwaite and T. Bottomore, eds., pp. 69–70. Oxford: Blackwell.

Crick, M.

1982 Anthropology of Knowledge. Annual Review of Anthropology 11:287–313.

1983 Anthropological Field Research: Meaning Creation and Knowledge Construction. *In* Semantic Anthropology, D. Parkin, ed., pp. 15–37. London: Academic Press.

1985 'Tracing' the Anthropological Self: Quizzical Reflections on Field Work, Tourism and the Ludic. Social Analysis 17:71–92.

1989 Representations of International Tourism in the Social Sciences: Sun, Sex, Savings and Servility. Annual Review of Anthropology 18:307–344.

1991 Tourists, Locals and Anthropologists: Quizzical Reflections on 'Otherness' in Tourist encounters and in Tourism Research. Australian Cultural History 10:6–18.

1994 Resplendent Sites, Discordant Voices. Sri Lankans and International Tourism. Chur: Harwood Academic Publishers.

1995 The Anthropologist as Tourist: An Identity in Question. *In* International Tourism: Identity and Change, M.-F. Lanfant, J. Allcock and E. Bruner, eds., pp. 205–223. London: Sage.

2003 Maldon Memories. Maldon: Maldon, Inc.

Dann, G.

1976 The Holiday was Simply Fantastic. Revue de Tourisme 3:19–23.

1977 Anomie, Ego-enhancement and Tourism. Annals of Tourism Research 4:184–194.

1981 Tourism Motivation: An Appraisal. Annals of Tourism Research 8:187–219.

1995 A Sociolinguistic Approach towards Changing Tourism Imagery. *In* Changes in Tourism: People, Places and Processes, R. Butler and D. Pearce, eds., pp. 114–136. London: Routledge.

1996 The Language of Tourism: A Sociolinguistic Perspective. Wallingford, Oxon: CAB International.

2000 Theoretical Advances in the Sociological Treatment of Tourism. *In* International Handbook of Sociology, S. Quah and A. Sales, eds., pp. 367–384. London: International Sociological Association.

Dann, G., ed.

2002 The Tourist as a Metaphor of the Social World. Oxon: CABI.

Dann, G., and E. Cohen

1991 Sociology and Tourism. Annals of Tourism Research 18:155–169.

Dann, G., D. Nash, and P. Pearce, eds.
 1988 Methodological Issues in Tourism Research. Annals of Tourism Research 15(1):1–58.
Davies, C.
 1999 Reflexive Ethnography: A Guide to Researching Self and Others. London: Routledge.
Dawson, L., V.-M. Fredrickson, and N. Graburn
 1974 Traditions in Transition: Culture Contact and Material Change. Berkeley: Lowie Museum.
de Alwis, A.
 1980 Tourism, the Greatest Movement for World Peace and Understanding. Colombo: Ceylon Tourism Board.
DeKadt, E.
 1992 Making the Alternative Sustainable: Lessons from Development for Tourism. *In* Tourism Alternatives: Potentials and Problems in the Development of Tourism, V. Smith and W. Eadington, eds., pp. 47–75. Philadelphia: University of Pennsylvania Press.
DeKadt, E., ed.
 1979 Tourism: Passport to Development? New York: Oxford University Press.
Denzin, N., and Y. Lincoln, eds.
 1993 Handbook of Qualitative Research. Thousand Oaks: Sage.
Duchet, R.
 1949 Le Tourism à Travers les Ages: Sa Place dans la Vie Moderne. Paris: Vigot Frères.
Duloum, J.
 1963 Naissance, Developpement et Declin de la Colonie Anglaise de Pau (1814–1914). Annals de La Faculté de Droit et des Sciences Économiques de l'Université d'Aix-Marseille 53:65–77.
Durkheim, E.
 1938[1895] The Rules of Sociological Method. New York: The Free Press.
 1915[1912] The Elementary Forms of Religious Life. London: Allen and Unwin.
Eliade, M.
 1974 The Myth of the Eternal Return. Princeton: Princeton University Press.
Esmeyer, L.
 1984 Marginal Mediterraneans. Foreign settlers in Malta: Their Participation in Society and Their Contribution to Development. Amsterdam: Anthropological–Sociological Centre, University of Amsterdam.
Farver, J. A.
 1984 Tourism and Employment in the Gambia. Annals of Tourism Research 11:249–266.
Finkelstein, M.
 1984 The American Academic Profession: A Synthesis of Scientific Inquiry Since World War II. Columbus: Ohio State University Press.
Forster, E.
 1964 The Sociological Consequences of Tourism. International Journal of Comparative Sociology 5:217–227.

Frank, A. G.
 1972 Lumpen Bourgeoisie and Lumpen-Development: Dependence, Class and Politics in Latin America. New York: Monthly Review Press.
Franklin, S.
 1984 Science as Culture, Cultures of Science. Annual Review of Anthropology 24:163–84.
Frey, N.
 1998 Pilgrim Stories: On and Off the Road to Santiago. Berkeley: University of California.
Friedlander, L.
 1965 Roman Life and Manners Under the Early Empire. London: Routledge.
Friedrichs, R. W.
 1970 A Sociology of Sociology. New York: The Free Press.
Geertz, C.
 1974 The Interpretation of Cultures. New York: Basic Books.
Giddens, A.
 1995 Epilogue: Notes on the Future of Anthropology. *In* The Future of Anthropology: Its Relevance to the Contemporary World, A. Ahmed and C. Shore, eds., pp. 272–277. London: Athlone.
Gilbert, E. W.
 1939 The Growth of Inland and Seaside Health Resorts in England. Scottish Geographical Magazine 53:116–135.
Goeldner, C.
 2003 How Tourism and Hospitality Research has Evolved: A North American Perspective. International Journal of Tourism Sciences 3:163–174.
Goeldner, C., and B. Ritchie
 2006 Tourism: Principles, Practices, Philosophies (10th ed.). Hoboken: Wiley.
Goffman, E.
 1959 The Presentation of Self in Everyday Life. Garden City, NY: Doubleday.
Goldfarb, G.
 1989 International Ecotourism: A Strategy for Conservation and Development. Policy Analysis Exercise for John F. Kennedy School of Government. Cambridge: Harvard University.
Gorer, G.
 1948 The American People, a Study in National Character. New York: W. W. Norton.
Gottschalk, L., C. Kluckhohn, and R. Angell, eds.
 1945 The Use of Personal Documents in History, Anthropology and Sociology (Bulletin 53). New York: Social Science Research Council.
Gouldner, A.
 1971 The Coming Crisis of Western Sociology. New York: Avon.
Graburn, N.
 1967 The Eskimos and 'Airport Art'. Transaction 4:28–33.
 1969 Art and Acculturative Processes. International Social Science Journal 21:457–468.
 1977 Tourism—The Sacred Journey. *In* Hosts and Guests: The Anthropology of Tourism, V. Smith, ed., pp. 17–32. Philadelphia: University of Pennsylvania Press.

1980 Teaching the Anthropology of Tourism. International Social Science Journal 32:56 -68.

1983a The Anthropology of Tourism. Annals of Tourism Research 10:9–33.

1983b To Pay, Pray and Play. Aix-en-Provence: Centre des Hautes Études Touristiques.

1989 Tourism: The Sacred Journey. *In* Hosts and Guests: The Anthropology of Tourism (2nd ed.), V. Smith, ed., pp. 21–36. Philadelphia: University of Pennsylvania Press.

2001 Secular Ritual: A General Theory of Tourism. *In* Hosts and Guests Revisited: Tourism Issues of the 21st Century, V. Smith and M. Brett, eds., pp. 42–50. Elmsford: Cognizant Communication Corp.

Graburn, N., ed.

1976 Ethnic and Tourist Arts: Cultural Expressions from the Fourth World. Berkeley: University of California.

Graburn, N., ed.

1983 The Anthropology of Tourism. Annals of Tourism Research 11(1):9–189.

Graburn, N., and J. Jafari

1991 Introduction: Tourism Social Science. Annals of Tourism Research 18:1–11.

Graburn, N., and J. Jafari, eds.

1991 Tourism Social Science. Annals of Tourism Research 10(1):1–169.

Greenwood, D.

1977 Culture by the Pound: An Anthropological Perspective on Tourism as Cultural Commoditization. *In* Hosts and Guests: The Anthropology of Tourism, V. Smith, ed., pp. 129–138. Philadelphia: University of Pennsylvania Press.

1989 Culture by the Pound: An Anthropological Perspective on Tourism as Cultural Commoditization. *In* Hosts and Guests: The Anthropology of Tourism (2nd ed.), V. Smith, ed., pp. 171–185. Philadelphia: University of Pennsylvania Press.

Hall, M.

2004 Reflexivity and Tourism Research: Situating Myself and/with Others. *In* Qualitative Research in Tourism: Ontologies, Epistemologies and Methodologies, J. Phillimore and L. Goodson, eds., pp. 137–155. London: Routledge.

Hall, D., M. Swain, and V. Kinnaird, eds.

2003 Gender and Tourism. Tourism Recreation Research 28(2):7–75.

Hallowell, A. I.

1965 The History of Anthropology as an Anthropological Problem. Journal of the History of the Behavioral Sciences 1:24–38.

Hammersley, M., and P. Atkinson

1995 Ethnography: Principles in Practice (2nd ed.). London: Routledge.

Handler, R., and E. Gable

1997 The New History in an Old Museum: Creating the Past at Colonial Williamsburg. Durham: Duke University Press.

Harrell-Bond, B.

1978 A Window on the Outside World: Tourism and Development in the Gambia. American Universities Field Staff Report 19.

Harris, M.
  1968 The Rise of Anthropological Theory: A History of Theories of Culture. London: Routledge.
Harrison, J.
  2003 Being a Tourist: Finding Meaning in Pleasure Travel. Vancouver: University of British Columbia.
Heiss, J., and D. Nash
  1967 Sources of Anxiety in Laboratory Strangers. Sociological Quarterly 8:215–221.
Hermans, D.
  1981 The Encounter of Agriculture and Tourism: A Catalan Case. Annals of Tourism Research 8:462–479.
Hobsbawn, E., and T. Ranger, eds.
  1983 The Invention of Tradition. Cambridge: Cambridge University Press.
Howell, B.
  1994 Weighing the Risks and Rewards of Involvement in Cultural Conservation and Heritage Tourism. Human Organization 53:150–159.
Hunt, E.
  1984 Holy Land Pilgrimage in the Later Roman Empire AD312–460. Oxford: Clarendon Press.
Jackson, E., and T. Burton
  1989 Mapping the Past. *In* Understanding Leisure and Recreation: Mapping the Past, Charting the Future, E. Jackson and T. Burton, eds., pp. 29–48. State College: Venture Publishing.
Jafari, J.
  1973 The Role of Tourism in the Socioeconomic Transformation of Developing Countries. MS thesis, Cornell University, Ithaca.
  1987 Tourism Models: The Sociocultural Aspects. Tourism Management 8:151–159.
  1990a Research and Scholarship: The Basis of Tourism Education. Journal of Tourism Studies 1(1):33–41.
  2001 Scientification of Tourism. *In* Hosts and Guests Revisited: Tourism Issues of the 21st Century, V. Smith and M. Brent, eds., pp. 28–41. Elmsford: Cognizant Communication Corp.
  2005 Tourism Gaining Cogency: From an Industry-Driven Force to a Public-Platform Choice. Cultural Diversity and Tourism 4:9–16. UNESCO.
Jafari, J., ed. in chief.
  1973 Annals of Tourism Research: A Social Science Journal. Oxford: Pergamon.
  1999 Annals of Tourism Research *en Español*. Palma de Mallorca: Universitat de les Illes Balears.
  2000 Encyclopedia of Tourism. London: Routledge.
Jurdao Arrones, F.
  1990 España en Venta. Madrid: Ediciones Endymion.
Kinnaird, V., and D. Hall, eds.
  1994 Tourism: A Gender Analysis. New York: Wiley.

Kitcher, P.
1993 The Advancement of Science. New York and Oxford: Oxford University Press.
Kottak, C.
1966 The Structure of Equality in a Brazilian Fishing Community. PhD Thesis, New York: Columbia University.
Krapf, K.
1961 Les pays en voie de developpement face au tourisme: introduction methodologique. Revue de Tourisme 16:82–89.
1964 La consommation touristique: une contribution a une theorie de la consommation. Aix-en-Provence: Centre des Hautes Études Touristiques.
Krippendorf, J.
1986 Tourism in the System of Industrial Society. Annals of Tourism Research 13:517–532.
1987 The Holiday Makers: Understanding the Impact of Leisure and Travel. London: Heinemann.
Kuhn, T.
1970 The Structure of Scientific Revolutions (2nd ed.).Chicago: University of Chicago Press.
1977 The Essential Tension: Selected Studies in Scientific Tradition and Change. Chicago: University of Chicago Press.
Kuper, A.
2004 Anthropology. *In* The Social Science Encyclopedia (3rd ed.), A. Kuper and J. Kuper, eds., pp. 24–34. London: Routledge.
Lanfant, M.-F.
1972 Les théories de loisir: Sociologies et ideologie. Paris: Presses Universitaires de France.
1980 Introduction: Tourism in the Process of Internationalization. International Social Science Journal 32(1):14–43.
1987 L'impact social et culturel du tourism international en question: Reponses sociologiques. Problems of tourism 10(1):3–34.
1992a Préface à l'ouvrage de Michel Picard. Tourisme culturel et culture touristique à Bali, pp. 5–12. Paris: L'Harmattan.
1992b International Tourism Reconsidered: The Principal of the Alternative. *In* Potential and Problems in the Development of Tourism, V. Smith and W. Eadington, eds., pp. 88–112. Philadelphia: University of Pennsylvania Press.
1995 Introduction. *In* International Tourism: Identity and Change, M.-F. Lanfant, J. Allcock and E. Bruner, eds., pp. 1–23. London: Sage Publications.
Lanfant, M.-F., J. Allcock, and E. Bruner, eds.
1995 International Tourism. Identity and Change. London: Sage.
Lanfant, M.-F., M. Picard, and J. De Weerdt
1982 Implications locales du Tourisme International. Paris: Centre d'Etudes Sociologiques, CNRS.

Langness, L.
  1965 The Life History in Anthropological Science. New York: Holt, Rinehart, and Winston.
Leach, E.
  1961 Rethinking Anthropology. London: Athlone Press.
Lee, R. L.
  1978 Who Owns Boardwalk: The Structure of Control of the Tourist Industry of Yucatan. *In* Tourism and Economic Change, V. Smith, ed., pp. 19–35. Studies in Third World Societies 6.
Lett, J.
  1989 (Epilogue) Touristic Studies in Anthropological Perspective by Theron Nuñez. *In* Hosts and Guests: The Anthropological Study of Tourism (2nd ed.), V. Smith, ed., pp. 275–279. Philadelphia: University of Pennsylvania Press.
Levi-Strauss, C.
  1963 Structural Anthropology. New York: Basic Books.
Lew, A., M. Hall, and A. Williams, eds.
  2004 A Companion to Tourism. Malden: Blackwell.
Lewenstein, B.
  1995 Book Review. Isis 86:145–146.
Lewis, H.
  2001 Boas, Darwin, Science and Anthropology. Current Anthropology 42:381–406.
Lodge, D.
  1984 Paradise News: A Novel. New York: Viking.
Löfgren, O.
  1999 On Holiday. Berkeley: University of California Press.
Lubell, B., J. F. MacCannell, and D. MacCannell
  1998 You are Here You Think: A San Francisco Bus Tour. *In* Reclaiming San Francisco: History, Politics, Culture, J. Brook, C. Carlsson and N. Peters, eds., pp. 137–150. San Francisco: City Lights Books.
Lukes, S.
  1972 Emile Durkheim: His Life and Work. New York: Harper & Row.
Lyotard, J.
  1984 The Postmodern Condition: A Report on Knowledge. Manchester: Manchester University Press.
MacCannell, D.
  1968 Structural Differentiation and Rigidity in 48 States of the United States. Unpublished PhD dissertation, Cornell University.
  1973 Staged Authenticity: On Arrangements of Social Space in Tourist Settings. The American Journal of Sociology 79(3):589–603.
  1976 The Tourist: A New Theory of the Leisure Class. New York: Shocken Books.
  1983 Erving Goffman (1922–1982). Semiotica 45(1/2):1–33.
  1990 Working in Other Fields. *In* Authors of Their Own Lives: Intellectual Autobiographies of Twenty American Sociologists, B. Berger, ed., pp. 165–189. Berkeley: The University of California Press.

1992 Empty Meeting Grounds: New York: Routledge.

1999 Epilogue. *In* The Tourist: A New Theory of the Leisure Class (2nd ed.), pp. 189–203. Berkeley: University of California Press.

2000 Symbolic Capital: Urban Design for Tourism. Journeys 1(1/2):157–182.

2001a Remarks on the Commodification of Cultures. *In* Hosts and Guests Revisited, V. Smith and M. Brent, eds., pp. 380–390. New York: Cognizant Communication Corp.

2001b Tourist Agency. Tourist Studies 1(1):23–37.

2001c The Bay's Edge: Between Pleasure and Decay. *In* Back to the Bay, Museum Catalogue, pp. 24–27. Yerba Buena: Center for Arts.

2001d Landscape Architecture's Time. *In* Revelatory Landscapes, pp. 18–27. San Francisco: Museum of Modern Art.

2002a The Ego-Factor in Tourism. The Journal of Consumer Research 29(1):146–151.

2002b Geographies of the Unconscious: Robert F, Heizer Versus Alfred Kroeber on the Drawing of American Indian Territorial Boundaries. Cultural Geographies 9:3–14.

MacCannell, J. F.

2002 Death Drive in Venice: Sophie Calle as Guide to the Future of Cities. The Journal of Culture and the Unconscious 2(1):55–79.

Mannheim, K.

1936 Ideology and Utopia: An Introduction to the Sociology of Knowledge. New York: Harcourt Brace.

Marcus, G., and M. Fisher

1986 Anthropology as Cultural Critique: An Experimental Moment in the Human Sciences. Chicago: University of Chicago Press.

Mauss, M.

1923–24 Essai sur le don: Forme et raison de l'échange dans les Societés Archaiques. L'année sociologique 1:30–186.

McCabe, S.

2002 The Tourist Experience and Everyday Life. *In* The Tourist as a Metaphor of the Social World, G. Dann, ed., pp. 61–76. Oxon: CABI Publishing.

McIntosh, R.

1972 Tourism: Principles, Practices, Philosophies. Columbus: Grid Publications.

Mead, M.

1955 Cultural Patterns and Technical Change. New York: New American Library.

Merquior, J. G.

1993 Western Marxism. *In* Social Thought, E. Outwaite and T. Bottomore, eds., pp. 710–712. Oxford: Blackwell.

Merton, R.

1968 Social Theory and Social Structure (Enlarged Edition). New York: The Free Press.

1996 On Social Structure and Science (edited and with an Introduction by Piotr Sztompka). Chicago: University of Chicago Press.

Miège, J.

1933 La Vie Touristique en Savoie. Revue de Géographie Alpine 23:749–817; 1934 24:5–213.

Mintz, S.
  1986 Sweetness and Power: The Place of Sugar in Modern History. New York: Penguin Books.
Mitchell, L.
  1979 The Geography of Tourism. Annals of Tourism Research 6:235–244.
Moon, O.
  1989 From Paddy Field to Ski Slope: The Revitalization of Tradition in Japanese Village Life. Manchester: Manchester University Press.
Murdock, G.
  1982 Outline of Cultural Materials. New Haven: Human Relations Area Files.
Musée Massena
  1934 Les Anglais dans le Comté de Nice et en Provence depuis le XVIIIme siècle.
Nash, D.
  1954 The American Composer: A Study in Social Psychology. PhD Thesis, University of Pennsylvania, Philadelphia.
  1963 The Ethnologist as Stranger: An Essay in the Sociology of Knowledge. Southwestern Journal of Anthropology 19:149–167.
  1970 A Community in Limbo: An Anthropological Study of an American Community Abroad. Bloomington: Indiana University Press.
  1977 Tourism as a Form of Imperialism. In Hosts and Guests: The Anthropological Study of Tourism, V. Smith, ed., pp. 33–47. Philadelphia: University of Pennsylvania Press.
  1979 Tourism in Pre-Industrial Societies. Aix-en-Provence: Centre des Hautes Études Touristiques.
  1981 Tourism as an Anthropological Subject. Current Anthropology 22(5):461–481.
  1984 The Ritualization of Tourism. Annals of Tourism Research 11:503–506.
  1989 Tourism as a Form of Imperialism. In Hosts and Guests: The Anthropology of Tourism (2nd ed.), V. Smith, ed., pp. 37–52. Philadelphia: University of Pennsylvania Press.
  1996 Anthropology of Tourism. Oxford: Elsevier.
  1999 A Little Anthropology (3rd ed.). Upper Saddle River: Prentice-Hall.
  2000 Ethnographic Windows on Tourism. Tourism Recreation Research 25:29–36.
  2004 New Wine in Old Bottles: An Adjustment in Priorities in the Anthropological Study of Tourism. In Qualitative Research in Tourism: Ontologies, Epistomologies and Methodologies, J. Phillimore and L. Goodsen, eds., pp. 170–184. London: Routledge.
Nash, D., and J. Heiss
  1967 The Stranger in Laboratory Culture Revisited. Human Organization 26:47–51.
Nash, D., and V. Smith
  1991 Anthropology and Tourism. Annals of Tourism Research 18:12–25.
Nash, D., and R. Wintrob
  1972 The Emergence of Self Consciousness in Ethnography. Current Anthropology 13:527–542.

Noronha, R.
   1979 Paradise Reviewed. *In* Tourism: Passport to Development, de Kadt, ed., pp. 177–204. New York: Oxford University Press.
Novak, D., and R. Lekachman
   1964 Development and Society: The Dynamics of Economic Change. New York: St. Martins Press.
Nuñez, T.
   1963 Tourism, Tradition, and Acculturation: Weekendismo in a Mexican Village. Ethnology 2:347–352.
   1977 Touristic Studies in Anthropological Perspective. *In* Hosts and Guests: The Anthropology of Tourism, V. Smith, ed., pp. 207–216. Philadelphia: University of Pennsylvania Press.
   1989 Touristic Studies in Anthropological Perspective. *In* Hosts and Guests: The Anthropology of Tourism (2nd ed.), V. Smith, ed., pp. 265–279. Philadelphia: University of Pennsylvania Press.
Parsons, T.
   1937 The Structure of Social Action: A Study in Social Theory with Special Reference to a Group of Recent European Writers. London: McGraw Hill.
   1949 Essays in Sociological Theory: Pure and Applied. Glencoe, IL: The Free Press.
   1951 The Social System: Glencoe, IL: The Free Press.
Parsons, T., and B. Barber
   1948 Sociology, 1941–1946. American Journal of Sociology 53:246–254.
Pearce, D.
   1993 Introduction. *In* Tourism Research: Critiques and Challenges, D. Pearce and R. Butler, eds., pp. 1–8. London: Routledge.
Pearce, P.
   1982 The Social Psychology of Tourist Behavior. New York: Pergamon Press.
Pfaffenberger, B.
   1983 Serious Pilgrims and Frivolous Tourists: The Chimera of Tourism in the Pilgrimages of Sri Lanka. Annals of Tourism Research 10:57–74.
Phillimore, J., and L. Goodson, eds.
   2004 Qualitative Research in Tourism: Ontologies, Epistomologies, and Methodologies. London: Routledge.
Picard, M.
   1973 Étude Documentaire sur le Tourisme: Approche Psycho-Sociologique. Paris: Publicis Conseil.
   1976 La Demande de Loisirs. Paris: Secrétariat d'Etat au Tourisme.
   1979 Sociétés et Tourisme. Réflexions pour la Recherche et L'action. Paris: UNESCO.
   1980 Sur quelques rapports entre la sociologie et l'économie politique dans l'étude du loisir. Loisir et Société 3:325–356.
   1990 "Cultural Tourism" in Bali: Cultural Performances as Tourist Attraction. Indonesia 49:37–74.
   1992 Tourisme culturel et culture touristique à Bali. Paris: L'Harmattan.

1996 Bali. Cultural Tourism and Touristic Culture. Singapore: Archipelago Press (revised, expanded and updated translation of Bali. Tourisme Culturel et culture touristique. Paris: L'Harmattan, 1992).

1997 Cultural Tourism, Nation-Building, and Regional Culture: The Making of a Balinese identity. *In* Tourism, Ethnicity, and the State in Asian and Pacific Societies, M. Picard and R. E. Wood, eds., pp. 181–214. Honolulu: University of Hawaii Press.

2002 Religion, tradition, et culture: la construction dialogique d'une identité Balinaise. L'Homme 163:107–136.

Picard, M., and J. Michaud, eds.

2001 Tourisme et sociétés locales en Asie Orièntale. Quebec Dept. d'anthropologie, Université Laval: 196 pp.

Picard, M., and R. E. Wood, eds.

1997 Tourism, Ethnicity, and the State in Asian and Pacific Societies. Honolulu: University of Hawaii Press.

Pickering, A.

1993 Science as Practice and Culture. Chicago: University of Chicago Press.

Pimlott, J. A. R.

1947 The Englishman's Holiday. London: Faber.

Pouris, C., and C. Beerli

1963 Culture et Tourisme. Paris: OECD.

Preister, K.

1986 Issue-Centered Social Impact Assessment. *In* Anthropological Praxis: Translating Knowledge into Action, R. Wulff and S. Fiske, eds., pp. 39–55. Boulder: Westview Press.

Pye, E., and T. B. Lin

1983 Tourism in Asia: The Economic Impact. Singapore: Singapore University Press.

Richter, L.

1983 Tourism, Politics and Political Science: A Case of Not So Benign Neglect. Annals of Tourism Research 10:313–336.

Riley, R., and L. Love

2000 The State of Qualitative Tourism Research. Annals of Tourism Research 27:164–187.

Ritchie, B.

1993 Tourism Research: Policies and Managerial Priorities for the 1990's and Beyond. *In* Tourism Research: Critiques and Challenges, D. Pearce and R. Butler, eds., pp. 201–216. London: Routledge.

Ritchie, B., P. Burns, and C. Palmer, eds.

2005 Tourism Research Methods. Oxford: CABI Publishing.

Rojek, C.

1985 Capitalism and Leisure Theory. New York: Tavistock.

1989 Leisure and Recreation Theory. *In* Understanding Leisure and Recreation: Mapping the Past, Charting the Future, E. Jackson and T. Burton, eds., pp. 69–88. State College: Venture Publishing.

Roseberry, W.
1996 The Unbearable Lightness of Anthropology. Radical History Review 65:5–25.
Rosenberg, H.
1988 A Negotiated World. Toronto: University of Toronto Press.
Rossides, D.
1978 The History and Nature of Sociological Theory. Boston: Houghton Mifflin.
Rubin, M.
1974 The Walls of Acre. New York, NY: Holt, Rinehart and Winston.
Russell, B.
1948 Human Knowledge: Its Scope and Limits. New York: Simon & Schuster.
Sahlins, M.
1962 Stone Age Economics. Chicago: Aldine.
Scheler, M.
1980[1924] Problems of a Sociology of Knowledge. London: Routledge.
Schippers, T.
1991 Regards Ethnologiques sur l'Europe. Terrain 17:146–152.
Schlechten, M.
1988 Tourisme Balnéaire ou Tourisme Rural Integré: Deux Modèles de Développement Sénégalais. Saint-Paul Fribourg, Suisse: Éditions Universitaires Fribourg Suisse.
Schuetz, A.
1944 The Stranger: An Essay in Social Psychology. American Journal of Sociology 49:499–507.
1964 Collected Papers. Martinus Nijhoff: The Hague.
Seale, C.
2001 Qualitative Research. *In* Readers Guide to the Social Sciences, J. Michie, ed., pp. 363–364. London: Fitzroy Dearborn Publishers.
Seligson, M., and J. Passé-Smith
1993 Development and Underdevelopment: The Political Economy of Inequality. Boulder: Lynne Rienner Publications.
Shapin, S., and S. Shaffer
1985 Leviathon and the Air Pump: Hobbes, Boyle, and the Experimental Life. Princeton: Princeton University Press.
Shore, C., and S. Wright
1999 Audit Culture and Anthropology: NeoLiberalism in British Higher Education. Journal of the Royal Anthropological Institute 5:557–575.
Simmons, L., ed.
1942 Sun Chief: The Autobiography of a Hopi Indian. New Haven: Yale University Press.
Smith, L.
1993 Biographical Method. *In* Handbook of Qualitative Research, N. Denzin and Y. Lincoln, eds., pp. 286–305.Thousand Oaks: Sage.
Smith, S.
1989 Book Review. Annals of Tourism Research 16:130–132.

Smith, V.

1977 Introduction. *In* Hosts and Guest: The Anthropology of Tourism, V. Smith, ed., pp. 1–14. Philadelphia: University of Pennsylvania Press.

1989 Introduction. *In* Hosts and Guests: The Anthropology of Tourism (2ⁿᵈ ed.), V. Smith, ed., pp. 1–17. Philadelphia: University of Pennsylvania Press.

1992 Introduction: The Quest in Guest. Annals of Tourism Research 19:1–18.

1994 A Sustainable Antarctic: Science and Tourism. Annals of Tourism Research 12:221–230.

Smith, V., ed.

1977 Hosts and Guests: The Anthropology of Tourism. Philadelphia: University of Pennsylvania Press.

1978a Tourism and Behavior. Studies in Third World Societies 5:1–100.

1978b Tourism and Economic Change. Studies in Third World Societies 6:1–152.

1989 Hosts and Guests: The Anthropology of Tourism. Philadelphia: University of Pennsylvania Press.

1992 Pilgrimage and Tourism: The Quest in Guest. Annals of Tourism Research 19(1):1–121.

Smith, V., and S. Wanhill, eds.

1986 Domestic Tourism. Annals of Tourism Research 13(3):329–489.

Smith, V., and W. Eadington, eds.

1992 Tourism Alternatives: Potentials and Problems in the Development of Tourism. Philadelphia: University of Pennsylvania Press.

Smith, V., and J. Splettstoesser, eds.

1994 Antarctic Tourism. Annals of Tourism Research 21(2):221–386.

Smith, V., and M. Brett, eds.

2001 Hosts and Guests Revisited: Tourism Issues of the 21ˢᵗ Century. Elmsford, NY: Cognizant Communication Corp.

Spencer, J., and W. Thomas

1948 Hill Stations and Summer Resorts of the Orient. Geographical Review 38:631–671.

SSRC (Social Science Research Council Seminar)

1954 Acculturation: An Exploratory Formulation. American Anthropologist 56:973–1002.

Stocking, G.

1983 Observers Observed: Essays on Ethnographic Fieldwork. Madison: University of Wisconsin Press.

Storey, J.

1996 Cultural Studies. *In* The Social Science Encyclopedia (2ⁿᵈ ed.), A. Kuper and J. Kuper, eds., pp. 159–161. London and New York: Routledge.

Strathern, M., ed.

2000 Audit Culture: Anthropological Studies in Accountability, Ethics and the Academy. London: Routledge.

Strozier, C.

2001 Heinz Kohut: The Making of a Psychoanalyst. New York: Farrar, Strauss and Giroux.

Swain, M. B.
  1977 Cuna Women and Ethnic Tourism: A Way to Persist and an Avenue to Change. *In* Hosts and Guests: The Anthropology of Tourism, V. Smith, ed., pp. 71–82. Philadelphia: University of Pennsylvania Press.
  1989a Gender Roles in Indigenous Tourism: Kuna Mola, Kuna Yala, and Cultural Survival. *In* Hosts and Guests: The Anthropology of Tourism (2nd ed.). V. Smith, ed., pp. 83–104. Philadelphia: University of Pennsylvania Press.
  1989b Developing Ethnic Tourism in Yunnan, China: Shilin Sani. Tourism Recreation Research, XVI(1):33–39.
  1990 Commoditizing Ethnicity in Southwest China. Cultural Survival Quarterly 14(1):26–29.
  2004 (Dis)Embodied Experiences and Power Dynamics in Tourism Research. *In* Qualitative Research in Tourism: Ontologies, Epistemologies and Methodologies, J. Phillimore and L. Goodson, eds., pp. 102–118. London: Routledge.
Swain, M. B., ed.
  1995 Gender in Tourism. Annals of Tourism Research 22(2):247–478.
Swain, M. B., and J. Momsen, eds.
  2002 Gender/Tourism/Fun? Elmsford: Cognizant Communication Corp.
Swain, M. B., M. Brent, and V. Long, eds.
  1998 Annals and Tourism Evolving: Indexing 25 Years of Publication. Annals of Tourism Research 25(Suppl.):991–1014.
Swain, M. B., and H. Xiao
  2003 Annals Index: Vols. 1–30 (1973–2003). Annals of Tourism Research 30:983–1048.
Teas, J.
  1988 I'm Studying Monkeys; What Do You Do? Youthful Travelers in Nepal. *In* Anthropological Research on Contemporary Tourism: Student Papers from Berkeley, N. Graburn, ed., Kroeber Anthropological Society papers Nos. 67/68.
Thomas, W. I., and F. Znaniecki
  1927 The Polish Peasant in Europe and America. New York: Dover.
Thurot, J.-M.
  1981 Reformuler la problématique de l'impact socio-culturel du tourisme. Revue de Tourisme 2:2–9.
Towner, J.
  1996 An Historical Geography of Recreation and Tourism in the Western World: 1540–1940. Chichester and New York: John Wiley and Sons.
Towner, J., and G. Wall
  1991 History and Tourism. Annals of Tourism Research 18:71–84.
Tribe, J.
  1997 The Indiscipline of Tourism. Annals of Tourism Research 24:638–657.
  2004 Knowing about Tourism: Epistemological Issues. *In* Qualitative Research in Tourism: Ontologies, Epistemologies, and Methodologies, J. Phillimore and L. Goodson, eds., pp. 46–62. London: Routledge.

Turner, L., and J. Ash
 1975 The Golden Hordes. International Tourism and the Pleasure Periphery. London: Constable.
Turner, V., and E. Turner
 1978 Image and Pilgrimage in Christian Culture. Oxford: Basil Blackwell.
UNESCO
 1966 Resolution on the Preservation and Presentation of the Cultural Heritage in Connection with the Promotion of Tourism. Paris: UNESCO.
Urry, J.
 2002 The Tourist Gaze (2nd ed.). London: Sage.
van den Berghe, P.
 1960 The Dynamics of Race Relations: An Ideal Type Study from South Africa. PhD Thesis, Harvard University.
 1979 Human Family Systems, New York: Elsevier.
 1980 Tourism as Ethnic Relations, A Case Study of Cuzco, Peru. Ethnic and Racial Studies 3:375–391.
 1981 The Ethnic Phenomenon. New York: Elsevier.
 1989 Stranger in their Midst. Niwot: University Press of Colorado.
 1990 From the Popocatepetl to the Limpopo. *In* Authors of their Own Lives, B. B. Berger, ed., pp. 410–431. Berkeley: University of California Press.
 1994 The Quest for the Other: Ethnic Tourism in San Cristóbal, Mexico. Seattle: University of Washington Press.
 1995 Marketing Mayas: Ethnic Tourism Promotion in Mexico. Annals of Tourism Research 22:568–588.
 2001 El Camino Inca: A Profile of Cuzco Tourists. International Journal of Hospitality and Tourism Administration 1:99–110.
van den Berghe, P., and J. Flores Ochoa
 2000 Tourism and Nativistic Ideology in Cuzco, Peru. Annals of Tourism Research 27:7–26.
van den Berghe, P., and C. Keyes
 1984 Tourism and Re-Created Ethnicity. Annals of Tourism Research 11:343–352.
van den Berghe, P., and G. Primov.
 1977 Inequality in the Peruvian Andes: Class and Ethnicity in Cuzco. Columbia, Missouri: University of Missouri Press.
Van der Werff, P.
 1980 Polarizing Implications of the Pescaia Tourist Industry. Annals of Tourism Research 7:197–223.
van Gennep, A.
 1960 [1908] The Rites of Passage. Chicago: University of Chicago Press.
Vermuelen, H., and A. Alvarez Roldan, eds.
 1995 Studies in the History of European Anthropology. London: Routledge.

Vidich, A., and S. Lyman
  1993 Qualitative Methods: Their History in Sociology and Anthropology. *In* Handbook of
    Qualitative Research, N. Denzin and Y. Lincoln, eds., pp. 23–59. Thousand Oaks: Sage.
von Wiese, L.
  1930 Fremdenverkehr als Zwichenmenschliche Beziehung. Archiv für Fremdenverkehr
    1(1):1–3.
Wade, P., ed.
  1997 Cultural Studies Will be the Death of Anthropology. Manchester: Group for
    Debates in Anthropological Theory.
Wallace, A.
  1970 Culture and Personality. New York: Random House.
Waller, S., and J. Lea
  1999 Seeking the Real Spain? Authenticity in Motivation. Annals of Tourism
    Research 26:110–129.
Wallerstein, I.
  1974 The Modern World System. New York: Academic Press.
  1984 The Development of the Concept of Development. *In* Sociological Theory,
    R. Collins, ed., pp. 102–116. San Francisco: Jossey Bass.
WCED (World Commission on Environment and Development)
  1987 Our Common Future. New York: Oxford University Press.
Weber, M.
  1958 The Protestant Ethic and the Spirit of Capitalism. New York: Scribner.
  1967 Economy and Society. New York: Bedminster Press.
Wolf, E.
  1982 Europe and the People without History. Berkeley: University of California
    Press.
Wood, R. E.
  1993 Tourism, Culture and the Sociology of Development. *In* Tourism in South-East
    Asia, M. Hitchcock, V. T. King and M. J. G. Parnwell, eds., pp. 48–70. London:
    Routledge.
World Tourism Organization
  2001 (Preliminary Report) World Tourism Trends.
Worsley, P.
  1984 The Three Worlds. Chicago: University of Chicago Press.
Yair, G., and N. Apeloig-Feldman
  2005 Sociology in Jerusalem: The Shadow of its History. Israeli Sociology 7:95–122.
    (In Hebrew).
Young, R.
  1977 The Structural Context of the Caribbean Tourist Industry: A Comparative Study.
    Journal of Rural Cooperation 5:657–672.

Young, R., and D. MacCannell
    1979 Predicting the Quality of Life in the United States. Journal of Social Indicators
        Research 6:23–40.
Zabel, D.
    1996 Sociology. *In* The Social Sciences: A Cross-Disciplinary Guide to Selected
        Sources, N. Herron, ed., pp. 187–207. Englewood: Libraries Unlimited.

Author Index

Subject Index